O UGHTEN
H OUSE
PUBLICATIONS

"Ascension Books for the Rising Planetary Consciousness"

❧ OTHER WORKS BY ERIC KLEIN ❧

The Inner Door, Vol. I and Vol. II

A sequel to *The Crystal Stair*, these two volumes contain additional guidance from the Masters regarding self-mastery and the ascension path.

Ascension Tapes

A collection of channeled messages and meditation tapes, each bringing loving messages from the Ascended Masters.

The Crystal Stair ❧

First Edition — November, 1990

Second Edition — July, 1992
Second Printing — December, 1992
Third Printing — April, 1993

Third Edition — February, 1994
Second Printing — September, 1994

THE CRYSTAL STAIR

A GUIDE TO THE ASCENSION

CHANNELED MATERIAL FROM
SANANDA (JESUS),
ASHTAR, ARCHANGEL MICHAEL, AND
ST. GERMAIN

BY

ERIC KLEIN

THIRD EDITION

Editing & Typography by Sara Benjamin-Rhodes
Cover Illustration by Cathie Beach
Published by Oughten House Publications
Livermore, California USA

THE CRYSTAL STAIR
A GUIDE TO THE ASCENSION
Channeled Material from Sananda (Jesus), Ashtar, Archangel Michael, and St. Germain

© 1990, 1992, 1994 by Eric Klein
Published 1990. Third Edition 1994.

00 99 98 97 96 95 94   0 9 8 7 6 5 4 3 2

THIRD EDITION

COVER ILLUSTRATION BY CATHIE BEACH
EDITING & TYPOGRAPHY BY SARA BENJAMIN-RHODES

PUBLISHED BY:
OUGHTEN HOUSE PUBLICATIONS
P.O. BOX 2008
LIVERMORE, CALIFORNIA, 94551-2008 USA

Library of Congress Cataloging-in-Publication Data
The Crystal Stair : a guide to the ascension / channeled material from
Sananda (Jesus), Ashtar, Archangel Michael, and St. Germain;
Eric Klein, -- 3rd ed.
        p.   cm.
    ISBN 1-880666-06-5 : $12.95
    1. Spirit writings.   2. Self-actualization (Psychology)
--Miscellanea.   I. Jesus Christ (Spirit)   II. Klein, Eric, 1951-
BF1290C785   1994
133.9"3--dc20   92-17157
                                            CIP
ISBN 1-880666-06-5, Trade Publication
        Printed in United States of America
    Printed with vegetable ink on acid-free paper

DEDICATION

With love and gratitude, I dedicate this book to Lord Sananda, the Ashtar Command, the Great White Brotherhood and all who serve the light.

ACKNOWLEDGMENT

Special thanks to Jenny Annear for her inspiring dedication to this project, to Robert Gerard for his 3-D wizardry, to Sara Benjamin for her wonderful editing assistance, and to Christine for her love and support.

THE IMPORTANCE OF DISCERNMENT

In editing a book for Oughten House, I strive to take it to the highest level of which I am capable. I draw upon my intuition and experience and try to catch anything that is not accurate or clear. However, there are as many pictures of reality as there are points of awareness to formulate them. There are many destiny patterns unfolding simultaneously. We each need to use our own discernment to distinguish what is "ours" and what is someone else's. No source of information is without its distortion. Even the clearest channels are not, nor have they ever been, 100% accurate. Even within information that is "mostly true," there is some information that is not true. Even within information that is "mostly false," there is some truth present.

Your greatest ally in finding your way to your own "destination" is your own discernment. No one can know your own answers except you. You cannot rely on anyone or anything outside of you: your answers all lie within you. We are all unique aspects of the One. There is no duplication whatsoever, which is pretty amazing in itself. As you read what is in these pages, take what is "yours" and embrace it. The rest may be there for someone else. If it helps you on your path, then it has served.

— Sara Benjamin-Rhodes, Managing Editor

Publisher's Note

The channeled material presented in the book, *The Crystal Stair*, is a form of documentary concerning spiritual matters. It consists of transmitted information. The reader's interpretation of this or any other channeled information is strictly subjective and reflects his or her personal beliefs.

The language used in this book has been transcribed with the intention of presenting the actual transmissions of the Masters, with the least possible alteration in meaning. Because of this, there are a few words used in unconventional ways. The essence of the material remains unchanged.

We at Oughten House extend our wholehearted appreciation and gratitude to each of our Literary Producers for making this publication possible: Marge and John Melanson, Barbara Rawles, Robin Drew, Irit Levy, Debbie Detwiler, Kiyo Monro, Alice Tang, Eugene P. Tang, Brad Clarke, Victor Beasley, Ruth Dutra, Nicole Christine, Dennis Donahue, Fred J. Tremblay, Kathy Cook, and Kimberley Mullen.

TABLE OF CONTENTS

∽ PREFACE ∾

In January of 1990, I was asked by Sananda to channel a series of weekly classes on the subject of ascension. These classes were given over a six week period, beginning in February of that year. They were to be followed by two similar courses (of five weeks each) lasting through most of that summer. During that time, Ashtar suggested the creation of a book containing the transcriptions of the best of these classes. He recommended that we not be overly concerned about the "literary merits" of the book, but rather, that we get the information out as quickly as possible.

Since the time of the publication of this material, Sananda's words (see Introduction) have proven truly prophetic, as this information has found its way into the hands of many lightworkers worldwide. It is my hope that this new edition will now find an even more expanded audience for this vital information.

I feel it is important to state, concerning this or any other channeled material, that this information is not meant to be taken as the gospel truth of the planetary ascension process. I have done my best to bring through the words and presence of the Masters with clarity, knowing always that within this multi-dimensional universe, there are many possible perspectives of any single event. As Ashtar has often said, "Channeling is a rather limited medium of communication."

Yet, in spite of the restrictions inherent in this form of communication, one point is very clear. That is, the need for each of us to bring through with trust and humility whatever we are blessed to receive from Spirit. I leave you with love and these pertinent quotes:

"A man attains perfection when his work is worship of God, from whom all things come and who is in all.

"Greater is thine own work, even if this be humble, than the work of another, even if this be great. When a man does the work God gives him, no sin can touch this man.

"And a man should not abandon his work, even if he cannot achieve it in full perfection; because in all work, there may be imperfection, even as in all fire there is smoke."

— *Bhagavad Gita*

"If you bring forth that is within you, what you bring forth will save you. If you do not bring forth what is within you, what you do not bring forth will destroy you."

— *Gnostic Gospel of St. Thomas*

Eric Klein
Santa Cruz, CA
April, 1992

INTRODUCTION

BY

SANANDA

Many have been served, and many more will be served by the channelings presented in this collection. It is our wish that this information be made public to assist in the mighty transformation now taking place on Earth. Ascension is and always has been the ultimate goal and end result of third-dimensional existence. What is happening on this world now is not new within the context of universal evolution — it has happened on many worlds and will occur again on newly evolving planets throughout the creation.

What is presented here is as an energetic reminder to those of you who have roles to play in the unfolding drama of the times. If this information triggers within you a sense of joy and excitement, if you feel an alignment with this perspective, consider the possibility that you are going to actively participate in it. If the information concerning "Earth Changes" causes fear, please be reminded that as in any birth process, there is a brief period of pain followed by a time of great joy.

So it will be in the birthing of the New Earth. Each ascending human will experience their own birth into the next dimension of consciousness against the backdrop of the powerful transition of the Earth herself. There is no way to describe in language the importance of this event. It remains for each of you to open to your divinity and to assume your rightful places in the vast ocean of love now crashing on your shores.

❧ Class One ❧

INTRODUCTION TO ASCENSION

❧ Sananda ❧

Hello. Nice to be here with you this evening on this auspicious occasion. I am Sananda, here to introduce you to a great adventure in your lives. I might say, to *re*-introduce you to something you have known on some level of yourselves for a very long time. So please make yourselves comfortable and be relaxed. We will be introducing you to the ascension process this evening. The first class is always the most challenging for us. There is so much to discuss that it is difficult to know where to begin. But with your help in the form of questions, we generally end up taking care of most of the information you need to know regarding the ascension and these times that you are living in.

These times are quite extraordinary. What is occurring now has not occurred on this world before. It is a transformation. There is an incredible amount of growth available. The opportunity to take a quantum leap into higher consciousness is now here for you. You may have a certain awareness of this in your lives. You may be in your own ways experiencing a quickening of growth, a heart opening, more light and love in your life, more desire to know the truth. This is a result of this increased energy that is occurring. What I am here to talk about, as well as the others who will speak to you in this series of classes, is the completion, or goal, of all of this transformation. You are not here on this planet to endlessly grow and process your emotions. This is part of a larger picture. This is just part of a growth towards a completion. And now at this time, through a special dispensation of the Father/Creator of the universe and all the universes, we are putting out the call to those beings such as yourselves, those Light Workers and Starseeds, who will be the first to learn about this opportunity to return to their true states of awareness, their true identities. This will culminate in the ascension process.

What is ascension? It is a great leap of experience on every level of your being. In general, you could say it is a leap from third-dimensional reality into a fifth-dimensional or higher state of consciousness, third-dimensional reality being what you now see and hear and taste and experience with your senses, all that appears to be solid or having this dimensionality of solidness. I would like to include in this definition (though they are more fourth-dimensional manifestations: thoughts and ideas, emotions, etc.) all of that which is existing in this planetary realm. You might say that the fifth dimension or higher, the ascended state, is a state of increased frequency of vibration. It is as if you have a prism and you shine white light through the prism, breaking it into many various colors, various wavelengths of light. You could say that the third-dimensional existence as you know it relates to that visible spectrum of light that you can see with your eyes, from the violet through the other colors. Ascension is a matter of going beyond this limited spectrum of experience. The nature of the universe does not change so much. The laws of physics do not change so much. But you expand and increase your frequency of vibration and your consciousness to a point where you can see those colors and move into those realms that are now invisible to you.

So part of the process is an awakening to your potentials, your hidden potentials. They have been hidden quite well, have they not? You have been using a certain percentage of your grey matter. Some of you are more aware through meditations and psychic powers, but nevertheless you have been existing within a certain limited framework of consciousness. So another difference between an ascended being and yourselves is that we have a one hundred percent mental capacity fully operating in our consciousness. And you have much less. I would say you use only ten to fifteen percent. Maybe I will give some of you the benefit of the doubt and say that you have used up to twenty percent. Congratulations. But you see, there is a great deal more for you to be aware of, a great deal more for you to experience. And it is very enjoyable to do so. It is very blissful and peaceful to be surrounded by this loving presence of the Father continually, to feel at one with the Creator. So an ascended being is one who has made that leap, who has at least attained to the level of awareness of the fifth dimension, who has gone beyond birth and death, who has attained that state of immortality wherein consciousness will no longer be broken by the sleep you know as death. Neither is there aging. You have seen pictures of Ascended Masters and they look the same pretty much all the time. If you have seen photographs of me (there are a few in existence), I have not changed much in 2,000 years or for even longer than that. So again, an aspect of ascension is that you will be free of birth and death. You will be free of all of the limitations of third-dimensional reality.

This transformation is not something that is intended to be selective for a very few individuals. It is something which is now occurring on a planetary scale. It is something that is going to be available to all human beings in this lifetime, in a very short time. You are hearing about it. You are in the first wave of those who have heard about it, of those who are interested. So this is not something that is an option. For you, only the timing is optional. This is not a new automobile I am selling you that you can decide whether to purchase or not. I am telling you something that is going to occur and is going to happen one way or the other. And it is for you to align yourselves and to open to the transformation if you wish to be among the first to take that leap of consciousness.

So why are you the first? Why are there so few who are ready to hear about this at this time? Why are you so different, you might ask. Why are your hearts a little bit more open? Why are your minds a little bit more open to this possibility? It is because you have somewhat higher origins. Those of you who are in this room with me now are what I would classify as Light Workers or Starseeds. You are, believe it or not, very evolved beings. You are very beautiful and courageous beings. You are among those who chose to leave the ascended state, to come here, to take third-dimensional incarnations many thousands of years ago in order that you might assist humanity, in order that you might assist in the transformation of this planet. It is time for you to realize your origins to some extent, and to begin to appreciate yourselves for who you are beyond your minds and your personalities, beyond your limited concepts of yourselves. This is why you are among the first to hear of this. This is why you are awake to the possibility. Many have heard these descriptions of the ascension and for some reason they do not awaken to that. For some reason they are somewhat sleepy or disbelieving. Their time will come. Now it is your time. So part of what we will be working on together in this series of classes, for those of you who choose to continue onwards, is the unveiling of your own higher Selves, the increased awareness of who you really are beyond your personalities and individual life experiences. You will begin to experience an expansion of your self-concept. You will begin to feel a great deal more of your true presence, your higher Self, as we do our best to connect you more strongly with that aspect of yourself. We are going to work on integrating you with that higher Self so that you do not feel separate from God or from your true self, so that you do not feel disempowered or helpless or lost here in this third-dimensional quagmire you call "planet Earth experience." There are many benefits to this process. Indeed, it is a process. So I congratulate you for your openness this evening, for having the courage and openness to come and hear about this. I encourage you to ask whatever questions you have about this. This is not an ordinary class that you are taking. This is not a workshop that will assist you in manifesting more money exclusively. This is a class that is cutting straight to the very essence of your beings. It is very transformational.

So what is occurring now that is different? Why is this time more powerful and intense? It is because the Earth itself is undergoing the initial phases of its transformation to the ascended state. The Earth as a third-dimensional manifestation has a very short time to continue. There will be incredible transformations of this planet and this solar system that you are inhabiting. All of the atoms and molecules of the Earth, of the solar system, and of every being in existence on the Earth are transforming towards a higher frequency and will soon be in the fifth dimension of experience. This is why this is not an optional experience for you. If you are inhabiting the planet Earth, know that you are here at this time for a purpose. You are Light Workers and you have been awaiting this time. A great deal has happened to you in your Earth lives, a lot of water under the bridge, a lot of lifetimes where you were trying your best to be ordinary citizens. Sometimes you were persecuted for being extraordinary citizens. Sometimes you were great teachers. Sometimes you were yogis and meditators in your caves. Sometimes you were white witches or any other sort of manifestation, trying your best to do your missions here, to channel the energy of God into the desert-like consciousness of the world. You have done a lot. You have been rather successful individually. Yet collectively I would say the change that is intended for this planet has not been proceeding as smoothly or as rapidly as we had hoped when this choice was made by you to incarnate here. So the original plan requires a little bit of a boost at this time. What has happened is that most of the Starseeds have fallen asleep themselves. This is why the world is so sleepy and why even the Starseeds are sleepy. Because there is an aura of sleep and confusion which surrounds the planet. The light has not broken through fully yet. But it is making great strides to do so.

So I ask you to open to the possibility of your higher Selves, your own divinity, and open to the possibility that you are ascended beings who descended at a certain time in history to do the work that you have been doing. And now it is time; your internal alarm clock has gone off and awakened you. You heard the word "ascension," or perhaps read some information about it, and your internal alarm clock went off. Something in you said, "This is for me." It is because you are programmed to awaken. You are programmed for this time, for you knew that no matter what occurred in your third-dimensional lifetimes you would not be left behind when the Hierarchy came to elevate the consciousness and to lift and transform. So now it is time, and you are receiving your wake up calls. You are waking up quite beautifully. There is more to do and experience. You will experience it. I will speak a little bit about the ascension process. Next week Ashtar will be here to speak in more detail within his area of expertise. You see, there is a great deal of involvement by the Ashtar Command and the extraterrestrial masters. There are many ships surrounding the Earth. They are not visible to you because they are in higher dimensions. They are not visible to your earthly radar. They are not visible to the space shuttles. But let me say the skies are swarming with ascended beings at this time who have been assisting with this work.

So what is the process? You have grown accustomed to reincarnational experience — that is, having your soul incarnate into a body and going through a lifetime of a certain number of years, experiencing death, and leaving your body to return again to the Earth. You have gone to some fourth-dimensional areas. There are heavens and hells galore, with many experiences. Yet always you return to the body, for this body is the platform from which your launch will take place into the fifth dimension. This is the intention, let me say, of having a physical body, at this time especially. I would say that your ascension will be all but identical to my own. You will not leave your bodies behind and go to a high state of consciousness. Your bodies will be transformed also. The molecules and atoms, your sub-atomic particles, all that you are, will be transformed and accelerated into the fifth dimension. So you do not have to die. Well, that's some good news. Despite the fact that human beings have grown so accustomed to dying that it has become a common awareness or common belief, I am telling you now: you do not have to die. And you will not.

The actual experience of ascension involves the lifting of your vibrational frequencies, which culminates in the physical lifting of your body in a high state of consciousness from the planet's surface into the waiting light vehicles. And yes, when I attained my ascension, I was lifted into the light vehicles also. You could say that I went up into the spaceships, if you prefer to view them as spaceships. So your experience will be the same as mine, although your requirements will be somewhat less than mine were. Fortunately you do not have to go through the trials and tests that I did. What I went through was for all of you and all of humanity. You could say that I paved the way for this process. And I have been waiting for you for a long time. So I am very excited to see the fruition of all the work we have been doing here for thousands of years. For thousands of years the Ashtar Command and ascended brotherhood have been working. For thousands of years we have been waiting for this time. And we are very happy and excited that our wait is all but over and that we will be reunited with those of our family. I am speaking of you now. And that we will have the opportunity to do some very vital work with the mass of humanity also. So you will be lifted. You may call it evacuation or you may call it ascension. These terms are related, but the evacuation refers to the lifting of your physical forms. The ascension refers to the experience of making the shift into the fifth dimension and beyond. This occurs shortly after the lifting. It is one process with two phases, you might say.* So this is available to you. We are making this available. It is above all available due to the love of the Father for his creation and for all of the innocent beings who are here, who have been here in this world, whose hearts are calling out for more love, truth and light, who have been influenced by darkness and confusion. So my recommendations to you, if you are interested in this process, and this is sounding and feeling like truth to you — prepare yourselves. Open your hearts and investigate this. Take this course. We will work with you on many levels. We will work with you intellectually and do our best to explain within the limitations of speech the information about the ascension. We will also work with you in your hearts, in your chakras, in your awakening, opening, balancing; in preparing you. If it is your desire to be among the first, we will do this.

The current plan calls for, and I might say that it is quite a brilliant plan in my opinion, three waves of ascension. The goal of course, as difficult as it may sound, is to have every human being on this planet experience the ascension in this lifetime. It is doubtful this will occur. We are going to do our best to harvest as many as we can who are ready. Therefore, we will have three waves of ascension. The first two waves being, for the most part, the returning of the Starseeds to their true states, the re-

* see Epilogue, p. 173

ascending of you who are originally ascended beings who have come here. It is our hope that many of those Light Workers who will awaken will avail themselves of the opportunity to be lifted in the first or second waves of ascension. The first wave is imminent. It is our hope that it will occur very soon. The sooner the better, in my opinion. Those who ascend within the first wave will be given the opportunity to return to Earth as Ascended Masters, to walk among humanity teaching and performing "miracles," sharing this incredible message, and assisting in the transformation of human beings. This is ultimately the purpose that you came here for. It is time for you to open to the possibility that you can complete your Earth missions and do this work from a higher perspective quite a bit more effectively than you have been, being as you have been enmeshed in third-dimensional life and its limitations.

So upon the ascension of the first wave there is an opportunity for choice. Many choices will be given to you. You can choose to return as an Ascended Master in a light body, having a body that is immortal, having the ability to materialize and de-materialize at will, to zip back and forth between the ships and the planet, to perform miracles, to create spontaneously out of the etheric substance, to heal, to do many wonderful things. In short, this is to attract a lot of attention. You haven't been attracting very much attention, have you? In all of your work, all of your meditations and your sharing has done some good. But for the most part it has only assisted in gathering the Starseeds back together again. It has not had a great deal of effect on humanity as a whole. It is a bit more profound of an effect we are hoping to have, as you return as Ascended Masters and create quite a ruckus and a stir. Being in the ascended state you will not be affected by negativity, doubt, fear, money, these sort of limitations. You will be able to be as radical and outrageous as you truly are and as you were before you took on the veils. The veils will be lifted from you. This is one choice. This is the choice that we are hoping many will accept. It is not mandatory to do so. If you as a Starseed choose to ascend in the first wave and to do some other service in another area with the Ashtar Command, or to return to your origins, this will be perfectly acceptable. As ascended beings you are always doing some form of service simply by being and showering your presence wherever you are. You have come from very many different places, different levels of consciousness, different angelic realms, different states, and you will have the opportunity to return to your soul families and points of origin. If you have not felt comfortable and entirely at home on Earth there is a very good reason for this. And it is good and it is a blessing that you have not. For it has kept you a little bit more awake and a bit more hopeful of something more. So here is the something more. It is coming your way on a silver platter with all of our light and all of our love.

I think I will speak about the Great White Brotherhood and the hierarchy of beings that are working at this time. You have heard of the Great White Brotherhood, perhaps. It is a service organization of beings who have ascended. You may have heard of the Ashtar Command or the extraterrestrial Ascended Masters, as you might call them. There is little difference between them. The Great White Brotherhood tends to be made up of many beings who have had Earth incarnations, but not exclusively. But those who are working most closely with you have generally had some Earth experience and have committed themselves to this particular sphere of activity, the Earth, this beautiful planet which is in need of so much assistance. So there is an organizational structure, you might say, to the work that we are doing. There is a chain of command proceeding from the Father/Creator through all of the angelic hosts and creator-gods, spirits, beings. Within this Earth sphere of activity I am the supreme commander over all of the Ashtar Command and its activities, and over the Ascended Masters of the Great White Brotherhood. This is my service. You might say that I am a coordinator of love. There is also a great deal of activity by the angelic hosts at this time. Archangel Michael and his legions are here for the protection and the transformation, and for the dispatching of those dark forces which have taken control of the Earth.

So you see there is a great deal about to occur. It has been occurring, but it is going to become much more physical and much more evident. As the Earth undergoes its transformation into the fifth dimension there will be much more of cataclysmic experience. The shaking and quaking and volcanic activities of the Earth will occur. Many of the transformations have begun; much flooding has occurred as you know, and earthquakes, etc. This will continue and it will increase in intensity. It is part of the process of the Earth's transformation. It is inevitable. It must occur. One of the by-products of this is that human beings will be shaken into another state of awareness. They will begin to question their lives and will begin to be a bit more open. Many of them will. Many of them will resort to a state of fear and panic. We are here to "save" as many as we can from the death experience and complete the cycle of this planet. It is a very incredible experience to be a part of. So tonight I am inviting each of you to take part in this, to take part in a big way, not as an innocent bystander but as an active participant, to return to your masterhood, to return to your God-nature, to take back the powers you have given away by being third-dimensionalized, to reawaken the other eighty-five percent of your brain, to accelerate your atoms, to ascend and to return to that full consciousness you have longed for many lifetimes.

I will speak about the requirements for this. Yes, we have requirements. I use the word rather facetiously, for compared to the requirements for those who have already ascended before this time, they are really rather easy requirements. First of all it is necessary to have some understanding of God, or some experience of God, to have an open heart towards that aspect of your higher Self. It does not matter so much how you philosophize or view this or label it, but to have an awareness of your Creator, your higher Self. You need to have an openness within your heart, to have an open heart and as best you can to love yourself unconditionally, for this is where it begins, and then to love unconditionally all that you see, all that you meet. In fact, to be a love radiator. Many of you are so beautiful it is redundant for me to speak of this. But nevertheless it is a requirement. It is not necessary for you to understand scientifically all that will occur in the ascension process. In fact, I do not think that anyone in this room could grasp it without a great deal of education. But there is some information you can study if you wish to understand intellectually how this occurs. I will recommend *The Keys of Enoch* book as a more scientific treatise on the Earth transformations, the ascension process and the role of the Hierarchy and extraterrestrial masters. However, it is not necessary for you to understand any more than the limited explanation I have already given you. It is more of an awareness, more of an expression of love in your heart, an openness to the process, and above all a desire, a longing to return, a longing to know your true completion and to complete your spiritual growth here on Earth. That's it. You see, it is not very difficult, is it? In fact, when the first wave of ascension occurs, if you are giving yourself to this process and desiring the ascension, you can have the experience of ascension even in your sleep. You do not need to become a great saint or yogi. If you are not meditating now, I would encourage you to begin. If you are, I would encourage you to continue and to focus a little bit more on this. It is not necessary for any of you to attain perfect self-mastery. I don't think that it is going to be possible within the time that is left, anyway. Know that you are already saints. Maybe that will make it easier for you. Know that you are returning to who you truly are, rather than developing a new aspect of your-selves. Truly you are going to see the veils removed around your own hearts and consciousness. I guarantee it. It will occur very soon in your lifetimes. We will take a great stride forward in our classes. Hopefully we can share this infor-mation and enough of the experience that you will go through any doubts or confusions. Of course your doubts will arise. You would not be human if you heard this information and did not have some skepticism about it. I encourage you to ask your questions. Know that there is part of you, your rational mind or your skeptical natures, which may never believe in this. We will be giving you a great deal of information and experience regarding the validity of this, though there will always be a part of you which has a little gnawing doubt that it will ever be occur-ring or that it is even possible. Know that you do not need to banish this part of your consciousness in order to have this experience. This is the part of you which will experi-ence it when it happens. And then you will know. Above all, love yourselves. Read the *Eagle's Wings* material*, as this is very beneficial.

So let me open the floor to questions at this time. Please feel free to be yourselves and ask me whatever you desire to ask. This does not mean I can answer all of your ques-tions. Within this framework of communication there are certain limitations, but I will do the best that I can.

"I don't have an understanding of what a Starseed or a Light Worker is, nor do I know how to find out whether I might be one or not."

I will tell you. You are one. There are many manifesta-tions of Light Workers and many experiences. There are many Starseeds, or Light Workers as I call them, who are completely unaware of anything relating to spirituality or meditation or ascension. You might say they are in a state of varying degrees of sleep. This is not a criticism of them

* see Readings Recommended by the Author, p. 177

as individuals. It is merely a statement of the power and density that exists on planet Earth. The veils are very thick here. If you are not clear whether you are a Starseed or Light Worker it is not an indication that you are not one, nor is it an indication that you are not going to have the opportunity to be an ascended being. You will have that opportunity. One of the aspects of unconditional love that is a requirement for this path is that we stop criticizing ourselves. We all carry within us ways of criticizing or judging our behaviors and levels of success. It is time for you to all love yourselves unconditionally, as well as you can, regardless of how well you are performing against your ideal goals and expected ways of being. So for you as an individual I would say if you can do some meditation and continue to come to these classes, we will work with you. If you continue through this course you will have quite an experience of awakening, quite an experience of your higher Self, much more than you have yet experienced. This is our intent and this is our promise to you. There is some exploration that needs to be done. It is the wisest course of action for any of you who are not quite certain about this, not quite sure of the truth of this. It is wise for you to continue to pursue this, to ask your questions and to make a full and thorough investigation. If what I am saying is true you have a lot to gain by doing this. And what I am saying is true.

"Could you comment on the term 'twin flame'?"

A twin flame is your equal and opposite double, or another aspect of your higher Self, a being which is completely connected with you. Or shall I say, a being who had their origins at the same time as you did. You might say that you were manifested at a certain point into individuality. You came from a twin flame combination. So if you are the feminine aspect of yourself, there is a masculine aspect, for lack of a better terminology. There is a being that is your ideal mate. One aspect of ascension is that generally you are reconnected with your twin flame essence. It is quite beautiful. The longing to be reconnected with the twin flame — to have the ideal relationship, the ideal love expression — is a very strong drive in human beings. It is the origin of your drive for relationship. At some level you are aware that somewhere there must be an ideal relationship because it feels so natural to you. So the twin flame is the perfect relationship for you, the being that is most completely aligned with you and is in fact part of you on some level. Many of your twin flame essences are not in physical form at this time. They are working from the ascended state. In fact I think some of you have twin flames whom you will be reuniting with upon your ascension. So if you are having trouble with finding the perfect mate for yourself, there may be a very good reason: he/she may not be here. As you grow spiritually there is something like a magnetic attraction which begins to occur between the twin flames. As they grow spiritually the magnetic attraction between them draws them together at a certain point. If they are not both in physical incarnation, the attraction will be completed when the ascension occurs. That is a book in itself. That is a little overview of the situation with regard to twin flames. It is quite a beautiful experience.

You also have soul families. You will be more and more reconnected with them as you grow, and especially after your ascension. There are beings who were created at the same time you were, in the same space and in the same way, who have the same characteristics as yourselves. And it is a very family type of feeling to be reunited with these. Most of your families are not in third-dimensional reality. Most of your connections are waiting for you to ascend, and then you will have a reunification with them. Upon your ascension you will be aware once again of who you really are and of these connections. It will be like waking up from a dream and remembering who you are. When you wake up in the morning you may be aware that you have just had a strange dream. And yet within thirty seconds you are awake and fully present in your normal consciousness and your normal personality. This is somewhat like the ascension process — that is, you awake from this third-dimensional experience to be reunited and reacquainted with your own higher Self, your own real personality, and then this life will be the dream.

"Sananda, those people who have been our parents in this lifetime or our children in this lifetime, is there a tendency for them to be part of our soul family?"

Not necessarily. It is possible, and there is a slight tendency, but it is a stronger relationship or connection than you might have in your ordinary relationships with your parents or children. Although if you are Starseeds or Light Workers chances are very good that your children are also. So there is an increased possibility that they are in your soul family. It is not necessarily the case that your parents are Light Workers. Some are, most are not.

"You said ascension would happen very quickly, and I realize the time element is difficult to translate, but what do you mean by 'quickly'?"

You are referring to when the first wave of ascension will occur?

"Yes."

I would say that it is imminent. Imminent to us may seem like a long time to you. Sometimes a day can seem like a long time to you in your reality. I would say give yourselves a time frame from between three weeks from now to five years from now. It must occur by then in my opinion. There are many variables which dictate the timing of this event. It is not in our control, even my own control. I wish that it were. But it is only from the highest source that the final word will come. We are hoping to collect as many Starseeds as we can in the first wave. In fact, we are calling the first wave the "leap of faith." For

those of you who go in the first wave will have little to go
on except our channeled messages, your own spiritual
experience of our presence, and your own belief and faith.
Those who come in the second and third wave will have
some visible experience that it is possible because they will
be face to face with someone who has done it already. So it
is impossible to give you an exact time, but let me say it is
likely that it could occur even this year. I would suggest
that your proper attitude would be that you are ready to
go at any time, but you are maintaining your responsibilities in your lives and are prepared to stay for as long as is
required. I do not think that it will be more than five years.
I think it will be much less than that. My opinion of what
the Creator has in mind is that He is waiting until the last
possible moment to gather as many Starseeds as possible
into the first wave, so that there are the maximum number
of Ascended Masters returning to do the maximum amount
of good, to cover the Earth with Christs. So if it takes a
little bit longer than you hope, it is because, in my opinion,
He is waiting until that last moment. The more who come
on the first wave, the more can be saved in subsequent
waves, and more will experience this. Again, the first and
second waves are primarily going to be made up of
Starseeds. The first wave will undoubtedly be Starseeds,
and only the small percentage of Starseeds who are awake
to this. The second wave will most likely be the majority
of Starseeds. Hopefully there will be some humans who
are not of that category who will be prepared to go. The
third wave will occur at the last moment, before and during
the major transformations and cataclysms, as you might
view them. I will call it the transformation of the Earth's
surface. At that point it will most likely not be possible to
sustain life on this planet. All this will likely occur within
this decade. I think Ashtar can give you more scientific
and specific information about that. Know that our goal is
to lift as many beings as possible from this world into their
higher state of awareness within these three waves. The
Earth will undergo its transformation. It will become a

fifth-dimensional entity, and afterwards there will be a repopulation of the Earth by beings who are compatible with fifth-dimensional reality. So you might say that no one will be able to be earthlings unless they have ascended.

"It has come to my attention that a great deal of self-healing needs to be done. I'm having trouble reconciling in my mind how a process like ascension can occur before the self-healing is done."

This is an excellent question. The self-healing that you are speaking of is something we are going to be addressing dramatically within this very course. Let me say that you have an emotional body that has been with you for many lifetimes. It has borne the brunt of a lot of negativity and fear and confusion. You are all to some extent scarred by this in your emotional bodies. If you have been working on yourselves, doing your healing and meditations, you have processed a great deal of it. If you are more new to this, then you may have a bit more work to do. Yet I would say that the transformation that is necessary is not something that will take a great deal of time. You do not need to be one hundred percent healed and whole emotionally or spiritually in order to ascend. It makes it easier for you to go through the process. It makes it more enjoyable perhaps, but there is nevertheless the opportunity for you to do so. We can work miracles with each of you. This is our intention. There were people from the first and second classes who did not necessarily meditate very much, but through the course of the class they began to meditate and feel a connection with their guidance, and by the end they were channeling Ascended Masters themselves. This is something that can occur as a result of your interactions with us. We will be working with you — especially if you choose this ascension path as your goal — quite directly and dramatically and showering you with our love and healing. We will be assisting you to release those limitations that you have accepted around yourselves — all the pain and suffering that each of you has absorbed — that to some extent still clings to your emotional bodies and beings. This can be surrendered and released. And it does not need to be painful. It does not need to be overly difficult. Though it will be challenging.

Let us assume that at the end of this class you feel a commitment to pursuing the ascension and to taking this course. You may feel you have a lot of work and healing to do. Just do the best that you can to open yourself to this process and to meditation. You can get some guidance in meditation if you desire. I will help you or others can help you. If you sincerely apply yourself and have that sincere desire in your heart, I do not see any reason why it is not possible for you to go. If you are not going in the first wave — if it is not your state to go in the first wave (perhaps you are not quite ready or you choose not to go at that time) — there will be another opportunity that occurs not too far after the first wave and you can in all likelihood be well prepared by that time. Don't give up on yourself and feel that you cannot experience the healing and make the first wave. You do not know when it will be. I would say to recognize that you are a very powerful and divine being. You have, as all have, accepted limitations and veils and accepted more of the pain of life and the density that exists here into yourself and into your body. This will be released. If you have a sincere desire, it will be released. You can participate in it. A lot of it will be occurring without your active participation. This is the time when miracles are going to occur. This is not as much of a miracle as you might think. So be positive and make your choice based not upon what you think is possible for you, but make your choice based on what you would like if anything were possible for you. You may be feeling in your heart that you are not worthy or ready for ascension. And yet your heart may be telling you that it would like to ascend more than anything in this world. You can choose to relate to that part of you which feels you can't do it, or you can choose to relate to the part of you that knows it wants to. So relate to that part of yourself. That's all you need to do basically. You will receive guidance and will be led to various experiences as you were led to this particular channeling. There are no accidents. We are not collecting any dead wood here. We are only collecting beautiful beings and you are all in that category. There will be more guidance. You can ask whatever questions you desire. You can ask for guidance concerning meditations. You can ask for a private session with this channel. He would be happy to do so. If you feel you would like a personalized experience, this is available to all. I am doing my best to communicate in this format in a rather general way.

"The people who over the years have claimed to see spaceships, are they seeing your ships or some third-dimensional ships?"

Let me say that there are other extraterrestrial beings in the Earth's sphere of activity aside from the divine beings of the Ashtar Command and the ascended brotherhood. There are beings who are of lesser stature spiritually. There are beings who are somewhat neutral in their attitude towards the Earth, or rather scientific. There are other beings who are downright negative in their effects upon humanity. Their ships are generally visible. You may at times see a ship of the Ashtar Command (they can of course materialize in the third dimension where you can witness them). In the future that will happen *en masse*. It is part of the plan. The Earth will be surrounded by ships visibly during the last stage of the final evacuation. For the most part we are remaining invisible in the fifth dimension. It is much safer. The Ashtar Command has contacted all the world leaders. The world leaders have not been very open to exchanging information and opening to their presence. For this reason, it is not entirely safe for the Ashtar Command to manifest in third-dimensional reality. The other ships that are here are something that you should be wary of, something that you should be rather concerned with in terms of their origins. If you see a ship visibly manifested I would not necessarily run up to it and say, "Here I am Ashtar, take me." They may take you, but not to Ashtar. There are beings that have made alliances with the secret governments. They are doing their best to confuse the issues here. The Ashtar Command is more powerful and enlightened and can take care of them when the time comes. If you see a spaceship, simply observe it and ask your heart or feeling nature if you feel a Christ vibration. I don't think this will happen, but if you should see a space being, first of all, if they do not look like a human being, I would be wary. Most of the negative extra-terrestrials do not look the same as we do. Human beings are the majority of the human creation in the universes. You might say that humanity is fashioned in the image of the Father. There are other beings who are not quite as beautiful to look at from your perspective. You would be surprised to know that they are not as beautiful to look at from our perspective. Some of them have no emotional bodies. In other words they have never experienced love. So you can detect them by their emanations. You will all be protected if you simply request to be protected from anything negative of this nature occurring to you. It is highly unlikely.

"Are the beings from the Pleiades a good group?"

The Pleiadians are of the positive. They are in the alliance of the Ashtar Command. The Pleiadians and the beings from the constellation of Orion are also positive. The stargate within the Orion constellation is an interdimensional doorway into other dimensions. It is through this doorway that many ascended beings come in their light vehicles.

"Sananda, is it true that there is a whole population of people in the Inner Earth?"

Yes. I would not necessarily call them all humans, but there are certain evolvements of beings. They are going to experience the culmination of their experience just as humanity does.

"Would they be considered the Yetis?"

No, that's a horse of a different color. These have spacecraft which they use to come into the Earth's atmosphere to a certain extent, but they can't travel interdimensionally as the Ashtar Command or the more evolved beings. I think if you will ask Ashtar your questions about the space beings he will be a little bit more informed. I am informed but I do not want to steal his thunder. Needless to say, there are beings throughout the universes. This is one galaxy and one universe. There are many universes. There are many dimensions of existence overlapping one another. There are beings of incredible power and magnificence existing. You might say the Earth exists at one of the far corners of one local universe. It is one of the more backward places in the creation. So what you experience by way of the Ashtar Command will be quite enlightening and surprising and delightful to you. As you resume your place in the hierarchy, as you experience the benefits of being an ascended being, you will come into a greater understanding of this hierarchy and of the incredible magnificence and beauty and purpose of the Creation. You have seen a horse with blinders on? A third-dimensional reality is like wearing blinders, only you might say the blinders go all the way around. When you begin to open to higher consciousness, there is a little crack in the blinders and a little bit of light comes in. You do not fully remove the blinders until you complete your Earth life and experience the ascension. Then they are fully removed and all of the wonders are made apparent to you. You see, it is very important for you to focus on ascension at this time. It is your next step. It is a chance that is much more than one in a million. It is more like one in a trillion. And you are here: you have physical bodies, you are Light Workers, you are hearing about this, you are very blessed beings. So stop thinking you are limited and that there is something wrong with you. You are special. You will feel your own specialness more and more.

"It was suggested in [the booklet] On Eagle's Wings* that we study The Urantia Book.* Why is this important?"

It is not entirely important. It is something for those who are more intellectually inclined, who require a bit more intellectual proof of reality and information about the ascension. There is a great deal about the life of Jesus from a more real perspective. In the Bible there is much missing. There is little direct mention in the Bible of the possibility for ascension for humanity. There is a great deal that has been twisted or left out. So this book has a bit more of the true story, and you can read this if you desire. It is very thick. It is very difficult reading in a way. *The Keys of Enoch** book is somewhat the same. But there are certain beings who require a great deal of proof-positive and verification.

"The last few months I have had feelings like I was dying. It intensified over the last two weeks, where I was having nightmares and panic attacks and a lot of things coming up regarding death. Astrologically I'm going through some kind of death. I'm to find a new way of relating to the world. I had problems sleeping. Since I made the decision to come here I've been sleeping fine and have felt better."

I think that you are intended to be here and intended to hear about this. If you are having an experience of death it is because your ego is transforming, or "dying," as they say. Some people need more of a kick in the pants to come here. But if you are here, it is no accident. Your higher Self has been trying to get your attention. It has gotten your attention and you are here. There is an aspect to this

* see Readings Recommended by the Author, p. 177

healing or growth that sometimes can feel like pain to you. It is because you are attached to your ego, your limited self. When your limited self undergoes expansion or healing, it feels like pain at times. One thing that we will be working on with all of you — and Archangel Michael will be working on specifically — will be severing your attachments to these limited experiences. He will be helping to cut your attachments to that process that your egos are going through. In fact you will be cutting your attachment to your ego all together. The transformation will continue. There is emotional healing which will be taking place. It will not always feel painless, but I think you will have a greater awareness of the perfection of it as you become more liberated in your experience, as you take on more power and feel that which you are longing for, feel it coming from your guides and your higher Self, feel it welling up within your heart, and have a more continual experience of love. This is very healing. I think this is one aspect you personally will appreciate a great deal. So we will be working with you. You may call on me for your emotional healing. I will give you a hint. Anyone here who has healing to go through, especially emotionally, if you call on me I will assist you. And I will come if you call my name with sincerity.

"Is the ascension process the same as what is described in the Bible as 'People will be taken up into the air,' especially as described by the Jehovah's Witnesses?"

Yes, the event that they are speaking of in Revelation is the last wave or the final evacuation process. The way it appears to occur to the innocent bystander is that the person next to you on the bus has just disappeared. And so it says that two people will be sitting together and one will be taken and the other will not. So this is more in reference to the final evacuation. It is the same process that you will undergo. You will be lifted. The Scriptures of the Revelation are accurate for the most part, though all prophecy needs some flexibility. We are reserving the right to do whatever we see fit to save this world. We will not be bound by any particular scripture or prophecy, although for the most part many of them are quite accurate. It is for all of you to be spontaneous and open-hearted and enjoy the action. There is a great deal of action occurring. You are going to have a ringside seat. In fact, if you choose to be Ascended Masters and return in that capacity, you will be the cause of a great deal of action. You will be the source of much scratching of heads and soul-searching by other beings.

"When you were in a body on this Earth as Jesus Christ, did you ever marry?"

No, I didn't. I knew a Mary.

"I have a friend who insists she was married to Jesus."

There are many beings who can feel that connection with me but, formally, no.

"Are you with a twin flame now?"

My twin flame is existing in another sphere at this time. So we are together on one level. We are aware of one another. But at the level that I work with the Ashtar Command and with you, no. This does not mean that you cannot propose to me if you so desire. I am available for love sessions. In fact it is my hope that you will all make many dates with me.

"The picture of you that is in this room, is that an accurate picture?"

Very close to my fifth-dimensional manifestation, the realm wherein I have a light body; yes, it is close. Wouldn't you like to know what you look like in a fifth-dimensional body? Let's get back to business.

"Can you describe it?"

I would say that upon your ascension you will attain to a more youthful age. Most will appear to be of the age of the early twenties or mid-twenties. This will be your appearance for as long as you have your ascended body. You will rarely depart from that. Let me also say, children of the Light Workers who ascend will ascend also, and will be accelerated to the same age that you are. So I'm warning you now that your parenting days are over.

"Can you define a child?"

It is a fine line at a certain point. But there is a fine line within each being where they become fully responsible for their own actions and choices. This usually occurs sometime in the late teens to the early twenties. If you have children that are on the borderline, know that if they are still dependent on you, there is an excellent chance they will ascend when you do. And the children will be the first to be evacuated during the final evacuation. In fact, all of the children of the Earth will be evacuated first. They are considered innocent beings.

So, my friends, I am afraid our time is up for this evening. Know that you will have many more opportunities to ask your questions. I ask you each, in the days ahead, to reflect upon what we have shared together this evening. And I hope you will decide to participate in this adventure we have been attempting to describe. Go within and ask for guidance. Perhaps we can meet again within your own hearts. This is where you will find the truth. Until next time, goodnight.

❧ Class Two ❧

THE ASHTAR COMMAND

⋘ Ashtar ⋙

Good evening, my dear friends. This is Ashtar. I am very happy to be here with you this evening, to share information and the love that we can share together in these momentous times. Please relax yourselves and be comfortable and I will give you an introduction. I would like to address some information concerning the Ashtar Command: our purpose, who we are, and what we are doing here speaking to you in this strange manner. I will give you the opportunity to ask me questions later on. I'm sure you will all have more.

So you have been introduced to this ascension idea, this plan of ours. Let me say it is a plan of the Christ's, under whose auspices we are working directly. I would like to speak a little bit about my role and the role of the Ashtar Command in fulfilling this. Perhaps it will put your mind more at ease about extraterrestrial ascended beings surrounding you. If this is a new idea to you then I am sure there is or has been at least a little bit of alarm, so I come to soothe you a little bit. You can see that I have no horns upon my head nor do I have green skin. We are human in appearance as you are. There are humans throughout the universe. The Earth is not the only inhabited planet, and as the Lord made man in His image, it is only logical that there are images of Him scattered throughout His creation. So, let me say that the Ashtar Command is an intergalactic alliance of etheric ships and human beings and angelic beings. We are here on a mission and we have been for many thousands of years. We have been monitoring and assisting in the evolvement of the planet and the consciousness of the human species. We have from time to time manifested physically, but largely we work spiritually. There may come a time — probably there will come a time — when you will see our ships, but it is a little too early for that yet. We are remaining in the fifth dimension. So we are surrounding you with millions of ships and many millions of volunteers, servants, and ascended beings. You cannot see us unless we lower our frequency to third-dimensional time and space. Nevertheless we are here and we are fully functioning. In fact, at this time our efforts have been redoubled and we have a great number of fleets surrounding the planet, doing much work.

Our work consists of many different areas. Largely, we are assisting in the elevation of consciousness during this period in which the planet is growing towards its ascension. We are assisting in evolvement. We are delivering our trainings to you in your sleep. We are delivering our telepathic messages to those of you who can hear and receive them. We are opening communication links each day. There are more and more of you who are opening to the aspects of channeling and telepathic communication with us. And when I say us, I am referring to the Ashtar Command and all of the Ascended Masters of the Great White Brotherhood. We are working in unison, you see. Each of us in our different areas of specialty, but as a coordinated effort. We are a very organized group of beings. We take time for fun and play as you do. In fact we have perfected it a little bit more than you have, for we have a little more freedom, and yet at the same time we are quite organized and impeccable in our manifestations. At least we try to be.

Aside from the work that we are doing with these communications and messages in enhancing individual spiritual growth, we are working with the planet, and we have been for some time, to assist the planet in maintaining balance. We have up until recently been working to deter activities along the fault lines. This activity has ceased. It is time now to allow this to occur and it is occurring (earthquakes, etc.). We have been working with our technology to assist in controlling somewhat the rotation of the Earth, controlling the wobble which will inevitably result in a new polar shift. We have been doing much to focus the light which is being broadcast from the Creator Himself throughout the universe. Specifically we have been working with energy grids. These are difficult to describe. They appear somewhat like meridian lines with various vortex points which surround your planet, and we use these grids to assist in balancing and controlling the rate and the nature of the spiritual ray which is emanating to your world. This is, as I have said, to assist in balancing, for your world is existing in a state of precarious balance. At this time we are doing everything we can, and have been for quite some time, to allow you and all of humanity to have the maximum time to develop spiritually and to be prepared for the change and the ascension which is taking place on this world.

With regard to ascension, I would say that the Earth herself is ascending. This is an unavoidable growth which must occur and it will result in some Earth changes. Most likely they will be quite dramatic. We are working with individual ascension especially strongly at this time because the time is so critical. We are attempting to reach as many beings as possible, especially the Starseed or volunteers — you who have been among us in the past and will return to be with us again. We are assisting all those on this planet who are open to spiritual growth and awareness at this time. All those who have love in their hearts are feeling this emanation that we are assisting in, and are receiving subconscious messages from us.

It gives me great pleasure to be here with you. Some of you are new to me, at least in this particular format, though we have been watching and observing all of you for some time. I must say you are branded individuals. You are all glowing a little bit more profoundly than most of your cohorts here on Earth. So it is very difficult for you to escape our attentions. Because you are glowing so much it makes it easier for us to connect with you and to find you no matter where you may try to hide, to share with you the love that we have, and the gifts that we have awaiting you. So it is a time of great celebration on our part and I think on your part. It is a matter of your assimilating this information and especially assimilating this new energy which is manifesting. As you do so, you will find your life becomes more and more of a celebration and there is more joy and love within you and things begin to look quite a bit more positive. You have been surrounded by negative thoughts and emanations for many lifetimes. We are deprogramming you in our way, not by brainwashing you but by showering you with so much love that you must melt. So if you have hardened your hearts a little bit in an effort to protect yourselves I understand this. It is part of your growth process, but love will melt this ice. For what we come to share is the same love that has been expressed by every master who has been here.

The Christ is our supreme commander. We work in conjunction with the archangels, specifically Archangel Michael. We are a broad-spectrum alliance of beings. We come from near and far in the universe and from other universes. We come as volunteers and servants and I will tell you why we come. It is because we have experienced so much love we don't know what to do with it. And we must share. So we come from the far corners of the universe, to areas which have yet to attain the restructuring and reordering that the Creator has ordained, and we come in a timely manner to assist. Now we will assist in your ascension.

So, I will speak a little bit about your individual ascension work, as this is the main focus of this class and our role in it. Let me say that there is a spiritual science to this ascension. It is involved with love. It is involved with spiritual growth primarily, but there is also a certain "high tech" aspect to it. This is where our etheric ships or merkabah vehicles come into play. We are here surrounding the planet and we are in touch with all of you and we are awaiting your evacuation and ascension. This is the physical lifting back into our ships where your ascension process will be completed. Those of you who are aware of and feel comfortable with the extraterrestrial or Space Brotherhood aspect of this ascension will have an experience of entering our ships upon the time of your lifting. There are other beings who have not this understanding, and if they were to find themselves in that situation would perhaps feel fear or disorientation. They will be feeling the ascension in somewhat different ways but they will also be lifted into the ships, though they may have the experience that they are being accompanied by angels rather than space beings. You see, there is very little difference or no difference.

So the first wave is what we are focusing on at this time, as we said in our previous class. As Sananda said concerning the first wave, it is to manifest as soon as there are sufficient volunteers. For our part we are ready on our end of things. We are continuing to align the energy grids and to focus the energy, to assist in the growing presence of God upon this planet and within this planet and within each of you. We are doing work to assist in the clearing of the emotional body of the Earth, the emotional aura which has contained much of negative emotions and negative projections. This manifests often as air pollution. We are working to clear this somewhat. All of this work makes the path of ascension all that much easier, as there are then less layers of density for you to go through. Nevertheless, we are mainly waiting for more volunteers who are interested in this first wave of ascension and who are willing to take the time and energy to prepare themselves for this. Sananda has already outlined the general ways you can prepare yourselves. I will say that at the time of your lifting, regardless of whether it is the first or subsequent liftings, your experience will be somewhat as he has outlined. You will be taken to a ship. You will be lifted physically as an etheric and physical being. You will be given an opportunity to make choices concerning your next manifestation. You could continue to work with planet Earth as an Ascended Master or you could return to one of the more spiritual realms from which you came. Some of you have sources that are extremely different from your current manifestations. Some of you are angelic beings and others are of the Space Brotherhood. Some are humans or other ascended beings. You will be reconnected with your original presence, who you truly are.

So given the information that you will receive at that time you will make a choice as to whether you desire to continue your work in this area. I recommend this as the most profound spiritual leap you could take: to become an Ascended Master and to return. There are many choices and the choice will be yours. You will receive training if you wish to be an Ascended Master and return to assist the remainder of humanity in their ascension process. All must be lifted or leave this planet in some way in the remaining years, in order to make way for the Earth's clearing. There will be much training offered to you. You will be able to experience a great deal of wonder at first until you re-acclimate yourself. You will be taken to one of the mother ships. There we will have a great celebration. We are growing impatient to be reunited with you as you are with us. You will find that it is likely some of you may have surpassed us in your spiritual evolvement. So I would recommend that you do not look at us as gods who are above you, who are to be worshipped, but rather as your brothers and sisters.

You will have the opportunity, if you choose, to remain upon the ships. The ships you will be housed in are quite large. There are of course shuttlecraft. There are platforms. There is one that is situated over this home, as this is one of the headquarters of the Ashtar Command. We have a communications platform ethereally located above this dwelling. You will be taken to the mother ships where you will be able to experience rest and relaxation as some of you are growing quite weary with third-dimensional limitation. It will be time for you to reacquaint yourself with your spiritual powers and your I AM presence. You will merge and become again ascended beings. You will have to be retrained in aspects of creativity and manifestation and with your powers and how to use them.

You will have no more need to struggle on a survival level. You will have what you desire instantaneously manifested by your own desire. This all ascended beings can do. In my opinion it is one of the unfortunate circumstances of this Earth life or third-dimensional life that all who are here are so limited and enslaved by the need to earn a livelihood to pay for food and lodging. All this takes so much time and energy. You have a very difficult time and very little energy left for even a minimum of spiritual work and service. Some of you have this somewhat beat, but most of humanity is still struggling for survival. So you will have to get used to having a lot more freedom. I think you will enjoy this. You will have to get used to being connected consciously and constantly with the Creator. You are working towards this now. Some of you are making great strides in your growth. Nevertheless, until your final ascension you will still have a remainder of limited ego or density around you. So regardless of the state that you attain (which can be quite expanded), there will still be a transformation which takes place at that last moment.

So what is it like living on an etheric fifth-dimensional ship? It is quite pleasant and aesthetic. Some of the ships are hundreds of miles in diameter. There are cycles such as you experience here of day and night — simulated cycles. Sunlight is processed in a way such as to still allow for a day and night experience. There are natural settings. We have forests, streams, lakes, and oceans full of creatures. We do not have poison oak, however. We have selected wisely from among all species. We have avoided anything of this sort. You might say it is a very Eden-like existence. It is similar to what the Earth will become after the Earth changes have occurred and the Earth has ascended to a fifth-dimensional entity.

There will be a time when those who are evacuated will be offered the opportunity to return to Earth as ascended beings and to recolonize the Earth. The Earth will be dramatically improved by that point. And those beings who inhabit the Earth will have the same Ascended Master capabilities as those of us on other planes do now. So there will be no need to have a "good credit rating." You will all have unlimited credit with the Creator. You will all use your credit wisely and responsibly to create manifestations that are in alignment with God's will. It will be automatic with you at that point. So there is no fear of misusing your powers. You will be purified to the extent that you will have no more desire to abuse the privileges that you will be receiving.

So after some time spent aboard the ships, you will have completed your training. Then you will be returning (those of you who decide to follow this course as Ascended Masters) to Earth, to exist here and to walk side by side with humans — to create quite a ruckus with your manifestations: your miracles, your ability to materialize and dematerialize at will, your ability to create out of etheric substance all that you require. I think you have heard of the powers of Sananda when he was here as Jesus. This is what I am referring to. As it is written in the Scriptures, it is our hope that you will do what he did and more. This is available to you. So we are hoping with this brilliant plan that with enough returnees as Ascended Masters manifesting throughout the globe, and dramatically doing so, we expect that this will create quite a stir. It should inspire many others to find out what is going on and to question this New Age that is manifesting. There will be much teaching and you will be trained. You will know how to protect yourselves from any negativity. And you will know how to read human beings, read their thoughts and feelings. You will have full use of the mind. And as Sananda said last week, you will be immortal and ever youthful. So when you return you will look a little bit younger and more radiant, but you will still look the same. You will still be the same being, though somewhat transformed.

So this is the work that we are doing in this class. It's to prepare you for all of this and to answer your questions which will arise. We will be working more and more experientially with you from this point onwards in the classes, to assist you in preparing yourselves and purifying and healing. This is to open your hearts to unconditional love for yourselves so that you can fulfill the requirements necessary to partake of this adventure. So if you have been bored up until now with your Earth life, and many of you have, having somewhat of a remembrance of what it is like to be an ascended being or creator-god, now your time of boredom is over. Now it is time to awaken and prepare yourselves. Make your decisions concerning this ascension process. You will not avoid it but you may perhaps postpone it a bit. But I say why postpone what is so blissful and so liberating? It is your destiny. Above and beyond all your worldly manifestations and missions and services, your ascension is your prime directive at this time. It is your primary service. By giving yourself to the ascension process you will realign your priorities somewhat and you will find it much simpler knowing where to put your energy. You will be more directed if you have not been until now. You will be more inspired to meditate. You will have more of a reason to meditate. You will feel a little bit more of an imminence. You will feel more of a presence around you if you will give yourself to this process. It is your choice. I am here as a recruiter. I will not make you sign anything, for you will sign in your own hearts. But I tell you that the joy and the love we have to offer and to share with you is far beyond what you have yet experienced. You can have the experience of day-to-day growth and closeness with the Ascended Masters. You can have easy access and communication with the Ashtar Command and the ascended brotherhood. In fact, this is part of our teaching and part of our preparation. This contact is to open you because it is very beneficial at this time. Do you have any questions for me?

"Is your general schedule still the same? In my business it would not be appropriate to line up long-term clients if I were to be leaving soon."

You are very responsible are you not? This is commendable. I would encourage you to live as if you were going to be here for another five years or so. Despite the fact that the first wave of ascension could occur at any time, there are no guarantees when. So it is not our wish that you or anyone else should throw your security up in the air. It is for you to continue to act as if you are going to be here. If you feel strongly inspired within to somewhat alter your schedule of work you may do so. I would like to add that it is your responsibility and not mine. If anyone here should quit their job and assume that in two days' time they will be on one of the ships, I don't want to hear about it. We are not giving any dates because it is not known by us when the exact date will be. There is only one being who knows the date and He has not communicated it to us.

"Who's that?"

Let me say the supreme commander, the Lord God Almighty. Even Sananda does not know. You may ask him and he will tell you the same thing. We are very patient because we understand that time and space are very important aspects of your third-dimensional reality. You must understand that for us it is quite different. For us one of your days passes like a wink of an eye or like a moment. But it also seems timeless to us. So it is very difficult for us to even speculate. We have made an effort to do so, saying that it could be as soon as this year. But this is a speculation. It is not a prediction.

"Will it be easier for us from now until the time until we ascend?"

I would say your spiritual work will be easier. Your material work will be easier if it is in alignment with your higher purpose. If your material work is not quite so aligned with your higher purpose or mission then perhaps you will feel a little bit of friction there. There will be some realigning occurring with you, most likely. But it won't be to the point where you need to dramatically alter your lifestyle. Your lifestyles are probably fine just as they are. But we do suggest that you meditate more and increase your amount of focused concentration in meditation. But do not dramatically alter your lifestyles. It is difficult because there is an emotional healing process that occurs when you accept this challenge to be on the spiritual path. As you know, this makes it sometimes difficult to feel fully functional in the material realm and your work situations. But for the most part there will be a great deal of clearing that takes place emotionally, so that you will all feel a great deal lighter as a result of the process. So there will be times that are challenging because your growth is being acceler-ated, but it will result in easier times for you.

"Do you need a certain percentage of volunteers or is it just the opening of the heart? How do you measure where the planet is en masse *in regards to reaching the goal of ascension?"*

With regards to the first wave, there is a certain critical mass which must be attained. It is probably somewhere between one or two thousand beings. That is our prediction as to the number that will be required. It could be more or less. But we think that if there were two thousand Starseeds who were ready to go on the first wave that it would probably be sufficient. Again, this is an estimate.

"Does the number 144,000 fit in with the ascension at all?"

You have been reading your *Keys of Enoch* book. 144,000 is a general estimate of the number of Starseeds or ascended beings who are here at this time. So you see there are roughly 144,000 of you who have taken this mission as Starseeds a long time ago. And we are only looking for a small percentage of that in order to make the first wave possible. So there is a percentage factor I suppose. But it is more of a love factor that we are looking for. It's more of an openness. Needless to say we had hoped there would be much more readiness. We had hoped that the situation here would have worked out somewhat differently. It has turned out that the vast majority of those who incarnated here as Starseeds have themselves fallen into a rather deep sleep and have been existing as if they were ordinary third-dimensional human beings. So there is going to be some shaking up required to even awaken them, let alone to awaken the mass of humanity which they have come to serve.

So I am honored to be with those of you who are awakened at this point. Know that you are in the minority. Even in the New Age movement, there are many beings who are somewhat familiar with New Age philosophy but have not yet opened themselves to this information and experience. There are many borderline cases and we are hoping to pull them in. We are hoping that many of you will assist us in doing so. That is the number one requirement: the numbers of human beings, the number of Starseeds. There are other factors but this is the prime one that you should concern yourselves with. First of all, be concerned with your own preparedness. Be clear about your own desire and readiness. And then network this information.

"I read that when we return to the Earth we will come with a connection to the ship for protection. Is this so?"

Yes, you will have some sort of jewelry. It will be something of a communication device but also something that will allow you to beam yourself back aboard instantaneously.

It sounds a lot like Star Trek. Was that channelled?"

It was not directly channeled but certain ideas were pulled in. There have been many motion pictures and things of that sort which have involved certain aspects of this. But it was not channeled directly. I think you will find there is much openness in the artistic community. They have the ability to channel certain lyrics or musical pieces or writings. This perhaps was inspired somewhat in this way.

"I'm having a problem balancing my meditation with my daily duties. Can you suggest how much we should be meditating?"

I would say that it is not necessary to create chaos in your life by avoiding your responsibilities in order to meditate. I think that if you begin the process with sincerity, and use quality rather than quantity at first, then you will automatically create the space wherein you will find yourself having more time to do so. If you utilize the time you have now to meditate, it will be a signal to your guides and teachers who are working with you that if you are given free time you utilize it wisely. Do not be overly concerned. Try to meditate at least twice a day. It is very good to take some retreat time if you can. I would recommend half a day a week for those who are accustomed to meditating. It will be quite an enhancement in your experience and in your consciousness of the presence of your guides and of your own higher Self manifesting. So it is relative. Begin with fifteen minute intervals or a half hour and work your way up. We will find a way to elevate you if your heart is sincere.

"Is there any protection technique you can authorize?"

Yes. Call upon Archangel Michael. Ask him to surround you with his blue light and to use his sword to cut your psychic connections with all human creations. You will find this is quite elevating, as it detaches you almost instantaneously from your personal attachments. I would say they are more likely to cause you distress than any other entities. This is sufficient.

"When we ascend, will there be a way of notifying family members of what happened or do they just find out the best way they can?"

This is a commonly asked question. There will be two ways that they can understand. Not everyone will, mind you. First, there will be those who are close enough to you to know that you are following an ascension path and that you will perhaps someday disappear. Those who are very close to you and who are spiritually oriented and who will not consider you crazy can be told this. I would not communicate it with others who are not open, as you will receive somewhat of a negative response. So those who are open to this and have been communicated with can be told that if you are to disappear at a certain time not to be alarmed because it will mean that you have ascended. Then there are ways to communicate with those other family members who are not so open. We have ways to communicate with them via messengers or messages. We can accommodate them if this is your wish. Of course we cannot spend our time dramatically reaching out and touching everyone you have met in your lives and manifesting before them and telling them that you have ascended. This is quite a job. If there is someone who is very close to you, then perhaps they can be comforted so they will know you have not perished or been in any danger. We have ways of connecting with people in ways they are open to receiving. Perhaps we could manifest a letter in their mailbox or have them visited by an angelic presence. And also their hearts will be telling them, and they will receive messages in their sleep, so that their subconscious will be prepared for the information that is presented to them. I would say for you it is important to be prepared to simply leave the scene and detach yourself from your relationships and attachments. This is the correct attitude for you to have. It is not beneficial to be overly concerned about those you leave behind, as you are leaving so that you may serve them better. Perhaps it will be possible for you to return in person and greet them by materializing in their living room. If you think they have a strong heart you may perhaps do this. We have addressed the issue of your children previously. They are of course of top priority with us, as they are with you.

"In regard to members of our family who are not awakened or not even near to being so, what can we do to make them ignite just a little bit without seeming too 'far out'?"

Unconditional love. You need not speak to someone with this information if they are not ready to hear it. Nevertheless, all hearts are open to receiving love. There is a way to love everyone and touch everyone's heart in a way that they are open to receiving. It may not be anything related to what you would consider a spiritual practice. It could be a foot massage. But whatever you do in a loving way for another enhances their spiritual growth. And the number one service you can do for them is to experience your own ascension, thereby shocking them into an awakened state. Your number one priority in service is to follow the ascension path, if this is your choice. You will do more as Ascended Masters than you have done as third-dimensional beings. You will be able to transmit much more love in ways that people can truly feel and be transformed by. This is your role at this time, and it is quite an honor that you have before you. In fact even to hear about this information at this time is an honor, as I am honored to bring you this communication.

Above all be aware that these times are non-standard, not "business as usual." These times are magnificent in their opportunities and possibilities. You have an opportunity that has been granted very few beings. The results of your accepting this challenge will be quite marvelous. You will receive a promotion in your evolvement. There is a spiritual hierarchy, and the closer you get to the ultimate God — the presence of the One Creator — the more opportunities and the more your experience will be: the more fringe benefits you will receive, the broader your choices of service, and you will have the opportunity to go beyond the realm from which you originally came. So if you were a seventh dimension angel perhaps you will be able to attain to a higher dimension and be that much closer to the Source. This is the ultimate longing for all of the beings who are in manifested creation, regardless of whether they are angelic presences or clouds of spiritual consciousness or physical forms or ascended physical forms. We all have the longing to be closer to the throne.

"Do Starseeds run in families or is there one here and one there in a family?"

I would say that all variations are possible. There is a likelihood that those in your immediate family are Starseeds also, though there is a possibility that some may not be. It is impossible for you to be able to tell completely even by their behavior. As I've said, of the many Starseeds who are here, the majority have fallen into a deep state of sleep. So the fact that they are not acting like Starseeds does not mean that they are not. It just means they are a little deeper undercover. I would not be concerned about this. They will find their right places.

"What happens to those who are not Starseeds who don't want to wake up and become ascended beings?"

Many will experience what you refer to as death if they do not make the choice to be evacuated as of the last lifting. They will be transported in spirit to a place that is fitting their level of evolvement. Those who make the choice to evacuate by the final evacuation, wherein all human beings will have the opportunity to leave — this is just before the cataclysmic events such as we have described will occur — those who have enough love in their hearts to give themselves to the lifting process, but who are not yet ready to ascend, will be kept and served in third-dimensional craft and will be transported to planets where they will feel more comfortable and can continue to work out their karma. Those who are not open to the lifting process will most likely experience the death process at that time. Their souls will be evacuated without their bodies. Those who are here in the guise of human beings but who are truly the Dark Lords and those other types of emanations will be dealt with summarily. Some will be returned to the central sun for restructuring. There are many beings upon this world who do not belong on this world, and who have created chaos from the moment they set foot upon this planet — who have enslaved other beings, the more innocent mass of humanity, with their various powers and power plays and desires for dominion. They are fallen angels. All are existing and all will be dealt with. There is a great deal of re-ordering that is taking place throughout the universe at this time. The re-ordering mechanism will have rearranged the Earth, and the Earth will be reordered in alignment with the will of the Father. So no being will be punished, but all beings will be taken to where they are more in company with those they are aligned with. Ascended beings will be with ascended beings and humans will be with other humans who have an innocence and openness to growth. And they will not be subjected to these powers and the dark presences. The powers and dark presences will be given opportunities to change their ways. But those who do not will most likely be disintegrated and be restructured. It is possible for a soul to die.

"It's hard for me to understand that if there are 144,000 Starseeds and you're trying to wake up 2,000, that so many have forgotten. I thought there were cellular remembrances that might trigger an understanding. And also, in our dream state I know we are working on this, so can they be contacted that way? I'm just amazed that we are in such bad shape. I just think if Starseeds agreed to this mission, then why can't this be more productive? How successful is the dream state awakening?"

Concerning the dream work we are doing: it is progressing and there are many beings who are borderline New Age people who have not yet awakened to this consciously. It is not so much that they are unawakened but that they have not gotten the information concerning this ascension yet. There are many who are on the verge of taking this challenge, but they need to have the information presented to them on a conscious level. In fact the very words "ascension" and "evacuation" are somewhat of an encoded message for them. There is a great deal of work that can be done, with as many channels as will give themselves and as many others who will network this information. There will be a great effect in doing so. We also are quite disappointed with the outcome of this experiment. But it has been millions of years since most of the Starseeds took this challenge and this is a long time to be subjected to materialism and third-dimensional limitations. So there is much wounding that has taken place in the external world within the emotional body. It has been very difficult to maintain awareness. So we are doing the best we can to work with all beings and to present this information to them in a teaching format, in training in their etheric bodies at night. But it is for the conscious communication to be directed towards them so they can awaken and give themselves to this. It is not enough that they have heard it in their sleep. They need to hear it consciously and they need to make a conscious mental and emotional choice concerning it. They need to bring their free will to bear and to recognize and understand their options and be willing to undergo the transformation that is necessary. So you can do a great deal simply by speaking to others who are open and sharing information, tapes and channeled messages. It is my hope that you will be inspired to do this.

"How does the book Keys of Enoch *fit in?"*

That is quite a volume. I would say it is very accurate in its presentation. It is from a very clear source. Those of you who desire may look into this, and I think you will find that everything that we have been addressing in this class is addressed in that New Age scripture. They refer to the space brotherhood as the Higher Evolution. So I think that your studies of *The Keys of Enoch* are very beneficial. Keep in mind that within every type of channeled message or scripture there is always a certain slight degree of misinformation. This is a very clear scripture, yet there is the necessity for you to always, in any channeling, use your own discretion and to take the words and teachings to heart to see if they are true for you. But I would encourage you and anyone else in your study of this, if you wish to learn more. This is more validation for what we are communicating. It is very helpful to hear this from another source and to see it written down, that there is such a thing as evacuation and ascension and space brotherhoods. You can read about our work from a more scientific standpoint than can be brought through this particular non-scientific channel. So it is an excellent work and I recommend it. Some of you may not be able to "get into it."

"I've reread it and have been studying it for a year now."

There are levels of understanding you see. Your subconscious self is understanding more and being awakened more than your understanding mentally. So it is good to read it even if you do not understand everything logically or intellectually. It is encoded with messages and activations for you. It has assisted in your growth, activating your spiritual awareness.

"I was wondering why other spiritual groups are not speaking about the ascension?"

A very controversial question. This is almost one that I am hesitant to respond to, for it may come as a criticism when it is not. There are many spiritual masters who are masters in certain areas of growth but have not entirely mastered their own ascension process or are not open to or receiving this particular information. This information will be more felt and more appreciated by those who are more humble and childlike in their aspect. Those who have an investment in a particular spiritual path, and in trying to understand things with regards to one particular training, may perhaps find it difficult to integrate this information. There are "comfort zones" in any spiritual path. It is difficult for some to leave the comfort of the teachings they have grown accustomed to and accept the possibility of this other information. This information has not been made that public as of yet. It has just begun to be made public in the past several years. The spiritual work that people have been doing has been preparing them for their ascension, no doubt. Yet it will be another step for them to awaken to this. I think that the first wave will be made up largely of volunteers who are very open, innocent, and humble in their demeanor. Of course this describes most of you. Those who have a large investment in a particular spiritual path will have to be shaken out of it a little bit more by the return of the Ascended Masters in physical form. So they are Starseeds no doubt, but some may be in their own comfort zones. Either that or they simply have not been presented with this information consciously, as of yet.

"Is this the Second Coming?"

Not quite yet. These are the preliminaries.

"When there are many Masters in the ascended state and many ascended beings on the planet is that the Second Coming? Is the Second Coming a multiplicity of Christs?"

I for one do not feel competent to predict what the Christ will do next. He is quite spontaneous. It has been written that he will return from the sky in the last days. I would not put it past him to do so. The Second Coming as referring to the Second Coming of the Christ ... in effect, it is the second coming, for you will be merged with your Christ bodies and there will be, in effect, thousands of Christs walking the face of the Earth. But the coming of that particular being that you refer to as the Christ will most likely only be manifested in the last days. Maybe not. It is up to Him. I can speak somewhat for those in my command as to what they will do, but for those who I am serving I would not begin to be so bold.

"Is Maitreya in London the Christ or is it Jesus or are they one and the same?"

Jesus, the Christ, is in an ascended state at this time, though there are avatars present upon the Earth at this time. Many spiritual masters are playing their roles consciously or subconsciously in this awakening of humanity. So this being will also attempt to do his part in his own way. As to whether or not he is a Christed entity you must judge that for yourself. I will not pass judgment in this way. It is part of your growth to discern truth from fiction. And it is a disservice on my part if I were to categorize and give you my impressions of every teaching or truth that has been spoken or given. It is part of your process to separate the wheat from the chaff. I would say that within every teaching there are truths and elements that are less focused on the truth. If you take it to your heart and it serves you in your process of growth, then do so. If not, then let it go by. There is no need to give yourself to any one incarnated spiritual master at this time. This is something which is being phased out. Of those masters who have had followings, who are more humble and aware, there are some who have already taken their devotees and given them to their own paths and have released the attachment to having a large number of followers. Others still have a desire to have followers. But it is being phased out, for it is a time when each individual being will become a Christ. There will only be Christs remaining on the Earth within a short time. Then there will be no more need to have teachers and devotees. That has served a purpose, but now I would give you the challenge to become masters yourselves. And you can do so directly, working with the Ascended Masters. If you desire to receive teaching from an incarnate master you may do so, but you will not receive anything more profound than you can in your own living rooms and through your own guidance and channeling. You are masters yourselves. This is the challenge that is before you and before the planet.

"Is Sananda's ship still sending healing to the Earth between 8:00 and 9:00 p.m. every evening, and are you the commander of Sananda's ship?"

Yes and yes. In fact the healing is more intensified at that time, but it is ongoing continuously. So at any time you may tune into his presence and be receiving it.

"Is the healing for all of the bodies, the spiritual, emotional, physical, oversoul? Is every body of the

multidimensional being getting healed?"

Yes. The whole package. We will be doing some work. Sananda himself will be with you again in another class, and he will be working specifically with healing the emotional body, as this is an important aspect of the work you will be doing. And if he follows the pattern of the last course, he will take you on a guided meditation and give you some assistance in releasing and healing your emotional bodies. This is the number one area where healing is required at this time. The power of love is such that it heals you throughout your entire being. It is very simple. Whether you understand that you have multiple bodies or not makes no difference. You can be healed simply by giving yourself to the love ray. We have made it so simple. In fact you must be somewhat simple to give yourself to this process. Many who are very sophisticated will find ways of avoiding it.

"Why are the fundamentalist Christian churches so violently against the New Age groups?"

They are afraid. They are afraid of losing their power. They are afraid that if the New Age does manifest, everyone will have an individual experience of God and there will no longer be a reason to go to a particular church or to donate to a particular cause. And they would find themselves suffering financially and in other ways. There is a great degree of impurity in the organized religions. Most of them will be the last to awaken and in fact many never will. They will probably be among those who refuse to. If you feel a fundamentalist bent in someone's nature, love them unconditionally but silently for your own protection. The Christ is love. The Christ is the presence that we are and the presence that we share. It is very simple. There is no need to bring fear, judgment, or criticism of others into it. The Christ was not critical even of those who were persecuting him. So let this be a guide to you. If anyone is persecuting you, then use his example. Do not expect it to be noticed. But do it for your own upliftment.

"Can you speak on the Seven Rays and are the Starseed incarnating on a particular or mixed ray?"

Very mixed. There are many different beings here from different sources, different angelic groups, different Ascended Masters. You are going to be reunited with your spiritual families. You will understand more of this as it occurs. This borders on the realm of very esoteric understanding. Let us simplify it and say that there are many volunteers from all over the universe, from all types of evolvements and from all types of manifestations. So you will feel yourself connecting with your true higher nature. If you happen to be an angelic presence, you will feel your angelic self more. You will be able to contact this and perhaps your angelic brethren will contact you. I'm sure they already have. There will be a reunification with your true families. It will not be such a feeling of division as there is existing here between families or tribes or governments. There will be a feeling of love and sharing, but there will also be this feeling of at-home-ness, a feeling of nurturance and being surrounded by beings whom you feel connected with internally, on a very deep level. The experience that you have longed for in your family life which has been rather imperfect here will be manifested in that way. You have been trying to experience the feeling of your spiritual family in your friendships and in your relationships. But it will be much more profound.

"Will this work help transform our physical bodies as well, like being in better shape or losing weight or being more healthy?"

You may be inspired to take steps in this area. Let me say that the more emotionally healthy you are and the more spiritually aligned you are, the easier it is to become healed, as most illnesses have their roots in the emotional body. So there will be a great deal of work done on an emotional level. It has already begun. It will assist you in releasing energies that have already caused within you certain patterns of illness. You will not necessarily receive a miraculous healing by the end of the course. I make no claims of this nature. But it will be a great enhancement to inspire you to take steps in that area. If you will approach your physical symptoms spiritually, emotionally, mentally, and physically, you will achieve your goals for yourselves at this time. If you approach them only physically, you will not clear out the emotional source of the illness entirely. And if you only approach it spiritually or emotionally, it will perhaps take longer to achieve the clearing of them. But you can be healed of many things that you felt were chronic and part of your makeup. As you become lighter and lighter you will find that your aches and pains begin to disappear, though I think it's likely that you will experience more aches and pains during the process. And then you will pass through that phase into a phase of being much lighter and more youthful.

So, I think there is still time to do a brief meditation before we close. At this point I will say goodbye until next time. Goodnight.

❧ Class Three ❧

CUTTING THE STRINGS

⇜ Sananda & Archangel Michael ⇝

Hello. Good to see all of you again and looking so bright. You have all been applying yourselves, I can see. You've been going through your transformations and changes. It is very joyful for us to see all of you so sincere in your path and so open in your hearts. We will do our best not to disappoint you. Know that all the work you are doing in meditation and in opening yourselves will be rewarded. So relax yourselves, be comfortable and enjoy yourselves. Let yourselves be a little bit loose this evening, not too frivolous and not too serious. And don't forget to breathe occasionally.

Tonight we will be talking about release, cutting the strings, letting go of attachment, or whatever you wish to label it. I like the term "cutting the strings," myself. You have all embarked on this journey to some degree. I think most of you are quite sincere in seeking to achieve the ascension. Tonight, myself and others will be assisting you in releasing those things that are holding you to the third-dimensional reality. The only effort required on your part is simply to relax and to allow and loosen your grip a little bit on your everyday lives. Allow yourselves for this evening to be in this moment and see what this moment has to offer you.

All of you have been enmeshed in what you would call a life experience. In fact you have been enmeshed in many life experiences, but the one that is most pervasive is this current one. Surrounding you in your lives are many physical, emotional, and mental experiences. These are your attachments or connections. You are all connected to your lives, to your activities, to your emotional traumas, and all the various parts of yourselves.

It could be said that your external lives in the world are reflections of your internal lives and the belief systems and feelings you have about yourselves. So you are sitting here in your lives surrounded by the mirror of what you feel about yourself. If you feel loving toward yourself you are most likely having a loving experience of life. If you feel guilty and fearful then you are most likely attracting lesser life experiences.

But I am here tonight to tell you not to worry and not to be concerned about the nature of these experiences. For whatever it is you are feeling, whatever it is you are experiencing, it is all going to be transformed. You will be releasing your attachments to third-dimensional reality in a gentle and easy manner. This is a lot of the work that we will be doing here. For the most part we are offering these particular classes so you can ascend gradually, so that you can prepare for the process, feel and savor it and not be traumatized by it.

As you begin to ascend and as you begin to lighten up you will feel where you are connected to the world and where you are attached to your personality and relationships. This is where you are stuck in your evolution at this point. So we are going to release these attachments with love in a very graceful and surgical manner, as you feel ready to do so. Know that what is required of each of you is not to drastically change your external lives, restructure your personalities or restructure your belief systems. We are going to take a little more subtle approach. We are going to get rid of everything! So no matter how refined your personality and your self-concept is, it doesn't matter. You will have to let go of it anyway.

You have all been perfecting yourselves. Too bad. Whether you are saints or devils it matters little. You have to release it all. For in growth we have to release what we are holding on to so that we will be open and empty to contain what is coming. What is coming to you now is a great deal of energy and a great deal of upliftment. You may have to release a little bit more than usual. You may have to release everything. This is nothing to fear and nothing to be overly concerned about. I am merely reflecting the reality of the situation. Those who are not prepared for the ascension will have dramatically less time to go through this same process. Many will not be able to do it. Many will be torn or fearful or attached and they will miss their opportunity.

Because of the work you have been doing and because you are the Light Workers and Starseeds we come to you first, knowing you will be receptive. And notice how receptive you are. Is it not amazing that so many people are receptive to this strange concept? It is because you are intended for it. It is a natural process for you and it is meant to be a natural process in this class and in all of the work that you do. It is not meant to be something that you feel a painful separation or a tearing away of your personality. We are here to assist you to gently release. The way that you release is by feeling that which is beginning to come to you as a blessing. You will feel this uplifting as a blessing and a beautiful new energy in your lives. And by opening and facing this new energy it becomes very easy to open your hands and release that which you have been holding on to. So you will never be empty here. You are to be filled constantly. We are just changing the fluid in your containers. We are giving you all an oil change.

Out with the old oil and in with the new! — the oil of love. You will all be functioning much more smoothly soon, with much less wear and tear on your internal parts. So how will this feel to you?

As you begin to feel yourself being lifted in consciousness and in vibrational frequency, you will find a strange phenomenon occurring in your life. You will begin noticing the things you have been attached to, things you have been experiencing, people you have been surrounded with and parts of your personality. They may begin to seem different to you. They may begin to seem a little bit heavy and a little bit more difficult to maintain. You may question yourself as to why you have been maintaining them at all. In the face of the great light and presence, you will have an easy time of releasing those imperfect aspects. Those things that you love about yourselves will remain, as they are the part of you that is true. The only thing that will fall away will be your attachment to that. In this process we are not concerned with the manifestations of your attachments, but rather, the cords that bind you to those experiences and manifestations.

This is what Archangel Michael is going to assist you in removing with his sword. You all have the "ties that bind." You all have connections emanating from your physical presences. These connections are mostly from your midsections, or your second and third chakras. You all have spiritual cords which connect you with all of the experiences of your lives, with all of the people that you are with, your careers and your various mechanisms of third-dimensional reality. You are all like octopi. So you will begin to feel or become aware of your cords of attachment in this process. There comes a time when they begin to feel constricting and a little bit uncomfortable. It is at that time that you may request and ask for Archangel Michael or any of the Masters to come and assist you in cutting your psychic connections to your old reality. You are headed for a new reality which will be superimposed upon the old one. So all of you will be having the experience of this simultaneous dimensionality of your lives. It will be infringing upon your old reality more and more. And more and more it will be pushing out the old.

The energy that is being expressed this evening and that is being showered upon all of you is that which will assist in enlightening you to your attachments and to your cords. It will show you that which will be released and will assist you in doing so. For you it is a process of opening, trusting, and surrendering. It is trusting that where you are going is better than where you have been. We hold onto things in our lives because they give us a feeling of security and safety. So there is always an aspect of faith required when we let go of that which has nurtured us and provided us with some limited degree of satisfaction. The satisfaction and security that is awaiting you is so incredible and so divine. I think that as you begin to experience it you will have little difficulty in surrendering to it, for it feels like your higher Self. It feels like your purpose and destiny. It feels like your own heart is growing and vibrating with the frequency of love. So you will have to have your hands free to accept all of these new gifts. Again this is not a transformation that you can consciously manifest or drive yourself into. It is something that will occur quite spontaneously in the unfolding of your process. It is more for you simply to relax and allow it.

Just as you may be feeling yourselves changing in your physical experience with regards to that which you eat and drink and imbibe, you have been receiving signals about changes and following them. So it will be with this that we are speaking of tonight. So relax, and we will take a moment to meditate, and then perhaps we can have an expert in the field come and speak to you about this.

Welcome my dear ones. This is Archangel Michael. It is lovely to be with you and bask in your presence this evening. Know that you are surrounded by the angelic host. We are showering you with our love and with our radiance as we are sharing in your radiance. We are all being lifted together. It is so beautiful.

I come this evening at the request of the Christ to assist you in letting go, to assist in severing your attachment to your limitations. You have been immersed in darkness for a very long time, yet you have not forgotten your higher Selves. You have not forgotten your purpose. It has not been easy for you to remember or to act upon this, yet you have done so. I am here to encourage you to continue on this path which will come to fruition very soon in your lives. Relaxation and breathing: this is surrender. In this moment practice surrender. Allow yourself to be lifted. Allow yourself to be surrounded by the light. There is nothing to fear in being lifted into your true state. If it is fearful to you it is only because you have grown accustomed to the third-dimensional reality and its ties. When you are reacquainted with your true states, you will find it strange that you ever were attached to the third-dimensional reality. All the dense energies that are still clinging to your emotional bodies and to your physical bodies will be shed. You will be shedding your old skins and will be reemerging with the true presence.

It is an exciting time. It is a time of great joy. Do not allow yourselves to give in to doubt and fear. Simply feel what you are feeling. If you are feeling a difficulty in your transformation, call upon me to assist you in severing those connections, with these things which are causing you discomfort. You have grown accustomed to discomfort and limitation. Many of those experiences which you are now releasing are those which in the past you held on to for satisfaction and security and some measure of peace. A greater peace comes to fill you up and your old shells are too small to contain it all.

So tonight we are lifting you. Consciously or unconsciously, you are being lifted in your frequency and in your experience and in your consciousness. Some of you may begin to feel that you are rising and that you are not in connection with the Earth so much as before. Some of you will still feel that you are in your ordinary circumstances. Regardless of your perception of the activity, be assured that we are working to lift you. It is our desire to teach you in this way, experientially, what it is to ascend. By taking small steps now you will already have taken many small steps up the ladder and you will feel comfortable and at ease when the ascension comes. You will not be traumatized by the process. If you are not traumatized by the process when you are reacquainted and reconnected with the Hierarchy, then you will not have so long of a time in transition before you can join in the experience of the Brotherhood and the sharing that exists.

Many who ascend will have to have a time of relaxation and reassimilation of their new environments. Many will be unable to appreciate at first just where they are and what has happened to them. They will need to have some training and some guidance and some gentle loving care. The same gentle loving care which you are receiving ahead of time, so that when you are with the Brotherhood you can enjoy and even assist in lifting the remainder.

There is so much to enjoy and experience. It is like a huge smorgasbord of delight. Fortunately, once you ascend you do not have to die, so you will have plenty of time to enjoy it all. The time is so limited in the third-dimensional reality. There is never enough time to achieve that which you desire to achieve. Just as you begin to get good at what you are doing, you begin to grow old and must leave. This will not occur in the future with you. You will have conscious memory of all your experiences. You will be able to grow indefinitely. You will be able to explore the universes and go wherever you desire to visit, depending on your level of evolvement and service.

As you arise you may begin to feel your connections to the Earth more strongly. You may begin to feel some heaviness or density in your second, third, and first chakras. It is almost like you are trying to float like a balloon but have many strings attached to you. If you desire, at these times you may perform this visualization:

Imagine yourself lifted high above the Earth, high in the clouds, and surrounded by the Angelic Host. Imagine yourself floating, but connected to the Earth by many strings or cords — dark rubbery cords that connect with you. And then, call upon me by name and imagine a bright blue sword of flame severing these cords and feel the lightness as you rise.

You need not worry that if you rise you will not be able to reconnect with your third-dimensional reality. It is always there waiting for you. At any time you desire you can rematerialize in the third-dimensional reality even after your ascension.

So tonight allow yourselves to float. Allow yourselves to rise. If you feel accompanied by angels, you are. There are more than enough angels to go around. It is their service ister to humanity and to assist in the upliftment. It gentle presence which comforts you through transist as they are the gentle presences that comfort those who have left their bodies in the death experience. This is much better than dying, is it not? The lightness that you will begin to feel in your bodies and in your emotions and in your presence will be a result of your releasing and rising into a higher frequency. And the rising into the higher frequencies results in the more dense energies falling away. At any time that you feel yourselves caught or bound to a dense energy call upon me. Ask me to be with you and to assist you in severing these psychic connections. This is not an escape from reality. It is an escape to reality.

Know that as you release your attachments you will not suddenly stop loving all the people in your lives that you have come to love and be with. It is the attachment to these beings which inhibits the flow of love. You can love much more profusely if you are free and open and channeling love. So nothing that you have been associated with out of love will be harmed in your ascension process. Those of you who have children and relationships may be concerned. But in all of your relationships you will be benefiting everyone in this process. For as you cut the cords of dense energy you can reestablish your connection with etheric cords of love energy, so that the purity of your experience can be shared with all those around you. The difference here is that these cords do not bind you.

So allow yourselves to feel more in your bodies if you are not. Allow yourselves to feel your own legs and your connection to the Earth. Let yourselves drift back a little bit into a workable functioning state. I tell you that the quality of experience you have with this process is a direct reflection of the amount that you apply yourselves in preparation for it. If you are preparing yourselves consciously in meditation then you will have a very enjoyable experience in ascension. It will be like a ride in an amusement park to you. It will be as if you were waiting in line for some time with your ticket in hand, and you finally get to go in the car and ride the hill up the roller coaster.

So I encourage you, as all the Masters have been, to meditate. If possible, meditate twice a day, morning and evening. This is the recommendation of Sananda. I will not suggest an amount of time to meditate. It is more a matter of you doing a little bit more than you have been and making it more of a quality time. Everyone has their own capacity. Do not limit yourself to a certain amount of time. And perhaps give yourself a time once a week when you can give yourself several hours to explore the inner realm, where you can practice ascending and releasing. And as you feel yourself rising and you feel your ties, then do the meditation we did this evening. You must raise yourselves a little bit so that I can get my sword under there. That is your task and that is your homework assignment for this week. Practice raising yourselves. Practice ascending in meditation and do not be overly attached to the results. Do not be overly self-critical.

It is happening to each of you. No one is being left out of the process. Some of you are more earthbound or grounded. Some of you are ready to take off at a moment's notice. Some of you are particularly angelic and fluttery. This is your nature. Love your nature. Those of you who are grounded are grounded for a reason. Those of you who are floaty are floaty for a reason. You will discover the reason as you proceed. You will understand the reason in totality as your ascension is completed. Then you will see the full perfection of your own self and all the lessons you have undergone and why you are the way you are. So know that you are beautiful the way you are. Again we are not here to perfect your personalities. We are here to share this experience and take you as you are. So if anyone is back to Earth enough to ask questions of me this evening, I will avail myself.

wondering about my pets. I'm real connected to and I'm wondering if they will be able to ascend is?"

It's a good opportunity for you to practice being an angel and working with beings who desire to ascend. You can begin working with your pets. You have but to shine your light upon them and shine the emanation of the light body. Visualize light surrounding them and it is possible they will be able to rise also. Strange as it may seem there is a bird heaven and a cat heaven and a dog heaven, just as your mothers told you when you were children. You may not be quite so attached to them as time goes on, but they will be provided for.

"If there are those of us who are more grounded, does this cause any more difficulty in lifting, in the actual ascension?"

Often it is more helpful to be grounded. If you are grounded this means you are connected to all of your chakras and you are able to bring the energy, the light energy, through to your entire body, which is required in order to ascend. So do not be self-critical about your particular experience as long as you are meditating and making an effort to surrender and open yourself to this process. It is more a matter of the openness of your heart and the love that you feel within you. These are the criteria. If you have an open heart you will be aligned by the Brotherhood and by the Angelic Host. They will work with you if you are open in your heart to receive this energy. The adjustments that are necessary within your chakras, within your body, your light body will be made. So there is a rebalancing which is to take place within all of you. Some of you may find yourselves feeling more grounded than you have. This is because the light energy is desiring to come through your entire form and not just stop at the heart chakra. You want to have a whole body where you are going, not just a half. So do not be concerned about this. I am quite adroit at wielding this blade. It only takes a fraction of an inch. If necessary I will take a chunk of earth with you. And it will be a blessed chunk of earth indeed.

"Will each of us go individually, like 'Beam me up, Scotty,' or will we go as a group?"

You will all go in the same way, as you said, "Beam me up, Scotty." Your various reactions to the process of ascension will be quite varied depending on your own levels of evolvement and your own levels of attachment. You will all undergo your own processes around this lifting, but the actual lifting will occur exactly the same for each. It is something we have perfected. So you will be lifted. Whether you all go at the same moment or not is still to be decided. All those who go in the first wave will go at approximately the same time on the same date, whether you are all together or whether you are separated. Those who are going with the first wave will meet again.

"Will we be able to see or perceive that others are lifting? Will we know or is this a very singular experience as it is occurring?"

You have your hands so full of experience at that time that even if you are seeking to have a group experience you will quickly lose track of the fact that you are with a group. Your own experience with your light body will take precedence. You will be so surrounded by light and energy and presence that you will not be concerned with anything that was around you prior to the initiation of the experience. So again, if you are in a group, if this should be the way that it would manifest, you will have the group experience prior to the lifting. Then there will be quite an experience of light and you may afterwards feel yourself again in the group but in a new location. There are many ways it can occur and many different variables involved. But the actual process of ascension does not vary. The actual manifestation of the light body is quite a scientific maneuver. There is little room for variation. Everything must be accomplished with perfection and with perfect alignment.

"What about the children? You said the children would go with us and that they would be made the age of eighteen. When we come back will they come back with us or will our work be separate? If they come back will they come back as Ascended Masters also? Will they stay the age of eighteen or will they be returned to the age they were previously? I have a curious son."

Your current relationship with your child will be quite different. You are now mother and child. You also have a soul relationship or a spiritual connection with this being. This is the kind of connection that will remain after your ascension. So you will recognize one another if you are to meet at that time. And yet you will not feel quite so motherly towards this being, as you will be more the same age. You will see one another as you truly are. Right now you are viewing one another through a very limited glass. You are viewing one another within your limited parameters, your roles. Your roles will be different while your beings will be the same.

Whatever opportunities for service are presented will be presented to each of you individually. Some will work together and some will not. It is all in accordance with what is most beneficial for the upliftment of the remnant of humanity. At the time of your ascension you will no longer have prejudice about being with different people. Perhaps you will remain with your twin flames. Perhaps you will work in groups. But the connections you have made in the Earth plane will feel quite different to you. In fact, they will feel quite different to you even before your ascension, as you begin to release more and more. So you may find your relationships in general shifting a little bit. They will still be of love. They will still be of healing and teaching. But they will not be of attachment.

"If we are not the grounded type, how can we facilitate the balancing of our chakras in this process?"

It is not something that you need to control. It is something you need to simply open to. In your meditation call upon your guides, Ashtar, myself, or Sananda, and ask us to manifest your light body. In order to manifest your light body you need to have your chakras aligned. This is all part of the process. So under that one broad category of request you will get quite a tune-up. And whatever you experience is appropriate. If you do not feel yourselves being focused in a more grounded way, it may be that is not required for you. If you feel yourselves being more grounded, then it is something necessary for you. It is an individual process with regards to the preparation.

Each of you have unique balancing to accomplish and a unique way of opening to do so. You all have various attachments of different sorts. You all have varying degrees of openness in your chakras. Some of you are very open. Some of you are very open in certain chakras and more closed in others. This will be opening so you may feel a little bit of processing going on. You may feel a great deal of processing going on. It is for you to trust and have faith and know that it is necessary for your growth, for the completion of your missions and tasks, and for your ascension.

"During meditation I feel very heavy. Could you comment on this?"

There will be some release that is in order for you, as far as emotional clouds. Your emotional body still contains densities from Earth lives — remembrances, that sort of thing. These will be released. It is always appropriate for you to follow your intuition in regards to this. If you are feeling yourselves, any of you, going through intense emotional release, then maybe you could avail yourself of someone's service who is accomplished at helping to release emotional traumas. As I said, this path is unique for each. Most of you simply can meditate your way to ascension. Some of you will meditate and feel yourselves encountering obstacles which seem very difficult to overcome, or some great heaviness that you can't quite get yourself to understand or to release. If your meditation and calling upon my services is not sufficient, then you can go to an expert in the field and perhaps try some hypnotherapy or something of this nature. Also take care of your physical health. You need to have a way to oxygenate yourself a little bit more. You may talk to this being on my right here. She is an expert in these physical health matters. She will open herself to serve you in this regard. Do not be concerned; you are all being provided for. You are all in the hands of God.

"You said the first wave of ascension could begin this year, possibly mid-year. Is it a year or two process? Or will this first wave of ascension last five years? What kind of timing can you give us on this?"

At this point it appears that the first wave could occur as soon as sometime this year. Hopefully sooner than later. There are many variables. As the time for the first wave approaches, you will be notified in ways that you cannot deny. You will be made aware. The second wave could be, I would say, within six months to several years after the first. The final wave will be at the last possible moment. So this may not occur for some years but it should be within this decade. The farther out the dates go in time the less predictable they are.

Time and space. Time and space. You will all have enough of time and space in the third dimension soon. You will see why it is so difficult for us to predict. We are existing in a universe which is multidimensional. So your views of a universe that has a beginning, middle and end are really quite limited and not totally appropriate to reality. In reality there is only one moment and within that moment many universes are occupying the same space in different dimensions. Just as we are with you now in this same space, but you cannot visually see us. Most of you cannot. It is because we are existing in a different dimension. Our frequency is higher and your senses cannot perceive at this frequency. So when you ascend you will also feel yourself surrounded by your friends and you will have bodies. You will have fifth-dimensional or higher bodies. But they will be much different, much lighter and much more enduring, much more filled with light. From that perspective you may say, "Wow, I still have hands and feet! Nothing has changed." For a moment you may feel that nothing has changed, and then you will begin to realize what has happened and what you have left behind and what you have gained. There are many dimensions in this universe, and many dimensions in the many universes.

"Will we still have a third-dimensional reality in the same way we do now or will it appear to look different?"

It will look quite comical to you. You will see it and remember having been within it and you will have many hearty laughs over all of your predicaments. You will be viewing it from a more detached and uplifted space. And even if you choose to remanifest from time to time as Ascended Masters, which it is our hope that many of you will do, it will still not be quite the same. You will be in your light bodies. Once you attain to the fifth dimension you have no more need to be bound. This is a liberation.

"I have a question about the time difference in the fifth and third dimension. If I'm on the ship being trained for, say three or four months, how long would that be in Earth time? Would it be like three days in Earth time?"

It is something like that, but it is much more flexible than you can now imagine. It could seem like ten years in "space time," and yet you could be put back onto the Earth within a matter of hours of your initial departure. You will be able to go through doorways of time and space, and perhaps you can enter wherever there is an entry point for you which is in alignment with your service. But yes, it will seem like you are with us for a longer period than it actually is in Earth time. The Earth time which transpires will be less than it seems. Again there are so many variables.

Imagine all the beings ascending, meeting in the mother ships, getting reacquainted with their own lineages and their own higher Selves, remembering who they are, being trained and showered with love and blessings, and making their choices as to the opportunities that are there for each of them. So there is quite a deal of work which has to be done. There is quite a deal of organization which must take place. We are very organized, despite the fact that some of us have wings. Despite the fact that some of us are space brothers we are not all that spacey. It gets less and less spacey as you continue, and more and more precise and simultaneously more and more expanded. Difficult to understand, I am aware.

So the time that occurs between the lift-off and the reemergence of the ascended beings is not really known. It is dependent on many variables. We hope that it is as soon as possible, for there are the remnant of the Starseeds which will need to be assisted in their transition also. The Starseeds who have not awakened at this point, who are just beginning to awaken or who are slumbering quite soundly in their third-dimensional nests, will need to be revived. So the first work that the ascended beings will do will be to revive these beings. And it will not be difficult, for you will have many powers and wonders to show them which will remind them of who they are as well. So it is hoped that there will be quite a clamor to be in the second wave.

You who are open to being in the first wave are in the minority, the vast minority. And those of you who are open to this process are truly to be honored, as you will be. You have much in store for you of surprise and wonder and much celebration. You will all be reacquainted with your own natures and your own alliance of beings. You have come from many corners of the universe, from many angelic spheres and many higher evolutions. Though you have the connection in Spirit which we all share, you also have your own particular history and source, your own particular family, your soul family and your group. And this all will be made clear to you. You will be made aware of this. It is quite a magnificent universe.

The alliance will continue until the Earth is liberated. Then you may wish to return to your sources or to other service. You will find that service is the prime directive of all enlightened and liberated beings. Service is the way that you feel your own magnificence flowing through, your own connection to the Father, and it is really quite addictive. The more you get of that energy the more you want. And so there is a general clamor for service. In fact, many who were not fully qualified also desired to be Starseeds at this time. You were the more qualified, believe it or not. It's hard to imagine from your perspectives.

"As returning teachers with fifth-dimensional bodies, will it be possible to distinguish Starseeds from humanity?"

Yes.

"So we'll know who to shake up and who to be gentle with?"

Yes. You will all have your powers of tact fully established and you will not harm anyone in your manifestations. You will be trained for your particular services. You will be reacquainted with the powers you have latent within you, which are awaiting you when you reconnect with your higher vehicles.

"We have been told to share the tapes of these classes if we think there are people open to this or who have expressed an interest in being part of this. In listening to the tapes will they get the same benefits that we are receiving? Is this their way of being reached at this time?"

Yes, you may share the tapes with those who are open to this. If they listen to the tapes, they can practice meditating while they listen and they'll receive the benefit of my presence. It is not necessary to graduate from this course in order to ascend.

"Michael, if one has the very true desire to go with the first wave, will that person most likely ascend?"

Yes. If you have a strong desire to do so this is an indication that you are meant to go at the first wave. Some are not to go with the first wave though we are not sure who they are. So do not ask me who is going and who is not in the first wave. This is too much pressure even for me. But know that if you do not go with the first wave you will instead be given, at the time of the ascension, further instruction. And you will understand why you are not going and what you are to do. It is very unlikely that any who are Starseed will not be going by the second wave.

So if you feel within yourself the desire to go with the first wave, then by all means pray and meditate. Call upon the manifestation of your light body. It is above all the desire of your heart which calls forth the powers that will assist you. This is a desire that you do not have to surrender. It is attached to devotion. Devotion is the desire of the heart to be with the beloved. You may find this desire growing as your others are lessening. Know that no one is overlooked. We are consciously connected with all of the Starseeds and all of humanity, whether they are conscious of us or not. We are working with each to open them and prepare them. No one will be left in the dust unless they desire to be.

"This is a personal question. I've received information that I am not to go on the first wave because I have something to complete before I go, even if at the time of ascension I would like to go. When the ascension happens, will I be given further clarification on that?"

Yes, though I would not be too strong in your beliefs about what your destiny is at this time. This opportunity for ascension with the first wave is additional to your other programming. Each of you have been on a program, a destiny course of uplifting humanity and doing various acts of service as you have been throughout your lifetimes. So this presentation of the ascension at this time comes as a kind of a shock. It's superimposed upon your other programming. I would suggest that you continue on the path as you have been and wait until ascension to make your decision. You need not believe that you are bound to any contracts unless you desire to be. This is an opportunity to surrender all of your unfinished business and to take another course.

"But I feel like my need to stay has to do with another being who wants to be born so it can ascend."

If I were you I would honor your feelings, honor your information, and also remain open. If you are open you will receive the correct guidance and will not be misled. Have no fear about this. Simply prepare yourself, and in your preparation all things will be made clear to you. It is not our desire to create more confusion in your lives. If you feel a strong inclination to wait for the second wave, then do so. All things can be accommodated. And this does not mean that you will not benefit from our services in this class. For of course, you will. You will simply be prepared. When the time comes you will be prepared. The preparation that we are doing with you is not something that will fade away or wear off with time. So regardless of how long a time it is after this particular set of classes ends and the ascension occurs, the work that you do here will be fully in effect. Liberate yourself from concern and simply be open. See what presents itself to you.

"Michael, even in using discretion in sharing this information about the ascension, I'm encountering fear in others. I've been telling them to think of it as part of

their spiritual growth because that's how I see it. Can you comment on this?"

Fear is the number one restriction to ascension. Fear is that which will inhibit the mass of humanity from ascending. We and you are here to eradicate this fear. We are here to reassure you. You who go on the first wave and return will be here to reassure others who are still in third-dimensional reality that there is nothing to fear. So when presenting this information you may encounter fear and confusion. This information does not go along with the programming even of those who are following a spiritual path. Many spiritual paths do not take into consideration that ascension is the ultimate goal. This is erroneous teaching, for ascension is the ultimate goal of spiritual growth. So you are right in saying ascension is part of spiritual growth. Simply say that ascension is the end result of spiritual growth and enlightenment on the third-dimensional plane of reality. It is the way that you access the next phase of your growth.

There is growth from the fifth dimension up through the other dimensions leading all the way to the very throne of God. You can reassure them that you are not believing in some strange manifestation of Space Brothers coming to take you away. Again we have cautioned you about this. If you have spoken of the Space Brothers to others and found resistance or fear, this is your responsibility. Don't say we didn't warn you! People will believe in Jesus Christ. They will believe in various Ascended Masters. They will even believe in angels. They will have a very difficult time believing and understanding the Ashtar Command. This has not been part of Earth programming, except for a few light beings and prophets.

It will become more and more part of life on the third dimension as time goes on. When the Earth is ready to feel the full manifestation of the Ashtar Command, it will manifest, so that there can be no doubt about their power and their benevolence. It is up to you in the meantime to experience the benevolence and share this with others who are open. Get the word out discreetly.

"The more I pursue ascension the more I am challenged by others about my beliefs. Can you comment?"

You will be challenged. It is one of the manifestations of the Fallen Brotherhood, the dark forces which cause separation and the dissemination of imperfect spiritual teachings. If the teachings do not account for the ascension they are not complete and we cannot give our stamp of approval on them. So you may benefit from these teachers for a time. But you will find yourself only rising to a certain level of awareness. Human beings attract the teachings that they can accept at the time.

You are each being tested in your faith, in your devotion and in your clarity. This is not necessarily an easy trip. It can be graceful and accomplished in a smooth way, yet there are always sticking points along the path. Some days it just feels like too much and you want to forget the whole thing — but you can't. You have all probably tried this by now. You will try again. When the Christ was present in his third-dimensional existence his closest disciples — those who were most blessed with his presence — still had their moments of doubt and denial. So this is a part of the testing process. Follow your heart's desire, as Ashtar has requested and recommended. Do not ask yourself what you think is possible. Instead ask yourself what you would desire to experience if anything were possible. It is much more close to reality to believe that anything is possible. So know that ascension is real, that it is real for you and you shall experience it.

"Michael, I've experienced a lot of physical discomfort in the last few years. I don't feel very light going through the process and I feel like I have to be physically healed or improved before I can ascend. Also, these physical

problems don't seem to make sense when I think of what's happening to me spiritually. Can you comment?"

Physical symptoms are a sign of your shift to a higher frequency of manifestation. I recommend that beings deal with the ascension both physically and spiritually. Meditate and ask for the manifestation of healing from Sananda the Christ and from your other teachers and guides. Ask for your light body as we have been recommending. Do not be concerned about how your body is reacting. All your bodies are being restructured cellularly. This is not always a comfortable process. It is part of the manifestation process. You are going through it in a more gentle and gradual way than many. Many who come after you will have an intensified period of adjustment to the ascension. On the physical level you might also get help from health professionals, acupuncture, etc. Love your body and follow your intuition but do not be overly concerned or attached to what you are feeling in your physical bodies. Your physical bodies are responding. They may respond in quite unusual ways to this ascension process. They may in fact feel more dense and heavy than ever and they may have their aches and pains and various other manifestations. This is part of the operation. It is simply for you to go through and you shall go through it as gracefully as possible. Know that it is the last time it will trouble you.

So it is time for us to do a little meditation. I wish you to know that you are not simply in the presence of one being who has chosen to come through and speak to you for the evening. You are also surrounded by other masters, ascended beings, guides and teachers and angels. There is an assortment of beings ministering to you. This is true in your ordinary meditations as well, but may not be as profoundly experienced at all times. Just relax and follow your breathing. If you feel an increased light at your third eye or in your upper chakras you may observe this. There will be a variety of experience available according to your various needs. We will not simply treat you as one body with the same energy when you are in a group. We will give each of you that which you are most in need of and most open to. Again, the more meditation that you can do in your lives, the higher level of experience you can have in our group meditations. Some meditations will feel profound and some will feel scattered. Do not judge yourself. The mind will also have its reaction to this increased frequency of energy. Sometimes the mind will become quite agitated and you will wonder if you've lost your ability to meditate. Do not be concerned with this. Spend your time and give your focus to your breath. You will receive what is needed, so have trust and faith. Let us meditate together for a bit.

Those of you who desire to remain in meditation may do so. We will not desert you. Those of you who desire to return may do so now. Gently. We wish you to know that we are always with you. And as a manifestation of this we will give you your homework assignment for the week. That is, call upon my presence each morning and each evening before retiring. Ask for my assistance in liberating you from that which is holding you back and you will find that it is quite effective. You will have the awareness that I am truly with you in your battle against limitation. Know that the light surrounds you always and know that you cannot fail.

Be at peace and love yourselves as the Christ loves you: unconditionally. Do not be concerned with your imperfections and your limitations. Love them all. They will not be with you for long. You may even savor those habits which are falling away. The last days of third-dimensional existence for you are to be enjoyed as much as you can enjoy them while undergoing this process. You will find yourselves going through days of intensity and days of great grace. Have faith and trust throughout all. Our blessings are with you. The magnitude of our love is immense. The magnitude of your beauty awaits you. So my floaty ones, until next time, goodnight.

❧ Class Four ❧

SERVICE

⋘ St. Germain ⋙

Good evening. This is St. Germain. It is a pleasure to join you this evening. I think you will find that as you progress along this path you will be laughing more and more. And your control will be less and less. We understand and enjoy it. Your joy is our joy. Your enjoyment is our enjoyment. It is our goal to share with you what we are experiencing. It is our service. So I am honored to be with you this evening, to have been selected to be the one to speak. I'll have you know that there is a great line of waiting Masters who would like to speak at this gathering. They would like to share your presence and share their experience with you. So I am honored to be selected. I have some things to share with you. Some guided meditations. And I would also like to address the subject of service and share with you my experience of what it is to be an ascended being — as much as I can share in this format.

Be relaxed and enjoy yourselves. Don't hesitate to burst out laughing. This is not a path of control. This is a path of spontaneity. I would like to share with you a little bit about what it is like to be serving as an Ascended Master. Once you have achieved this state of ascension, once you have liberated yourselves from third-dimensional slavery, you will find that you have a great deal more time on your hands. You will not have to work jobs. You will not have to do any number of activities that you are doing now to simply maintain your existence. So you will find that you have a great deal of time on your hands, and enjoyable experiences constantly. And it will become clear to you that your greatest joy is to assist others and share that which you are experiencing. As I said, there is a long line of beings who desire to speak to you and it is for this reason. It is our joy to share our experience as Masters and as teachers. For it is in service that we grow and experience more. So you will find, if you have not already begun to, a shift in your consciousness. It will be quite dramatic upon ascension, the shift from worldly concerns regarding your survival, to service. And you will find yourselves seeking the correct niche for yourself as a servant of the light.

All the beings in the universe, in all of the universes who are aligned with the Father, have the same dilemma. It is a problem that we share. We cannot get enough of the Father's love. The more we get the more we desire. And He cannot give us enough. For the more He gives the more we receive and the more He has to give. This is the nature of the universe. It is service and sharing. The hierarchy of beings who are serving are always eager to find a new way to express their love, a new way to focus the light through themselves to assist others. This is truly what service is. It is not a matter of good deeds or noble activities. Service is simply those actions which you perform coming from the inner plane of love in connection with your divine breath, surrendering to the Holy Spirit. You might say that service is the root of all Creation. The universes are always expanding, new creations occurring constantly, new opportunities for service. New opportunities to shower forth that light which is flowing through. And when you align more and more with that light within you, you will find a great desire within you to share it spontaneously, in just the same way that you were laughing previously. You will find the desire to share this energy spontaneously. And it will be this desire of your heart which will counsel you and direct you in your next phase of service.

Imagine yourselves free from all your worldly concerns. Imagine yourselves now if you did not have to earn money — if you did not need money, if you did not need to manifest any of the third-dimensional needs — and having within your experience, within your body, within your spirit, an incredible well of love and light. This is where you are headed. And this is the impetus behind all of the Masters who incarnate upon the Earth, all the enlightened and ascended beings. No matter where they manifest, they all share the common thread of service. They all share that experience of the Father's love, knowing that it is the ultimate high, the ultimate experience, the ultimate enjoyment. And the ultimate good that they can do for themselves and others. Some will serve by their spontaneous laughter, by their lack of inhibition. Some will serve as teachers, instructing others in the nature of the universe and in the nature of spiritual growth. There is much to teach here in this world. There is much darkness and confusion. So to align yourselves with this light — to liberate yourselves is the first step in uplifting those who are not as fortunate as yourselves. This is always your free will, of course. But I speak from experience when I say that you will all have a strong desire to serve. You will all feel much gratitude and love upon the completion of your third-dimensional mission. I am not saying you are not already experiencing this, but it will be as a more focused ray. At this time you are still unaware of your true potential, of the true potential of your presence and who you truly are. Each of you has a discovery, or a series of discoveries to make, concerning your own nature, your own true selves. When you align with this, what you truly are, you will find a great deal more light able to come through and you will be channeling directly through your presence, directly through your bodies, through your hearts and spiritual presence. You will find yourselves aligned with the highest will. You will find yourselves free of confusion and knowing in each moment how to proceed, where to turn all your energy, in what way and to what degree. So now the feelings that you have about serving and opening to share, though they are sincere, they are not one hundred percent aligned with your higher Selves and with the ways that it is possible to come through you.

So this is why the Masters, the Ashtar Command, the Angelic Hosts are all pressing forward with this ascension program. It is because there is so much to do. There is so much work to be done, so much to be experienced. There is a great need for volunteers. Volunteers to ascend and to return with a focused ray of light — with a direct and powerful manifestation of love and Christ energy — to demonstrate visibly to others what is possible in the human life, especially at this time. It is a dramatic gesture that we are making, and one that you will be able to share in if you desire. So those of you who enjoy the human drama will be able to participate in drama at a higher level. Do not fear that you will be left out of the play. You will be the source of much drama. Indeed there will be a need to train those who return in how to deal with the reactions of the multitudes, for those of you who desire to, let us say, "go for it" with maximum velocity — maximum service — will create quite a stir. There is a place for everyone. There is a service. There is the opportunity for choice, but I am telling you will likely feel this as your prime directive. It was your prime directive in incarnating in the physical plane to begin with. It was a very dramatic gesture on your part. Unfortunately many who did so got caught up in the drama. This is one reason why we are remedying the situation in a series of waves rather than all at once. It is a gentle reminder at first, a moderately gentle reminder second, before the more serious reminder of the Earth changes. So there is much that I would like to share, much that we on our side would like to share of an experiential nature. Before I begin this, I would like to ask if you have questions concerning what I have spoken of so far regarding service. Then we will have some guided meditation.

⚜

"I would like to ask if we could choose to come back and serve in a way that we are already involved with?"

Yes, by all means, you have free choice. Though your realm will be greatly expanded. If you are a healer you will be able to channel a great deal more healing energy, and you will be able to heal spontaneously, as the Christ was able to, and achieve much more dramatic results. All of your desires and talents can be and will be utilized if you so desire. This experience is to be shared and spontaneously expressed. You can do so in music if you desire also. Whatever it is you feel. It is the experience that is important. The service that you do is basically simply sharing an experience. The format is not nearly as important as the experience.

"I hear terms like the Mother Earth, the Mother Mary, Father the God ... so what is this all about?"

The Mother is quite present. The Mother focuses the love of the very source of creation. The source of creation is that which I refer to as the Father. It is less of a gender, but it is a way to describe it. The Mother energy is the Mother-God focusing the Father's energy, and attuning it with her love and her presence. So we are not in a male universe exclusively. We are in a balanced universe. You will understand this more and more. It is beyond our ability to express. Let us say that there is a divine Father energy and a divine Mother energy and those two combine in various ways to create. And if you are a devotee of the

Mother you perhaps will find yourself becoming a goddess yourself. I think you are already becoming one, and expressing that aspect. So you will be enhanced in what you are rather than expected to alter yourselves to fit into a given pattern. What you are is beautiful and a divine expression. There are many creator-beings: the Father, the Mother, the Elders who create, the Elohim. There is a hierarchy. There is much of creation coming through the Elohim and the Elders in creating universes.

I think the easiest way to describe it is that there is a source of light. That source of light focuses itself through various of its own creations, refining itself as it focuses through different hierarchies of creator-gods and beings to the point where it reaches a third-dimensional reality and solid creation. So what this solid creation is, truly, is a focused and solidified light energy. It is the same light energy that is at the source of the universe. It is the energy of the Father. Perhaps you feel that you are sitting on solid earth and pillows and chairs. You are sitting on light. You are light. All is light. It is simply focused in this way on this plane. On the higher planes and dimensions it is somewhat less focused, somewhat more etheric. So there is the ability there to take that etheric energy and to create. And the higher you proceed up the hierarchy the more light you have to work with and the more you can create. You have all seen and experienced the difficulties of manifesting in the third dimension. How many of you have desired to manifest things which have not happened, or have had obstruction to manifestation? It is much more difficult on the third dimension to manifest. This is one reason why we are recommending upgrading yourselves. Are you all tired of struggling and doing affirmations? I assure you I am tired of hearing them. They have assisted in this process of us coming and lifting you but we are getting tired of hearing it. You can listen to it for a while when you have ascended. It is my hope that I will be out of range. Of course, I am joking. It is a pleasure to assist, but there are so many obstructions with manifesting here on the third dimension.

All of you have a great deal of spiritual presence and essence and a great desire to serve. You would all like to be free from money worries and able to manifest that which is in your hearts to manifest, because you are by nature serving beings. You are the light beings, the Starseeds, and you have come to serve. So we have found that it is a little too dense here for you to really unleash your full potentials. And I think you will agree with me that it has not been an easy task. You have had to focus your energies on so much of a survival level that the remaining energy you have had to focus has been dissipated. This is not to say that it is impossible. But it is far too slow of an experience for this time. This time requires dramatic, punctual, effective, experienced manifestation. It is easier to do so from a higher platform.

"Is resurrection coming to our ascension?"

Resurrection and ascension are basically the same, within this context.

"Can you explain to me what is keeping the Ascended Masters from speaking to other beings?"

They are speaking constantly to all of you. All of you are receiving messages from your guides. It is a matter of your openness and receptivity. Many of you are already open to receiving messages and are quite attuned to doing so. There were many who have had the opportunity to channel. Many still do and many are learning to. But not as many have taken advantage of the opportunity as we had hoped. It was our design to have more channels to work in this particular way. Others channel in other ways: by healing, by music, etc. There are many ways of channeling the divine presence. But to answer your question, there is much density.

"Could you comment on why I have been experiencing so much intensity lately?"

There has been an intensification this week of the energy, especially for those who are preparing for the ascension. You might say we are in the final stages. So all that is of density with each of you and with all of those who are desiring the ascension is being removed. This takes the form of emotional release and physical release. Believe me, we understand. We are aware of the discomforts some of you are experiencing. Probably all of you are experiencing various aspects of this. What you are doing is surrendering to the process. And in surrendering to the process you are releasing your own limited existence, your own limited desires, all that you have held close to you for security and a feeling of nurturing and safety. Your "comfort zone," let us say. We are seeking to have this transition be as smooth as possible, but there is no getting around some discomfort. This is why we have been so direct in asking each of you to meditate as much as you can to assist you in doing this, in letting go. For the more you meditate the easier it is for you to be cleansed, or to release. So much is happening on very deep levels of yourselves, often times it is subconscious. Perhaps you feel that you are losing something. You may feel overcome with sorrow, feeling you have lost something, or that you are leaving something without even having an idea of what it is you are sorry or crying about. This is part of the process. It need not be a great deal of the process, but nevertheless it is there. As you approach closer and closer to the final experience you will feel yourselves letting go of more and more. This is nothing which is being taken from you without your consent. It is something that is being purged from your system because you are desiring to increase the frequency of your vibration. Ascension is simply increasing the frequency of your vibration. So all that is of dense and lower vibration is being shaken loose. Physically speaking, your cells and your DNA codes are being readjusted. There is so much occurring within your physical bodies. This is the source of your ailments, your mysterious health problems. And the same can be said of your emotional bodies, which hold the memory of all you have experienced on the Earth. Much you have experienced has been of a sorrowful or painful nature. Even though it may have been painful and sorrowful, there is still a tendency to hold on to that which you know. You have all assimilated into your emotional bodies and personalities these experiences. So it may feel that you are losing part of yourself. This can be a bit frightening. It can give way to occasional fears. The way to counteract this and to overcome it is simply to give yourself to the light and to know and experience directly that aspect of yourself which is growing larger and larger, so that you will be experiencing what you are receiving as you are experiencing what you are releasing. So you are not alone. None of you are alone in the particular process. And there are many more outside of this class who are going through the same process.

"I'm feeling a conflict. I'm feeling like sleeping a lot but at the same time I feel like there is much that needs to be done and time is short. I've been surrendering to the sleep. Is this need to sleep just part of the physical transition process? Will I move through it and get back to work? Am I trying to evade something?"

It is a common occurrence, and it is an aspect of loving yourself to listen to your body's needs. There are times, of course, when it is not practical, but if you ask for guidance and assistance, perhaps your life can be arranged in such a way that you can accommodate these increased demands of your body. There is not nearly so much to accomplish as you might believe. At least from our perspective. It is not our desire that you each run around and prepare yourselves as if you were about to experience the death process. If it is your desire to lessen your responsibilities and make more time for meditation and preparation then that is all the better. But you are perfectly in alignment. You are not trying to evade the issue by sleeping. You are merely allowing your body the opportunity to transmute. It is very stressful on the physical organism when all the cells and molecules of the body are being renewed, restructured, and increased in frequency. You may find yourselves feeling worn out and tired even though you may look at your day and feel that you didn't do anything much. So honor your bodies.

Guidance, receptivity — these are part of the process also. You are being drawn into a realm of more and more spontaneity, more receptivity to moment-to-moment input and messages and experiences. The more you can learn to exist like this, the easier it will be for you to surrender to that moment when you find yourself being lifted. You may have already found moments in your sleep or in meditation where you feel the lifting process beginning. If you have experienced this, there may be a part of you which is still a bit afraid of it, some desire to hold on to the Earth consciousness. So we are trying to make this as gradual as possible by assisting you in a gradual ascension, by working with you in your sleep and in your meditations. When you call upon your light body, it responds, and more and more you will find that you feel the actual presence of your light body coming down over you. This is your Christ overself. The Christ overself will come down over you, around you, and through you. And you will rise with it. This is why we ask that you call upon your light bodies every time you meditate, to get used to the process. It does not have to come to you as a shock. It can come to you as a gradual upliftment. Those things that you are releasing can be released gradually and gracefully so that they need not be so upsetting to your normal lives. You can find yourselves being more spontaneous and happy. It is meant to be enjoyed.

"Yesterday, I had to be in a musical event. Right before that I had a very emotional situation at home. When I

got there my heart was closed and I couldn't sing. It was a good message for me on how I handled this situation. I just close down so I don't feel. But then I can't do my work. Is there another way to not allow these vibrations to hit me and yet still remain open to the love and the music?"

The only way to truly rid yourself of this experience is to acknowledge that if you did not have these emotions in you, then you would not be affected by them. So there is a mirror effect here for you. You may feel that someone is dumping on you or giving you negativity, but if you were not on some level attracting this experience as a teaching for yourself, you would not bring it to you.

So I can give you all the advice in the world about calling on your teachers and guides and Sananda to surround you with light. This is always beneficial. But this will not protect you from your own lessons. So I suggest that you look within and see how it is within yourself that you are still attracting these experiences. They may be coming simply so that you can see what there is to release. It is a matter of releasing this within yourself. Release density from your own emotional body. Then you will not attract it from without. So, because you desire to open your heart and sing, perhaps it will be an added impetus to release that which restricts you from doing so. I'm sure you have already heard some of the ways to release. I think at this point in your growth it is a matter for you to call upon Sananda and ask him what is appropriate.If you are feeling a large emotional charge within your emotional body, it may not be appropriate to try to meditate it away. It is more important to express it in a non-harmful way. Perhaps therapeutically, or to scream and jump around. At other times you can meditate and ask Sananda to remove it. If you call upon me by name, and ask for the violet flames to surround those emotions with transmuting violet flame, that will assist in carrying it off as well. You can attack it from every different angle, spiritually and therapeutically. Above all, do not be overly attached. For as you release things there is a tendency to seek to reincorporate that experience as a part of yourselves. You will begin to feel perhaps that you are a terrible person because you are experiencing anger and rage, when in fact the anger and rage are leaving you. So don't pull it back into yourself with self-judgment and guilt. Allow it to go. Maybe it will be the last time you will have to experience this.

It is an individual path. There is nothing I can say to handle all situations for all beings. This is why it is necessary to connect with your own guidance, your own higher Selves, so that you have a guide within you to ask. It is our wish that each of you have the ability to call upon your guides and to hear our responses. If you can hear our replies, then you can channel your own healing. You can channel your own guidance. You will not require any external source. This is the ultimate desire of we who come through.

"I have been told that Kuan Yin would like to work with me. Is this true? How can I do that?"

Kuan Yin is a very powerful teacher — a very beautiful, clear, and sharp presence. A very focused and powerful ray. In your work with us we will be opening you and your channeling ability so that you can accept energies from other beings as well. You can request her presence in your meditations, and if you can get yourself to the inner peace you will see what she feels like to you. Know that when you speak her name or call for her she is hearing and will make herself available to you. It is no great mystery or difficulty. It is truly a simple act of prayer and a request on your part for her presence. If you desire, you could perhaps request that this one attempt to channel her for you. I am certain he would be most pleased to make this attempt, as he has not yet channeled this particular energy. So there are two ways you can approach the increasing of this connection. Also there may be others in this vicinity who can channel her energy as well. You are a powerful being and your femininity and hers are in alignment. Her power and yours will be merging as you develop.

So, I think it is time to do some meditation together. Know that we are assisting you week by week in your focus and in your concentration and your ability to go within. Know that in meditating at this time you are achieving incredible benefits. Much more so than you were just a few months ago. And now that we are in the final countdown phase there is an increase even more exponentially. So every breath that you take in meditation is a great release and a great liberation for you. You are closing in on your ultimate destinies.

Relax. Align yourself and attune with your own breathing. Listen to your breath as it flows in and out of your body. We are going to take each of you individually into your own inner sanctuary. I would like you to imagine yourselves walking, approaching a pyramid, one large enough for you to enter and comfortably inhabit. It is an individual pyramid just for you. As you approach you see the stones. They are perfectly connected one upon the other, geometrically perfect. And over the doorway of the pyramid, a doorway which is big enough for you to enter, you may stand there and if there are any inscriptions over the door you may read them — whatever you see or visualize there for yourself. This is your inner sanctuary.

So you enter, and you find in the center of the pyramid a beautiful floor, a beautiful seat — something perfectly comfortable for you to sit on in meditation. Inside the pyramid it is very still. There are no external vibrations penetrating. You are completely insulated from external vibration, from three-dimensional reality and all of its manifestations. There is a dim light filtering through from above you. Just be there and meditate within this structure. It is your sanctuary. You will find in this space more stillness, more peace. The only energies that are within this pyramid are your own ener-

gies. So by controlling your own focus and concentration you can completely still all vibration except for the vibration of the inner self and the breath. In your meditation you may begin to feel the feeling of the higher Self, you may begin to see the light of your higher Self, for your third eyes are being opened. Your crown chakras are being opened. And the light is flowing through. You may, if you are still enough and attuned enough, be able to hear the energy of light, the music of the spheres. You may be able to hear a high ringing sound, any number of tones. This is the way your higher Self or God sounds. This is the way atoms and molecules and planets and galaxies sound in their movements. If you wish to hear this music you can cover your ears a little bit. There is a bone or cartilage that is at the outside of the orifice of your ear, sort of a flap. If you wish to you can close off your hearing by pressing in upon it. (You can get earplugs for this also.) Now you know what this little strange appendage is for!

So you are experiencing the stillness and the presence of your higher Self within your pyramid sanctuary. And now I would like each of you to call forth the presence of your light bodies, and we will assist in bringing them down and bringing you up to connect. If you feel yourself drifting in meditation. simply return to your breath. You are having the benefit of this experience regardless of whether you are visualizing it or feeling it. Some of you are good at visualizing. Some of you are good at hearing. Some of you are good at feeling. So there is a feeling to God and a way to see God and a way to hear God to accommodate all of your individual abilities. So now I would like you to imagine another pyramid — a pyramid of light above your sanctuary pyramid — of the same dimensions, of the same size and shape as your pyramid. It is slowly descending — slowly descending until it merges with your pyramid, occupying the same space, activating your pyramid, activating your experience. Your light bodies are now surrounding you. Some of you will have a profound experience of this. Some of you will not be quite so aware. Be assured it is manifesting for each of you regardless of your judgment of the experience. Release your judgment and simply be. The light body comes to *you. It superimposes itself upon you. It merges with you and activates the transformation.*

❧

If you are enjoying your present experience you may remain there. There is no need to stop if you are experiencing the bliss of the light around you. I would like to ask others of you who have questions concerning this particular meditation, this visualization, any of the aspects — then you may ask me. This will be your homework assignment for the week. It is my desire that you do this at least once a day. Let it be as a precursor to your meditations. Any questions?

"When we go into our pyramid do we call on our light body and then meditate after that?"

Meditate first briefly, feel yourself attuned, and then call upon your light body. In that way you can feel the transformation consciously. Bringing down the pyramid of light is a way for you to visualize your light body coming down over you and around you. It does not always look like a pyramid. This is simply one way it can manifest. If you desire to call upon myself, Sananda or Ashtar or any of the Ascended Masters or angels, you can accommodate all of us in your pyramid. We will be pleased to join you. The main experience to call for is your own higher Self, your own light body. This is like practicing ascension. If you practice, you will be better at it when the time comes. When you feel the light body descending and your own vibrational frequency rising, you will feel more comfortable with the process.

Again I would like to say that some of you have been meditating for a long time. Some have not. Those of you who are better at focusing and meditating will perhaps have a more profound experience. Perhaps not. Regardless of what you feel yourself experiencing, know that when you do this exercise you will be attracting and manifesting the light body. Have no doubt about this. Your request in this is sacred to us and we await it. If you care to do this exercise six times a day, feel free to do so. You can remain in your inner sanctuary as long as you desire. You are free in that space. The more you are cleansed and purified in preparation, the more of an experience you will have in doing this. It will get so that you will have experiences that feel so profound and so powerful that you will ask yourself whether or not "this is it." "This may be it. I may be going now." You will have a good opportunity to let go and to experience the surrender aspect. For in that moment of ascension there is a point when you consciously surrender to the process and allow it to take place. Where you consciously say "yes" to the process. It will do you no harm to say yes to the process in your practice sessions. You never know. There is much work that we will be doing with you prior to the ascension. But there is no harm in being prepared. We will be assisting you and leaving you (after these classes) in a state, hopefully, where you will be so attuned to the process that you will be prepared. So whenever it occurs, you will already know what to do. You will welcome it and not be afraid. Again, this is a matter of joy and happiness and love and reunion. A matter of reuniting with your own light bodies and families, and with those awarenesses that you have lost in your three-dimensional incarnations.

There is a great deal waiting for you. There is memory to be recalled. There is experience to share, and there are many honors to be bestowed upon you after your triumph. Truly it is a triumph for each of you to have come this far, to have opened yourself to this present level of experience and openness to the ascension process, regardless of anything that comes afterwards. This will result in a great many blessings and a great liberation to you upon your ascension. The work that you do prior to ascension does a great deal to determine what avenues and opportunities are available to you. Not all will be having the same level of opportunity upon ascension. You will come into your true natures and true presence, and because of the works you have done in this lifetime, in other lifetimes, and especially in preparation for the ascension, you may have the opportunity to go beyond the fifth dimension into other dimensions, to explore realms that are indescribable. There is liberation from the third dimension. This is ascension. And there is further growth. So the more time you can spend in your inner sanctuary, the more you will be earning yourself good merits. You will be able to be in the company of greater and greater, higher and higher incarnations of consciousness.

It is our desire to prepare you for the maximum experience. You already know about ascension. You are already meditating and preparing yourself for it. In a way, the remainder of these classes will be preparing you for that which comes afterwards. This is why I have been discussing service with you this evening. You will be expanded beyond your dreams. You will be able to experience so much more light. You will be able to take in so much more and to bear so much more. You are channels of divine light. In your present condition you have a limited opening through which the light can flow. The more you ascend to the higher levels of awareness, the higher dimensionality you achieve, the wider and wider your channel becomes, the more you can share and receive. It is really quite an experience to have a maximum charge of divine love flowing through you. This is what I personally attain to. And one reason for the work that I am doing here this evening. It is an act of service for you and also for myself. For I, too, desire the maximum experience, the maximum growth. And as the universe is being restructured dramatically, there are new opportunities for all of us. We will all be promoted.

So, it has been my pleasure to be with you again. I am honored to have been a part of this ongoing experience and ongoing experiment. I will say to you now that this experiment is being accomplished and it is extremely successful. It is a successful experiment. So you are all to be congratulated. You are all radiating and shining much more brightly. The mind is like a wayward child. It will do what it will, and it will pass its aspersions upon all and have its doubts and confusions and its drama. This will be with you for some time. This is something you are being liberated from. But do not allow this to sway you in your dedication and devotion. For it is your devotion which will ultimately create your place in the Heaven Worlds — your devotion, the love in your heart for the Creator, the openness to merge with and to serve that beautiful energy. So the blessings of all of the masters are with you. Sananda sends his warmest regards. Archangel Michael has been with us this evening, surrounding us from a distance with his beautiful wings. He asks me to ask if any of you have remembered your homework assignment for last week: to call upon him with his sword to sever your ties, your attachments. You may continue if you have not been doing this exercise.

So our love is with you. We will see you again next time. Do not forget your inner sanctuaries. We are keeping your place warm. Goodnight.

❧ Class Five ❧

HEALING THE EMOTIONAL BODY

❈ Sananda ❈

Good evening. Welcome to class number five. This is Sananda. Allow yourselves to relax and breathe. This focuses your energy and concentration. Let the cares of the day drain away from your bodies. So how are we all doing? I thought so. Well, tonight we will be working on healing the emotional body, bringing through some soothing energy for you. This is a very important subject. Perhaps the most important. This is love. Love is that which will heal you, that which will be your ticket into the next phase. So tonight we will be opening your heart centers and working with you in this way, to achieve some balance and amplify the love experience for you. I hope you will all enjoy this.

You have all been seeking love for your entire lifetime. Well, you are about to find it. You will find an amplified version of that which you have already been experiencing. Love is a difficult thing to achieve while you are in the third-dimensional reality, as you all know. You have been trying in many ways to grasp on to this elusive experience. It has been scarce here. It will be more abundant in the future, much more abundant. The fact that it is scarce in the third-dimensional reality is an aberration. It is not the rule in the universe. Actually, love is the essential ingredient, the essential building block of all the universe. So you volunteers have come here to bring a little bit more love to an atmosphere which has been quite devoid of it. You have all succeeded in various degrees, but now it is time for you to return to your true state and your true allotment of this precious elixir. For you can only share that which you have in abundance. Most of you are still struggling to have even enough for yourselves. Tonight we will open you to a little bit more of this energy and increase your abundance of love.

You have all been in existence for many lifetimes. You have all received many impressions in your emotional bodies. In this lifetime in particular, you have received many scars or impressions that are not altogether positive. Because of the density and negativity of the Earth plane you have all been, to some extent, victimized by the negative effects of the lack of love. So the emotional body recalls this. The emotional body tends to hold experience within it until such time as it is allowed to release that experience. So you have all been in your growth patterns experiencing various types of emotional release and healing. Much has been accomplished, yet there is a little more to do. But it will be assisted by us. We will amplify your love and also the grace which surrounds you, in releasing any remaining darkness that has clung to your emotional bodies.

So what will be the most beneficial way to heal yourselves? I would say it would be to take a nice long bath in a pool of love. The love will enter your spaces. It will enter your wounded emotional body and heal you. You have very many concepts around the term and experience of love. Truly it is an experience and not something that you can understand. Each of you has done many crazy things in the name of love, have you not? Things which you ordinarily would find completely illogical. You will jump at the chance to perform if there is some love at the end of that experience. So I will tell you that there is a great deal of love at the end of this ascension experience. And let this be the carrot at the end of the stick for some of you. You have been seeking this experience intensely. There is so much love that is waiting to surround you. There is so much that it is an experience of bliss. I would say bliss is the experience of having too much love. In your third-dimensional reality you probably cannot conceive of having too much love. But it is possible and you will all experience it. Perhaps you will even ask us to turn down the juice a little bit, believe it or not. For love can be very explosive. It can be very expanding. It has a tendency to melt the boundaries of your limited identity to the point where you feel a oneness or a merging with all of creation. And you will all experience this. This is an aspect of where you are headed. This is integral to the ascension process.

You have many judgments and criticisms and opinions about your own particular experience and your own identity around the issue of love. You all have varying degrees of belief in your deservedness. You have judgments about yourselves concerning your past performance in this area, and in your ability to open your heart to receive and to give. I think tonight would be a good chance to erase the blackboard and start with a clean slate — to release all of your self judgments and self criticisms around this issue. Your judgments and beliefs around this issue are just as faulty as your judgments and beliefs around other issues in your lives. So if you are feeling that you cannot possibly open to such a high degree of love, sharing and giving and openness — if you feel that you are not a particularly open individual — this is a belief which must be eradicated. These beliefs will trip you up in your ability to bathe in that pool of love. All that is required ... it is not a matter of deserving; it is a matter of being outrageous enough to take the leap into it. It is there. The pool of love is there within you. Most of you have withheld from yourselves this experience because your programming told you that you did not deserve it, or it had to come in a certain package or a certain relationship. I am here to tell you that you need not be in a relationship to experience the depths of love. A relationship can mirror your experience but it cannot in itself take you to the depths. You yourself must provide the outrageous behavior of leaping into the pool of love.

So you have all done so many crazy things to receive this experience of love. I think it is time for you to do one more final crazy thing — leave the world as an ascended being. Love ultimately is your ticket — not your idea about your capability to love, but the simple fact that you are open to it. So tonight, be open to the possibility that you can be in a state of bliss, that it is in fact your true state. All these things that you have overlaid upon and around this experience will fall away, leaving you with your own true nature. Your own true nature is bliss. It is what you are. It is what is happening in your atoms right now. The reason we have all been so adamant about asking you to meditate, is so that you can still your mind and relax your stranglehold upon your true nature enough to experience it. Experience that essence. So the importance of love in the ascension process is critical. You do not need to be overly concerned about where you are at with this openness to love and being a loving being. This will only lead you to more self-criticism and judgment. Know that those beings who have love in their hearts for the Creator and for themselves will be able to ascend. If you have limitations around this, perhaps regarding your own deservedness, they will most likely be healed, for you have all stated your intention to ascend. In doing so you have unleashed many incredibly powerful transformations in your lives, and one of these is the unlimiting of your love capability. So do not judge yourself if you do not feel at this time that you are able to love unconditionally. This is your goal. You do not need to be perfect in order to ascend. But I will tell you how to begin. Begin by loving yourselves. The amount of love that you share with and for yourself does a great deal to decide how much love you can experience in other ways. All concepts about deservedness are to be immediately discarded if possible. If you can, be as little children who do not look at themselves with a critical eye or a judgmental eye, but only know that they desire love and will cry for it if they do not receive it. They will long for it until they are feeling completed in that experience. This is the proper attitude towards love and devotion, to be as a little child. A child knows what feels good and a child will go for that feeling regardless of anything else, regardless of any external circumstances. It is a direct approach. So I invite you all to be a little more childlike. If you are finding yourself in an experience that is lacking in love within yourselves, do not rationalize the situation by telling yourself, "Well, the reason I am feeling this is because of this and that and these reasons and these judgments and criticisms and these circumstances." You see how sophisticated you have all become. It's to the point where you can quite often rationalize your desire for love right out the window. So stop rationalizing and if you feel the need for more love, ask for it. If you feel the desire for unconditional love, ask for it. It is available to you. Because of where you are in your evolution and because of your commitment, it is even more available to you. It becomes more available with each passing day. So allow yourselves to be more childlike.

If you are feeling a bit out in the cold or lacking in nurturance, ask for that. And do whatever you can in your way to provide the nurturance and love that you desire. Whatever it is, give yourself those treats. Give yourself that time, that extra time to sleep or meditate or do something that you love. It is not time to withhold from yourself anything that is of a positive and good feeling. It is time to spoil yourselves as you would spoil your own children. And we will follow your example. We will follow through and provide you with a little extra juice.We are encouraging all to do this at this time. The way that we encourage you is to allow you a little bit more of that which you desire. So if you are praying for love and trying to nurture yourself, you will create a little bit of a vacuum wherein we can amplify the presence of the experience. If you have an experience of an abundance, you will have something to share. And this is the most useful experience in the love spectrum: sharing it. It is very difficult to keep to yourself. If you try to keep an overabundance to yourself, it ends up stagnating. Pretty soon you will find yourself wondering where it went. So spoil yourselves and very soon you will find yourselves having an abundance. And you can spoil your loved ones. You can spoil those you see on the street with a kind word. Love does not need to be a mushy affair. It can be as simple as a kind word or a hello — these are aspects of love also — friendliness, compassion. All the attributes of love are to be shared and experienced when you have the essential juice. If you do not have the essential juice, your attempts to be compassionate will only come off as being phony and hollow. So focus upon that juice. Fill yourself with it. Meditation is an excellent time. A little bit later we will be sharing with you a technique, a guided meditation, which will assist you in spoiling yourselves and healing your emotional bodies. You have been kicked around and your emotional bodies recall this. If you feel a difficulty in opening up to unconditional love at this time it is because you have done so in the past and have received less than positive feedback. So do not judge yourselves if you feel a difficulty in opening up to unconditional love. You have a valid and very good reason for feeling this. Begin in a simple way with loving yourself. You will not give yourself a bad time by loving yourself.

So there is much of emotional balancing and healing, some emotional release which has been underway, as you all know. Many of you have been experiencing this. This is all part of the drama of the ascension process. At times you may feel you are farther from the truth or farther from the ascension than you were last week at this time.

If you are feeling these kinds of feelings, it is most likely that you are undergoing this emotional cleansing and healing. It is not something you should be overly alarmed about. It is to be surrendered to. Love yourselves and do the best that you can. It is difficult to meditate at those times when you are undergoing this process. It is easy at that time to judge yourself, to feel that you are not doing a very good job. Forget about that. You are all doing wonderfully. And we are extremely pleased with the progress that you are making. I have to say that this group has been quite a success. Almost beyond our expectations. The openness which you have brought to this gathering and to this process gives us hope. And it gives us great joy. And this great joy and hope and love will be reflected back to you. You are experiencing it at various times now in your meditations and lives. You will experience it much more dramatically upon your ascension. You will all be very embarrassed at the response that you receive. This is no small matter that you are undertaking. So allow the process to continue. If you feel yourselves being stuck at any particular point in emotional cleansing or release, call on us for extra help. And follow your guidance.

Now is not the time to withhold healing from yourselves. It is a time to heal. Again, you do not need to make yourselves perfect in order to ascend. The process will occur. None of you will miss the boat unless you have a radical change of heart between now and then. We are simply seeking to make it more conscious and more smooth and easy. We hope to make the end result more magnificent. You will all have honors bestowed upon you. The more work you do now the more honors you will receive and the more opportunities you will have. You are all free spirits and desire to have many options in your lives. Continue this ascension program and you will have a great deal to chose from. We love you so much. What you need to do is tap into our love for you. This will show you how to love yourselves. Many of you have forgotten or have limited your expression of self love. Perhaps you feel guilty of loving yourself too much. Perhaps you feel it is not right or egotistical. You see, there are so many ways that you limit yourselves. I ask you, can you surrender all of your ideas and become as little children? Simple and direct. Call out for what you desire. You do not need to think about whether you deserve to experience it. A child simply calls out for what it desires. Do not be afraid to be too outrageous. You cannot be too outrageous at this time. You are all still too conservative. Believe it or not, here in Santa Cruz, in this bastion of outrageous free love, you are all limiting yourselves. So if *you* can't do it, what are they going to do in Chicago? They need to see someone succeeding in this process and see that it is possible. Since you are the most outrageous batch we could find, and despite the fact that you were in much need of repair, we have decided to go for it with you. I am only kidding. You are all beautiful beings. Very radiant. You do not see yourselves as we see you. But if you could, then ninety percent of your problems would be over. For ninety percent of your problems are in your own beliefs and judgments about yourself. So now is the time to forget about the past. Forget about anything you have done in the past. You are all forgiven, all of your outrageous crimes. Anything you did in the past, you did feeling that it was the right thing to do. You are all honorable beings.

Now the floodgates are opening, and what we are asking is for you to stand in front of the stream and be the first to be drowned in love. Many more will follow. This entire planet will become a love planet. There will not be a being on this planet without an open heart. At this time there are many who have been feeding you the false programming that tells you you deserve less. Many who have — out of their own ignorance and desire for dominion — sought to keep you and the other innocent beings down, from experiencing your birthright. So it is for you to be among the first, to be examples. Perhaps it is only walking around with a smile on your face or a light in your eyes. That smile and that light will increase dramatically when you have made your leap. So love yourselves as we love you. We are all going to take a vacation together this evening. You deserve to be on a continual vacation and you are headed in that direction. It is not irresponsible. It is irresponsible to withhold it from yourselves. Withholding it from yourselves withholds it from humanity. For you are the channels to bring this message of the permanent vacation to all of those who are still slaving away. You see, there is a great deal of joy in this message. You will have a favorable response. There will be some diehards who refuse and who prefer to keep their noses to the grindstone. You will allow them to do so. But most are childlike and desire freedom and love. These are the ones you will reach and connect with. So, have you any questions?

"I heard through another channel that there will be equal chaos in the Heavens as there is on Earth during this process. I'm not clear on this."

You need to get cable! You will get more channels that way. You will soon have a selector in your own body. You have one now but have not learned how to operate it fully. Then you will be able to tune into many channels.

Yes, there is a great deal of activity in space, as you say. This is not so much for you to be concerned with. You are to focus yourself on your own ascension process and your own growth here. There is little you can do about space. We are taking care of space. There is a housecleaning that is in effect. And it is a universal experience. It is not limited to the planet Earth. There is a new wave of energy that has proceeded from the Creator himself through all the channels and through all of creation. It is a reordering of the universe, a reordering of the creation. So what you are experiencing here in your corner of the galaxy is simply a result of this. So those beings who have been out of alignment with love and with the will of the Father are being dealt with. There are many planets. There are many beings with space travel capability who have not come into alignment fully. So they are being instructed. If they are offering resistance, they are being dealt with more forcefully. Many beings have come to the planet Earth, extraterrestrial beings not of the Ashtar Command, but lesser beings who have come here in physical ships in their physical bodies. One result of the housecleaning which has been in effect is that it has pushed them from their home bases out into farther reaches of the galaxy. They are seeking a place where they can be left alone to do their high jinks. So there are many who are uninvited guests upon the planet Earth. When the wave of ascension hits the planet Earth, it is going to sweep them a bit farther out into the galaxy.

The way the galaxy is structured is that there is a core, or central sun, around which the stars and star systems revolve. At the center of each of the galaxies is the Higher Evolution. As you proceed outward from the center, there is less of perfection and more of chaos. Planet Earth exists a little bit on the edges of this galaxy, so the housecleaning has taken a little bit longer to reach here. And those beings who were a little bit closer to the center, who were performing their high jinks, have been asked to surrender or have fled as their planets have also been cleaned up. So there will be some rather spectacular star wars. You will be made aware of them as your ascension is completed. At this point there is little you can do or little to worry about. But know that this planet is not alone in the overall restructuring and reordering of the universe. All are due for advancement at the completion of this cycle. The Ascended Masters will be advanced as well. So there will be many vacancies. We are hoping you will assume some of these empty chairs, some of these services. This is the way of the universe. Expansion and evolution without end. As we have said, you can never get too much of love. So it has been set up so that there is continual growth.

"I've found myself in a lot of conflict with people lately and I don't really know what to do about it. Is that going to happen often?"

It is a good opportunity for you to forgive. I think the main lesson here is to forgive yourselves for anything that you feel less about. You will attract experiences that mirror the feelings you have toward yourself, so perhaps in your cleansing and emotional healing you are releasing feelings of unworthiness or conflicts you have held concerning yourself. They are being mirrored to you externally. So do not sink to the level of reflecting negativity. Try to reflect only love. This is a good challenge for you in unconditional love. It is always appropriate to forgive whether you feel you are right or wrong. Whether you feel you have been wronged or persecuted. It is a test of your ability to forgive.

"Is there a way to be angry and loving at the same time — to feel angry and be able to express it in a loving way? Or is anger something that we shouldn't feel?"

At this point you can express it with love. Expressing anger with love is simply expressing your feelings, or what is at the core of your anger. So there is a way to share the fact that you are angry without expressing negativity upon another being. It is sharing your feelings. If you feel that you are angered by something someone has done, you can express to them that something they did caused you to feel anger. You did not feel it was right, you felt that you were being persecuted, perhaps, or treated unjustly. So look beneath the anger. See why it is you are feeling anger. And if there is someone there to share those feelings with, then do so. You can also release anger in an extreme way: have a fit; pound on some inanimate pillows which cannot feel your rage. It is all right to release rage at this point if you do not have a way to release it more gently. Seek to forgive yourself and others. But do not "stuff" your feelings, for they need to be released. You are all undergoing a releasing process. Often it is at such a deep level that you do not even know why you are feeling what you are feeling. Simply allow the feelings to flow through. Allow yourself to feel what you feel. As for the future, anger will become obsolete. It won't be long before you do not feel it any more. You will feel power. Perhaps you will feel a focused power or directness which may feel similar to anger, but it is not.

"Knowing I will be ascending soon, it is hard to proceed with my day to day activities with excitement and enthusiasm. I feel very blasé about my life."

I understand. I couldn't do it myself. Many of us who have graduated from your state have chosen to remain Ascended Masters and not incarnate because of the daily grind of third-dimensional reality. The ascension process will put you through some changes in your outlook.

"Sananda, how do we live with that feeling, especially when you are dealing with another person who is real 'here.' My partner sees anything that I do for myself as selfish. He heard one of my tapes of this class and thought I was really out of it and crazy. How do I deal with that? I feel like I'm leaving, but not just yet, so I'm stuck with the situation and his attitude."

There are ways of being present and ways of being not present. I think that as you grow in this experience you will become more and more present when you are present. So for you it is a matter of being fully present in the situation that you are in when you are in this relationship or connection. Be there. Be fully present and responsive and receptive. You do not need to forsake your responsibilities. In fact it is a good exercise to be perfecting yourself *in* your responsibilities. Certain things will be able to fall away that are unnecessary, while others are not. You must still provide for your children and do your work. Each of you have responsibilities that you must maintain. So give yourself to the task at hand. As difficult as it may seem, try to bring in more of your presence to that moment. It is a matter of being in the moment. In the moment when you are there you are not leaving. You are there. So be there. You do not need to subject yourself to negativity. It is difficult, I know, but you have given yourself this test at this time. So accept responsibility for it. Know that as you release your own judgments about yourself you will not receive judgments from external sources. So perhaps his judgments about your irresponsibility are reflections of your own feelings of irresponsibility about yourself.

In this process there is much emotional transformation and release. This is why we are here with this topic this evening. None of you are immune from this. Some of you will have more intensity to deal with than others. It is part of the process, so accept that it is part of your growth. If you are feeling different emotionally, if you are feeling from time to time that you are going through heaviness or despair and doubt, I tell you you will go through these. There is a part of you which will attempt to throw a blanket of doubt over this entire process. This is part of the battle. As the time draws to a close, and as the countdown progresses, you will find perhaps more of a battle with the part of you which will desperately seek to place you back in ordinary reality. This is where your faith will come in. But when you are experiencing this, and having difficulty meditating and connecting with your guidance and higher Self, that is where you will be tested in your faith. It is not something that cannot be overcome. You are receiving so much assistance. View these situations as clouds passing before the sun. You know the sun is there. You know the cloud will pass and the sun will shine upon you again. Again, this is not a small task you are undertaking. Very few have achieved this. It is difficult to believe when you look around you and see the world progressing and proceeding in a fairly normal way. It is difficult to believe you could be ascending when you see everyone around you going about their business as usual, and even you yourselves doing your particular responsibilities as if nothing was different. This is the challenge of the first wave. Those who take the remaining opportunities to ascend will have ample physical evidence that the world is not "business as usual."

"Last night I was startled awake and I felt actual fear over the ascension process and thought I would like to be asleep when it happens."

So you desire an anesthetic! This can be provided if you still desire it as the time approaches. By then you might have gone through the fear to the point where you will be wide-eyed and excited about it.

"Sananda, is it true that fear and doubt are tools to help us test our faith and inner courage to move on to a higher state of consciousness, and that doubt actually exists in higher consciousness throughout?"

Fear and doubt do exist but they are not the creations of the Supreme Being. Fear and doubt exist as challenges. It is true that by overcoming fear and doubt you gain strength and faith. So for all beings who have found themselves in the reality of the third dimension, or cut off from their Source, they will have to go through this test of faith, through doubt and fear. But there is a point where these are no longer applicable and present. This is the realm that we are seeking to take you to. There are always challenges to growth, but the challenges will not come in such a negative fashion. The challenges will come as opportunities to you, or as choices. So you will always feel yourselves being guided and perhaps stretched a little bit to experience new and higher dimensions of reality. There are tests of this nature, but they are in no way quite so dense. You are moving beyond these.

"I'm having a hard time with food and finding something that I can eat. There are so many resistances to things. Is this personal for me because of my particular

body, or is it part of the process? Also, I'm feeling some kind of emotional pressure, like I'm about to explode!"

The situation is temporary. It is a cleansing for you. I think you are being shaken a little bit. I think you are being somewhat forcefully shaken and awakened. This is quite confronting and attention-grabbing when your very sustenance comes into question. You may have many relationship problems and this sort of thing, but when you cannot eat any more, your higher Self is giving you quite an attention grabber. I think the two questions are interconnected. What is the emotional experience you are referring to?

"I feel pressure inside of me building up."

Despite the uncomfortableness you are feeling, it is temporary and it is part of the process.

"Should I stop eating for the time being?"

I think you may have to eat lightly, but this emotional thing is desiring to release. It desires to explode, just as you are experiencing. It will come to a head very shortly and you will then be able to eat more normally. I cannot tell you what it is. But you will not starve to death and you will not explode. There is perhaps part of you which is resisting expansion or the spiritual explosion that you are undergoing. So maybe it requires a bit of blasting. I would meditate more and ask your higher Self and guides to assist you in releasing that which is desiring to be released. Perhaps it is an attachment to a particular experience. It can be so subconscious that you may not even know. Perhaps you will never know what it is or what it was. But you are elevating your frequency and the density is seeking to hold you back from doing this. You will have to allow yourself to explode spiritually, I think.

"I have had a lot of little questions about what it's like for an ascended being who returns to the Earth. What about sleeping at night, rent, making love? What is their

day-to-day experience of third-dimensional reality as an ascended being?"

I assure you there will be no desire to have sexual intercourse with a member of unascended humanity. You will view things quite differently. As for your accommodations, there will be no need to make reservations or pay rent. You will all be given instructions and it will be different for each of you. Let me say, these types of things will be the least of your problems. You can sleep aboard ship each night if you desire to sleep. You can go back and forth as often as you like. You will be able to pop in and out. You will not be bound to this reality as you are bound now. This is the basis of your question. You have only this experience in your memories and so of course you will wonder about these things. But all will be explained to you and your training will be quite complete. Because of your conscious states you will have little difficulty in remembering your lessons. Nowadays you have less recall. If you learn something now, you often forget much of it because of the state of affairs here and the lower capacity of the mind at this time. After you have ascended you will be able to have total recall of what you are taught and your training will be remembered. It will be much easier.

"Do you mean that we will have recall of things we learned previous to the ascension as well?"

Yes, you will have a higher perspective on what you learned in your previous lifetimes, and you will be made more aware of your experiences during your Earth sojourn. If you have the desire to look back at your lifetimes, you can do so. You will not forget anything that you have learned. This will be a training for you as well as an exercise in service. So you will be more aware rather than less aware. There is much that has happened to all of you that you will not desire to be made aware of. But all experience has been beneficial to your learning and growing, and conscious of it or not you will have the full benefit of the experience. You may not recall exactly why or how you know how to do something, or how you know how to respond to a certain situation, but you will know how to respond. Your memories and teachings will not be lost. It will all make more sense to you.

"Will we be able to know our past lifetimes?"

Yes. If you desire this, you will be able to see your full range and full spectrum of lifetimes. We have movie theaters for viewing. You can go into your own individual movie theater to see a replay. I think it will be less fascinating to you than you might expect.

"I would think that if we could do this, we can use it with other individuals. If we could tap that in them, then we could use it to help awaken them."

Yes, you have been doing this. This was your goal and you have succeeded to some degree in doing this. You have touched many human beings, and those are the ones who will respond to this in the second and third waves of evacuation. So your work has not been lost. All of the rays of love and hope you have showered upon humanity — none were wasted. It's impossible to waste love. It seems to radiate in all directions endlessly. Some of the love that you have channeled in your earlier lifetimes is now reaching other planets.

"How would this ascension affect our families? If we ascend before them, will they freak out? Will they be taken care of in this?"

It will be a shock to them of a beneficial nature. So if they are shocked by your disappearance when you ascend, it will be a shock which will have a beneficial effect in the long run. But I assure you most of humanity will undergo a "freaking out" or shocking period which will make your disappearance seem small in comparison. So many of the things you are worried about leaving behind, like confused family members and unpaid debts — these will be the least of humanity's concerns as the energy increases and as the Earth changes progress. People will not be so concerned about these matters. They will be more concerned with maintaining their life and livelihoods and existence and growing spiritually. Growing spiritually will be much higher on the priority list. So the fact that you disappear and shock someone will shock them into questioning life a little bit more and will give them a head start on the program. There are ways to communicate with those beings who require communication. They will be notified of your whereabouts and they can be assisted in understanding. We can reach many. Perhaps you will return and reach them yourselves. There are innumerable options.

It is time for our meditation. This is the good part. This is the part I have been waiting for. It's vacation time. Relax and breathe. All of your concerns and emotional situations and processing will fall away. If not tonight, they will fall away in the near future. I ask you to put them on the back burner and focus in the present moment on what you are doing here and now. Trust that we are taking care of you in all of these regards. All of your unanswered questions are being taken care of. We are going to go into our inner sanctuary as St. Germain has guided you. Simply breathe and relax.

Imagine before you a pyramid of stone large enough for you to enter through a doorway. You enter the doorway. You enter a small room with a chair for you to sit upon. There is a little bit of light streaming in from above, just enough for you to see and feel comfortable. Make yourself comfortable. This is your inner sanctuary. It is insulated from the vibrations of the world. It is insulated from all negativity and vibration of the third-dimensional reality. In this space there is only your breath and your higher Self and myself. We are going to bring down the light pyramid and superimpose it upon the stone pyramid. You may begin to experience your light body in the form of a pyramid of light, in the exact dimensions of the pyramid that you are within. It will superimpose itself over the top of your stone pyramid. Allow it to descend at whatever rate is comfortable until it is completely encircling you. If you are having trouble visualizing — perhaps you are more of a feeling person than a visualizer — there is no harm in this. Simply breathe and meditate and feel. Imagine the feeling of this. Feel the activation of the light body surrounding you. You are completely within it. Now you are insulated within that space. Now we are going to take a little trip in our merkabah vehicle via the imagination and the etheric body. You have but to remain relaxed and breathe. We are going on vacation. As you meditate, you are being transported. If you are desiring an intensification of the experience of your light body you may ask and it will be provided. We are moving inter-dimensionally. You may feel yourself sitting here but you are also traveling.

You may feel yourself settling down now. You are landing, so to speak. It is as if you have flown through the air and landed. And there is the doorway directly before you in the side of the pyramid. You can rise and visualize yourself proceeding. You walk out the doorway and find yourself on a beautiful island, a beautiful South Pacific island. This is a vacation spot just for you. You have your own island. It is a small but beautiful island just for yourself. It feels very beautiful to you. The air is the perfect temperature. The light is beautiful. The ocean is a beautiful blue. The sky is blue. We are going to spend a little bit of time on this island. It is an island of healing and balance where you can go whenever you feel the need.

So as you walk out of your pyramid towards the beach, you will notice that this island has one unique characteristic that is different from what you have experienced before. The beach of this island is composed of tumbled crystals. As you walk out onto the beach you see these beautiful clear quartz crystals. You can feel them with your bare feet as you walk upon the beach. You feel them beneath your feet as they disappear under the beautiful blue ocean. You may walk into the water and feel it upon your feet. You may wade in it. You may experience it. As you do so, you begin to become curious about your situation and where you are, and you decide to explore. You wish to circumnavigate the island, to venture along the beach. As you begin to walk along the shore, you notice that the beach of stones is changing color. It becomes a beautiful black stone beach of obsidian. You walk on this. You feel these stones. You may sit upon them. You may wade and pick them up and feel them. You may lie down upon them with your legs in the water. You may experience them in whatever way you desire. As you do so, as you are connecting with this area of the beach of the obsidian stones, your first chakra is opened and cleansed. You feel a healing energy. You feel a sense of release and relaxation in your first chakra. This is a feeling of security, of groundedness and connection with the Earth and the energy of the black stones.

After you have experienced this for a little bit, you again feel curious and continue your walk. You come to a section of beach composed of dark reddish stones. They are beautiful tumbled garnets. You are enjoying the interplay of the water upon the stones, and the feeling of your feet connecting with them. They are a beautiful color and you are attracted to it. You may wish to sit upon this beach, or lie upon the stones, or stand and feel the energy. As you do so, your second chakra is relaxed and is opened. There is a feeling of release and relaxation as this energy works within you and your body absorbs the energy. There is a healing that takes place. There is a release of any accumulated tension in this part of your body.

Again you become curious and go on to the next portion of the beach. You find that it is a beautiful beach of bright, gold-colored citrine stones. They are golden. As you experience this beach you feel your third chakra opening. You feel your power center relaxing. You feel the beautiful healing energy penetrating and rising through your body. You feel this energy balancing your lower chakras in perfect alignment and perfect balance. All tension is released. We move on to the next beach. It is of beautiful rose quartz, pinkish in color. It is beautiful clear rose quartz, more clear than any you have seen. As you touch upon this area of the beach with your bare feet you feel your heart opening. You feel an expansion and a beautiful depth of love flowing from your heart throughout your body. It flows from your heart and through your lower chakras, down into the stones and into the Earth. All tension is removed from your heart center. There is a great expansion which takes place. There is great relaxation. It is a feeling of love and nurturance, of unconditional acceptance and trust. You find that you can relax totally in this trust and love. You can release all fears and cares and know that you are One and you are loved and nurtured.

As you begin to walk again you are feeling very free and very relaxed. You are almost floating as you walk upon the next beach, which is of beautiful blue stones. They are the color of lapis lazuli. The color is deep and rich. As you experience this beach you feel your throat center opening. You feel all tension within your throat being relaxed and released. You feel in alignment with your heart and all of your chakras. You feel the connection between the heart chakra and the throat, releasing your freedom of expression. And you can feel the blue light energy of these stones surrounding your throat. It is expanding and relaxing.

You move along to the next beach. It is of beautiful amethyst stones. They are deep violet and purple. This beach is particularly beautiful to you and you desire to sit upon it and feel the water at your feet. As you do so you feel the activation and opening of your third eye chakra. You may see the light within you. You may feel that beautiful pulsating light coming to you in waves. Just as the waves of the purple sea caress your feet you may feel the waves of light. Your third eye center is cleared. It is opened and connected with your heart and throat chakra in perfect alignment and balance. Now, as you move along the beach, you find you have circumnavigated the entire island, returning back to the beach of the clear quartz stones. Now your experience of this beach is emphasized in the opening of your crown chakra. As you stand or sit upon these stones, you feel complete alignment of the light energy coming through your crown, through the top of your head, through all of your chakras as a completely balanced and aligned experience of relaxation. There is no more tension within your chakras or within your emotional body. You simply breathe, and feel this balance and this health.

Now, I direct your attention back to your footsteps. Follow your own footsteps through the sand back to your pyramid vehicle. Know that you can take this journey whenever you desire, especially when you feel the need for emotional balance or healing. When you feel the need for a vacation, you have reservations. So know that in leaving this island you can return at any time. You can return and explore and spend as much time as you wish upon any or all of the beaches. For now it is time to re-enter your pyramid and seat yourself. Feel the door closing. Again you are surrounded by the beautiful bright light. Allow the light pyramid to descend around you. At the point that your light pyramid aligns completely with your stone pyramid, you are ready to return. Simply breathe and you will again be transported. So I say to you my dear ones, this is your island of love. You can enter the sanctuary of your light pyramid and journey to the sanctuary of your island of love at any time. The balance that is achieved in this way is most healing to the emotional body and aligns you.

Now your pyramids are settling back down to Earth. You are reintegrating with your physical body, yet you are still feeling that beautiful balance, relaxation, and openness. You have given this as a gift to your own bodies on your journey. You may remain in meditation as your pyramid rises above you and returns from whence it came.

❦

So it is with great joy that I thank you this evening for your very active participation. We have called upon you to use your visualization, your minds and your consciousness a little bit more actively this evening. But the results have been very successful. In fact I am in an extreme experience of bliss to be within your auras at this time. So love yourselves and above all, allow, accept, trust. You are undergoing an incredible experience, an incredible transformation. You will succeed. We have not lost a Starseed yet in all of our work. Enjoy the process. Enjoy the beautiful experience of meditation. Please call on me whenever you feel the need of extra healing for your emotional bodies, or in releasing. I will assist in every way that I am allowed. Goodnight, my friends.

❧ Class Six ❧

FINAL INSTRUCTION

⇒ Ashtar & Sananda ⇐

Good evening. This is Ashtar. So, you have all made it one way or another through storms and strange trials to be here this evening. I thank you for your dedication. As you know, this is our last class in this particular series. We will consider it a sort of "wrap up." I'll discuss a few things with you and give you an opportunity to ask any more questions that you might have.

You have been involved and will continue to be involved with a great deal of transformative energy in your lives. In fact, the more responsibility that you take on in your ascension, in your conscious ascension, the more you will find yourselves quickening in your growth and in your development. For truly the ascension is and can be a gradual process culminating in the final event. It is our hope that you will all take to heart the matters that we have discussed, the tips that we have given you in this course and utilize them. Focus your energies. I think you will find it easier to await for your final lifting if you are experiencing a lifting on a day-to-day basis. This is what you will experience if you apply yourself in your meditations and request help from us, from your guidance. Call upon your light bodies as we have discussed. You will experience more and more the feeling of lifting, the feeling of expansion, and you will find yourselves coming face to face with your limitations as we have discussed previously. This will be an indication to you, not that you are doing something wrong, but that you are in fact expanding beyond old limitations and beliefs, old creations. You are entering a new realm of consciousness, and you will grow at whatever rate you can achieve within your own level of dedication and your own abilities, your own capacities, let me say.

This is a uniquely individual path. Each of you has a goal. Your goal may be the same. In experiencing the goal, it may be quite similar in those last moments when you feel the lifting taking place. And yet all of the processing and the preparation and experiences you have prior to this event are uniquely your own. You may share with one another and have a great deal in common and support one another, but you are each on an individual path: unwinding the illusion that has surrounded you, releasing, and learning to be one with your higher Selves, your God-Selves. It is my sincere hope that each of you will practice your meditations, your affirmations. Follow our guidance. Tune into our guidance individually and in groups, however you feel comfortable. And in doing so it is my hope you will have an incredible journey.

This is a path of joy, a path of love, a path of increased peace. It is a path upon which you can increase your powers of manifestation, your powers of healing, your powers of connection with guidance. All of the blessings of Spirit, all of the gifts of Spirit are enhanced when one begins to give themselves to the ascension process, which is another way of saying ... a very direct way of giving yourself to the God-presence within. So I would like to say (and it is very important to note) that in the days to follow, those of you who are pursuing your paths will each find individually —

each uniquely — your own guidance, your own motivations, your own inspirations.

You will find ways to connect with other human beings in loving ways, in healings, in channelings, etc. And it is my wish to tell you that whatever you are feeling drawn to, whatever is inspiring, is important for you. There are no limitations that are to be placed upon you. If you are on the ascension path, any work that you do in spiritual growth areas will ultimately enhance your ascension process. So feel free to be spontaneous in your lives. Open yourselves to guidance and to the magic that takes place when you do so. It can be a very magical life.

There is a tendency that we have noticed among you, and among others throughout the world who are waiting for the ascension. There is a tendency to long to give up your worldly life a little bit prematurely. There is a sincere desire within you for the ascension. For you are awakening to that longing that is within you, that has been within you for a very long time. But now it is presenting itself openly to your hearts and to your consciousness. So you are faced with a situation where you have work to do to prepare yourself, and also you must work to maintain your life experiences, your responsibilities. So I would like to give you some hints and tips about what I feel is appropriate to your particular situation, concerning your waiting and the work that you have yet to do.

As we have said, we have no way of informing you at this time when the first wave will be. It is important you know that it will happen. And it is our hope that it will happen very soon. But it is also our intention to communicate to you that you are to live as if you were going to be here for some time. It is not appropriate behavior for you to throw all of your responsibilities out the window and wait for the ships. This is rather dysfunctional behavior which may result in your having more to deal with, more unnecessary chaos financially and in other ways. So it is my hope that you will find the balance in your hearts. It is there.

There is a great deal of excitement at first upon hearing about ascension. But as you assimilate the information and begin more and more to walk upon the path, it becomes more integrated into your life. It becomes something that you can manage to work upon, manage to grow towards in a balanced way, in a way that does not detract or cause you the feelings of impatience so often. Those feelings will arise. Those longings will arise, but it is my intention that they not be overpowering to you. They are part of the path. It is necessary to connect with your inner longing, to connect with the part of you which longs to be one again, which longs for that completion, that merging, that reconnection.

So what can you do? Here you are existing in this world, making the best of things. Now you know about the ascension. You have the path to walk upon. You have some guidance to follow. You have some Masters to call upon. Yet you are still face to face with your daily realities. So first of all I would like to recommend, as we have been saying all along, that you continue your meditations. Continue to call upon the manifestation of your light body. And continue, above all, to call upon myself or Sananda or any of the other Masters on a daily basis. Take time each day to do this, in whatever way works for you. It is more and more important that you have a strong sense of guidance internally. It is important that you have an experience of the ascension process unfolding for you. If this becomes merely another New Age philosophy, you will find yourselves drifting perhaps a little bit in a less direct path, in a less intensified growth pattern. It is our hope that you will continue to dedicate yourselves to this in your own ways, and to find the strength you need to prepare for the day. The day is coming. And it will be a certain date or a certain time. Call upon us to fill your lives with joy in the meantime.

You have been taking this course, as we call it, in contacting us. You have strengthened and enhanced your connection with us dramatically. You have placed yourselves somewhat out of the crowd a little bit. You have chosen to accept the ascension process. You have volunteered, though the true volunteering doesn't come until those last moments when you make your final choice. You have (philosophically at least) volunteered to ascend; and in doing so you have increased your contact with us. You have increased our ability to work with you in more intense and more beautiful ways, more powerful ways. So, continue with this and know that this is strong with you.

So, as I have said in the past, know that the ascension can occur at any time in the near future. It is our plan that it will. There is no way of knowing the exact date. And we will not be able to give you an exact date even in the future. We can only give you our impressions. But it is our hope that you will live as if you are going to be here for some years. At least for some years to come, so as to have a smooth and enjoyable time. Know that the last days you spend upon this planet are intended for you to experience as a great joy and love and peace and excitement. Your last days on this planet are intended to be enjoyed and can be enjoyed. For you will find as a benefit to this ascension work, all the release work that is occurring will result in your having an experience of life that is much lighter and much more enjoyable. Your very presence and your health and well-being will increase, as well as your ability to contact the great ocean of love and healing within yourselves. So it is a time of joy and celebration. Again, do not wait for that day. You can celebrate now. Share with one another and support one another. Open to the miracles that are taking place.

Your Ascended Master training can begin long before you are an Ascended Master. So if you are feeling a strong drive within you to take the ascension path, and you want to be one of those who returns as an Ascended Master to teach — if this is your desire — know that your training has begun. It begins from the moment that you make that decision. There will be periods for each of you, most likely, when you will find yourselves dealing with doubts and fears. You will find times when your own mind will tell you that it is all crazy and that it will never happen. I am telling you this in advance so that when it happens you can remember that, "I told you so." These are like clouds that you walk through. It is not for you to be dissuaded or to put a huge amount of energy into this, but know that it will arise. For your faith will be tested. One of the prerequisites to those who are going on the first wave will be a rather fully developed sense of faith.

Again, the prerequisites for ascension at this time — for you and for the rest of humanity who choose to accept it — are much less than in the past. Those individuals who have ascended by their own work and by their own diligence had to pass quite a few more tests than you will have to pass. Nevertheless, there is an element of testing. There is an element of faith and trust which you will be developing more and more, which will be tested in certain ways. As you pass the tests, you will feel yourself ascending a little bit at a time and waiting joyfully for the main event. This is necessary. This aspect of faith is very important. And in saying faith, I do not mean blind faith. I do not mean believing something that you have heard from some external source, but your own heart's knowledge of what is true for you. So again, it is all important that you experience the ascension process within you, so you feel the miraculous growth that is taking place. And let this be the source of your faith.

When you find yourselves confused, when you find yourselves walking through what seems to be a dark tunnel on the path, call upon us. Seek that silence wherein we can speak to you, and share with you our love. We have ways and means of connecting with all of you. You see, you are part of the family now. There is an ever growing family of Light Workers, of Starseeds. And you are the volunteers, the first wave volunteers, though it is not necessary for you to choose the first wave if you do not desire it at that time. I am grouping you together. Another aspect of this waiting period that you are in ... it is extremely important and helpful for you to maintain some contact with others in your group and to support one another. You can meditate together. You can channel for one another. You can come to the groups that are occurring at this home. This is somewhat of a center for Starseed support groups. But know that you are not alone. You have your ascended family working with you. You also have a more and more extensive family of beings, of humans here who are awake to this process and can assist you, who can share with you their own experience in ways that are very uplifting. In sharing your experience you will find that you are not alone, that others are experiencing strange transmutations in their physical forms as well. You are not going crazy, though sometimes you may feel that it is too much for you. You may feel waves of energy and waves of release. All of this is part of the path. You see, you have chosen a rather intense path of growth here. Perhaps some of you feel you have stumbled upon it. Nevertheless, you are responsible for choosing it. So continue to assume this responsibility and you will find the rewards are truly remarkable. So, I would like to also speak this evening a little bit about what you can expect in those final days and hours and moments. As near as I can express it to you in a way that is applicable for all. As I said, each of you will have your own experience of ascension. And it may appear to manifest to you a bit differently from others. Yet in general you will have the same overall experience. There is no way that we can inform you far in advance, at this point at least, for we are not privy to that information. We will not know ourselves when the final moment will be until perhaps an hour or two before it occurs. Yet we will have our hunches and feelings as you do. And we are ever prepared. I would say that in the days before the first wave, those who are qualified for this event may feel a great deal of intensification of the release process. You may feel a stirring up of your emotional bodies, a stirring up of those belief patterns and whatever is remaining in you to process. You may find a great deal of release occurring, an intensification. If you begin to feel this in your lives, perhaps you could focus more on your meditation. Give yourselves to our counseling. This will prepare you for the lifting if it is to occur at that time.

In the final hours before the lifting takes place, you will feel a connection, you will feel the presence of your guides. You may feel myself, or Sananda, or other ascended beings who you are working with. You will not be alone at that time. You will feel an intensification of the presence of your guides. And at that time you will begin to feel a great deal of inner peace and clarity. Again I am speaking generally. But I think this will be true for ninety-nine percent of you. You will at that time feel the presence of your guidance, and in this calm and ease you will most likely be drawn to meditation, drawn towards quiet and peaceful surroundings where you can give yourself to Spirit, where you can enjoy the experience of surrendering. For you will have an experience of those areas where you are attached to the world. You will feel your connections, your attachments with your earthly life and those relationships you have had. And there you will have your opportunity to choose whether you wish to relinquish these attachments or remain behind. I sincerely request that you open yourselves to letting go at that time. What you let go of will be taken care of. It is not so important as you think, and what you are going towards is much more important than you can know at this time. So there will be a sense of trust that you will be exhibiting, a sense of faith. And this is why there is a necessity for you to pass these tests of faith and trust. For in that final moment and final hour you will have to give yourself with faith to the process. It will feel a bit more intense or powerful, and slightly different from your usual meditations. So there will be an element of faith there where you are letting go to a new experience. You will be lifted. You will be lightening up. You will be more etheric than you have been. You will be taken through a stage where you will feel this. And it is quite enjoyable, this peaceful, etheric experience, even though you will be conscious that you are in your bodies and meditating.

And there will come the time when you, sitting with your guides in silence, will be presented with an internal, very pronounced vision of a window — some sort of an opening. It will perhaps look like a window to you, or a doorway opening up, though it will not be quite as subtle as the light that you meditate on within. It will be more pronounced than that. In fact you will be able to see it with your eyes open or closed. It will be that evident. In general this will be the experience. If it appears in a slightly different way for you, do not hesitate. Go with your faith and trust. Go with your feeling. In that final moment you will make the choice on your own to walk through that window or to remain behind. You will be with your guides prior to that moment and immediately following, but in that exact moment that you walk through the window or doorway into the light you will be on your own. You will have the feeling that you are on your own. For it is your individual choice to do so.

Let me say that this entire experience I am speaking of will happen quite spontaneously. You need not remember consciously all that I am saying now. You need not have a picture in your mind and wait for it to occur. It will occur spontaneously. You will know what to do. You have been prepared sufficiently for that. So do not be afraid that if you forget something I am saying now you will not make it. In fact, if you are asleep at that time you will have the same experience in your sleep state and will have the same choice. And you will, if you are ready, walk through in your sleep state. So it cannot be that difficult if you can do it in your sleep. So have no fear that you will miss the boat or make a mistake. And as you walk through the light window you will perhaps be able to see on the other side a panorama, some sort of scene, and you will see guides waiting for you and you will again be connected with guidance immediately following this. You will be lifted at this time. This is the critical moment. This is the moment in which you make your final choice. Up until that point it is a theoretical, philosophical, and somewhat less than experiential acceptance of the ascension. I think most of you will not hesitate. The nature of this class, and the importance of it, has been to prepare you to such an extent that in your hearts there is something that knows now what to do, that knows now this is for you. This comes with the work we have been doing.

So you will be lifted. You will be in your physical form, though more ethereal in nature, more light feeling. But you will still be in your body at this time. You will be lifted into a ship. And you will be acclimated and you will at that time make your choices. You will have choices presented to you as to what you desire, what path you wish to choose. You will have free will as to whether you wish to choose the ascension path and return to the Earth as an Ascended Master, or whether you wish to remain in spirit, to return to your prior state of spirituality or an exalted state. For you will be due for promotions after your Earth service. So you will be acquainted with what is available to you at that time. And each will have different choices. It is our hope that many will choose the ascension path and return as ascended teachers. I think out of your compassion most of you will do that. But there is no judgment or criticism. It is your choice. This is somewhat of a description of what will occur during the first wave of the evacuation.

There is one other area I would like to address. First, I will let all that sink in a little bit. And you may ask questions in a few moments. You see, it is one thing to discuss the ascension theoretically or philosophically, and quite another to actually be presented with the fact that it will actually happen to you. As you proceed along your path you will come more face to face with the truth in this. Then you will have to process your reactions to that. But there is always a great deal of grace and light and love surrounding the path, so it is not all that difficult to find your way and to continue. It is a very inspiring path to walk. So have no fear. Fear will arise, but it will not have its source in the ascension. It will have its source in previous experiences on Earth coming up to be released. You will have no need to fear. Soon you will be liberated from it and from all earthly limitations. You will be restored to your more natural state. You will be overjoyed, and we will be overjoyed. We are waiting for you with open arms. It has been a long time that you have been here. And we have waited a long time even to be able to present this information in this way. We have waited a long time, until the time was right to present it. Now we are presenting it, and it gives us great joy. So know that though you are waiting and it may seem like forever ... sometimes a month or a week can seem like forever if you are feeling impatience, but know that even if it were to take another five years, it is still the wink of an eye to us and to you in your overall existence. So try to have an awareness that time is truly illusory here.

So the last item I would like to address is service. I would like to make some recommendations to you, those of you who are feeling inspired to assist in this process. For those of you who are feeling you would like to get on with it and do whatever you can, I will recommend some simple ways you can assist us. In fact, your lives will become service. This has always been the intention of your hearts. You have gotten bogged down in survival issues and limitations. It has been very difficult to give yourself totally to selfless service. But there will be a time when you have nothing else to do but enjoy yourselves and play and do service. So you can begin this. This is part of your Ascended Master training. You can begin it now.

Primarily, number one, your service is to yourselves: to nurture yourselves, to facilitate your growth on this path. This is your primary responsibility. It is extremely important that you take responsibility for your own preparation for ascension. Whatever you feel drawn to do, whatever feels appropriate to you, this is of prime importance. I would say from my perspective that this takes precedence over all else. I am not telling you, again, to quit your jobs and go meditate in the mountains. You will not need to do this. You will be able to find appropriate ways to focus on this work. Nevertheless, this is your number one priority. *Suggested* priority, I might add. Number two, do whatever you can to network this information, to reach out to other Starseeds who are not yet aware of this process and this imminent event. For as you know, we are requiring a certain critical mass, a certain number of volunteers. Otherwise the ascension will not have the needed impact, and there is definitely a need for a great impact at this time to turn the events of the world around. So share this information with those who are open to it. If you have friends in other parts of the country, if you have people that you know might be interested, you can send them tape recordings. You can send them channelings. You can direct them to other people, to this particular channel or to others for more information. This is very important at this time.

So, giving yourself to serving in this way enhances your own growth experience. This is not something you need to feel hysterical about. In fact, I am hoping you will address this in a rather calm and centered fashion. No one need run out into the streets screaming about the ascension or post ads in all the newspapers and this sort of thing. This is something to be accomplished from heart to heart. And only through the heart is this truth to be communicated. The intellectual information is communicated, but it is the heart which responds. Remember that.

So do what you can. If you feel inspired, do what you can. And again, I would say continue to be connected in your groups. You may avail yourselves of the channelings that occur here. There is quite a Starseed group and it is very supportive. Or gather together among yourselves or with others for support and sharing. So, I have probably forgotten something that I meant to say tonight, but I will open the floor to questions.

"When we ascend and we are at this point where we make our choice, and if we make a choice to come back down to continue doing our work on Earth, are we considered ascended at that time?"

Yes, you will be ascended before you return. And you will never be de-ascended again. You will return in your light bodies.

"Also, at that time will we be lifted from third-dimensional being to the fifth?"

Yes. To fifth or beyond.

"I'm attending a metaphysical business success class in San Jose. I have shared this in the class and my leader has told me several times not to give up my body to any group. From everything I've heard I don't see where I'm giving up my body on this."

You are not giving up your body. You are evolving it. You will still have the same body. It will be more evolved. Your leader is not understanding. It is a natural part of spiritual growth. The ascension is the completion of spiritual growth on this planet. It is not leaving your body in the hands of some other group or some master or some strange cult of some type. It is necessary for you to take your body with you. You cannot ascend without a body. So in a way, it is much safer than dying wherein your body goes into the earth and you leave it behind. You have left many bodies. So perhaps you could point out the paradox to her. Beings leave their bodies all the time.

"Can you talk about the purpose of the ascension if we would not choose to come back and help the Earth? If that's why we are here as Starseeds, our mission was to help the planet at this time of transition. What is the purpose of having a choice of going on to another realm and not coming back? Is it because of the cataclysmic events that are coming?"

The cataclysmic events will not harm you if you are an ascended being on the Earth, for you can instantaneously beam to an area of safety. The purpose in your coming here was in large measure to assist humanity in evolvement. But it was also to assist yourselves. It was also to enhance your own growth, you see. So it is perfectly acceptable for you to take your Earth sojourn as a growth experience, to know that you have done some good here and to move on to your liberation. There is no criticism if you choose this. You are undoubtedly feeling a strong desire to return and this is appropriate for you. But there are other reasons why beings have chosen as Starseeds to come here. This is a large part of it, but being here on the Earth has enhanced your spiritual growth and progress many times, despite what you may feel that you have experienced here, the density that you have encountered. The end result of your leaving here as an ascended being is that it has served you. So you see, it is appropriate if one chooses to simply return to a more spiritual state. Because in the time that you have been here on the Earth you have been doing service. It is not that you have done nothing. Up until the point you ascend you will all have done a great deal to assist others and to share love and to work upon the evolvement. So some may feel that their work is done. And others may feel like they would like to have one last shot at doing what they can do. So it is not necessarily a selfish choice to leave, to not come back. There are some who have wearied themselves to quite an extent by being here and doing a great deal of service. It may be appropriate for them to let others carry on from here. You will not be leaving the realm of service if you choose to move on. The nature of the universe is that all beings that are aligned with the God-presence are doing service in their own ways. So if you do not choose to return to Earth as an Ascended Master, to do that service, there will be other service opportunities that you will choose from.

So you see, all of your choices will involve various service opportunities. It will be your heart's desire to serve at that point. It is the longing of all beings who are experiencing the God-presence, to share it in whatever way they feel is appropriate. So this is one aspect of service: returning. Very important, but not the only one.

"I've been noticing that there has been a lot of emotional upheaval in the last few days, particularly in my life. What's that all about?"

I believe that Sananda addressed this to quite an extent last week. There is an emotional clearing that is taking place. Energies have been stored within your emotional body. They could be from this lifetime, they could be from many lifetimes ago. It could be an accumulated effect. But there are energies that you have been carrying around in your emotional body which are too dense for you to take with you in your ascension. So they are leaving. And the only ways they can leave is through expression, through release, or through meditation. In general, emotions are expressed as feelings as they are being released. So you are being cleared a little bit. When they come to the surface — and you may not even understand what they are representing to you — simply know that they are leaving you. There are certain ways and means that the world has, and the Masters have, to press those buttons which will cause you to once again re-experience those and release them and be lighter. You need to lighten up if you are going to rise. So do not be overly concerned. You may feel that you are a little bit crazy. You may feel a little bit strange. Some of you have grown accustomed to being "very together people," as the saying goes. Very functional and grounded and organized. Perhaps you will find a space of time for some few hours or some few days when you feel totally at a loss to cope with reality. You are entering a new territory here. That is why, again, faith and trust and the meditation connection with your guides are so important. If you can connect with us, we can assist you by explaining to you so you will have an understanding. You need not necessarily have an understanding in order to do the work, but it helps. Again this is why it is important to continue to connect with one another and to share, for you will be going through processes. Sometimes very intense ones. It helps to have another who understands the process to share with.

"Can you say something about the rainbow rays, rainbow bands, and how we can utilize them in our lives to reach a higher frequency?"

I think you will need to phrase your question in a language that the channel understands.

"There is a hierarchy of Rainbow Beings, cosmic beings, who are working with some of us now. Can you tell us anything about how we can utilize the rainbow ray in parts of our bodies to uplift our own frequency, to let more light in? Do you know anything about that?"

I would say that this is a more complex description of the work that we are already doing with you. You see, there are many beings who are connecting with you. Many different levels of reality. And each one of these beings has a particular frequency. And this frequency can be said to express as a color, or as a feeling, or in other ways. So if you were to view the spectrum of the beings that are working with you, the various groups of beings could be said to represent the rainbow. I would say that it is not so important that you have an intellectual understanding of this, but if you feel this is important to you, you may pursue it. But know that in your work, in your simple meditations and preparations for ascension, all of this is being accomplished. We have a great deal more going on with you than we can express in this way. We are simplifying this message so as to reach the most beings and to make it as simple and easy as possible. We are using many high technologies and spiritual sciences, and this rainbow ray is one way of describing an aspect of the work that is being done not only by us but by the other angelic hierarchies.

"I've heard that the Brotherhood has said that it's time now to gather the Starseeds and take them home. Can you say something more about this?"

You will be gathered in the lifting and ascension process. You will be taken home, for your origins are quite diverse, you see. You are from many different sections of the universe. You will return to your homes, or choose to remain as an Earth master for a time. But ultimately, after your work here is done, you will have the opportunity to return to that home planet or area that you emanated from, if you feel drawn to it or homesick for this particular manifestation. Some of you will feel more at home with the Earth after having been here for so long. But nevertheless the universe will open its doors to you. You will be able to travel through the dimensions, experience the marvels of creation — and whatever level of evolvement you have attained, you will be returned to that level of the cosmic hierarchy or beyond. You will be able to approach much nearer to the throne of the Creator than you are now.

"When you are channeling through a person and that person needs to ask you a question, would you automatically know that that person is asking you a question, or should the person say what the question is?"

I would say, speak your mind if you have a question. If you are channeling ... you are feeling the presence of Ashtar, yes? We are enjoying your presence. You are doing well. Try not to doubt yourself so much. If you have a question you may ask Duncan to ask you the question. Or you may ask it yourself mentally. You may say, "Ashtar, what about this?" Try it and see if you get better answers than those that come through this channel, and share with us. I think you will get a good response.

"What does it take to get a spaceship over your house? Are there any advantages by which we would want to have this? There's one over this house. I would sure like to have one if it meant doing the work. I would like to experience it even in a dream state."

You may ask this channel, these two that are sitting here, their experiences of being lifted. They can share with you what it is like. It can be quite enjoyable. At the same time it can feel quite natural. Nothing to write home about at times. I would say that if you are meant to be somewhat of a command center, as this place is, there will be a platform in place over that abode. It is a communication center. The channel who is existing here, the channels who are here, are connecting more and more with the beings who are operating this platform. It is somewhat of a telepathic communications station. A stable platform, you might say. It is difficult to understand intellectually. Let it be an experience for you. The channel is perplexed himself about how to deal with this aspect of his connection with this particular ship. We are trying to explain it to him, though he is a little dense!

Ask and you shall receive. This is part of the connection we are asking you all to make. Connect with your guidance. The Ashtar Command has completely functional operators on duty twenty-four hours a day to take your calls. So please respond and develop yourselves in this way, and you too can have this wonderful experience of channeling or receiving messages.

"After ascending to the ship, if your decision is to go into the spirit realm rather than return, what happens to your body?"

It is altered or rematerialized in a different form.

"But you keep your body?"

Well it depends upon where you came from, you see. If you are heading towards a higher-dimensional state where there is only light and energy, then your body may be transformed to such an extent that it no longer looks like a body. There are different manifestations in different levels of awareness, you see. The physical body is in one sense the crown of creation. It's meant to be a perfect manifestation, a reflection of the God-presence. As it is said that God created man in his own image. It is more true than you can know. Yet there are many different manifestations. There are many levels of bodies also. The third-dimensional body and the fifth-dimensional body look somewhat similar. But as you proceed up the ladder of expanded presence, I would say for you to wait and see. This will be explained to you if it is pertinent for you. You will know and be reacquainted with where you came from at the time of your lifting. Let it be sort of a surprise package for you. You are finding out who you really are, but you will not understand who you truly are until your ascension. And some of you will be quite surprised how you have limited yourselves to such a tiny package. You have all surrounded your great cosmic beings with limited beliefs to such an extent that you feel rather powerless or small. When you ascend you will feel quite a bit more powerful and expanded. You will realize why it was difficult to maintain third-dimensional form.

"Is there anything Dark Forces can do to stop this?"

Ultimately, no. If you were to fall under the sway of false teachings or doubt or fear — all of the chaos that is present here on this world — in effect you would be allowing the dark forces to affect you personally and your particular readiness for the ascension. Nevertheless, the ascension itself cannot be affected by them. They are attempting as best they can to keep humanity in a state of confusion and fear. So if you fall into fear, know that you are perhaps being influenced by them. At the same time, I must say that fears will arise spontaneously as a result of your taking this path, as you realize more and more what you are getting into. The part of you which clings to third-dimensional reality — your egos — at times may feel fear. This is a natural response. But if you do not indulge in it, I would say the Dark Forces will not be able to harm you. They are not fully aware of their own limitations.

"The term 'The Great White Brotherhood' ... does 'White' refer to race and does 'Brotherhood' refer to just the males, or does it include males and females?"

The Great White Brotherhood is a name to label all of the Ascended Masters. It is not a racial description. There are Ascended Masters of both sexes and of all colors. The Great White Brotherhood is a label used to describe the organization of a group of beings who have ascended. There is a great hierarchy you see, an organizational structure. It is somewhat of a service organization at a higher level of consciousness with a higher purpose. So it is a group that you will be joining soon.

"Why is it that Ascended Masters have chosen not to manifest on the Earth plane but to use channels at this stage?"

As you say, it is at this stage that we are not manifesting. There will be a time, there have *been* times, when we have manifested to a few individuals who were ready and who had a particular purpose for this to happen. In general, this is your time to shine. There is also an element of faith and trust that we have discussed. It is part of the opportunity that you have in coming here, in taking this ascension path — the opportunity to enhance your own growth by ascending. And it is involved with faith. So we have been given instructions that it is not time for us to manifest. Some of you have been calling on us to do so. We would like to. At certain times we may. But we are receiving our orders from on high. And it is for you to ascend and return and for you to be the Ascended Masters. If we were to all converge upon the Earth at this time it would create quite a stir, but as we discussed before, you are here not only to serve humanity but to serve yourselves and to grow spiritually. So it is somewhat out of respect for the Starseeds who have chosen to be here, out of respect for their process and their path. We do not wish to rob them of the experience that we had ourselves at an earlier time. Let me just say that God works in strange ways. Is this not a strange way to communicate?

"My father is 83 years old. It seems like he is just about ready to leave the planet. What happens to his soul?"

All beings who have left their bodies and who are in the intermediate state awaiting new bodies, who are in the nonphysical state, will attain to a level of experience based upon their particular evolvement. So whatever he has earned in his own lifetimes, he will be taken to that state. He may end up on another planet. He may end up as an ascended being if he is so evolved. He may end up back upon the Earth as one of the New Age children. It is solely dependent on his level of evolvement. But all of the beings who are disembodied and not in physical forms will receive their just rewards.

"Is this what is meant when the Bible talks about all the dead coming back again? Everybody will be going into a new life form?"

Yes, this is somewhat the case. Those souls who are in the astral belt, as I would refer to it, are waiting in their various heavens and hells for another incarnation. This will all be restructured. There will be no more need for a fourth dimension, or an astral plane, when the Earth has attained to the fifth dimension. So there are very many options for these beings. It is difficult to enumerate them. All I will say to you is that those who have earned positive rewards will go to positive places. And those who have not will go to less evolved places where they can work out their karma. None of the beings who are not worthy of ascension will remain upon the Earth. Only those who have attained to a certain level of evolvement will return to Earth.

"Considering the sequence of waves of ascension, at which point would it be expected that the Christ will be here?"

Well, I myself would not begin to speak for him. I would say, in my opinion, it will be at the last stage, in the final evacuation. During that stage and if it occurs. He has free will also. He is a slippery rascal. When you get to know him personally, you may find your conceptions a little bit expanded. He has quite a sense of humor. He is, you might say, the perfect manifestation of mankind. And also One with the Source. So it has been written that he will return. And if this prophecy is to hold true then it would be at the final evacuation, the third wave. You see, that is one reason why it is an element of faith for all of you. You have not seen such miracles occurring physically. It is a test for you. It is a leap of faith. If you take the leap of faith you will be rewarded for doing so.

"What is the difference in criteria between our ascension path and that of Jesus?"

You have it much easier. Those beings who have ascended prior to you, the Ascended Masters who have gone through the Earth school and ascended, have had to develop extreme focus, extreme surrender, have had to be alone many years and many lifetimes of meditation to achieve the ascension. They have had to exhibit levels of faith and trust beyond that which you will have to manifest. They have had to pass through a much more stringent course of training. Because the time was not right for this mass ascension. The door was not quite so open, so they had to force matters a little bit by their own power and will and by calling continually for grace and assistance.

Fortunately for them, those who succeeded were rewarded, and many of them are speaking to you through this channel and others now. So know that the door is more open. The cosmic timing and the cosmic grace is flowing more now. It is more important now to simply be of unconditional love and apply yourselves sincerely. You do not need to master all of the duality of life. You do not need to conquer and have self-mastery over all of your emotions. That is a very intense path. There are more dimensions to the Earth life and ascension of Jesus than we have discussed in this course. That subject is a course in itself.

"You mentioned the New Age babies. Considering we have a limited amount of time now, what are the roles of these babies? What is their life span and what is their consciousness level — the babies that are coming to families now?"

A great deal of the births that are taking place now are very evolved beings who are coming here to lend their support, knowing that they will not be here long. They know that they will be lifted in the ascension waves. But they are making a gesture in manifesting in physical form in this sphere, to assist with the critical mass by adding to the love energy that is here. So many of the beings who are being born now are Starseeded children.

"You say a great deal of them are ... Does that mean that some aren't?"

Yes, there are some who are not. The distinction is that in order to be a Starseed baby you have to have been an ascended being already and then take a third-dimensional body. A regular being need only have a normal course of evolution and need not have progressed beyond the fourth dimension.

"So one may still be involved in the karmic cycle and one may not?"

Yes.

"If we are Starseeds, does that mean that we have ascended before?"

You are getting the picture. Know that if you are Starseeds, you were ascended beings or angelic beings — highly evolved beings —who chose to come here and take on third-dimensional reality: these bodies and all the other bodies you have had. So you are, in your ascension, *re-*ascending. While those who have not been ascended beings — those beings who are of the normal human species — will be ascending (if they do so) for the first time. So you will be reacquainted with who you were and also who you have grown to be. You know the expression "getting yourselves together?" You have higher Selves you need to be getting together with, your higher aspects, you see. So your light bodies are waiting for you. Those beings who have not been ascended do not have light bodies as of yet. Their light bodies will be created upon their lifting, if they are qualified for that.

"If they were qualified, you mean, to love?"

Yes, that is the main criteria. For the final evacuation, it is love and openness to God, willingness to release fear and limitations and negative emotions, mainly fear.

"Is your etheric body different from your light body?"

Yes. They are close but not exactly the same.

"Do our light bodies dwell within us as well as somewhere else?"

They are dwelling multidimensionally. That is why you have to call them down in your meditations and feel them re-merging with you, feel them surrounding you. That is the meditation you experienced last week, the aspect of calling down the light pyramid. This is a way of representing your light body. So there are light vehicles, your merkabah vehicles, waiting for you to reconnect with and to reacquaint yourself with, so you can use them to travel throughout the universe.

So I think it is time for us to focus a little bit. Know that your unanswered questions will be answered. I think we have answered all that you need to know at this time. We cannot satisfy all of your curiosity, for your mental capacity is not capable of understanding fully until you have the experience. This is not an insult to your intelligence. It is only a reflection of your predicament. If you are inspired to do so, call upon your light body to surround you with its presence. We will do a short meditation as it is getting late.

Hello. This is Sananda. It seems that you need some calming down this evening. You are all very lively. I am coming through simply to congratulate you on passing this course. You have all received passing marks from me. Your diplomas will not be handed out until later on — I think you know what I mean. You will have to rise to a little bit higher level to receive them. I come only to share my love for a moment, to tell you how much I love all of you, to encourage you to continue with your ascension work, with your processes. Love one another. Share with one another. Call upon me. Call upon Ashtar, Archangel Michael, any of the Ascended Masters that you are working with or the Angelic Host. This work that you are doing now is extremely important. It is extremely important for yourselves. It is extremely important for this planet. So continue and enjoy yourselves. I have been honored to bring you this field of study and to put together this course for you.

And whatever you can do to share this information in a clear and loving way with those who are open, again I will encourage you to do so. You have faculties and facilities to do this that we have not. You can dial telephones and this sort of thing, write letters. This is all important work. But above all, love yourselves. Nurture yourselves. Honor yourselves. Do not criticize or judge yourselves anymore. You may stop doing that right now. I give you my permission. I would make it an order except you have free will. Enjoy yourselves. I will be connecting with each of you in your meditations. Until next time, goodnight.

⋘ EPILOGUE ⋙

In 1991, approximately one year after the original ascension classes, I was taken by the Masters on an etheric journey. Though aware of my body seated in its usual meditation spot, my conscious awareness was somehow lifted high above it. I rose upward through energy fields of light and into a large lightship. Once there, I found myself seated in a small council chamber. Ashtar and Sananda were seated at my right, and around an oval table were seated many members of the Command and other Masters.

To my great surprise, just as I was beginning to wonder what I was doing in such lofty company, Sananda turned and asked me if I was ready to make my report! To the great astonishment of my normal conscious mind (which was definitely along for the ride), I saw myself stand and I listened with fascination as a rather detailed report of my Earth mission experiences and thoughts poured out of me, to be thoughtfully (and at times tearfully) received by all present. I continued to listen as my "higher Self" channeled my "Earth self," describing the challenges and sorrows experienced by the Starseeds over many lifetimes of service on this planet. My report focused most directly on the apparently limited success that had been achieved in awakening the Starseeds and in uplifting the mass consciousness of humanity.

At the close of the talk, again to my great surprise, Ashtar turned and asked me what course of action I would recommend! My response was not quite so surprising — I recommended that all Starseeds be immediately evacuated!

At that point Ashtar turned to the council and asked the Commanders for their response. The vast majority raised their hands, signifying agreement. As I took my seat, Sananda said that this recommendation would be taken under consideration, and that he would inform me of his decision. I was then returned in the same way I had come, back to my usual meditation place, filled with the intense love and compassion of the Masters.

Two days later, in my morning meditation, Sananda again filled me with his light and presence, saying that he was honoring his promise to report back with the results of his deliberations and with the guidance he himself had received from higher sources. He said that it would not be highest wisdom to immediately evacuate the Starseeds from the surface of the Earth, as this would be detrimental to the Divine Plan. He said that this course of action was indeed possible, but that it would abandon humanity and close the door to those preparing to make the shift into higher consciousness. He asked that we, as Lightworkers, continue for a short time more to pursue the completion of our mission, with compassion and trust. He said that although our desire for ascension or evacuation could not be immediately fulfilled, he would initiate a "new dispensation" of love and support for all humans on the ascension path — a ray of love from his heart to ours, that would make our last days on Earth more joyful and more connected to Source. He said that this dispensation would greatly accelerate our growth and our ability to manifest positive results in our spiritual work.

From my own perspective, I can definitely say that in the past several years there does seem to have been a powerful renewal of interest in spiritual growth in general, and in the ascension specifically. With abundant grace from the Masters, this information alone (in the form of tape recordings and now published as *The Crystal Stair*) has reached many thousands in all corners of the English-speaking world. With the planned publication of future editions in foreign-language translations, these channelings will undoubtedly touch many more. The wide acceptance of this work continues to inspire the hope that, as lightworkers, we may succeed in our Earth mission, far beyond my initial expectations.

Although this third edition has been re-edited, only superficial changes have been made (punctuation, etc.). Even though my present understanding of ascension and evacuation does exceed what came through originally, I feel it would be inappropriate to modify the text in any way. Therefore, I have chosen to maintain the purity of the original channelings by leaving them intact, and will refer the reader to later messages, available on tape and in the *Inner Door* volumes, for further study.

However, I have been guided to comment generally on two points in this epilogue. First, regarding the time factor and predictions concerning when the first and subsequent waves will occur, the Masters have said that the timing of these waves cannot be accurately predicted far in advance, even by them. Ashtar has stated that the energy field of the Earth has been very beneficially altered as a result of the mass activation of Lightworkers that has taken place in recent years. This activation, as well as many other factors, will continue to affect the timing and details of the Plan. We have been asked to continue on our spiritual path with compassion and in service to humanity, as we await our rebirth into the higher dimensions. This completion will take place in God's time, and only with our surrender to the Divine Plan.

A second point, regarding the usage and meaning of the words "ascension" and "evacuation," should also be addressed here. In these original channelings, these words were sometimes used interchangeably (perhaps due to my own inexperience with this terminology, though more probably due to the sense we received at the time that, as the situation looked rather dismal for the success of the Earth volunteers' mission, evacuation seemed by far the most probable way our return to the higher dimensions could be accomplished.) Later messages have refined our understanding somewhat, though this understanding can never be complete until we have also completed our personal experience of the ascension process.

In later channelings, the Masters have communicated that it is most probable that the first two waves will be those of ascension — in the same way it has been experienced by the Masters of the "Great White Brotherhood" (i.e. a period of spiritual practice resulting in the direct transformation of the consciousness and physical body into a higher-dimensional body of light). The lightships, or merkabah, are involved in this process, though only in their fifth-dimensional manifestation. In the evacuation, which will likely involve those people belonging to the third wave, the lightships will lower their frequencies to be compatible with those of the third-dimensional octave, in order to lift human beings physically for protection from the Earth changes resulting from Mother Earth's own final cleansing and ascension. Some evacuated humans will be prepared to attain the ascension at that time, while other beneficial options will be experienced by most in this final "sifting and sorting" of humanity.

Again, the necessity for mass evacuations depends on many factors, and may or may not occur on a global scale. The success of lightworkers has already done much to heal the planet and lessen the severity of some of the Earth changes. It is our continuing responsibility to open to the energies now being transmitted from higher dimensions, in order to allow this planet and ourselves the maximum opportunity for graceful healing and transformation.

— Eric Klein
Santa Cruz, California
January, 1994

READINGS SUGGESTED BY THE AUTHOR

On Eagle's Wings by Ariana Sheran (available through Oughten House Publications)

On Earth Assignment, *Project Earth Evacuation*, and *Ashtar, A Tribute* by Tuella. (may be out of print; check with your local booksellers for availability)

Conclave: Meetings of the Ones, *Vols. I, II, III, IV* by Tuieta. (available from: Portals of Light, P.O. Box 15621, Ft. Wayne, IN 46885)

E. T. 101 The Cosmic Instruction Manual by Diana Luppi. Intergalactic Council Publications (available through Oughten House Publications)

Unveiled Mysteries (4th edition, 1974), and *The Magic Presence (3rd edition, 1939)* by Godfrey Ray King, St. Germain Press (available at New Age bookstores)

The Keys of Enoch by J. J. Hurtak, Academy of Future Science, 1972 (available at New Age bookstores)

The Urantia Book by The Urantia Foundation (available at New Age bookstores)

Serapis Bey: Dossier On the Ascension by Mark Prophet, Summit University Press, 1967

ABOUT THE AUTHOR

Eric Klein

Eric Klein was initiated and began his spiritual path of meditation and service in 1972. He began conscious channeling of the Masters in 1986 and evolved into a period of inner instruction from many ascended teachers. The first public channelings began in 1988 with weekly evening gatherings, which then evolved into more specific classes and workshops under guidance from Sananda.

Eric and his wife, Christine, continue to live in Santa Cruz, California. Christine is an acupuncturist and also a channel. Together, they have traveled extensively across the United States, channeling and teaching workshops in support of the personal and planetary ascension process. They continue to channel the Masters, including Sananda, Ashtar, Archangel Michael, St. Germain, Kuan Yin, Kuthumi, El Morya, Mother Mary, Serapis Bey, Hilarion, and others.

ABOUT THE PUBLISHER AND LOGO

The name "Oughten" was revealed to the publisher fourteen years ago, after three weeks of meditation and contemplation. The combined effect of the letters carries a vibratory signature, signifying humanity's ascension on a planetary level.

The logo represents a new world rising from its former condition. The planet ascends from the darker to the lighter. Our experience of a dark and mysterious universe becomes transmuted by our planet's rising consciousness — glorious and spiritual. The grace of God transmutes the dross of the past into gold, as we leave all behind and ascend into the millennium.

ABOUT THE ARTIST

Reverend Cathie Beach is a clairvoyant healer who lives in Santa Cruz, California. Besides illustrating book covers, she creates personalized, healing drawings. The images may be symbolic or abstract, and the colors resonate with an individual's energy system, giving support and balance. Many people are now using these drawings for gentle healing and personal empowerment. For additional information, please contact Oughten House.

PUBLISHER'S COMMENT

Our mission and purpose is to publish ascension books and complementary material for all peoples and all children worldwide.

We currently serve over twenty authors who have books, manuscripts, and numerous tapes in production. Most of our authors channel Sananda, Ashtar, Archangel Michael, St. Germain, Archangel Ariel, Hilarion, Mother Mary, and Kwan Yin. They need your support to get their channeled messages to all nations. Oughten House Publications welcomes your interest and petitions your overall support and association in this momentous and timely endeavor.

We urge you to share the information with your friends, and to join our network of spiritually-oriented people. Our financial proceeds are recycled into producing new ascension books and expanding our distribution worldwide. If you have the means to contribute or invest in this process, then please contact us.

OUGHTEN HOUSE PUBLICATIONS

Our imprint includes books in a variety of fields and disciplines which emphasize the rising planetary consciousness. Literature which relates to the ascension process is our primary line. We are also cultivating a line of thoughtful and beautifully illustrated children's books, which deal with spirituality, angels, mystical realms, and God, the Creator. Our third line of books deals with societal matters, personal growth, poetry, and publications about extraterrestrials.

The list that follows is only a sample of our current offerings. To obtain a complete catalog, contact us at the address shown at the back of this book.

Ascension Books & Books for the Rising Planetary Consciousness

The Crystal Stair: A Guide to the Ascension, by Eric Klein. — ISBN 1-880666-06-5, $12.95

An Ascension Handbook A practical, in-depth, how-to manual on the ascension process, by Tony Stubbs. — ISBN 1-880666-08-1, $11.95

Bridge Into Light: Your Connection to Spiritual Guidance A how-to book on meditating and channeling, by Pam and Fred Cameron. — ISBN 1-880666-07-3, $11.95

The Inner Door: Channeled Discourses from the Ascended Masters on Self-Mastery and Ascension, by Eric Klein.

Volume One: ISBN 1-880666-03-0, $14.50
Volume Two: ISBN 1-880666-16-2, $14.50

What Is Lightbody? Offers a twelve-level model for the ascension process, leading to the attainment of our Light Body. Recommended in *An Ascension Handbook*, this book gives many invocations, procedures, and potions to assist us on our journey home. Related tapes available. By Tashira Tachi-ren — ISBN 1-880666-25-1, $11.95 (Available first quarter, 1995)

Lady From Atlantis Millenium after millenium, male rulers have repeatedly failed to bring peace to this planet. Now Ascended Lady Master Shar Dae returns to modern America, to pursue her goal of world peace and the ending of duality. By Robert V. Gerard — ISBN 1-880666-21-9, $12.95 (Available late December, 1994)

Intuition by Design Increase your "Intuition Quotient" through the use of this book and its accompanying set of 36 cards. A valuable tool for applying your intuitive intelligence to all aspects of the decision-making process in your life. By Victor R. Beasley, Ph.D. — ISBN 1-880666-22-7, $21.95

Transformational Tools

We offer an ever-expanding selection of transformational tools to assist you in your journey back to mastery. These include books and tapes, with such titles as *The Thymus Chakra Handbook*, *Reality Maintenance 101*, *Angels of the Seven Rays,* and a series of tapes by Tashira Tachi-ren. For information on these and other titles in this category, please call or write for our free catalog.

Children's Books and Tapes

Books and tapes in this category include titles such as *Nature Walk*, *Mary's Lullaby*, *Song of Gothar*, and *Bear Essentials of Love*. Although primarily intended for children and adults who interact with children, they speak to the "child" within us all. For a full list of titles in this category, please call or write for our free catalog.

Discourses & Channeled Material

Hear the voices and experience the energies of our authors, on companion tapes to *Bridge Into Light* and *The Extraterrestrial Vision*. In addition, we offer many tapes on other spiritual and metaphysical subjects, such as *Parallel Realities*, *Birthing the Era of God*, *The Feminine Aspect of God*, and *Preparation for Ascension*. They are listed and described in our free catalog. Write or call for your copy now!

Music Tapes

We carry many titles of spiritually-based music, including both vocal and instrumental types. They collectively comprise a cornucopia of moods and sounds. Create your own "ascension chamber" whenever you play them — at home or wherever your journey takes you. For a listing of available titles, call or write for our free catalog. A reply card is bound into this book for your convenience, or you may reach us at the location listed on page 187.

Other Ascension Tools and Materials

We distribute many other items to assist you on your spiritual path. They include Ascension Cards and titles such as *The Extraterrestrial Vision*, *An Act of Faith*, *The P'taah Tapes*, *Earth's Birth Changes: St. Germain through Azena*, *On Eagle's Wings*, *E.T. 101*, and many more. Ask for our free catalog; we stand ready to serve you!

READER NETWORKING AND MAILING LIST

The ascension process presents itself as a new dimension and reality for many of us on Planet Earth. Oughten House Publications now stands in the midst of many Starseeds and Lightworkers who seek to know more. Thousands of people worldwide are reaching out to find others of like mind and to network with them.

You have the opportunity to stay informed and be on our networking mailing list. Send us the enclosed Information Reply Card or a letter. We will do our best to keep you and your network of friends up to date with ascension-related literature, materials, author tours, workshops, and channelings.

If you have a network database or small mailing list you would like to share, please send it along.

CATALOG REQUESTS AND BOOK ORDERS

Catalogs will gladly be sent upon request. Book orders must be prepaid: check, money order, international coupon, VISA, MasterCard, Discover Card accepted. Include shipping and handling (US postal book rate): $3.50 first book; add 50¢ for each additional book. Send orders to:

OUGHTEN HOUSE PUBLICATIONS
P.O. Box 2008
Livermore • California • 94551-2008 • USA
Phone (510) 447-2332
Fax (510) 447-2376

ATTENTION: BUSINESSES AND SCHOOLS!

OUGHTEN HOUSE books are available at quantity discounts with bulk purchases for educational, business, or sales promotional use. For details, please contact the publisher at the above address.

❅ *Notes* ❅

❊ *Notes* ❊

❋ *Notes* ❋

❀ *Notes* ❀

❋ *Notes* ❋

Foreword

Anne Frank kept a diary from 12 June 1942 to 1 August 1944. Initially, she wrote it strictly for herself. Then, one day in 1944, Gerrit Bolkestein, a member of the Dutch government in exile, announced in a radio broadcast from London that after the war he hoped to collect eyewitness accounts of the suffering of the Dutch people under the German occupation, which could be made available to the public. As an example, he specifically mentioned letters and diaries.

Impressed by this speech, Anne Frank decided that when the war was over she would publish a book based on her diary. She began rewriting and editing her diary, improving on the text, omitting passages she didn't think were interesting enough and adding others from memory. At the same time, she kept up her original diary. In the scholarly work *The Diary of Anne Frank: The Critical Edition* (1989), Anne's first, unedited diary is referred to as version *a*, to distinguish it from her second, edited diary, which is known as version *b*.

The last entry in Anne's diary is dated 1 August 1944. On 4 August 1944, the eight people hiding in the Secret Annexe were arrested. Miep Gies and Bep Voskuijl, the two secretaries working in the building, found Anne's diaries strewn all over the floor. Miep Gies tucked them away in a desk drawer for safekeeping. After the war, when it became clear that Anne was dead, she gave the diaries, unread, to Anne's father, Otto Frank.

After long deliberation, Otto Frank decided to fulfil his daughter's wish and publish her diary. He selected material from versions *a* and *b*, editing them into a shorter version later referred to as version *c*. Readers all over the world know this as *The Diary of a Young Girl*.

In making his choice, Otto Frank had to bear several points in mind. To begin with, the book had to be kept short so that it would fit in with a series put out by the Dutch publisher. In addition, several passages dealing with Anne's sexuality were omitted; at the time of the diary's initial publication, in 1947, it was not customary to write openly about sex, and certainly not in books for young adults. Out of respect for the dead, Otto Frank also omitted a number of unflattering passages about his wife and the other residents of the Secret Annexe. Anne Frank, who was thirteen when she began her diary and fifteen when she was forced to stop, wrote without reserve about her likes and dislikes.

When Otto Frank died in 1980, he willed his daughter's manuscripts to the Netherlands State Institute for War Documentation in Amsterdam. Because the authenticity of the diary had been challenged ever since its publication, the Institute for War Documentation ordered a thorough investigation. Once the diary was proved, beyond a shadow of a doubt, to be genuine, it was published in its entirety, along with the results of an exhaustive study. *The Critical Edition* contains not only versions *a*, *b* and *c*, but also articles on the background of the Frank family, the circumstances surrounding their arrest and deportation, and the examination into Anne's handwriting, the document and the materials used.

The Anne Frank–Fonds (Anne Frank Foundation) in Basle (Switzerland), which as Otto Frank's sole heir had also inherited his daughter's copyrights, then decided to have a new, expanded edition of the diary published for general readers. This new edition in no way affects the integrity of the old one originally edited by Otto Frank, which brought the diary and its message to millions of people. The task of compiling the expanded edition was given to the writer and translator Mirjam Pressler. Otto Frank's original selection has now been supplemented with passages from Anne's *a* and *b* versions. Mirjam Pressler's definitive edition, approved by the Anne Frank–Fonds, contains approximately 30 per cent more material and is intended to give the reader more insight into the world of Anne Frank.

In writing her second version (*b*), Anne invented pseudonyms for the people who would appear in her book. She initially wanted to call herself Anne Aulis, and later Anne Robin. Otto Frank opted to call his family by their own names and to follow Anne's wishes with regard to the others. Over the years, the identity of the people who helped the families in the Secret Annexe has become common knowledge. In this edition, the helpers are now referred to by their real names, as they so justly deserve to be. All other persons are named in accordance with the pseudonyms in *The Critical Edition*. The Institute for War Documentation has arbitrarily assigned initials to those persons wishing to remain anonymous.

The real names of the other people hiding in the Secret Annexe are:

THE VAN PELS FAMILY
(from Osnabrück, Germany):
Auguste van Pels (born 9 September 1900)
Hermann van Pels (born 31 March 1898)
Peter van Pels (born 8 November 1926)
Called by Anne, in her manuscript: Petronella, Hans and Alfred van Daan; and in the book: Petronella, Hermann and Peter van Daan.

FRITZ PFEFFER
(born 30 April 1889, in Giessen, Germany):
Called by Anne, in her manuscript and in the book: Albert Dussel.

The reader may wish to bear in mind that much of this edition is based on the *b* version of Anne's diary, which she wrote when she was about fifteen years old. Occasionally, Anne went back and commented on a passage she had written earlier. These comments are clearly marked in this edition. Naturally, Anne's spelling and linguistic errors have been corrected. Otherwise, the text has basically been left as she wrote it, since any attempts at editing and clarification would be inappropriate in a historical document.

Ik zal hoop ik aan jou alles kunnen
toevertrouwen, zoals ik het nog aan
niemand gekund heb, en ik hoop dat
je voor grote steun aan me zult zijn.
                    Anne Frank. 12 Juni 1942.

I hope I will be able to confide everything
to you, as I have never been able to confide
in anyone, and I hope you will be a great
source of comfort and support.

12 JUNE 1942

I hope I will be able to confide everything to you, as I have never been able to confide in anyone, and I hope you will be a great source of comfort and support.

COMMENT ADDED BY ANNE ON
28 SEPTEMBER 1942:
So far you truly have been a great source of comfort to me, and so has Kitty, whom I now write to regularly. This way of keeping a diary is much nicer, and now I can hardly wait for those moments when I'm able to write in you.

Oh, I'm so glad I brought you along!

I'll begin from the moment I got you, the moment I saw you lying on the table among my other birthday presents. (I went along when you were bought, but that doesn't count.)

On Friday, 12 June, I was awake at six o'clock, which isn't surprising, since it was my birthday. But I'm not allowed to get up at that hour, so I had to control my curiosity until quarter to seven. When I couldn't wait any longer, I went to the dining-room, where Moortje (the cat) welcomed me by rubbing against my legs.

A little after seven I went to Daddy and Mummy and then to the living-room to open my presents, and *you* were the first thing I saw, maybe one of my nicest presents. Then a bouquet of roses, some peonies and a potted plant. From Daddy and Mummy I got a blue blouse, a game, a bottle of grape juice, which to my mind tastes a bit like wine (after all, wine is made from grapes), a puzzle, a jar of cold cream, 2.50 guilders and a gift token for two books. I got another book as well, *Camera Obscura* (but Margot already has it, so I exchanged mine for something else), a plate of homemade biscuits (which I made myself, of course, since I've become quite an expert at making biscuits), lots of sweets and a strawberry tart from Mother. And a letter from Grammy, right on time, but of course that was just a coincidence.

Then Hanneli came to pick me up, and we went to school. During break I handed out biscuits to my teachers and my class, and then it was time to get back to work. I didn't arrive home until five, since I went to gym with the rest of the class. (I'm not allowed to take part because my shoulders and hips tend to get dislocated.) As it was my birthday, I could decide which game my classmates would play, and I chose volleyball. Afterwards they all danced around me in a circle and sang 'Happy Birthday'. When I got home, Sanne Ledermann was already there. Ilse Wagner, Hanneli Goslar and Jacqueline van Maarsen came home with me after gym, since we're in the same class. Hanneli and Sanne used to be my two best friends. People who saw us together used to say, 'There goes Anne, Hanne and Sanne.' I only met Jacqueline van Maarsen when I started at the Jewish Lyceum, and now she's my best friend. Ilse is Hanneli's best friend, and Sanne goes to another school and has friends there.

They gave me a beautiful book, *Dutch Sagas and Legends*, but they gave me Volume II by mistake, so I exchanged two other books for Volume I. Aunt Helene brought me a puzzle, Aunt Stephanie a darling brooch and Aunt Leny a terrific book: *Daisy Goes to the Mountains*.

This morning I lay in the bath thinking how wonderful it would be if I had a dog like Rin Tin Tin. I'd call him Rin Tin Tin too, and I'd take him to school with me, where he could stay in the caretaker's room or by the bicycle racks when the weather was good.

I had my birthday party on Sunday afternoon. The Rin Tin Tin film was a big hit with my classmates. I got two brooches, a bookmark and two books.

I'll start by saying a few things about my school and my class, beginning with the other children.

Betty Bloemendaal looks rather poor, and I think she probably is. She lives on an obscure street in West Amsterdam, and none of us knows where it is. She does very well at school, but that's because she works so hard, not because she's clever. She's pretty quiet.

Jacqueline van Maarsen is supposedly my best friend, but I've never had a real friend. At first I thought Jacque would be one, but I was badly mistaken.

D.Q.* is a very nervous girl who's always forgetting things, so the teachers keep giving her extra homework as a punishment. She's very kind, especially to G.Z.

E.S. talks so much it isn't funny. She's always touching your hair or fiddling with your buttons when she asks you something. They say she can't stand me, but I don't care, because I don't like her much either.

Henny Mets is a nice girl with a cheerful disposition, except that she talks in a loud voice and is really childish when we're playing outside. Unfortunately, Henny has

* Initials have been assigned at random to those persons who prefer to remain anonymous.

a girlfriend named Beppy who's a bad influence on her because she's dirty and vulgar.

J.R. – I could write a whole book about her. J. is a detestable, sneaky, stuck-up, two-faced gossip who thinks she's so grown-up. She's really got Jacque under her spell, and that's a shame. J. is easily offended, bursts into tears at the slightest thing and, to top it all, is a terrible show-off. Miss J. always has to be right. She's very rich, and has a wardrobe full of the most adorable dresses that are much too old for her. She thinks she's gorgeous, but she's not. J. and I can't stand each other.

Ilse Wagner is a nice girl with a cheerful disposition, but she's extremely finicky and can spend hours moaning and groaning about something. Ilse likes me a lot. She's very clever, but lazy.

Hanneli Goslar, or Lies as she's called at school, is a bit on the strange side. She's usually shy – outspoken at home, but reserved with other people. She blabs whatever you tell her to her mother. But she says what she thinks, and lately I've come to appreciate her a great deal.

Nannie van Praag-Sigaar is small, funny and sensible. I think she's nice. She's pretty clever. There isn't much else you can say about Nannie.

Eefje de Jong is, in my opinion, terrific. Though she's only twelve, she's quite the lady. She treats me like a baby. She's also very helpful, and I like her.

G.Z. is the prettiest girl in our class. She has a nice face, but is a bit stupid. I think they're going to hold her back a year, but of course I haven't told her that.

And sitting next to G.Z. is the last of us twelve girls, me.

There's a lot to be said about the boys, or maybe not so much after all.

Maurice Coster is one of my many admirers, but pretty much of a pest.

Sallie Springer has a filthy mind, and rumour has it that he's gone all the way. Still, I think he's terrific, because he's very funny.

Emiel Bonewit is G.Z.'s admirer, but she doesn't care. He's pretty boring.

Rob Cohen used to be in love with me too, but I can't stand him any more. He's an obnoxious, two-faced, lying, snivelling little twit with an awfully high opinion of himself.

Max van de Velde is a farm boy from Medemblik, but a decent sort, as Margot would say.

Herman Koopman also has a filthy mind, just like Jopie de Beer, who's a terrible flirt and girl-chaser.

Leo Blom is Jopie de Beer's best friend, but has been spoiled by Jopie's dirty mind.

Albert de Mesquita came from the Montessori School and jumped a year. He's really clever.

Leo Slager came from the same school, but isn't as clever.

Ru Stoppelmon is a short, goofy boy from Almelo who transferred to this school in the middle of the year.

C.N. does whatever he's not supposed to.

Jacques Kocernoot sits behind us, next to C., and we (G. and I) laugh ourselves stupid.

Harry Schaap is the most decent boy in our class. He's nice.

Werner Joseph is nice too, but all the changes taking place lately have made him too quiet, so he seems boring.

Sam Salomon is one of those tough guys from the rough part of town. A real brat. (Admirer!)

Appie Riem is pretty Orthodox, but a brat too.

SATURDAY, 20 JUNE 1942

*W*riting in a diary is a really strange experience for someone like me. Not only because I've never written anything before, but also because it seems to me that later on neither I nor anyone else will be interested in the musings of a thirteen-year-old schoolgirl. Oh well, it doesn't matter. I feel like writing, and I have an even greater need to get all kinds of things off my chest.

'Paper has more patience than people.' I thought of this saying on one of those days when I was feeling a little depressed and was sitting at home with my chin in my hands, bored and listless, wondering whether to stay in or go out. I finally stayed where I was, brooding. Yes, paper *does* have more patience, and since I'm not planning to let anyone else read this stiff-backed notebook grandly referred to as a 'diary', unless I should ever find a real friend, it probably won't make a bit of difference.

Now I'm back to the point that prompted me to keep a diary in the first place: I don't have a friend.

Let me put it more clearly, since no one will believe that a thirteen-year-old girl is completely alone in the world. And I'm not. I have loving parents and a sixteen-year-old sister, and there are about thirty people I can call friends. I have a throng of admirers who can't keep their adoring eyes off me and who sometimes have to resort to using a broken pocket mirror to try and catch a glimpse of me in the classroom. I have a family, loving aunts and a good home. No, on the surface I seem to have everything, except my one true friend. All I think about when I'm with friends is having a good time. I can't bring myself to talk about anything but ordinary everyday things. We don't seem to be able to get any closer, and that's the problem. Maybe it's my fault that we don't confide in each other. In any case, that's just how things are, and unfortunately they're not liable to change. This is why I've started the diary.

To enhance the image of this long-awaited friend in my imagination, I don't want to jot down the facts in this diary the way most people would do, but I want the diary to be my friend, and I'm going to call this friend *Kitty*.

Since no one would understand a word of my stories to Kitty if I were to plunge right in, I'd better provide a brief sketch of my life, much as I dislike doing so.

My father, the most adorable father I've ever seen, didn't marry my mother until he was thirty-six and she was twenty-five. My sister Margot was born in Frankfurt am Main in Germany in 1926. I was born on 12 June 1929. I lived in Frankfurt until I was four. Because we're Jewish, my father emigrated to Holland in 1933, when he became the Managing Director of the Dutch Opekta Company, which manufactures products used in making jam. My mother, Edith Holländer Frank, went with him to Holland in September, while Margot and I were sent to Aachen to stay with our grandmother. Margot went to Holland in December, and I followed in February, when I was plonked down on the table as a birthday present for Margot.

I started right away at the Montessori nursery school. I stayed there until I was six, at which time I started in the first form. In the sixth form my teacher was Mrs Kuperus, the headmistress. At the end of the year we were both in tears as we said a heartbreaking farewell, because I'd been accepted at the Jewish Lyceum, where Margot also went to school.

Our lives were not without anxiety, since our relatives in Germany were suffering under Hitler's anti-Jewish laws. After the pogroms in 1938 my two uncles (my mother's brothers) fled Germany, finding safe refuge in North America. My elderly grandmother came to live with us. She was seventy-three years old at the time.

After May 1940 the good times were few and far between: first there was the war, then the capitulation and then the arrival of the Germans, which is when the trouble started for the Jews. Our freedom was severely restricted by a series of anti-Jewish decrees: Jews were required to wear a yellow star; Jews were required to turn in their bicycles; Jews were forbidden to use trams; Jews were forbidden to ride in cars, even their own; Jews were required to do their shopping between 3.00 and 5.00 p.m.; Jews were required to frequent only Jewish-owned barbershops and beauty salons; Jews were forbidden to be out on the streets between 8.00 p.m. and 6.00 a.m.; Jews were forbidden to go to theatres, cinemas or any other forms of entertainment; Jews were forbidden to use swimming pools, tennis courts, hockey fields or any other athletic fields; Jews were forbidden to go rowing; Jews were forbidden to take part in any athletic activity in public; Jews were forbidden to sit in their gardens or those of their friends after 8.00 p.m.; Jews were forbidden to visit Christians in their homes; Jews were required to attend Jewish schools, etc. You couldn't do this and you couldn't do that, but life went on. Jacque always said to me, 'I don't dare do anything any more, 'cause I'm afraid it's not allowed.'

In the summer of 1941 Grandma fell ill and had to have an operation, so my birthday passed with little celebration. In the summer of 1940 we didn't do much for my birthday either, since the fighting had just ended in Holland. Grandma died in January 1942. No one knows how often *I* think of her and still love her. This birthday celebration in 1942 was intended to make up for the others, and Grandma's candle was lit along with the rest.

The four of us are still doing well, and that brings me to the present date of 20 June 1942, and the solemn dedication of my diary.

SATURDAY, 20 JUNE 1942

Dearest Kitty!

*L*et me get started right away; it's nice and quiet now. Father and Mother are out and Margot has gone to play ping-pong with some other young people at her friend Trees's. I've been playing a lot of ping-pong myself lately. So much that five of us girls have formed a club. It's called 'The Little Dipper Minus Two'. A really silly name, but it's based on a mistake. We wanted to give our club a special name; and because there were five of us, we came up with the idea of the Little Dipper. We thought it consisted of five stars, but we turned out to be wrong. It has seven, like the Big Dipper, which explains the 'Minus Two'. Ilse Wagner has a ping-pong set, and the Wagners let us play in their big dining-room whenever we want. Since we five ping-pong players like ice-cream, especially in the summer, and since you get hot playing ping-pong, our games usually end with a visit to the nearest ice-cream parlour that allows Jews: either Oasis or Delphi. We've long since stopped hunting around for our purses or money – most of the time it's so busy in Oasis that we manage to find a few generous young men of our acquaintance or an admirer to offer us more ice-cream than we could eat in a week.

You're probably a little surprised to hear me talking about admirers at such a tender age. Unfortunately, or not, as the case may be, this vice seems to be rampant at our school. As soon as a boy asks if he can cycle home with me and we start talking, nine times out of ten I can be sure he'll become enamoured on the spot and won't let me out of his sight for a second. His ardour eventually cools, especially since I ignore his passionate glances and pedal blithely on my way. If it gets so bad that they start rambling on about 'asking Father's permission', I swerve slightly on my bike, my satchel falls, and the young man feels obliged to get off his bike and hand it to me, by which time I've switched the conversation to another topic. These are the most innocent types. Of course, there are those who blow you kisses or try to take hold of your arm, but they're definitely knocking on the wrong door. I get off my bike and either refuse to make further use of their company or act as if I'm insulted and tell them in no uncertain terms to go on home without me.

There you are. We've now laid the basis for our friendship. Until tomorrow.

Yours, Anne

Dearest Kitty,

Our entire class is quaking in its boots. The reason, of course, is the forthcoming meeting in which the teachers decide who'll move up to the next form and who'll be kept back. Half the class is making bets. G.Z. and I laugh ourselves silly at the two boys behind us, C.N. and Jacques Kocernoot, who have staked their entire holiday savings on their bet. From morning to night, it's 'You're going to pass', 'No, I'm not', 'Yes, you are', 'No, I'm not'. Even G.'s pleading glances and my angry outbursts can't calm them down. If you ask me, there are so many dummies that about a quarter of the class should be kept back, but teachers are the most unpredictable creatures on earth. Maybe this time they'll be unpredictable in the right direction for a change.

I'm not so worried about my girlfriends and myself. We'll make it. The only subject I'm not sure about is maths. Anyway, all we can do is wait. Until then, we keep telling each other not to lose heart.

I get along pretty well with all my teachers. There are nine of them, seven men and two women. Mr Keesing, the old fogey who teaches maths, was annoyed with me for ages because I talked so much. After several warnings, he assigned me extra homework. An essay on the subject 'A Chatterbox'. A chatterbox, what can you write about that? I'd worry about that later, I decided. I jotted down the title in my notebook, tucked it in my bag and tried to keep quiet.

That evening, after I'd finished the rest of my homework, the note about the essay caught my eye. I began thinking about the subject while chewing the tip of my fountain pen. Anyone could ramble on and leave big spaces between the words, but the trick was to come up with convincing arguments to prove the necessity of talking. I thought and thought, and suddenly I had an idea. I wrote the three pages Mr Keesing had assigned me and was satisfied. I argued that talking is a female trait and that I would do my best to keep it under control, but that I would never be able to cure myself of the habit, since my mother talked as much as I did, if not more, and that there's not much you can do about inherited traits.

Mr Keesing had a good laugh at my arguments, but when I proceeded to talk my way through the next lesson, he assigned me a second essay. This time it was supposed to be on 'An Incorrigible Chatterbox'. I handed it in, and Mr Keesing had nothing to complain about for two whole lessons. However, during the third lesson he'd finally had enough. 'Anne Frank, as punishment for talking in class, write an essay entitled "'Quack, Quack, Quack,' Said Mistress Chatterback".'

The class roared. I had to laugh too, though I'd nearly exhausted my ingenuity on the topic of chatterboxes. It was time to come up with something else, something original. My friend Sanne, who's good at poetry, offered to help me write the essay from beginning to end in verse. I jumped for joy. Keesing was trying to play a joke on me with this ridiculous subject, but I'd make sure the joke was on him.

I finished my poem, and it was beautiful! It was about a mother duck and a father swan with three baby ducklings who were bitten to death by the father because they quacked too much. Luckily, Keesing took the joke the right way. He read the poem to the class, adding his own comments, and to several other classes as well. Since then I've been allowed to talk and haven't been assigned any extra homework. On the contrary, Keesing's always making jokes these days.

Yours, Anne

WEDNESDAY, 24 JUNE 1942

Dearest Kitty,

It's sweltering. Everyone is huffing and puffing, and in this heat I have to walk everywhere. Only now do I realize how pleasant a tram is, but we Jews are no longer allowed to make use of this luxury; our own two feet are good enough for us. Yesterday at lunchtime I had an appointment with the dentist on Jan Luykenstraat. It's a long way from our school on Stadstimmertuinen. That afternoon I nearly fell asleep at my desk. Fortunately, people automatically offer you something to drink. The dental nurse is really kind.

The only mode of transport left to us is the ferry. The ferryman at Josef Israëlkade took us across when we asked him to. It's not the fault of the Dutch that we Jews are having such a bad time.

I wish I didn't have to go to school. My bike was stolen during the Easter holidays, and Father gave Mother's bike to some Christian friends for safekeeping. Thank goodness the summer holidays are almost here; one more week and our torment will be over.

Something unexpected happened yesterday morning. As I was passing the bicycle racks, I heard my name being called. I turned around and there was the nice boy I'd met the evening before at my friend Wilma's. He's Wilma's second cousin. I used to think Wilma was nice, which she is, but all she ever talks about is boys, and that gets to be a bore. He came towards me, somewhat shyly, and introduced himself as Hello Silberberg. I was a little surprised and wasn't sure what he wanted, but it didn't take me long to find out. He asked if I would allow him to accompany me to school. 'As long as you're headed that way, I'll go with you,' I said. And so we walked together. Hello is sixteen and good at telling all kinds of funny stories.

He was waiting for me again this morning, and I expect he will be from now on.

Anne

Dearest Kitty,

*U*ntil today I honestly couldn't find the time to write to you. I was with friends all day Thursday, we had company on Friday, and that's how it went until today.

Hello and I have got to know each other very well this past week, and he's told me a lot about his life. He comes from Gelsenkirchen and is living with his grandparents. His parents are in Belgium, but there's no way he can get there. Hello used to have a girlfriend named Ursula. I know her too. She's perfectly sweet and perfectly boring. Ever since he met me, Hello has realized that he's been falling asleep at Ursul's side. So I'm kind of a pep tonic. You never know what you're good for!

Jacque spent Saturday night here. Sunday afternoon she was at Hanneli's, and I was bored stiff.

Hello was supposed to come over that evening, but he rang about six. I answered the phone, and he said, 'This is Helmuth Silberberg. May I please speak to Anne?'

'Oh, Hello. This is Anne.'

'Oh, hello, Anne. How are you?'

'Very well, thanks.'

'I just wanted to say I'm sorry but I can't come tonight, though I would like to have a word with you. Is it all right if I come by and pick you up in about ten minutes?'

'Yes, that's fine. Bye-bye!'

'Okay, I'll be right over. Bye-bye!'

I hung up, quickly changed my clothes and did my hair. I was so nervous I leaned out of the window to watch for him. He finally showed up. Miracle of miracles, I didn't rush down the stairs, but waited quietly until he rang the bell. I went down to open the door, and he got right to the point.

'Anne, my grandmother thinks you're too young for me to be seeing you on a regular basis. She says I should be going to the Lowenbachs', but you probably know that I'm not going out with Ursul any more.'

'No, I didn't know. What happened? Did you two have an argument?'

'No, nothing like that. I told Ursul that we weren't suited to each other and so it was better for us not to go out together any more, but that she was welcome at my house and I hoped I would be welcome at hers. Actually, I thought Ursul was hanging around with another boy, and I treated her as if she were. But that wasn't true. And then my uncle said I should apologize to her, but of course I didn't feel like it, and that's why I broke up with her. But that was just one of the reasons.

'Now my grandmother wants me to see Ursul and not you, but I don't agree and I'm not going to. Sometimes old people have really old-fashioned ideas, but that doesn't mean I have to go along with them. I need my grandparents, but in a certain sense they need me too. From now on I'll be free on Wednesday evenings. You see, my grandparents made me sign up for a wood-carving class, but actually I go to a club organized by the Zionists. My grandparents don't want me to go, because they're anti-Zionists. I'm not a fanatical Zionist, but it interests me. Anyway, it's been such a mess lately that I'm planning to leave. So next Wednesday will be my last meeting. That means I can see you Wednesday evening, Saturday afternoon, Saturday evening, Sunday afternoon and maybe even more.'

'But if your grandparents don't want you to, you shouldn't go behind their backs.'

'All's fair in love and war.'

Just then we passed Blankevoort's Bookshop and there was Peter Schiff with two other boys; it was the first time he'd said hello to me in ages, and it really made me feel good.

Monday evening Hello came over to meet Father and Mother. I had bought a cake and some sweets, and we had tea and biscuits, the works, but neither Hello nor I felt like sitting stiffly on our chairs. So we went out for a walk, and he didn't deliver me to my door until ten past eight. Father was furious. He said it was very wrong of me not to get home on time. I had to promise to be home by ten to eight in future. I've been asked to Hello's on Saturday.

Wilma told me that one night when Hello was at her house, she asked him, 'Who do you like best, Ursul or Anne?'

He said, 'It's none of your business.'

But as he was leaving (they hadn't talked to each other the rest of the evening), he said, 'Well, I like Anne better, but don't tell anyone. Bye!' And whoosh . . . he was out of the door.

In everything he says or does, I can see that Hello is in love with me, and it's kind of nice for a change. Margot would say that Hello is a decent sort. I think so too, but he's more than that. Mother is also full of praise: 'A good-looking boy. Nice and polite.' I'm glad he's so popular with everyone. Except with my girlfriends. He thinks they're very childish, and he's right about that. Jacque still teases me about him, but I'm not in love with him. Not really. It's all right for me to have boys as friends. Nobody minds.

Mother is always asking me who I'm going to marry when I grow up, but I bet she'll never guess it's Peter, because I talked her out of that idea myself, without batting an eyelash. I love Peter as I've never loved anyone, and I tell myself he's only going around with all those other girls to hide his feelings for me. Maybe he thinks Hello and I are in love with each other, which we're not. He's just a friend, or as Mother puts it, a suitor.

Yours, Anne

SUNDAY, 5 JULY 1942

Dear Kitty,

The examination results were announced in the Jewish Theatre on Friday. My report wasn't too bad. I got one D, a C− in algebra and all the rest Bs, except for two B+s and two B−s. My parents are pleased, but they're not like other parents when it comes to grades. They never worry about reports, good or bad. As long as I'm healthy and happy and not too cheeky, they're satisfied. If these three things are all right, everything else will take care of itself.

I'm just the opposite. I don't want to be a bad pupil. I was accepted at the Jewish Lyceum on a conditional basis. I was supposed to stay at the Montessori School, but when Jewish children were required to go to Jewish schools, Mr Elte finally agreed, after a great deal of persuasion, to accept Lies Goslar and me. Lies also passed this year, though she has to repeat her geometry exam.

Poor Lies. It isn't easy for her to study at home; her baby sister, a spoiled little two-year-old, plays in her room all day. If Gabi doesn't get her way, she starts screaming, and if Lies doesn't look after her, Mrs Goslar starts screaming. So Lies has a hard time doing her homework, and as long as that's the case, the extra tuition she's been getting won't help much. The Goslar household is really a sight. Mrs Goslar's parents live next door, but eat with the family. Then there's the hired help, the baby, the always absent-minded and absent Mr Goslar and the always nervous and irritable Mrs Goslar, who's expecting another baby. Lies, who's all thumbs, gets lost in the mayhem.

My sister Margot has also got her report. Brilliant, as usual. If we had such a thing as 'cum laude', she would have passed with honours, she's so clever.

Father has been home a lot lately. There's nothing for

him to do at the office; it must be awful to feel you're not needed. Mr Kleiman has taken over Opekta, and Mr Kugler, Gies & Co., the company dealing in spices and spice substitutes that was set up in 1941.

A few days ago, as we were taking a stroll around our neighbourhood square, Father began to talk about going into hiding. He said it would be very hard for us to live cut off from the rest of the world. I asked him why he was bringing this up now.

'Well, Anne,' he replied, 'you know that for more than a year we've been sending our clothes, food and furniture to other people. We don't want our belongings to be seized by the Germans. Nor do we want to fall into their clutches ourselves. So we'll leave of our own accord and not wait to be hauled away.'

'But when, Father?' He sounded so serious that I felt scared.

'Don't you worry. We'll take care of everything. Just enjoy your carefree life while you can.'

That was it. Oh, may these sombre words not come true for as long as possible.

The doorbell's ringing, Hello's here, time to stop.

Yours, Anne

Dearest Kitty,

*I*t seems like years since Sunday morning. So much has happened it's as if the whole world had suddenly turned upside down. But as you can see, Kitty, I'm still alive, and that's the main thing, Father says. I'm alive all right, but don't ask where or how. You probably don't understand a word I'm saying today, so I'll begin by telling you what happened Sunday afternoon.

At three o'clock (Hello had left but was supposed to come back later), the doorbell rang. I didn't hear it, since I was out on the balcony, lazily reading in the sun. A little while later Margot appeared in the kitchen doorway looking very agitated. 'Father has received a call-up notice from the SS,' she whispered. 'Mother has gone to see Mr van Daan.' (Mr van Daan is Father's business partner and a good friend.)

I was stunned. A call-up: everyone knows what that means. Visions of concentration camps and lonely cells raced through my head. How could we let Father go to such a fate? 'Of course he's not going,' declared Margot as we waited for Mother in the living-room. 'Mother's gone to Mr van Daan to ask whether we can move to our hiding place tomorrow. The van Daans are going with us. There will be seven of us altogether.' Silence. We couldn't speak. The thought of Father off visiting someone in the Jewish Hospital and completely unaware of what was happening, the long wait for Mother, the heat, the suspense – all this reduced us to silence.

Suddenly the doorbell rang again. 'That's Hello,' I said.

'Don't open the door!' exclaimed Margot to stop me. But it wasn't necessary, since we heard Mother and Mr van Daan downstairs talking to Hello, and then the two of them came inside and shut the door behind them. Every time the bell rang, either Margot or I had to tiptoe downstairs to see if it was Father, and we didn't let anyone else in. Margot and I were sent from the room, as Mr van Daan wanted to talk to Mother alone.

When she and I were sitting in our bedroom, Margot told me that the call-up was not for Father, but for her. At this second shock, I began to cry. Margot is sixteen – apparently they want to send girls her age away on their own. But thank goodness she won't be going; Mother had said so herself, which must be what Father had meant when he talked to me about our going into hiding. Hiding . . . where would we hide? In the city? In the country? In a house? In a shack? When, where, how . . . ? These were questions I wasn't allowed to ask, but they still kept running through my mind.

Margot and I started packing our most important belongings into a satchel. The first thing I stuck in was this diary, and then curlers, handkerchiefs, schoolbooks, a comb and some old letters. Preoccupied by the thought of going into hiding, I stuck the craziest things in the satchel, but I'm not sorry. Memories mean more to me than dresses.

Father finally came home around five o'clock, and we rang Mr Kleiman to ask if he could come by that evening.

Mr van Daan left and went to get Miep. Miep arrived and promised to return later that night, taking with her a bag full of shoes, dresses, jackets, underwear and stockings. After that it was quiet in our flat; none of us felt like eating. It was still hot, and everything was very strange.

We had rented out our big upstairs room to a Mr Goldschmidt, a divorced man in his thirties, who apparently had nothing to do that evening, since despite all our polite hints he hung around until ten o'clock.

Miep and Jan Gies came at eleven. Miep, who's worked for Father's company since 1933, has become a close friend, and so has her husband Jan. Once again, shoes, stockings, books and underwear disappeared into Miep's bag and Jan's deep pockets. At eleven-thirty they too disappeared.

I was exhausted, and even though I knew it'd be my last night in my own bed, I fell asleep right away and didn't wake up until Mother called me at five-thirty the next morning. Fortunately, it wasn't as hot as Sunday; a warm rain fell throughout the day. The four of us were wrapped in so many layers of clothes it looked as if we were going off to spend the night in a refrigerator, and all that just so we could take more clothes with us. No Jew in our situation would dare leave the house with a suitcase full of clothes. I was wearing two vests, three pairs of pants, a dress, and over that a skirt, a jacket, a raincoat, two pairs of stockings, heavy shoes, a cap, a scarf and lots more. I was suffocating even before we left the house, but no one bothered to ask me how I felt.

Margot stuffed her satchel with schoolbooks, went to get her bicycle and, with Miep leading the way, rode off into the great unknown. At any rate, that's how I thought of it, since I still didn't know where our hiding place was.

At seven-thirty we too closed the door behind us; Moortje, my cat, was the only living creature I said good-bye to. According to a note we left for Mr Goldschmidt, she was to be taken to the neighbours, who would give her a good home.

The stripped beds, the breakfast things on the table, the pound of meat for the cat in the kitchen – all of these created the impression that we'd left in a hurry. But we weren't interested in impressions. We just wanted to get out of there, to get away and reach our destination in safety. Nothing else mattered.

More tomorrow.

Yours, Anne

Dearest Kitty,

So there we were, Father, Mother and I, walking in the pouring rain, each of us with a satchel and a shopping bag filled to the brim with the most varied assortment of items. The people on their way to work at that early hour gave us sympathetic looks; you could tell by their faces that they were sorry they couldn't offer us some kind of transport; the conspicuous yellow star spoke for itself.

Only when we were walking down the street did Father and Mother reveal, little by little, what the plan was. For months we'd been moving as much of our furniture and apparel out of the flat as we could. It was agreed that we'd go into hiding on 16 July. Because of Margot's call-up notice, the plan had to be moved forward ten days, which meant we'd have to make do with less orderly rooms.

The hiding place was located in Father's office building. That's a little hard for outsiders to understand, so I'll explain. Father didn't have a lot of people working in his office, just Mr Kugler, Mr Kleiman, Miep and a twenty-three-year-old typist named Bep Voskuijl, all of whom were informed of our coming. Mr Voskuijl, Bep's father, works in the warehouse, along with two assistants, none of whom were told anything.

Here's a description of the building. The large warehouse on the ground floor is used as a workroom and storeroom and is divided into several different sections, such as the stockroom and the milling room, where cinnamon, cloves and a pepper substitute are ground.

Next to the warehouse doors is another outside door, a separate entrance to the office. Just inside the office door is a second door, and beyond that a stairway. At the top of the stairs is another door, with a frosted window on which the word 'Office' is written in black letters. This is the big front office – very large, very light and very full. Bep, Miep and Mr Kleiman work there during the day. After passing through an alcove containing a safe, a wardrobe and a big stationery cupboard, you come to the small, dark, stuffy back office. This used to be shared by Mr Kugler and Mr van Daan, but now Mr Kugler is its only occupant. Mr Kugler's office can also be reached from the passage, but only through a glass door that can be opened from the inside but not easily from the outside. If you leave Mr Kugler's office and proceed through the long, narrow passage past the coal store and go up four steps, you find yourself in the private office, the show-piece of the entire building. Elegant mahogany furniture, a linoleum floor covered with rugs, a radio, a fancy lamp, everything first class. Next door is a spacious kitchen with a water-heater and two gas rings, and beside that a lavatory. That's the first floor.

A wooden staircase leads from the downstairs passage to the second floor. At the top of the stairs is a landing, with doors on either side. The door on the left takes you up to the spice storage area, attic and loft in the front part of the house. A typically Dutch, very steep, ankle-twisting flight of stairs also runs from the front part of the house to another door opening on to the street.

The door to the right of the landing leads to the 'Secret Annexe' at the back of the house. No one would ever suspect there were so many rooms behind that plain grey door. There's just one small step in front of the door,

1st Floor   *2nd Floor*   *3rd Floor*

and then you're inside. Straight ahead of you is a steep flight of stairs. To the left is a narrow hallway opening on to a room that serves as the Frank family's living-room and bedroom. Next door is a smaller room, the bedroom and study of the two young ladies of the family. To the right of the stairs is a 'bathroom', a windowless room with just a sink. The door in the corner leads to the lavatory and another one to Margot's and my room. If you go up the stairs and open the door at the top, you're surprised to see such a large, light and spacious room in an old canalside house like this. It contains a gas cooker (thanks to the fact that it used to be Mr Kugler's laboratory) and a sink. This will be the kitchen and bedroom of Mr and Mrs van Daan, as well as the general living-room, dining-room and study for us all. A tiny side room is to be Peter van Daan's bedroom. Then, just as in the front part of the building, there's an attic and a loft. So there you are. Now I've introduced you to the whole of our lovely Annexe!

Yours, Anne

FRIDAY, 10 JULY 1942

Dearest Kitty,

I've probably bored you with my long description of our house, but I still think you should know where

I've ended up; how I ended up here is something you'll work out from my next letters.

But first, let me continue my story, because, as you know, I hadn't finished. After we arrived at 263 Prinsengracht, Miep quickly led us through the long passage and up the wooden staircase to the next floor and into the Annexe. She shut the door behind us, leaving us alone. Margot had arrived much earlier on her bike and was waiting for us.

Our living-room and all the other rooms were so full of stuff that I can't find the words to describe it. All the cardboard boxes that had been sent to the office in the last few months were piled on the floors and beds. The small room was filled from floor to ceiling with linen. If we wanted to sleep in properly made beds that night, we had to get going and tidy up the mess. Mother and Margot were unable to move a muscle. They lay down on their bare mattresses, tired, miserable and I don't know what else. But Father and I, the two cleaner-uppers in the family, started in right away.

All day long we unpacked boxes, filled cupboards, hammered nails and tidied up the mess, until we fell exhausted into our clean beds at night. We hadn't eaten a hot meal all day, but we didn't care; Mother and Margot were too tired and keyed up to eat, and Father and I were too busy.

Tuesday morning we started where we left off the night before. Bep and Miep went shopping with our ration coupons, Father worked on our black-out screens, we scrubbed the kitchen floor, and were once again busy from morning to night. Until Wednesday, I didn't have a chance to think about the enormous change in my life. Then for the first time since our arrival in the Secret Annexe, I found a moment to tell you all about it and to realize what had happened to me and what was yet to happen.

Yours, Anne

Dearest Kitty,

*F*ather, Mother and Margot still can't get used to the chiming of the Westertoren clock, which tells us the time every quarter of an hour. Not me, I liked it from the start; it sounds so reassuring, especially at night. You no doubt want to hear what I think of being in hiding. Well, all I can say is that I don't really know yet. I don't think I'll ever feel at home in this house, but that doesn't mean I hate it. It's more like being on holiday in some strange pension. Kind of an odd way to look at life in hiding, but that's how things are. The Annexe is an ideal place to hide in. It may be damp and lopsided, but there's probably not a more comfortable hiding place in all of Amsterdam. No, in all of Holland.

Up till now our bedroom, with its blank walls, was

very bare. Thanks to Father – who brought my entire postcard and film-star collection here beforehand – and to a brush and a pot of glue, I was able to plaster the walls with pictures. It looks much more cheerful. When the van Daans arrive, we'll be able to build cupboards and other odds and ends out of the wood piled in the attic.

Margot and Mother have recovered somewhat. Yesterday Mother felt well enough to cook split-pea soup for the first time, but then she was downstairs talking and forgot all about it. The beans were scorched black, and no amount of scraping could get them out of the pan.

Last night the four of us went down to the private office and listened to England on the wireless. I was so scared someone might hear it that I literally begged Father to take me back upstairs. Mother understood my anxiety and went with me. Whatever we do, we're very afraid the neighbours might hear or see us. We started off immediately the first day sewing curtains. Actually, you can hardly call them that, since they're nothing but scraps of fabric, varying greatly in shape, quality and pattern, which Father and I stitched crookedly together with unskilled fingers. These works of art were tacked to the windows, where they'll stay until we come out of hiding.

The building on our right is a branch of the Keg Company, a firm from Zaandam, and on the left is a furniture workshop. Though the people who work there are not on the premises after hours, any sound we make might travel through the walls. We've forbidden Margot to cough at night, even though she has a bad cold, and are giving her large doses of codeine.

I'm looking forward to the arrival of the van Daans, which is set for Tuesday. It will be much more fun and also not as quiet. You see, it's the silence that makes me so nervous during the evenings and nights, and I'd give anything to have one of our helpers sleep here.

It's really not that bad here, since we can do our own cooking and can listen to the wireless in Daddy's office. Mr Kleiman and Miep, and Bep Voskuijl too, have helped us so much. We've already preserved loads of rhubarb, strawberries and cherries, so for the time being I doubt we'll be bored. We also have a supply of reading material, and we're going to buy lots of games. Of course, we can't ever look out of the window or go outside. And we have to be quiet so the people downstairs can't hear us.

Yesterday we had our hands full. We had to pit two crates of cherries for Mr Kugler to preserve. We're going to use the empty crates to make bookshelves.

Someone's calling me.

Yours, Anne

COMMENT ADDED BY ANNE ON 28 SEPTEMBER 1942: *Not being able to go outside upsets me more than I can say, and I'm terrified our hiding place will be discovered and that we'll be shot. That, of course, is a fairly dismal prospect.*

They were all so nice to me a month ago because of my birthday, and yet every day I feel myself drifting further away from Mother and Margot. I worked hard today and they praised me, only to start picking on me again five minutes later.

You can easily see the difference between the way they deal with Margot and the way they deal with me. For example, Margot broke the vacuum cleaner, and because of that we've been without light for the rest of the day. Mother said, 'Well, Margot, it's easy to see you're not used to working; otherwise, you'd have known better than to yank the plug out by the cord.' Margot made some reply, and that was the end of the story.

But this afternoon, when I wanted to rewrite something on Mother's shopping list because her handwriting is so hard to read, she wouldn't let me. She ticked me off again, and the whole family got involved.

I don't fit in with them, and I've felt that clearly in the last few weeks. They're so sentimental together, but I'd rather be sentimental on my own. They're always saying how nice it is with the four of us, and that we get along so well, without giving a moment's thought to the fact that I don't feel that way.

Daddy's the only one who understands me, now and again, though he usually sides with Mother and Margot. Another thing I can't stand is having them talk about me in front of outsiders, telling them how I cried or how sensibly I'm behaving. It's horrible. And sometimes they talk about Moortje and I can't bear that. Moortje is my weak spot. I miss her every minute of the day, and no one knows how often I think of her; whenever I do, my eyes fill with tears. Moortje is so sweet, and I love her so much that I keep dreaming she'll come back to us.

I have plenty of dreams, but the reality is that we'll have to stay here until the war is over. We can't ever go outside, and the only visitors we can have are Miep, her husband Jan, Bep Voskuijl, Mr Voskuijl, Mr Kugler, Mr Kleiman and Mrs Kleiman, though she hasn't come because she thinks it's too dangerous.

COMMENT ADDED BY ANNE IN SEPTEMBER 1942:
Daddy's always so nice. He understands me perfectly, and I wish we could have a heart-to-heart talk sometime without my bursting instantly into tears. But apparently that has to do with my age. I'd like to spend all my time writing, but that would probably get boring.

Up till now I've only confided my thoughts to my diary. I still haven't got round to writing amusing sketches that I could read aloud at a later date. In the future I'm going to devote less time to sentimentality and more time to reality.

Dear Kitty,

I've deserted you for an entire month, but so little has happened that I can't find a newsworthy item to relate every single day. The van Daans arrived on 13 July. We thought they were coming on the fourteenth, but from the thirteenth to sixteenth the Germans were sending out call-up notices right and left and causing a lot of unrest, so they decided it would be safer to leave a day too early than a day too late.

Peter van Daan arrived at nine-thirty in the morning (while we were still at breakfast). Peter's going on sixteen, a shy, awkward boy whose company won't amount to much. Mr and Mrs van Daan came half an hour later. Much to our amusement, Mrs van Daan was carrying a hatbox with a large chamber pot inside. 'I just don't feel at home without my chamber pot,' she exclaimed, and it was the first item to find a permanent place under the divan. Instead of a chamber pot, Mr van D. was lugging a collapsible tea table under his arm.

From the first, we ate our meals together, and after three days it felt as if the seven of us had become one big family. Naturally, the van Daans had much to tell about the week we'd been away from civilization. We were especially interested in what had happened to our flat and to Mr Goldschmidt.

Mr van Daan filled us in: 'Monday morning at nine, Mr Goldschmidt phoned and asked if I could come over.

I went straight away and found a very distraught Mr
Goldschmidt. He showed me a note that the Frank family
had left behind. As instructed, he was planning to take
the cat to the neighbours, which I agreed was a good
idea. He was afraid the house was going to be searched,
so we went through all the rooms, tidying up here and
there and clearing the breakfast things off the table. Suddenly I saw a notepad on Mrs Frank's desk, with an
address in Maastricht written on it. Even though I knew
Mrs Frank had left it on purpose, I pretended to be
surprised and horrified and begged Mr Goldschmidt to
burn this incriminating piece of paper. I swore up and
down that I knew nothing about your disappearance, but
that the note had given me an idea. "Mr Goldschmidt,"
I said, "I bet I know what this address refers to. About
six months ago a high-ranking officer came to the office.
It seems he and Mr Frank grew up together. He promised
to help Mr Frank if it was ever necessary. As I recall, he

was stationed in Maastricht. I think this officer has kept his word and is somehow planning to help them cross over to Belgium and then to Switzerland. There's no harm in telling this to any friends of the Franks who come asking about them. Of course, you don't need to mention the part about Maastricht." And after that I left. This is the story most of your friends have been told, because I heard it later from several other people.'

We thought it was extremely funny, but we laughed even harder when Mr van Daan told us that certain people have vivid imaginations. For example, one family living on our square claimed they saw all four of us riding by on our bikes early in the morning, and another woman was absolutely positive we'd been loaded into some kind of military vehicle in the middle of the night.

Yours, Anne

FRIDAY, 21 AUGUST 1942

Dear Kitty,

*N*ow our Secret Annexe has truly become secret. Because so many houses are being searched for hidden bicycles, Mr Kugler thought it would be better to have a bookcase built in front of the entrance to our hiding place. It swings out on its hinges and opens like a door. Mr Voskuijl did the carpentry work. (Mr Voskuijl has been told that the seven of us are in hiding, and he's been most helpful.)

Now whenever we want to go downstairs we have to duck and then jump. After the first three days we were all walking around with bumps on our foreheads from banging our heads against the low doorway. Then Peter cushioned it by nailing a towel stuffed with wood shavings to the door frame. Let's see if it helps!

I'm not doing much schoolwork. I've given myself a holiday until September. Father wants to start giving me lessons then, but we have to buy all the books first.

There's little change in our lives here. Peter's hair was washed today, but that's nothing special. Mr van Daan and I are always at loggerheads with each other. Mummy always treats me like a baby, which I can't stand. For the rest, things are going better. I don't think Peter's got any nicer. He's an obnoxious boy who lies around on his bed all day, only rousing himself to do a little carpentry work before returning to his nap. What a clot!

Mummy gave me another one of her dreadful sermons this morning. We take the opposite view on everything. Daddy's a sweetheart; he may get cross with me, but it never lasts longer than five minutes.

It's a beautiful day outside, nice and hot, and in spite of everything, we make the most of the weather by lounging on the folding bed in the attic.

Yours, Anne

COMMENT ADDED BY ANNE ON
21 SEPTEMBER 1942:
Mr van Daan has been as nice as pie to me recently. I've said nothing, but have been enjoying it while it lasts.

WEDNESDAY, 2 SEPTEMBER 1942

Dearest Kitty,

*M*r and Mrs van Daan have had a terrible argument. I've never seen anything like it, since Mother and Father wouldn't dream of shouting at each other like that. The argument was based on something so trivial it didn't seem worth wasting a single word on it. Oh well, to each his own.

Of course, it's very difficult for Peter, who gets caught in the middle, but no one takes Peter seriously any more, since he's hypersensitive and lazy. Yesterday he was beside himself with worry because his tongue was blue instead of pink. This rare phenomenon disappeared as quickly as it came. Today he's walking around with a thick scarf on because he's got a stiff neck. His Highness has been complaining of lumbago too. Aches and pains in his heart, kidneys and lungs are also par for the course. He's an absolute hypochondriac! (That's the right word, isn't it?)

Mother and Mrs van Daan aren't getting along very well. There are enough reasons for the friction. To give you one small example, Mrs van D. has removed all but three of her sheets from our communal linen cupboard. She's assuming that Mother's can be used for both families. She'll be in for a nasty surprise when she discovers that Mother has followed her lead.

Furthermore, Mrs van D. is miffed because we're using her china instead of ours. She's still trying to find out what we've done with our plates; they're a lot closer than she thinks, since they're packed in cardboard boxes in the attic, behind a load of Opekta advertising material. As long as we're in hiding, the plates will remain out of her reach. Since I'm always having accidents, it's just as well! Yesterday I broke one of Mrs van D.'s soup bowls.

'Oh!' she angrily exclaimed. 'Can't you be more careful? That was my last one.'

Please bear in mind, Kitty, that the two ladies speak abominable Dutch (I don't dare comment on the gentlemen: they'd be highly insulted). If you were to hear their bungled attempts, you'd laugh your head off. We've given up pointing out their errors, since correcting them doesn't help anyway. Whenever I quote Mother or Mrs van Daan, I'll write proper Dutch instead of trying to duplicate their speech.

Last week there was a brief interruption in our monotonous routine. This was provided by Peter – and a book about women. I should explain that Margot and Peter are allowed to read nearly all the books Mr Kleiman lends us. But the adults preferred to keep this special book to themselves. This immediately piqued Peter's curiosity. What forbidden fruit did it contain? He sneaked off with it when his mother was downstairs talking, and took himself and his booty to the loft. For two days all was well. Mrs van Daan knew what he was up to, but kept mum until Mr van Daan found out about it. He threw a fit, took the book away and assumed that would be the end of the business. However, he'd neglected to take his son's curiosity into account. Peter, not in the least fazed by his father's swift action, began thinking up ways to read the rest of this vastly interesting book.

In the mean time, Mrs van D. asked Mother for her opinion. Mother didn't think this particular book was suitable for Margot, but she saw no harm in letting her read most other books.

'You see, Mrs van Daan,' Mother said, 'there's a big difference between Margot and Peter. To begin with,

Margot's a girl, and girls are always more mature than boys. Second, she's already read many serious books and doesn't go looking for those which are no longer forbidden. Third, Margot's much more sensible and intellectually advanced, as a result of her four years at an excellent school.'

Mrs van Daan agreed with her, but felt it was wrong as a matter of principle to let youngsters read books written for adults.

Meanwhile, Peter had thought of a suitable time when no one would be interested in either him or the book. At seven-thirty in the evening, when the entire family was listening to the wireless in the private office, he took his treasure and stole off to the loft again. He should have been back by eight-thirty, but he was so engrossed in the book that he forgot the time and was just coming down the stairs when his father entered the room. The scene that followed was not surprising: after a slap, a whack and a tug-of-war, the book lay on the table and Peter was in the loft.

This is how matters stood when it was time for the family to eat. Peter stayed upstairs. No one gave him a moment's thought; he'd have to go to bed without his dinner. We continued eating, chatting merrily away, when suddenly we heard a piercing whistle. We lay down our forks and stared at each other, the shock clearly visible on our pale faces.

Then we heard Peter's voice through the chimney: 'I won't come down!'

Mr van Daan leapt up, his napkin falling to the floor,

and shouted, with the blood rushing to his face, 'I've had enough!'

Father, afraid of what might happen, grabbed him by the arm and the two men went to the attic. After much struggling and kicking, Peter ended up in his room with the door shut, and we went on eating.

Mrs van Daan wanted to save a piece of bread for her darling son, but Mr van D. was adamant. 'If he doesn't apologize this minute, he'll have to sleep in the loft.'

We protested that going without dinner was enough punishment. What if Peter were to catch cold? We wouldn't be able to call a doctor.

Peter didn't apologize, and returned to the loft. Mr van Daan decided to leave well enough alone, though he did note the next morning that Peter's bed had been slept in. At seven Peter went to the attic again, but was persuaded to come downstairs when Father spoke a few friendly words to him. After three days of sullen looks and stubborn silence, everything was back to normal.

Yours, Anne

MONDAY, 21 SEPTEMBER 1942

Dearest Kitty,

*T*oday I'll tell you the general news here in the Annexe. A lamp has been mounted above my divan bed so that in future, when I hear the guns going off, I'll be able to pull a cord and switch on the light. I can't use it at the moment because we're keeping our window open a little, day and night.

The male members of the van Daan contingent have built a very handy wood-stained food safe, with real screens. Up till now this glorious cupboard has been located in Peter's room, but in the interests of fresh air it's been moved to the attic. Where it once stood, there's now a shelf. I advised Peter to put his table underneath the shelf, add a nice rug and hang his own cupboard where the table now stands. That might make his little cubbyhole more comfy, though I certainly wouldn't like to sleep there.

Mrs van Daan is unbearable. I'm continually being scolded for my incessant chatter when I'm upstairs. I simply let the words bounce right off me! Madame now has a new trick up her sleeve: trying to get out of washing the pots and pans. If there's a bit of food left at the bottom of the pan, she leaves it to spoil instead of transferring it to a glass dish. Then in the afternoon when Margot is stuck with cleaning all the pots and pans, Madame exclaims, 'Oh, poor Margot, you have so much work to do!'

Every other week Mr Kleiman brings me a couple of books written for girls my age. I'm enthusiastic about the *Joop ter Heul* series. I've enjoyed all of Cissy van Marxveldt's books very much. I've read *The Zaniest Summer* four times, and the ludicrous situations still make me laugh.

Father and I are currently working on our family tree, and he tells me something about each person as we go along.

I've begun my schoolwork. I'm working hard at French, cramming five irregular verbs into my head every day. But I've forgotten much too much of what I learned in school.

Peter has taken up his English with great reluctance. A few schoolbooks have just arrived, and I brought a large supply of exercise-books, pencils, rubbers and labels from home. Pim (that's our pet name for Father) wants me to help him with his Dutch lessons. I'm perfectly willing to teach him in exchange for his assistance with French and other subjects. But he makes the most unbelievable mistakes!

I sometimes listen to the Dutch broadcasts from London. Prince Bernhard recently announced that Princess Juliana is expecting a baby in January, which I think is wonderful. No one here understands why I take such an interest in the Royal Family.

A few nights ago I was the topic of discussion, and we all decided I was an ignoramus. As a result, I threw myself into my schoolwork the next day, since I have little desire to still be in the first form when I'm fourteen or fifteen. The fact that I'm hardly allowed to read anything was also discussed. At the moment, Mother's reading *Gentlemen, Wives and Servants*, and of course I'm not allowed to read it (though Margot is!). First I have to be more intellectually developed, like my genius of a sister. Then we discussed my ignorance of philosophy, psychology and physiology (I immediately looked up these big words in the dictionary!). It's true, I don't know anything about these subjects. But maybe I'll have learned more by next year!

I've come to the shocking conclusion that I have only one long-sleeved dress and three cardigans to wear in the winter. Father's given me permission to knit a white jumper; the wool isn't very pretty, but it'll be warm, and that's what counts. Some of our clothing was left with friends, but unfortunately we won't be able to get to it until after the war. Provided it's still there, of course.

I'd just finished writing something about Mrs van Daan when she walked into the room. Thump, I slammed the book shut.

'Hey, Anne, can't I even take a peek?'

'No, Mrs van Daan.'

'Just the last page then?'

'No, not even the last page, Mrs van Daan.'

Of course, I nearly died, since that particular page contained a rather unflattering description of her.

There's something happening every day, but I'm too tired and lazy to write it all down.

Yours, Anne

Dearest Kitty,

*F*ather has a friend, a man in his mid-seventies named Mr Dreher, who's sick, poor and deaf as a post. At his side, like a useless appendage, is his wife, twenty-seven years younger and equally poor, whose arms and legs are loaded with real and fake bracelets and rings left over from more prosperous days. This Mr Dreher has already been a great nuisance to Father, and I've always admired the saintly patience with which he handled this pathetic old man on the phone. When we were still living at home, Mother used to advise him to put a gramophone in front of the receiver, one that would repeat every three minutes, 'Yes, Mr Dreher' and 'No, Mr Dreher', since the old man never understood a word of Father's lengthy replies anyway.

Today Mr Dreher phoned the office and asked Mr Kugler to come and see him. Mr Kugler wasn't in the mood and said he would send Miep, but Miep cancelled the appointment. Mrs Dreher called the office three times, but since Miep was reportedly out the entire afternoon, she had to imitate Bep's voice. Downstairs in the office as well as upstairs in the Annexe, there was great hilarity. Now each time the phone rings, Bep says 'That's Mrs Dreher!' and Miep has to laugh, so that the people on the other end of the line are greeted with an impolite giggle. Can't you just picture it? This has got to be the greatest office in the whole wide world. The bosses and the office girls have such fun together!

Some evenings I go to the van Daans for a little chat. We eat 'mothball biscuits' (biscuits that were stored in a wardrobe that was mothproofed) and have a good time. Recently the conversation was about Peter. I said that he often pats me on the cheek, which I don't like. They asked me in a typically grown-up way whether I could ever learn to love Peter like a brother, since he loves me like a sister. 'Oh, no!' I said, but what I was thinking was, 'Oh, ugh!' Just imagine! I added that Peter's a bit stiff, perhaps because he's shy. Boys who aren't used to being around girls are like that.

I must say that the Annexe Committee (the men's section) is very creative. Listen to the scheme they've come up with to get a message to Mr Broks, an Opekta Co. sales representative and friend who's surreptitiously hidden some of our things for us! They're going to type a letter to a shop owner in southern Zeeland who is, indirectly, one of Opekta's customers and ask him to fill out a form and send it back in the enclosed self-addressed envelope. Father will write the address on the envelope himself. Once the letter is returned from Zeeland, the form can be removed and a handwritten message confirming that Father is alive can be inserted in the envelope. This way Mr Broks can read the letter without suspecting a ruse. They chose the province of Zeeland because it's close to Belgium (a letter can easily be smuggled across the border) and because no one is allowed to travel there without a special permit. An ordinary salesman like Mr Broks would never be granted a permit.

Yesterday Father put on another act. Groggy with sleep, he stumbled off to bed. His feet were cold, so I lent him my bed socks. Five minutes later he flung them to the floor. Then he pulled the blankets over his head because the light bothered him. The lamp was switched off, and he gingerly poked his head out from under the covers. It was all very amusing. We started talking about the fact that Peter says Margot is a 'busy bee'. Suddenly Daddy's voice was heard from the depths: 'A busybody, you mean.'

Mouschi, the cat, is becoming nicer to me as time goes by, but I'm still somewhat afraid of her.

Yours, Anne

SUNDAY, 27 SEPTEMBER 1942

Dearest Kitty,

*M*other and I had a so-called 'discussion' today, but the annoying part is that I burst into tears. I can't help it. Daddy is *always* nice to me, and he also understands me much better. At moments like these I can't stand Mother. It's obvious that I'm a stranger to her; she doesn't even know what I think about the most ordinary things.

We were talking about maids and the fact that you're supposed to refer to them as 'domestic help' these days. She claimed that when the war is over, that's what they'll want to be called. I didn't quite see it that way. Then she added that I talk about 'later' so often and that I act as if I were such a lady, even though I'm not, but I don't think building sand-castles in the air is such a terrible thing to do, as long as you don't take it too seriously. At any rate, Daddy usually comes to my defence. Without him I wouldn't be able to stick it out here.

I don't get along with Margot very well either. Even though our family never has the same kind of outbursts they have upstairs, I find it far from pleasant. Margot's and Mother's personalities are so alien to me. I understand my girlfriends better than my own mother. Isn't that a shame?

For the umpteenth time, Mrs van Daan is sulking. She's very moody and has been removing more and more of her belongings and locking them up. It's too bad Mother doesn't repay every van Daan 'disappearing act' with a Frank 'disappearing act'.

Some people, like the van Daans, seem to take special delight not only in raising their own children but in helping others raise theirs. Margot doesn't need it, since she's naturally good, kind and clever, perfection itself, but I seem to have enough mischief for the two of us. More than once the air has been filled with the van Daans' admonitions and my cheeky replies. Father and Mother always defend me fiercely. Without them I wouldn't be able to jump back into the fray with my usual composure. They keep telling me I should talk less, mind my own business and be more modest, but I seem doomed to failure. If Father weren't so patient, I'd have long ago given up hope of ever meeting my parents' quite moderate expectations.

If I take a small helping of a vegetable I loathe and eat potatoes instead, the van Daans, especially Mrs van Daan, can't get over how spoiled I am. 'Come on, Anne, eat some more vegetables,' she says.

'No, thank you, ma'am,' I reply. 'The potatoes are more than enough.'

'Vegetables are good for you; your mother says so too. Have some more,' she insists, until Father intervenes and upholds my right to refuse a dish I don't like.

Then Mrs van D. really flies off the handle: 'You should have been at our house, where children were brought up the way they should be. I don't call this a proper upbringing. Anne is terribly spoiled. I'd never allow that. If Anne were my daughter . . .'

This is always how her tirades begin and end: 'If Anne were my daughter . . .' Thank goodness I'm not.

But to get back to the subject of raising children, yesterday a silence fell after Mrs van D. finished her little speech. Father then replied, 'I think Anne is very well brought up. At least she's learned not to respond to your interminable sermons. As far as the vegetables are concerned, all I have to say is look who's calling the kettle black.'

Mrs van D. was soundly defeated. The pot calling the kettle black refers of course to Madame herself, since she can't tolerate beans or any kind of cabbage in the evening because they give her 'wind'. But I could say the same. What a twit, don't you think? In any case, let's hope she stops talking about me.

It's so funny to see how quickly Mrs van Daan flushes. I don't, and it secretly annoys her no end.

Yours, Anne

MONDAY, 28 SEPTEMBER 1942

Dearest Kitty,

I had to stop yesterday, though I was nowhere near finished. I'm dying to tell you about another one of our clashes, but before I do I'd like to say this: I think it's odd that grown-ups quarrel so easily and so often and about such petty matters. Up till now I always thought bickering was just something children did and that they outgrew it. Of course, there's sometimes a reason to have a 'real' quarrel, but the verbal exchanges that take place here are just plain bickering. I should be used to the fact that these squabbles are daily occurrences, but I'm not and never will be as long as I'm the subject of nearly every discussion. (They refer to these as 'discussions' instead of 'quarrels', but Germans don't know the difference!) They criticize everything, and I mean everything, about me: my behaviour, my personality, my manners; every inch of me, from head to toe and back again, is the subject of gossip and debate. Harsh words and shouts are constantly being flung at my head, though I'm absolutely not used to it. According to the powers that be, I'm supposed to grin and bear it. But I can't! I have no intention of taking their insults lying down. I'll show them that Anne Frank wasn't born yesterday. They'll sit up and take notice and keep their big mouths shut when I make them see they ought to attend to their own manners instead of mine. How dare they behave like that! It's simply barbaric. I've been astonished, time and again, at such rudeness and most of all . . . at such stupidity (Mrs van Daan). But as soon as I've got used to the idea, and that shouldn't take long, I'll give them a taste of their own medicine, and then they'll change their tune! Am I really as bad-mannered, headstrong, stubborn, pushy, stupid, lazy, etc., etc., as the van Daans say I am? No, of course not. I know I have my faults and shortcomings, but they blow them all out of proportion! If you only knew, Kitty, how I seethe when they scold and mock me. It won't take long before I explode with pent-up rage.

But enough of that. I've bored you long enough with my quarrels, and yet I can't resist adding a highly interesting dinner conversation.

Somehow we landed on the subject of Pim's extreme diffidence. His modesty is a well-known fact, which even the stupidest person wouldn't dream of questioning. All of a sudden Mrs van Daan, who feels the need to bring herself into every conversation, remarked, 'I'm very modest and retiring too, much more so than my husband!'

Have you ever heard anything so ridiculous? This

sentence clearly illustrates that she's not exactly what you'd call modest!

Mr van Daan, who felt obliged to explain the 'much more so than my husband', answered calmly, 'I have no desire to be modest and retiring. In my experience, you get a lot further by being pushy!' And turning to me, he added, 'Don't be modest and retiring, Anne. It will get you nowhere.'

Mother agreed completely with this viewpoint. But, as usual, Mrs van Daan had to add her two penn'orth. This time, however, instead of addressing me directly, she turned to my parents and said, 'You must have a strange outlook on life to be able to say that to Anne. Things were different when I was growing up. Though they probably haven't changed much since then, except in your modern household!'

This was a direct hit at Mother's modern child-rearing methods, which she's defended on many occasions. Mrs van Daan was so upset her face turned bright red. People who flush easily become even more agitated when they feel themselves getting hot under the collar, and they quickly lose to their opponents.

The non-flushed mother, who now wanted to have the matter over and done with as quickly as possible, paused for a moment to think before she replied. 'Well, Mrs van Daan, I agree that it's much better if a person isn't overmodest. My husband, Margot and Peter are all exceptionally modest. Your husband, Anne and I, though not exactly the opposite, don't let ourselves be pushed around.'

Mrs van Daan: 'Oh, but Mrs Frank, I don't understand what you mean! Honestly, I'm extremely modest and retiring. How can you say that I'm pushy?'

Mother: 'I didn't say you were pushy, but no one would describe you as having a retiring disposition.'

Mrs van D.: 'I'd like to know in what way I'm pushy! If I didn't look out for myself here, no one else would, and I'd soon starve, but that doesn't mean I'm not as modest and retiring as your husband.'

Mother had no choice but to laugh at this ridiculous self-defence, which irritated Mrs van Daan. Not exactly a born debater, she continued her magnificent account in a mixture of German and Dutch, until she got so tangled up in her own words that she finally rose from her chair and was just about to leave the room when her eye fell on me. You should have seen her! As luck would have it, the moment Mrs van D. turned around I was shaking my head in a combination of compassion and irony. I wasn't doing it on purpose, but I'd followed her tirade so intently that my reaction was completely involuntary. Mrs van D. wheeled around and gave me a tongue-lashing: hard, Germanic, mean and vulgar, exactly like some fat, red-faced fishwife. It was a joy to behold. If I could draw, I'd like to have sketched her as she was then. She struck me as so comical, that silly little scatterbrain! I've learned one thing: you only really get to know a person after a row. Only then can you judge their true character!

Yours, Anne

Dearest Kitty,

*T*he strangest things happen to you when you're in hiding! Try to picture this. Because we don't have a bath, we wash ourselves in a tin tub, and because there's only hot water in the office (by which I mean the entire lower floor), the seven of us take turns making the most of this great opportunity. But since no two of us are alike and we are all plagued by varying degrees of modesty, each member of the family has selected a different place to wash. Peter takes a bath in the office kitchen, even though it has a glass door. When it's time for his bath, he goes round to each of us in turn and announces that we shouldn't walk past the kitchen for the next half hour. He considers this measure to be sufficient. Mr van D. takes his bath upstairs, reasoning that the safety of his own room outweighs the difficulty of having to carry the hot water up all those stairs. Mrs van D. has yet to take a bath; she's waiting to see which is the best place. Father washes in the private office and Mother in the kitchen behind a fireguard, while Margot and I have declared the front office to be our bathing grounds. Since the curtains are drawn on Saturday afternoon, we scrub ourselves in the dark, while the one who isn't in the bath looks out of the window through a chink in the curtains and gazes in wonder at the endlessly amusing people.

A week ago I decided I didn't like this spot and have been on the lookout for more comfortable quarters. It was Peter who gave me the idea of setting my tin bath in the spacious office lavatory. I can sit down, turn on the light, lock the door, pour out the water without anyone's help, and all without the fear of being seen. I used my lovely bathroom for the first time on Sunday and, strange as it may seem, I like it better than any other place.

The plumber was at work downstairs on Wednesday, moving the water pipes and drains from the office lavatory to the passage so the pipes won't freeze during a cold winter. The plumber's visit was far from pleasant. Not only were we not allowed to run water during the day, but the lavatory was also out of bounds. I'll tell you how we handled this problem; you may find it unseemly of me to bring it up, but I'm not so prudish about matters of this kind. On the day of our arrival, Father and I improvised a chamber pot, sacrificing a preserving jar for this purpose. For the duration of the plumber's visit, preserving jars were put into service during the daytime to hold our calls of nature. As far as I was concerned, this wasn't half as difficult as having to sit still all day and not say a word. You can imagine how hard that was for Miss Quack, Quack, Quack. On ordinary days we have to speak in a whisper; not being able to talk or move at all is ten times worse.

After three days of constant sitting, my backside was stiff and sore. Nightly calisthenics helped.

Yours, Anne

THURSDAY, 1 OCTOBER 1942

Dear Kitty,

Yesterday I had a horrible fright. At eight o'clock the doorbell suddenly rang. All I could think of was that someone was coming to get us, you know who I mean. But I calmed down when everybody swore it must have been either pranksters or the postman.

The days here are very quiet. Mr Levinsohn, a little Jewish chemist, is doing some experiments for Mr Kugler in the kitchen. Since he's familiar with the entire building, we're in constant dread that he'll take it into his head to go and have a look at what used to be the laboratory. We're as still as baby mice. Who would have guessed three months ago that quicksilver Anne would have to sit so quietly for hours on end, and what's more, that she could?

Mrs van Daan's birthday was the twenty-ninth. Though we didn't have a large celebration, she was showered with flowers, simple gifts and good food. Apparently the red carnations from her spouse are a family tradition.

Let me pause a moment on the subject of Mrs van Daan and tell you that her attempts to flirt with Father are a constant source of irritation to me. She pats him on the cheek and head, pulls up her skirt and makes so-called witty remarks in an effort to get Pim's attention. Fortunately, he finds her neither pretty nor charming, so he doesn't respond to her flirtations. As you know, I'm quite the jealous type, and I can't abide her behaviour. After all, Mother doesn't act that way towards Mr van D., which is what I told Mrs van D. right to her face.

From time to time Peter can be very amusing. He and I have one thing in common: we like to dress up, which makes everyone laugh. One evening we made our appearance, with Peter in one of his mother's skin-tight dresses and me in his suit. He wore a hat; I had a cap on. The grown-ups split their sides laughing, and we enjoyed ourselves every bit as much.

Bep bought new skirts for Margot and me at The Bijenkorf. The fabric is hideous, like the sacks that potatoes come in. Just the kind of thing the department stores wouldn't dare sell in the olden days, now costing 24.00 guilders (Margot's) and 7.75 guilders (mine).

We have a nice treat in store: Bep's ordered a correspondence course in shorthand for Margot, Peter and me. Just you wait, by this time next year we'll be able to take perfect shorthand. In any case, learning to write a secret code like that is really interesting.

I have a terrible pain in my index finger (on my left hand), so I can't do any ironing. What luck!

Mr van Daan wants me to sit next to him at the table, since Margot doesn't eat enough to suit him. That's all right with me, I like changes. There's always a tiny black cat roaming around the yard, and it reminds me of my dear sweet Moortje. Another reason I welcome the change is that Mummy's always carping at me, especially at the table. Now Margot will have to bear the brunt of it. Or rather, won't, since Mother doesn't make such sarcastic remarks to her. Not to that paragon of virtue! I'm always teasing Margot about being a paragon of virtue these days, and she hates it. Maybe it'll teach her not to be such a goody-goody. High time she learned.

To end this hodgepodge of news, a particularly amusing joke told by Mr van Daan:

What goes click ninety-nine times and clack once?
A centipede with a clubfoot.

Bye-bye, Anne

Dear Kitty,

*E*verybody teased me quite a bit yesterday because I lay down on the bed next to Mr van Daan. 'At your age! Shocking!' and other remarks along those lines. Silly, of course. I'd never want to sleep with Mr van Daan the way they mean.

Yesterday Mother and I had another run-in and she really kicked up a fuss. She told Daddy all my sins and started to cry, which made me cry too, and I already had such an awful headache. I finally told Daddy that I love 'him' more than I do Mother, to which he replied that it was just a passing phase, but I don't think so. I simply can't stand Mother, and I have to force myself not to snap at her all the time, and to stay calm, when I'd rather slap her across the face. I don't know why I've taken such a terrible dislike to her. Daddy says that if Mother isn't feeling well or has a headache, I should volunteer to help her, but I'm not going to because I don't love her and don't enjoy doing it. I can imagine Mother dying someday, but Daddy's death seems inconceivable. It's very mean of me, but that's how I feel. I hope Mother will *never* read this or anything else I've written.

I've been allowed to read more grown-up books lately. *Eva's Youth* by Nico van Suchtelen is currently keeping me busy. I don't think there's much of a difference between this and books for teenage girls. Eva thought that children grew on trees, like apples, and that the stork plucked them off the tree when they were ripe and brought them to the mothers. But her girlfriend's cat had kittens and Eva saw them coming out of the cat, so she thought cats laid eggs and hatched them like chickens, and that mothers who wanted a child also went upstairs a few days before their time to lay an egg and brood on it. After the babies arrived, the mothers were pretty weak from all that squatting. At some point, Eva wanted a baby too. She took a woollen scarf and spread it on the ground so the egg could fall into it, and then she squatted down and began to push. She clucked as she waited, but no egg came out. Finally, after she'd been sitting for a long time, something did come, but it was a sausage instead of an egg. Eva was embarrassed. She thought she was ill. Funny, isn't it? There are also parts of *Eva's Youth* that talk about women selling their bodies on the street and asking loads of money. I'd be mortified in front of a man like that. In addition, it mentions Eva's menstruation. Oh, I long to have my period – then I'll really be grown up.

Daddy is grumbling again and threatening to take away my diary. Oh, horror of horrors! From now on, I'm going to hide it.

Anne Frank

I imagine that . . .
 I've gone to Switzerland. Daddy and I sleep in one room, while the boys'★ study is turned into a sitting-room, where I can receive visitors. As a surprise, they've bought new furniture for me, including a tea table, a desk, armchairs and a divan. Everything's simply wonderful. After a few days Daddy gives me 150 guilders – converted into Swiss money, of course, but I'll call them guilders – and tells me to buy everything I think I'll need, all for myself. (Later on, I get a guilder a week, which I can also use to buy whatever I want.) I set off with Bernd and buy:

    3 cotton vests @ 0.50 = 1.50
    3 cotton knickers @ 0.50 = 1.50
    3 wool vests @ 0.75 = 2.25
    3 wool knickers @ 0.75 = 2.25
    2 petticoats @ 0.50 = 1.00
    2 bras (smallest size) @ 0.50 = 1.00
    5 pyjamas @ 1.00 = 5.00
    1 light dressing-gown @ 2.50 = 2.50
    1 thick dressing-gown @ 3.00 = 3.00
    2 bed jackets @ 0.75 = 1.50
    1 small pillow @ 1.00 = 1.00
    1 pair of lightweight slippers @ 1.00 = 1.00

★ Anne's cousins Bernhard (Bernd) and Stephan Elias.

1 pair of warm slippers @ 1.50 = 1.50
1 pair of summer shoes (school) @ 1.50 = 1.50
1 pair of summer shoes (best) @ 2.00 = 2.00
1 pair of winter shoes (school) @ 2.50 = 2.50
1 pair of winter shoes (best) @ 3.00 = 3.00
2 aprons @ 0.50 = 1.00
25 handkerchiefs @ 0.05 = 1.25
4 pairs of silk stockings @ 0.75 = 3.00
4 pairs of kneesocks @ 0.50 = 2.00
4 pairs of socks @ 0.25 = 1.00
2 pairs of thick stockings @ 1.00 = 2.00
3 skeins of white wool (underwear, cap) = 1.50
3 skeins of blue wool (sweater, skirt) = 1.50
3 skeins of variegated wool (cap, scarf) = 1.50
Scarves, belts, collars, buttons = 1.25

Plus 2 school dresses (summer), 2 school dresses (winter), 2 good dresses (summer), 2 good dresses (winter), 1 summer skirt, 1 good winter skirt, 1 school winter skirt, 1 raincoat, 1 summer coat, 1 winter coat, 2 hats, 2 caps. For a total of 108.00 guilders.

2 handbags, 1 ice-skating outfit, 1 pair of skates, 1 case (containing powder, skin cream, foundation cream, cleansing cream, suntan lotion, cotton wool, first-aid kit, rouge, lipstick, eyebrow pencil, bath salts, bath powder, eau-de-Cologne, soap, powder puff).

Plus 4 sweaters @ 1.50, 4 blouses @ 1.00, miscellaneous items @ 10.00 and books, presents @ 4.50.

FRIDAY, 9 OCTOBER 1942

Dearest Kitty,

Today I have nothing but dismal and depressing news to report. Our many Jewish friends and acquaintances are being taken away in droves. The Gestapo is treating them very roughly and transporting them in cattle-trucks to Westerbork, the big camp in Drenthe to which they're sending all the Jews. Miep told us about someone who'd managed to escape from there. It must be terrible in Westerbork. The people get almost nothing to eat, much less to drink, as water is available only one hour a day, and there's only one lavatory and sink for several thousand people. Men and women sleep in the same room, and women and children often have their heads shaved. Escape is almost impossible; many people look Jewish, and they're branded by their shorn heads.

If it's that bad in Holland, what must it be like in those faraway and uncivilized places where the Germans are sending them? We assume that most of them are being murdered. The English radio says they're being gassed. Perhaps that's the quickest way to die.

I feel terrible. Miep's accounts of these horrors are so

heartrending, and Miep is also very distraught. The other day, for instance, the Gestapo deposited an elderly, crippled Jewish woman on Miep's doorstep while they set off to find a car. The old woman was terrified of the glaring searchlights and the guns firing at the English planes overhead. Yet Miep didn't dare let her in. Nobody would. The Germans are generous enough when it comes to punishment.

Bep is also very subdued. Her boyfriend is being sent to Germany. Every time the planes fly over, she's afraid they're going to drop their entire bomb load on Bertus's head. Jokes like 'Oh, don't worry, they can't all fall on him' or 'One bomb is all it takes' are hardly appropriate in this situation. Bertus is not the only one being forced to work in Germany. Trainloads of young men depart daily. Some of them try to sneak off the train when it stops at a small station, but only a few manage to escape unnoticed and find a place to hide.

But that's not the end of my lamentations. Have you ever heard the term 'hostages'? That's the latest punishment for saboteurs. It's the most horrible thing you can imagine. Leading citizens – innocent people – are taken prisoner to await their execution. If the Gestapo can't find the saboteur, they simply grab five hostages and line them up against the wall. You read the announcements of their death in the paper, where they're referred to as 'fatal accidents'.

Fine specimens of humanity, those Germans, and to think I'm actually one of them! No, that's not true, Hitler took away our nationality long ago. And besides, there are no greater enemies on earth than the Germans and the Jews.

Yours, Anne

Dear Kitty,

I'm terribly busy. Yesterday I began by translating a chapter from *La Belle Nivernaise* and writing down vocabulary words. Then I worked on an *awful* maths problem and translated three pages of French grammar besides. Today, French grammar and history. I simply refuse to do that wretched maths every day. Daddy thinks it's awful too. I'm almost better at it than he is, though in fact neither of us is any good, so we always have to call on Margot's help. I'm also working away at my shorthand, which I enjoy. Of the three of us, I've made the most progress.

I've read *The Storm Family*. It's quite good, but doesn't compare with *Joop ter Heul*. Anyway, the same words can be found in both books, which makes sense because they're written by the same author. Cissy van Marxveldt is a terrific writer. I'm definitely going to let my own children read her books too.

Moreover, I've read a lot of Körner plays. I like the way he writes. For example, *Hedwig*, *The Cousin from Bremen*, *The Governess*, *The Green Domino*, etc.

Mother, Margot and I are once again the best of friends. It's actually a lot nicer that way. Last night Margot and I were lying side by side in my bed. It was incredibly cramped, but that's what made it fun. She asked if she could read my diary once in a while.

'Parts of it,' I said, and asked about hers. She gave me permission to read her diary as well.

The conversation turned to the future, and I asked what she wanted to be when she was older. But she wouldn't say and was quite mysterious about it. I gathered it had something to do with teaching; of course, I'm not absolutely sure, but I suspect it's something along those lines. I really shouldn't be so nosy.

This morning I lay on Peter's bed, after first having chased him off it. He was furious, but I didn't care. He might consider being a little more friendly to me from time to time. After all, I did give him an apple last night.

I once asked Margot if she thought I was ugly. She said that I was okay and had nice eyes. A little vague, don't you think?

Well, until next time!

Anne Frank

PS. This morning we all took turns on the scale. Margot now weighs 9 stone 6 pounds, Mother 9 stone 10, Father 11 stone 1, Anne 6 stone 12, Peter 10 stone 8, Mrs van Daan 8 stone 5, Mr van Daan 11 stone 11. In the three months since I've been here, I've gained 19 pounds. A lot, huh?

Dearest Kitty,

*M*y hand's still shaking, though it's been two hours since we had the scare. I should explain that there are five fire extinguishers in the building. The office staff stupidly forgot to warn us that the carpenter, or whatever he's called, was coming to fill the extinguishers. As a result, we didn't bother to be quiet until I heard the sound of hammering on the landing (across from the bookcase). I immediately assumed it was the carpenter and went to warn Bep, who was eating lunch, that she couldn't go back downstairs. Father and I stationed ourselves at the door so we could hear when the man had left. After working for about fifteen minutes, he laid his hammer and some other tools on our bookcase (or so we thought!) and banged on our door. We turned white with fear. Had he heard something after all and did he now want to check out this mysterious-looking bookcase? It seemed so, since he kept knocking, pulling, pushing and jerking on it.

I was so scared I nearly fainted at the thought of this total stranger managing to discover our wonderful hiding place. Just when I thought my days were numbered, we heard Mr Kleiman's voice saying, 'Open up, it's me.'

We opened the door at once. What had happened? The hook fastening the bookcase had got stuck, which is why no one had been able to warn us about the carpenter. After the man had left, Mr Kleiman came to get Bep, but couldn't open the bookcase. I can't tell you how relieved I was. In my imagination, the man I thought was trying to get inside the Secret Annexe had kept growing and growing until he'd become not only a giant but also the cruellest Fascist in the world. Whew. Fortunately, everything worked out all right, at least this time.

We had lots of fun on Monday. Miep and Jan spent the night with us. Margot and I slept in Father and Mother's room for the night so the Gieses could have our beds. The menu was drawn up in their honour, and the meal was delicious. The festivities were briefly interrupted when Father's lamp caused a short circuit and we were suddenly plunged into darkness. What were we to do? We did have fuses, but the fuse box was at the rear of the dark warehouse, which made this a particularly unpleasant job at night. Still, the men ventured forth, and ten minutes later we were able to put away the candles.

I was up early this morning. Jan was already dressed. Since he had to leave at eight-thirty, he was upstairs eating breakfast by eight. Miep was busy getting dressed, and I found her in her vest when I came in. She wears the same kind of long underwear I do when she cycles. Margot and I threw on our clothes as well and were upstairs earlier than usual. After a pleasant breakfast, Miep headed downstairs. It was pouring outside and she was glad she didn't have to cycle to work. Daddy and I made the beds, and afterwards I learned five irregular French verbs. Quite industrious, don't you think?

Margot and Peter were reading in our room, with

Mouschi curled up beside Margot on the divan. After my irregular French verbs, I joined them and read *The Woods Are Singing for All Eternity*. It's quite a beautiful book, but very unusual. I'm almost finished.

Next week it's Bep's turn to spend the night.

Yours, Anne

THURSDAY, 29 OCTOBER 1942

My dearest Kitty,

I'm very worried. Father's ill. He's covered with spots and has a high temperature. It looks like measles. Just think, we can't even call a doctor! Mother is making him perspire in hopes of sweating out the fever.

This morning Miep told us that the furniture has been removed from the van Daans' flat on Zuider-Amstellaan.

We haven't told Mrs van D. yet. She's been so '*nerven-mässig*'★ lately, and we don't feel like hearing her moan and groan again about all the beautiful china and lovely chairs she had to leave behind. We had to abandon most of our nice things too. What's the good of grumbling about it now?

Father wants me to start reading books by Hebbel and other well-known German writers. I can read German fairly well by now, except that I usually mumble the words instead of reading them silently to myself. But that'll pass. Father has taken the plays of Goethe and Schiller down from the big bookcase and is planning to read to me every evening. We've started off with *Don Carlos*. Encouraged by Father's good example, Mother pressed her prayer book into my hands. I read a few prayers in German, just to be polite. They certainly sound beautiful, but they mean very little to me. Why is she making me act so religious and devout?

Tomorrow we're going to light the stove for the first time. The chimney hasn't been swept in ages, so the room is bound to fill with smoke. Let's hope the thing draws!

Yours, Anne

★ Nervous.

Dear Kitty,

*B*ep stayed with us Friday evening. It was fun, but she didn't sleep very well because she'd drunk some wine. For the rest, there's nothing special to report. I had an awful headache yesterday and went to bed early. Margot's being exasperating again.

This morning I began sorting out an index card file from the office, because it'd fallen over and got all mixed up. Before long I was going barmy. I asked Margot and Peter to help, but they were too lazy, so I put it away. I'm not crazy enough to do it all by myself!

Anne Frank

PS. I forgot to mention the important news that I'm probably going to have my period soon. I can tell because I keep finding a whitish smear in my panties, and Mother predicted it would start soon. I can hardly wait. It's such a momentous event. Too bad I can't use sanitary towels, but you can't get them any more, and Mummy's tampons can be used only by women who've had a baby.

COMMENT BY ANNE ON 22 JANUARY 1944:
I wouldn't be able to write that kind of thing any more.

Now that I'm rereading my diary after a year and a half, I'm surprised at my childish innocence. Deep down I know I could never be that innocent again, however much I'd like to be. I can understand the mood changes and the comments about Margot, Mother and Father as if I'd written them only yester-

day, but I can't imagine writing so openly about other matters.
It embarrasses me greatly to read the pages dealing with subjects
that I remembered as being nicer than they actually were. My
descriptions are so indelicate. But enough of that.

I can also understand my homesickness and yearning for
Moortje. The whole time I've been here I've longed uncon-
sciously – and at times consciously – for trust, love and physical
affection. This longing may change in intensity, but it's always
there.

THURSDAY, 5 NOVEMBER 1942

Dear Kitty,

The British have finally scored a few successes in Africa and Stalingrad hasn't fallen yet, so the men are happy and we had coffee and tea this morning. For the rest, nothing special to report.

This week I've been reading a lot and doing little work. That's the way things ought to be. That's surely the road to success.

Mother and I are getting along better lately, but we're *never* close. Father's not very open about his feelings, but he's the same sweetheart he's always been. We lit the stove a few days ago and the entire room is still filled with smoke. I prefer central heating, and I'm probably not the only one. Margot's a stinker (there's no other word for it), a constant source of irritation, morning, noon and night.

Anne Frank

Dearest Kitty,

M other's nerves are very much on edge, and that doesn't bode well for me. Is it just a coincidence that Father and Mother never scold Margot and always blame me for everything? Last night, for example, Margot was reading a book with beautiful illustrations; she got up and put the book aside for later. I wasn't doing anything, so I picked it up and began looking at the pictures. Margot came back, saw 'her' book in my hands, knitted her brow and crossly demanded the book back. I wanted to look through it a bit more. Margot got angrier by the minute, and Mother butted in: 'Margot was reading that book; give it back to her.'

Father came in, and without even knowing what was going on, saw that Margot was being wronged and lashed out at me: 'I'd like to see what you'd do if Margot was looking at one of your books!'

I promptly gave in, put the book down and, according to them, left the room 'in a huff'. I was neither huffy nor cross, but merely sad.

It wasn't right of Father to pass judgement without knowing what the issue was. I would have given the book to Margot myself, and a lot sooner, if Father and Mother hadn't intervened and rushed to take Margot's part, as if she were suffering some great injustice.

Of course, Mother took Margot's side; they always take each other's sides. I'm so used to it that I've become completely indifferent to Mother's rebukes and Margot's moodiness. I love them, but only because they're Mother and Margot. I don't give a dash about them as people. As far as I'm concerned, they can go jump in the lake. It's different with Father. When I see him being partial to Margot, approving Margot's every action, praising her, hugging her, I feel a gnawing ache inside, because I'm mad about him. I model myself on Father, and there's no one in the world I love more. He doesn't realize that he treats Margot differently from me: Margot just happens to be the cleverest, the kindest, the prettiest and the best. But I have a right to be taken seriously too. I've always been the clown and mischief-maker of the family; I've always had to pay double for my sins: once with scoldings and then again with my own sense of despair. I'm no longer satisfied with the meaningless affection or the supposedly serious talks. I long for something from Father that he's incapable of giving. I'm not jealous of Margot; I never have been. I'm not envious of her brains or her beauty. It's just that I'd like to feel that Father really loves me, not because I'm his child, but because I'm me, Anne.

I cling to Father because my contempt of Mother is growing daily and it's only through him that I'm able to retain the last ounce of family feeling I have left. He doesn't understand that I sometimes need to vent my feelings for Mother. He doesn't want to talk about it, and he avoids any discussion involving Mother's failings.

And yet Mother, with all her shortcomings, is tougher for me to deal with. I don't know how I should behave. I can't very well confront her with her carelessness, her sarcasm and her hard-heartedness, yet I can't continue to take the blame for everything.

I'm the opposite of Mother, so of course we clash. I don't mean to judge her; I don't have that right. I'm simply looking at her as a mother. She's not a mother to me – I have to mother myself. I've cut myself adrift from them. I'm charting my own course, and we'll see where it leads me. I have no choice, because I can picture what a mother and a wife should be and can't seem to find anything of the sort in the woman I'm supposed to call 'Mother'.

I tell myself time and again to overlook Mother's bad example. I only want to see her good points, and to look inside myself for what's lacking in her. But it doesn't work, and the worst part is that Father and Mother don't realize their own inadequacies and how much I blame them for letting me down. Are there any parents who can make their children completely happy?

Sometimes I think God is trying to test me, both now and in the future. I'll have to become a good person on my own, without anyone to serve as a model or advise me, but it'll make me stronger in the end.

Who else but me is ever going to read these letters?

Who else but me can I turn to for comfort? I'm frequently in need of consolation, I often feel weak, and more often than not, I fail to meet expectations. I know this, and every day I resolve to do better.

They aren't consistent in their treatment of me. One day they say that Anne's a sensible girl and entitled to know everything, and the next that Anne's a silly noodle who doesn't know a thing and yet imagines she's learned all she needs to know from books! I'm no longer the baby and spoiled little darling whose every deed can be laughed at. I have my own ideas, plans and ideals, but am unable to articulate them yet.

Oh well. So much comes into my head at night when I'm alone, or during the day when I'm obliged to put up with people I can't abide or who invariably misinterpret my intentions. That's why I always come back to my diary – I start there and end there because Kitty's always patient. I promise her that, despite everything, I'll keep going, that I'll find my own way and choke back my tears. I only wish I could see some results or, just once, receive encouragement from someone who loves me.

Don't condemn me, but think of me as a person who sometimes reaches bursting point!

Yours, Anne

Dearest Kitty,

Yesterday was Peter's birthday, his sixteenth. I was upstairs by eight, and Peter and I looked at his presents. He received a game of Monopoly, a razor and a cigarette lighter. Not that he smokes so much, not at all; it just looks so distinguished.

The biggest surprise came from Mr van Daan, who reported at one that the English had landed in Tunis, Algiers, Casablanca and Oran.

'This is the beginning of the end,' everyone was saying, but Churchill, the British Prime Minister, who must have heard the same thing being repeated in England, declared, 'This is not the end. It is not even the beginning of the end. But it is, perhaps, the end of the beginning.' Do you see the difference? However, there's reason for optimism. Stalingrad, the Russian city that has been under attack for three months, still hasn't fallen into German hands.

In the true spirit of the Annexe, I should talk to you about food. (I should explain that they're real gluttons up on the top floor.)

Bread is delivered daily by a very nice baker, a friend of Mr Kleiman's. Of course, we don't have as much as we did at home, but it's enough. We also purchase ration books on the black market. The price keeps going up; it's already risen from 27 to 33 guilders. And that for mere sheets of printed paper!

To provide ourselves with a source of nutrition that

will keep, aside from the hundred tins of food we've stored here, we bought three hundred pounds of beans. Not just for us, but for the office staff as well. We'd hung the sacks of beans on hooks in the hallway, just inside our secret entrance, but a few seams split under the weight. So we decided to move them to the attic, and Peter was entrusted with the heavy lifting. He managed to get five of the six sacks upstairs intact and was busy with the last one when the sack broke and a flood, or rather a hailstorm, of brown beans went flying through the air and down the stairs. Since there were about fifty pounds of beans in that sack, it made enough noise to raise the dead. Downstairs they were sure the house was falling down around their heads. Peter was stunned, but then burst into peals of laughter when he saw me standing at the bottom of the stairs, like an island in a sea of brown, with waves of beans lapping at my ankles. We promptly began picking them up, but beans are so small and slippery that they roll into every conceivable corner and hole. Now each time we go upstairs, we bend over and hunt around so we can present Mrs van Daan with a handful of beans.

I almost forgot to mention that Father has recovered from his illness.

Yours, Anne

PS. The radio has just announced that Algiers has fallen. Morocco, Casablanca and Oran have been in British hands for several days. We're now waiting for Tunis.

Dearest Kitty,

Great news! We're planning to take an eighth person into hiding with us!

Yes, really. We always thought there was enough room and food for one more person, but we were afraid of placing an even greater burden on Mr Kugler and Mr Kleiman. But since reports of the dreadful things being done to the Jews are getting worse by the day, Father decided to sound out these two gentlemen, and they thought it was an excellent plan. 'It's just as dangerous, whether there are seven or eight,' they noted rightly. Once this was settled, we sat down and mentally went through our circle of acquaintances, trying to come up with a single person who would blend in well with our extended family. This wasn't difficult. After Father had rejected all the van Daan relatives, we chose a dentist named Albert Dussel. He lives with a charming Christian lady who's quite a bit younger than he is. They're probably not married, but that's beside the point. He's known to be quiet and refined, and he seemed, from our superficial acquaintance with him, to be nice. Miep knows him as well, so she'll be able to make the necessary arrangements. If he comes, Mr Dussel will have to sleep in my room instead of Margot, who will have to make do with the folding bed.★ We'll

★ After Dussel arrived, Margot slept in her parents' bedroom.

ask him to bring along something to fill cavities with.

Yours, Anne

Dearest Kitty,

*M*iep came to tell us that she'd been to see Dr Dussel. He asked her the moment she entered the room if she knew of a hiding place and was enormously pleased when Miep said she had something in mind. She added that he'd need to go into hiding as soon as possible, preferably Saturday, but he thought this was highly improbable, since he wanted to bring his records up to date, settle his accounts and attend to a couple of patients. Miep relayed the message to us this morning. We didn't think it was wise to wait so long. All these preparations require explanations to various people who we feel ought to be kept in the dark. Miep went to ask if Dr Dussel couldn't manage to come on Saturday after all, but he said no, and now he's scheduled to arrive on Monday.

I think it's odd that he doesn't jump at our proposal. If they pick him up on the street, it won't help either his records or his patients, so why the delay? If you ask me, it's stupid of Father to humour him.

Otherwise, no news.

Yours, Anne

Dearest Kitty!

*M*r Dussel has arrived. Everything went smoothly. Miep told him to be at a certain place in front of the post office at 11.00 a.m., when a man would meet him, and he was at the appointed place at the appointed time. Mr Kleiman went up to him, announced that the man he was expecting to meet was unable to come and asked him to drop by the office to see Miep. Mr Kleiman took a tram back to the office while Mr Dussel followed on foot.

It was eleven-twenty when Mr Dussel tapped on the office door. Miep asked him to remove his coat, so the yellow star couldn't be seen, and brought him to the private office, where Mr Kleiman kept him occupied until the cleaning lady had gone. On the pretext that the private office was needed for something else, Miep took Mr Dussel upstairs, opened the bookcase and stepped inside, while Mr Dussel looked on in amazement.

In the mean time, the seven of us had seated ourselves around the dining-table to await the latest addition to our family with coffee and cognac. Miep first led him into the Frank family's room. He immediately recognized our furniture, but had no idea we were upstairs, just above his head. When Miep told him, he was so astonished he nearly fainted. Thank goodness she didn't leave him in suspense any longer, but brought him upstairs. Mr Dussel sank into a chair and stared at us in dumbstruck silence, as though he thought he could read the truth on our faces. Then he stuttered, '*Aber* . . . but are you *nicht* in Belgium? The officer, the auto, they were not coming? Your escape was not working?'

We explained the whole thing to him, about how we'd deliberately spread the rumour of the officer and the car to throw the Germans and anyone else who might come looking for us off the track. Mr Dussel was speechless in the face of such ingenuity, and could do nothing but gaze around in surprise as he explored the rest of our lovely and ultra-practical Annexe. We all had lunch together. Then he had a short nap, joined us for tea, put away the few belongings Miep had been able to bring here in advance and began to feel much more at home. Especially when we handed him the following typewritten rules and regulations for the Secret Annexe (a van Daan production):

PROSPECTUS AND GUIDE TO THE SECRET ANNEXE
A Unique Facility for the Temporary Accommodation of Jews and Other Dispossessed Persons

Open all year round: Located in beautiful, quiet, wooded surroundings in the heart of Amsterdam. No private residences in the vicinity. Can be reached by trams 13 or 17 and also by car and bicycle. For those to whom such transport has been forbidden by the German authorities, it can also be reached on foot. Furnished and unfurnished rooms and apartments are available at all times, with or without meals.

Price: Free.

Diet: Low-fat.

Running water in the bathroom (sorry, no bath) and on various inside and outside walls. Cosy stoves for heating.

Ample storage space for a variety of goods. Two large, modern safes.

Private radio with a direct line to London, New York, Tel Aviv and many other stations. Available to all residents after 6.00 p.m. No listening to forbidden broadcasts, with certain exceptions, i.e. German stations may only be tuned in to listen to classical music. It is absolutely forbidden to listen to German news bulletins (regardless of where they are transmitted from) and to pass them on to others.

Rest hours: From 10.00 p.m. to 7.30 a.m.; 10.15 a.m. on Sundays. Owing to circumstances, residents are required to observe rest hours during the daytime when instructed to do so by the Management. To ensure the safety of all, rest hours must be strictly observed!!!

Free-time activities: None allowed outside the house until further notice.

Use of language: It is necessary to speak softly at all times. Only the language of civilized people may be spoken, thus no German.

Reading and relaxation: No German books may be

read, except for the classics and works of a scholarly nature. Other books are optional.

Calisthenics: Daily.

Singing: Only softly, and after 6.00 p.m.

Films: Prior arrangements required.

Lessons: A weekly correspondence course in shorthand. Courses in English, French, maths and history offered at any hour of the day or night. Payment in the form of tuition, e.g. Dutch.

Separate department for the care of small household pets (with the exception of vermin, for which special permits are required).

Mealtimes:

> *Breakfast:* At 9.00 a.m. daily except public holidays and Sundays; at approximately 11.30 a.m. on Sundays and public holidays.
>
> *Lunch:* A light meal. From 1.15 p.m. to 1.45 p.m.
>
> *Dinner:* May or may not be a hot meal. Mealtime depends on news broadcasts.

Obligations with respect to the Supply Corps: Residents must be prepared to help with office work at all times.

Baths: The tin bath is available to all residents after 9.00 a.m. on Sundays. Residents may wash in the downstairs lavatory, kitchen, private office or front office, as they choose.

Alcohol: For medicinal purposes only.

The end.

Yours, Anne

Dearest Kitty,

Just as we thought, Mr Dussel is a very nice man. Of course he didn't mind sharing a room with me; to be honest, I'm not exactly delighted at having a stranger use my things, but you have to make sacrifices for a good cause, and I'm glad I can make this small one. 'If we can save even one of our friends, the rest doesn't matter,' said Father, and he's absolutely right.

The first day Mr Dussel was here, he asked me all sorts of questions – for example, what time the cleaning lady comes to the office, how we've arranged to use the bathroom and when we're allowed to go to the lavatory. You may laugh, but these things aren't so easy in a hiding place. During the daytime we can't make any noise that might be heard downstairs, and when someone else is there, like the cleaning lady, we have to be extra careful. I patiently explained all this to Mr Dussel, but I was surprised to see how slow he is to catch on. He asks everything twice and still can't remember what you've told him.

Maybe he's just confused by the sudden change and he'll get over it. Otherwise, everything is fine.

Mr Dussel has told us much about the outside world we've missed for so long. He had sad news. Countless friends and acquaintances have been taken off to a dreadful fate. Night after night, green and grey military vehicles cruise the streets. They knock on every door, asking whether any Jews live there. If so, the whole family is immediately taken away. If not, they proceed to the next house. It's impossible to escape their clutches unless you go into hiding. They often go around with lists, knocking only on those doors where they know there's a big haul to be made. They frequently offer a bounty, so much per head. It's like the slave hunts of the olden days. I don't mean to make light of this; it's much too tragic for that. In the evenings when it's dark, I often see long lines of good, innocent people, accompanied by crying children, walking on and on, ordered about by a handful of men who bully and beat them until they nearly drop. No one is spared. The sick, the elderly, children, babies and pregnant women – all are marched to their death.

We're so fortunate here, away from the turmoil. We wouldn't have to give a moment's thought to all this suffering if it weren't for the fact that we're so worried about those we hold dear, whom we can no longer help. I feel wicked sleeping in a warm bed, while somewhere out there my dearest friends are dropping from exhaustion or being knocked to the ground.

I get frightened myself when I think of close friends who are now at the mercy of the cruellest monsters ever to stalk the earth.

And all because they're Jews.

Yours, Anne

Dearest Kitty,

*W*e don't really know how to react. Up till now very little news about the Jews had reached us here, and we thought it best to stay as cheerful as possible. Every now and then Miep used to mention what had happened to a friend, and Mother or Mrs van Daan would start to cry, so she decided it was better not to say any more. But we bombarded Mr Dussel with questions, and the stories he had to tell were so gruesome and dreadful that we can't get them out of our heads. Once we've had time to digest the news, we'll probably go back to our usual joking and teasing. It won't do us or those outside any good if we continue to be as gloomy as we are now. And what would be the point of turning the Secret Annexe into a Melancholy Annexe?

No matter what I'm doing, I can't help thinking about those who are gone. I catch myself laughing and remember that it's a disgrace to be so cheerful. But am I supposed to spend the whole day crying? No, I can't do that. This gloom will pass.

Added to this misery there's another, but of a more personal nature, and it pales in comparison to the suffering I've just told you about. Still, I can't help telling you that lately I've begun to feel deserted. I'm surrounded by too great a void. I never used to give it much thought, since my mind was filled with my friends and having a good time. Now I think either about unhappy things or about myself. It's taken a while, but I've finally realized that Father, no matter how kind he may be, can't take the place of my former world. When it comes to my feelings, Mother and Margot ceased to count long ago.

But why do I bother you with this foolishness? I'm terribly ungrateful, Kitty, I know, but when I've been scolded for the umpteenth time and have all these other woes to think about as well, my head begins to reel!

Yours, Anne

SATURDAY, 28 NOVEMBER 1942

Dearest Kitty,

We've been using too much electricity and have now exceeded our ration. The result: excessive economy and the prospect of having the electricity cut off. No light for a fortnight; that's a pleasant thought, isn't it? But who knows, maybe it won't be so long! It's too dark to read after four or four-thirty, so we while away the time with all kinds of crazy activities: telling riddles, doing calisthenics in the dark, speaking English or French, reviewing books – after a while everything gets boring. Yesterday I discovered a new pastime: using a good pair of binoculars to peek into the lighted rooms of the neighbours. During the day our curtains can't be opened, not even an inch, but there's no harm when it's so dark.

I never knew that neighbours could be so interesting. Ours are, at any rate. I've come across a few at dinner, one family making a cine-film and the dentist opposite working on a frightened old lady.

Mr Dussel, the man who was said to get along so well with children and to absolutely adore them, has turned out to be an old-fashioned disciplinarian and preacher of unbearably long sermons on manners. Since I have the singular pleasure (!) of sharing my far too narrow room with His Excellency, and since I'm generally considered to be the worst behaved of the three young people, it's all I can do to avoid having the same old scoldings and admonitions repeatedly flung at my head and to pretend not to hear. This wouldn't be so bad if Mr Dussel weren't such a telltale and hadn't singled out Mother to be the recipient of his reports. If Mr Dussel's just read me the riot act, Mother lectures me all over again, this time throwing the whole book at me. And if I'm really lucky, Mrs van D. calls me to account five minutes later and lays down the law as well!

Really, it's not easy being the badly brought-up centre of attention of a family of nit-pickers.

In bed at night, as I ponder my many sins and exaggerated shortcomings, I get so confused by the sheer amount of things I have to consider that I either laugh or cry, depending on my mood. Then I fall asleep with the strange feeling of wanting to be different from what I am or being different from what I want to be, or perhaps of behaving differently from what I am or want to be.

Oh dear, now I'm confusing you too. Forgive me, but

I don't like crossing things out, and in these times of scarcity, tossing away a piece of paper is clearly taboo. So I can only advise you not to reread the above passage and to make no attempt to get to the bottom of it, because you'll never find your way out again!

Yours, Anne

MONDAY, 7 DECEMBER 1942

Dearest Kitty,

Hanukkah and St Nicholas' Day nearly coincided this year; they were only one day apart. We didn't make much of a fuss with Hanukkah, merely exchanging a few small gifts and lighting the candles. Since candles are in short supply, we lit them for only ten minutes, but as long as we sing the song, that doesn't matter. Mr van Daan made a menorah out of wood, so that was taken care of too.

St Nicholas' Day on Saturday was much more fun. During dinner Bep and Miep were so busy whispering to Father that our curiosity was aroused and we suspected they were up to something. Sure enough, at eight o'clock we all trooped downstairs through the passage in pitch darkness (it gave me the shivers, and I wished I was safely back upstairs!) to the alcove. We could switch on the light, since this room doesn't have any windows. When that was done, Father opened the big cupboard.

'Oh, how wonderful!' we all cried.

In the corner was a large basket decorated with colourful paper and a mask of Black Peter.

We quickly took the basket upstairs with us. Inside was a little gift for everyone, including an appropriate verse. Since you're familiar with the kinds of poems people write each other on St Nicholas' Day, I won't copy them down for you.

I received a doll, Father got bookends, and so on. Well anyway, it was a nice idea, and since the eight of us had never celebrated St Nicholas' Day before, this was a good time to begin.

Yours, Anne

PS. We also had presents for everyone downstairs, a few things left over from the Good Old Days; plus Miep and Bep are always grateful for money.

Today we heard that Mr van Daan's ashtray, Mr

Dussel's picture frame and Father's bookends were made by none other than Mr Voskuijl. How anyone can be so clever with his hands is a mystery to me!

THURSDAY, 10 DECEMBER 1942

Dearest Kitty,

*M*r van Daan used to be in the meat, sausage and spice business. He was hired for his knowledge of spices, and yet, to our great delight, it's his sausage talents that have come in handy now.

We ordered a large amount of meat (under the counter, of course) that we were planning to preserve in case there were hard times ahead. Mr van Daan decided to make bratwurst, sausages and mettwurst. I had fun watching him put the meat through the mincer: once, twice, three times. Then he added the remaining ingredients to the minced meat and used a long pipe to force the mixture into the casings. We ate the bratwurst with sauerkraut for lunch, but the sausages, which were going to be preserved, had to dry first, so we hung them over a pole suspended from the ceiling. Everyone who came into the room burst into laughter when they saw the dangling sausages. It was such a comical sight.

The kitchen was a shambles. Mr van Daan, clad in his wife's apron and looking fatter than ever, was working away at the meat. Wha᷈ with his bloody hands, red face and spotted apron, he looked like a real butcher. Mrs van D. was trying to do everything at once: learning Dutch out of a book, stirring the soup, watching the meat, sighing and moaning about her broken rib. That's what happens when old (!) ladies do such stupid exercises to get rid of their fat behinds! Dussel had an eye infection and was sitting next to the stove dabbing his eye with camomile tea. Pim, seated in the one ray of sunshine coming through the window, kept having to move his chair this way and that to stay out of the way. His rheumatism must have been bothering him because he was slightly hunched over and was keeping an eye on Mr van Daan with an agonized expression on his face. He reminded me of those aged invalids you see in the poorhouse. Peter was romping around the room with Mouschi, the cat, while Mother, Margot and I were peeling boiled potatoes. When you get right down to it, none of us was doing our work properly, because we were all so busy watching Mr van Daan.

Dussel has opened his dental practice. Just for fun, I'll describe the session with his very first patient.

Mother was ironing, and Mrs van D., the first victim, sat down on a chair in the middle of the room. Dussel, unpacking his case with an air of importance, asked for some eau-de-Cologne, which could be used as a disinfectant, and Vaseline, which would have to do for wax. He looked in Mrs van D.'s mouth and found two teeth that made her wince with pain and utter incoherent cries every time he touched them. After a lengthy examination (lengthy as far as Mrs van D. was concerned, since it actually took no longer than two minutes), Dussel began to scrape out a cavity. But Mrs van D. had no intention of letting him. She flailed her arms and legs until Dussel finally let go of his probe and . . . it remained stuck in Mrs van D.'s tooth. That really did it! Mrs van D. lashed out wildly in all directions, cried (as much as you can with an instrument like that in your mouth), tried to remove it, but only managed to push it in even farther. Mr Dussel calmly observed the scene, his hands on his hips, while the rest of the audience roared with laughter. Of course, that was very mean of us. If it'd been me, I'm sure I would have yelled even louder. After a great deal of squirming, kicking, screaming and shouting, Mrs van D. finally managed to yank the thing out, and Mr Dussel went on with his work as if nothing had happened. He was so quick that Mrs van D. didn't have time to pull any more shenanigans. But then, he had more help than he's ever had before: no fewer than two assistants; Mr van D. and I performed our job well. The whole scene resembled one of those engravings from the Middle Ages entitled 'A Quack at Work'. In the mean time, however, the patient was getting restless, since she had to keep an eye on 'her' soup and 'her' food. One thing is certain: it'll be a while before Mrs van D. makes another dental appointment!

Yours, Anne

Dearest Kitty,

I'm sitting here nice and cosy in the front office, peering out through a chink in the heavy curtains. It's dark, but there's just enough light to write by.

It's really strange watching people walk past. They all seem to be in such a hurry that they nearly trip over their own feet. Those on bicycles whiz by so fast I can't even tell who's on the bike. The people in this neighbourhood aren't particularly attractive to look at. The children especially are so dirty you wouldn't want to touch them with a bargepole. Real slum kids with runny noses. I can hardly understand a word they say.

Yesterday afternoon, when Margot and I were taking a bath, I said, 'What if we took a fishing rod and reeled in each of those kids one by one as they walked by, stuck them in the tub, washed and mended their clothes and then . . .'

'And then tomorrow they'd be just as dirty and tattered as they were before,' Margot replied.

But I'm babbling. There are also other things to look at: cars, boats and the rain. I can hear the tram and the children and I'm enjoying myself.

Our thoughts are subject to as little change as we are. They're like a merry-go-round, turning from the Jews to food, from food to politics. By the way, speaking of Jews, I saw two yesterday when I was peeking through the curtains. I felt as though I were gazing at one of the

Seven Wonders of the World. It gave me such a funny feeling, as if I'd denounced them to the authorities and was now spying on their misfortune.

Opposite us is a houseboat. The captain lives there with his wife and children. He has a small yapping dog. We know the little dog only by its bark and by its tail, which we can see whenever it runs round the deck. Oh, what a shame, it's just started raining and most of the people are hidden under their umbrellas. All I can see are raincoats, and now and again the back of a stocking-capped head. Actually, I don't even need to look. By now I can recognize the women at a glance: gone to fat from eating potatoes, dressed in a red or green coat and worn-out shoes, a shopping bag dangling from their arms, with faces that are either grim or good-humoured, depending on the mood of their husbands.

Yours, Anne

TUESDAY, 22 DECEMBER 1942

Dearest Kitty,

The Annexe was delighted to hear that we'll all be receiving an extra quarter of a pound of butter for Christmas. According to the newspaper, everyone is entitled to half a pound, but they mean those lucky souls who get their ration books from the government, not

Jews in hiding like us who can only afford to buy four rather than eight ration books on the black market. Each of us is going to bake something with the butter. This morning I made two cakes and some biscuits. It's very busy upstairs, and Mother has informed me that I'm not to do any studying or reading until all the household tasks have been finished.

Mrs van Daan is lying in bed nursing her bruised rib. She complains all day long, constantly demands that the bandages be changed and is generally dissatisfied with everything. I'll be glad when she gets back on her feet and can clean up after herself because, I must admit, she's extraordinarily hardworking and neat, and as long as she's in good physical and mental condition, she's quite cheerful.

As if I don't hear 'shh, shh' enough during the day because I'm always making 'too much' noise, my dear room-mate has come up with the idea of saying 'shh, shh' to me all night too. According to him, I shouldn't even turn over. I refuse to take any notice of him, and the next time he shushes me, I'm going to shush him right back.

He gets more exasperating and egotistical as the days go by. Except for the first week, I haven't seen even one of the biscuits he so generously promised me. He's particularly infuriating on Sundays, when he switches on the light at the crack of dawn to exercise for ten minutes.

To me, the torment seems to last for hours, since the chairs I use to make my bed longer are constantly being jiggled under my sleepy head. After rounding off his limbering-up exercises with a few vigorous arm swings, His Lordship begins dressing. His underwear is hanging on a hook, so first he lumbers over to get it and then lumbers back, past my bed. But his tie is on the table, so once again he pushes and bumps his way past the chairs.

But I mustn't waste any more of your time griping about disgusting old men. It won't help matters anyway. My plans for revenge, such as unscrewing the light bulb, locking the door and hiding his clothes, have unfortunately had to be abandoned in the interests of peace.

Oh, I'm becoming so sensible! We've got to be reasonable about everything we do here: studying, listening, holding our tongues, helping others, being kind, making compromises and I don't know what else! I'm afraid my common sense, which was in short supply to begin with, will be used up too quickly and I won't have any left by the time the war is over.

Yours, Anne

WEDNESDAY, 13 JANUARY 1943

Dearest Kitty,

This morning I was constantly interrupted, and as a result I haven't been able to finish a single thing I've begun.

We have a new pastime, namely, filling packets with powdered gravy. The gravy is one of Gies & Co.'s products. Mr Kugler hasn't been able to find anyone else to fill the packets, and besides, it's cheaper if we do the job. It's the kind of work they do in prisons. It's incredibly boring and makes us dizzy and giggly.

Terrible things are happening outside. At any time of night and day, poor helpless people are being dragged out of their homes. They're allowed to take only a rucksack and a little cash with them, and even then, they're robbed of these possessions on the way. Families are torn apart; men, women and children are separated. Children come home from school to find that their parents have disappeared. Women return from shopping to find their houses sealed, their families gone. The Christians in Holland are also living in fear because their sons are being sent to Germany. Everyone is scared. Every night hundreds of planes pass over Holland on their way to German cities, to sow their bombs on German soil. Every hour hundreds, or maybe even thousands, of people are being killed in Russia and Africa. No one can keep out of the conflict, the entire world is at war, and even though the Allies are doing better, the end is nowhere in sight.

As for us, we're quite fortunate. Luckier than millions of people. It's quiet and safe here, and we're using our money to buy food. We're so selfish that we talk about 'after the war' and look forward to new clothes and shoes, when actually we should be saving every penny to help others when the war is over, to salvage whatever we can.

The children in this neighbourhood run around in

thin shirts and wooden clogs. They have no coats, no socks, no caps and no one to help them. Gnawing on a carrot to still their hunger pangs, they walk from their cold houses through cold streets to an even colder classroom. Things have got so bad in Holland that hordes of children stop passers-by in the streets to beg for a piece of bread.

I could spend hours telling you about the suffering the war has brought, but I'd only make myself more miserable. All we can do is wait, as calmly as possible, for it to end. Jews and Christians alike are waiting, the whole world is waiting, and many are waiting for death.

Yours, Anne

Dearest Kitty,

I'm seething with rage, yet I can't show it. I'd like to scream, stamp my foot, give Mother a good shaking, cry and I don't know what else because of the nasty words, mocking looks and accusations that she hurls at me day after day, piercing me like arrows from a tightly strung bow, which are nearly impossible to pull from my body. I'd like to scream at Mother, Margot, the van Daans, Dussel and Father too: 'Leave me alone, let me have at least one night when I don't cry myself to sleep with my eyes burning and my head pounding. Let me get away, away from everything, away from this world!' But I can't do that. I can't let them see my doubts, or the wounds they've inflicted on me. I couldn't bear their sympathy or their good-humoured derision. It would only make me want to scream even more.

Everyone thinks I'm showing off when I talk, ridiculous when I'm silent, insolent when I answer, cunning when I have a good idea, lazy when I'm tired, selfish when I eat one bite more than I should, stupid, cowardly, calculating, etc., etc. All day long I hear nothing but what an exasperating child I am, and although I laugh it off and pretend not to mind, I do mind. I wish I could ask God to give me another personality, one that doesn't antagonize everyone.

But that's impossible. I'm stuck with the character I was born with, and yet I'm sure I'm not a bad person. I do my best to please everyone, more than they'd ever suspect in a million years. When I'm upstairs, I try to laugh it off because I don't want them to see my troubles.

More than once, after a series of absurd reproaches, I've snapped at Mother: 'I don't care what you say. Why don't you just wash your hands of me – I'm a hopeless case.' Of course, she'd tell me not to talk back and virtually ignore me for two days. Then suddenly all would be forgotten and she'd treat me like everyone else.

It's impossible for me to be all smiles one day and venomous the next. I'd rather choose the golden mean, which isn't so golden, and keep my thoughts to myself. Perhaps sometime I'll treat the others with the same contempt as they treat me. Oh, if only I could.

Yours, Anne

FRIDAY, 5 FEBRUARY 1943

Dearest Kitty,

Though it's been ages since I've written to you about the squabbles, there's still no change. In the beginning Mr Dussel took our soon-forgotten clashes very seriously, but now he's grown used to them and no longer tries to mediate.

Margot and Peter aren't exactly what you'd call 'young'; they're both so quiet and boring. Next to them,

I stick out like a sore thumb, and I'm always being told, 'Margot and Peter don't act that way. Why don't you follow your sister's example!' I hate that.

I confess that I have absolutely no desire to be like Margot. She's too weak-willed and passive to suit me; she lets herself be swayed by others and always gives way under pressure. I want to have more backbone! But I keep ideas like these to myself. They'd only laugh at me if I offered this in my defence.

During meals the air is filled with tension. Fortunately, the outbursts are sometimes held in check by the 'soup eaters', the people from the office who come up to have a cup of soup for lunch.

This afternoon Mr van Daan again brought up the fact that Margot eats so little. 'I suppose you do it to keep your figure,' he added in a mocking tone.

Mother, who always comes to Margot's defence, said in a loud voice, 'I can't stand that stupid chatter of yours a minute longer.'

Mrs van D. turned red as a beetroot. Mr van D. stared straight ahead and said nothing.

Still, we often have a good laugh. Not long ago Mrs van D. was entertaining us with some bit of nonsense or other. She was talking about the past, about how well she got along with her father and what a flirt he was. 'And you know,' she continued, 'my father told me that if a gentleman ever got fresh, I was to say, "Remember, sir, that I'm a lady," and he'd know what I meant.' We split our sides laughing, as if she'd told us a good joke.

Even Peter, though he's usually quiet, occasionally

gives rise to hilarity. He has the misfortune of adoring foreign words without knowing what they mean. One afternoon we couldn't use the lavatory because there were visitors in the office. Unable to wait, he went to the toilet but didn't flush it. To warn us of the unpleasant smell, he tacked a sign to the door: 'RSVP – gas!'. Of course, he meant 'Danger – gas!' but he thought 'RSVP' looked more elegant. He didn't have the faintest idea that it meant 'please reply'.

Yours, Anne

SATURDAY, 27 FEBRUARY 1943

Dearest Kitty,

*P*im is expecting the invasion any day now. Churchill has had pneumonia, but is gradually getting better. Gandhi, the champion of Indian freedom, is on one of his umpteenth hunger strikes.

Mrs van D. claims she's fatalistic. But who's the most afraid when the guns go off? None other than Petronella van Daan.

Jan brought along the episcopal letter that the bishops addressed to their parishioners. It was beautiful and inspiring. 'People of the Netherlands, stand up and take action. Each of us must choose our own weapons to fight for the freedom of our country, our people and our religion!

Give your help and support. Act now!' This is what they're preaching from the pulpit. Will it do any good? It's definitely too late to help our fellow Jews.

Guess what's happened to us now? The owner of the building sold it without informing Mr Kugler and Mr Kleiman. One morning the new landlord arrived with an architect to look the place over. Thank goodness Mr Kleiman was in the office. He showed the gentlemen all there was to see, with the exception of the Secret Annexe. He claimed he'd left the key at home and the new owner asked no further questions. If only he doesn't come back demanding to see the Annexe. In that case, we'll be in big trouble!

Father emptied a card file for Margot and me and filled it with index cards that are blank on one side. This is to become our reading file, in which Margot and I are supposed to note down the books we've read, the author and the date. I've learned two new words: 'brothel' and 'coquette'. I've bought a separate exercise-book for new words.

There's a new division of butter and margarine. Each person is to get their portion on their own plate. The distribution is very unfair. The van Daans, who always make breakfast for everyone, give themselves one and a half times more than they do us. My parents are much too afraid of an argument to say anything, which is a shame, because I think people like that should always be given a taste of their own medicine.

Yours, Anne

THURSDAY, 4 MARCH 1943

Dearest Kitty,

*M*rs van D. has a new nickname – we've started calling her Mrs Beaverbrook. Of course, that doesn't mean anything to you, so let me explain. A certain Mr Beaverbrook often talks on the English radio about what he considers to be the far too lenient bombardment of Germany. Mrs van Daan, who always contradicts everyone, including Churchill and the news reports, is in complete agreement with Mr Beaverbrook. So we thought it would be a good idea for her to be married to him, and since she was flattered by the notion, we've decided to call her Mrs Beaverbrook from now on.

We're getting a new warehouse employee, since the old one is being sent to Germany. That's bad for him but good for us because the new one won't be familiar with the building. We're still afraid of the men who work in the warehouse.

Gandhi is eating again.

The black market is doing a booming business. If we had enough money to pay the ridiculous prices, we could stuff ourselves silly. Our greengrocer buys potatoes from the 'Wehrmacht' and brings them in sacks to the private office. Since he suspects we're hiding here, he makes a point of coming during lunchtime, when the warehouse employees are out.

So much pepper is being ground at the moment that we sneeze and cough with every breath we take. Everyone who comes upstairs greets us with an 'ah-CHOO'. Mrs van D. swears she won't go downstairs; one more whiff of pepper and she's going to be ill.

I don't think Father has a very nice business. Nothing but pectin and pepper. As long as you're in the food business, why not make sweets?

A veritable thunderstorm of words came crashing down on me again this morning. The air flashed with so many coarse expressions that my ears were ringing with 'Anne's bad this' and 'van Daans' good that'. Fire and brimstone!

Yours, Anne

WEDNESDAY, 10 MARCH 1943

Dearest Kitty,

We had a short circuit last night, and besides that, the guns were booming away until dawn. I still haven't got over my fear of planes and shooting, and I crawl into Father's bed nearly every night for comfort. I know it sounds childish, but wait till it happens to you! The ack-ack guns make so much noise you can't hear your own voice. Mrs Beaverbrook, the fatalist, practically burst into tears and said in a timid little voice, 'Oh, it's so awful. Oh, the guns are so loud!' – which is another way of saying 'I'm so scared'.

It didn't seem nearly as bad by candlelight as it did in

the dark. I was shivering, as if I had a temperature, and begged Father to relight the candle. He was adamant: there was to be no light. Suddenly we heard a burst of machine-gun fire, and that's ten times worse than anti-aircraft guns. Mother jumped out of bed and, to Pim's great annoyance, lit the candle. Her resolute answer to his grumbling was, 'After all, Anne is not an ex-soldier!' And that was the end of that!

Have I told you any of Mrs van D.'s other fears? I don't think so. To keep you up to date on the latest adventures in the Secret Annexe, I should tell you this as well. One night Mrs van D. thought she heard loud footsteps in the attic, and she was so afraid of burglars, she woke her husband. At that very same moment, the thieves disappeared, and the only sound Mr van D. could hear was the frightened pounding of his fatalistic wife's heart. 'Oh, Putti!' she cried. (Putti is Mrs van D.'s pet name for her husband.) 'They must have taken all our sausages and dried beans. And what about Peter? Oh, do you think Peter's still safe and sound in his bed?'

'I'm sure they haven't stolen Peter. Stop being such a ninny, and let me get back to sleep!'

Impossible. Mrs van D. was too scared to sleep.

A few nights later the entire van Daan family was awakened by ghostly noises. Peter went to the attic with a torch and – scurry, scurry – what do you think he saw running away? A swarm of enormous rats!

Once we knew who the thieves were, we let Mouschi sleep in the attic and never saw our uninvited guests again . . . at least not at night.

A few evenings ago (it was seven-thirty and still light), Peter went up to the loft to get some old newspapers. He had to hold on tightly to the trapdoor to climb down the ladder. He put down his hand without looking, and nearly fell off the ladder from shock and pain. Without realizing it, he'd put his hand on a large rat, which had bitten him in the arm. By the time he reached us, white as a sheet and with his knees knocking, the blood had soaked through his pyjamas. No wonder he was so shaken – stroking a rat isn't much fun, especially when it takes a chunk out of your arm.

Yours, Anne

FRIDAY, 12 MARCH 1943

Dearest Kitty,

*M*ay I introduce: Mother Frank, the children's advocate! Extra butter for the youngsters, the problems facing today's youth – you name it, and she defends the younger generation. After a skirmish or two, she always gets her way.

One of the jars of pickled tongue has gone off. A feast for Mouschi and Boche.

You haven't met Boche yet, despite the fact that she was here before we went into hiding. She's the warehouse and office cat, who keeps the rats at bay in the storeroom.

Her odd, political name can easily be explained. For a while the firm of Gies & Co. had two cats: one for the warehouse and one for the attic. Their paths crossed from time to time, which invariably resulted in a fight. The warehouse cat was always the aggressor, while the attic cat was ultimately the victor, just as in politics. So the warehouse cat was named the German, or 'Boche', and the attic cat the Englishman, or 'Tommy'. Some time after that they got rid of Tommy, but Boche is always there to amuse us when we go downstairs.

We've eaten so many brown beans and haricot beans that I can't stand to look at them. Just thinking about them makes me sick.

Our evening serving of bread has been cancelled.

Daddy just said that he's not in a very cheerful mood. His eyes look so sad again, the poor man!

I can't tear myself away from the book *A Knock at the Door* by Ina Bakker Boudier. This family saga is extremely well written, but the parts dealing with war, writers and the emancipation of women aren't very good. To be honest, these subjects don't interest me much.

Terrible bombing raids on Germany. Mr van Daan is grumpy. The reason: the cigarette shortage.

The debate about whether or not to start eating the tinned food ended in our favour.

I can't wear any of my shoes, except my ski boots, which are not very practical around the house. A pair of straw sandals that were purchased for 6.50 guilders were worn down to the soles within a week. Maybe Miep will be able to dig up something on the black market.

It's time to cut Father's hair. Pim swears that I do such a good job he'll never go to another barber after the war. If only I didn't nick his ear so often!

Yours, Anne

THURSDAY, 18 MARCH 1943

My dearest Kitty,

Turkey's entered the war. Great excitement. Anxiously awaiting radio reports.

FRIDAY, 19 MARCH 1943

Dearest Kitty,

In less than an hour, joy was followed by disappointment. Turkey hasn't entered the war yet. It was only a cabinet minister talking about Turkey giving up its neutrality some time soon. The newspaper-seller in Dam Square was shouting 'Turkey on England's side!' and the papers were being snatched out of his hands. This was how we'd heard the encouraging rumour.

Thousand-guilder notes are being declared invalid.

That'll be a blow to the black marketeers and others like them, but even more to people in hiding and anyone else with money that can't be accounted for. To turn in a thousand-guilder note, you have to be able to state how you came by it and provide proof. They can still be used to pay taxes, but only until next week. The five-hundred notes will lapse at the same time. Gies & Co. still had some unaccounted-for thousand-guilder notes, which they used to pay their estimated taxes for the coming years, so everything seems to be above board.

Dussel has received an old-fashioned, foot-operated dentist's drill. That means I'll probably be getting a thorough check-up soon.

Dussel is terribly lax when it comes to obeying the rules of the house. Not only does he write letters to his Charlotte, he's also carrying on a chatty correspondence with various other people. Margot, the Annexe's Dutch teacher, has been correcting these letters for him. Father has forbidden him to keep up the practice and Margot has stopped correcting the letters, but I think it won't be long before he starts up again.

The Führer has been talking to wounded soldiers. We heard him on the radio, and it was pathetic. The questions and answers went something like this:

'My name is Heinrich Scheppel.'

'Where were you wounded?'

'Near Stalingrad.'

'What kind of wound is it?'

'Two frostbitten feet and a fracture of the left arm.'

This is an exact report of the hideous puppet show

aired on the radio. The wounded seemed proud of their wounds – the more the better. One was so beside himself at the thought of shaking hands (I presume he still had one) with the Führer that he could barely say a word.

I happened to drop Dussel's soap on the floor and step on it. Now there's a whole piece missing. I've already asked Father to compensate him for the damages, especially since Dussel only gets one bar of inferior wartime soap a month.

Yours, Anne

THURSDAY, 25 MARCH 1943

Dearest Kitty,

Mother, Father, Margot and I were sitting quite pleasantly together last night when Peter suddenly came in and whispered in Father's ear. I caught the words 'a barrel falling over in the warehouse' and 'someone fiddling with the door'.

Margot heard it too, but was trying to calm me down, since I'd turned white as chalk and was extremely nervous. The three of us waited while Father and Peter went downstairs. A minute or two later Mrs van Daan came up from where she'd been listening to the radio and told us that Pim had asked her to turn it off and tiptoe upstairs. But you know what happens when you're trying to be quiet – the old stairs creaked twice as loud. Five minutes later Peter and Pim, the colour drained from their faces, appeared again to relate their experiences.

They had positioned themselves under the staircase and waited. Nothing happened. Then all of a sudden they heard a couple of bangs, as if two doors had been slammed shut inside the house. Pim bounded up the stairs, while Peter went to warn Dussel, who finally presented himself upstairs, though not without kicking up a fuss and making a lot of noise. Then we all tiptoed in our stockinged feet to the van Daans on the next floor. Mr van D. had a bad cold and had already gone to bed, so we gathered around his bedside and discussed our suspicions in a whisper. Every time Mr van D. coughed loudly, Mrs van D. and I nearly had a nervous fit. He kept coughing until someone came up with the bright idea of giving him codeine. His cough subsided immediately.

Once again we waited and waited, but heard nothing. Finally we came to the conclusion that the burglars had taken to their heels when they heard footsteps in an otherwise quiet building. The problem now was that the chairs in the private office were neatly grouped around the radio, which was tuned to England. If the burglars had forced the door and the air-raid wardens were to notice it and call the police, there could be very serious repercussions. So Mr van Daan got up, pulled on his coat and trousers, put on his hat and cautiously followed Father down the stairs, with Peter (armed with a heavy hammer, to be on the safe side) right behind him. The ladies (including Margot and me) waited in suspense until the men returned five minutes later and reported that there was no sign of any activity in the building. We agreed not to run any water or flush the toilet; but since everyone's stomach was churning from all the tension, you can imagine the stench after we'd each had a turn in the lavatory.

Incidents like these are always accompanied by other disasters, and this was no exception. Number one: the Westertoren bells stopped chiming, and I'd always found them so comforting. Number two: Mr Voskuijl left early last night, and we weren't sure if he'd given Bep the key and she'd forgotten to lock the door.

But that was of little importance now. The night had just begun, and we still weren't sure what to expect. We were somewhat reassured by the fact that between eight-fifteen – when the burglar had first entered the building and put our lives in jeopardy – and ten-thirty, we hadn't heard a sound. The more we thought about it, the less likely it seemed that a burglar would have forced a door so early in the evening, when there were still people out on the streets. Besides that, it occurred to us that the warehouse manager at the Keg Company next door might still have been at work. What with the excitement and the thin walls, it's easy to mistake the sounds. Besides, your imagination often plays tricks on you in moments of danger.

So we went to bed, though not to sleep. Father and Mother and Mr Dussel were awake most of the night, and I'm not exaggerating when I say that I hardly got a wink of sleep. This morning the men went downstairs to see if the outside door was still locked, but all was well!

Of course, we gave the entire office staff a blow-by-blow account of the incident, which had been far from pleasant. It's much easier to laugh at these kinds of things after they've happened, and Bep was the only one who took us seriously.

Yours, Anne

PS. This morning the toilet was clogged, and Father had to stick a long wooden pole and fish out several pounds of excrement and strawberry recipes (which is what we use for toilet paper these days). Afterwards we burned the pole.

SATURDAY, 27 MARCH 1943

Dearest Kitty,

*W*e've finished our shorthand course and are now working on improving our speed. Aren't we clever! Let me tell you more about my 'time killers' (this is what I call my courses, because all we ever do is try to make the days go by as quickly as possible so we're that much closer to the end of our time here). I adore mythology, especially the Greek and Roman gods. Everyone here thinks my interest is just a passing fancy,

since they've never heard of a teenager with an appreciation of mythology. Well then, I suppose I'm the first!

Mr van Daan has a cold. Or rather, he has a scratchy
throat, but he's making an enormous to-do over it. He
gargles with camomile tea, coats the roof of his mouth
with a tincture of myrrh and rubs Vick on his chest, nose,
gums and tongue. And to top it off, he's in a foul mood!

Rauter, some German bigwig, recently gave a speech.
'All Jews must be out of the German-occupied territories
before 1 July. The province of Utrecht will be cleansed
of Jews [as if they were cockroaches] between 1 April and
1 May, and the provinces of North and South Holland
between 1 May and 1 June.' These poor people are being
shipped off to filthy slaughterhouses like a herd of sick
and neglected cattle. But I'll say no more on the subject.
My own thoughts give me nightmares!

One good piece of news is that the Labour Exchange
was set on fire in an act of sabotage. A few days later the
Register Office also went up in flames. Men posing as
German police bound and gagged the guards and managed to destroy some important documents.

Yours, Anne

Dearest Kitty,

I'm not really in the mood for pranks (see the date). On the contrary, today I can safely quote the saying 'Misfortunes never come singly'.

First, Mr Kleiman, our merry ray of sunshine, had another bout of gastro-intestinal haemorrhaging yesterday and will have to stay in bed for at least three weeks. I should tell you that his stomach has been bothering him quite a bit, and there's no cure. Second, Bep has flu. Third, Mr Voskuijl has to go into hospital next week. He probably has an ulcer and will have to undergo surgery. Fourth, the managers of Pomosin Industries came from Frankfurt to discuss the new Opekta deliveries. Father had gone over the important points with Mr Kleiman, and there wasn't enough time to give Mr Kugler a thorough briefing.

The gentlemen arrived from Frankfurt, and Father was already shaking at the thought of how the talks would go. 'If only I could be there, if only I were downstairs,' he exclaimed.

'Go and lie down with your ear to the floor. They'll be brought to the private office, and you'll be able to hear everything.'

Father's face cleared, and yesterday morning at ten-thirty Margot and Pim (two ears are better than one) took up their posts on the floor. By noon the talks weren't finished, but Father was in no shape to continue his listening campaign. He was in agony from having to lie for hours in such an unusual and uncomfortable position. At two-thirty we heard voices in the passage, and I took his place; Margot kept me company. The conversation was so long-winded and boring that I suddenly fell asleep on the cold, hard linoleum. Margot didn't dare touch me for fear they'd hear us, and of course she couldn't shout. I slept for a good half-hour and then awoke with a start, having forgotten every word of the important discussion. Luckily, Margot had paid more attention.

Yours, Anne

FRIDAY, 2 APRIL 1943

Dearest Kitty,

Oh my, another item has been added to my list of sins. Last night I was lying in bed, waiting for Father to tuck me in and say my prayers with me, when Mother came into the room, sat on my bed and asked very gently, 'Anne, Daddy isn't ready. What if I listen to your prayers tonight?'

'No, Mumsie,' I replied.

Mother got up, stood beside my bed for a moment and then slowly walked towards the door. Suddenly she turned, her face contorted with pain, and said, 'I don't want to be angry with you. I can't make you love me!'

A few tears slid down her cheeks as she went out of the door.

I lay still, thinking how mean it was of me to reject her so cruelly, but I also knew that I was incapable of answering her any other way. I can't be a hypocrite and pray with her when I don't feel like it. It just doesn't work that way. I felt sorry for Mother – very, very sorry – because for the first time in my life I noticed she wasn't indifferent to my coldness. I saw the sorrow in her face when she talked about not being able to make me love her. It's hard to tell the truth, and yet the truth is that she's the one who's rejected me. She's the one whose tactless comments and cruel jokes about matters I don't think are funny have made me insensitive to any sign of love on her part. Just as my heart sinks every time I hear her harsh words, that's how her heart sank when she realized there was no more love between us.

She cried half the night and didn't get any sleep. Father has avoided looking at me, and if his eyes do happen to meet mine, I can read his unspoken words: 'How can you be so unkind? How dare you make your mother so sad!'

Everyone expects me to apologize, but this is not something I can apologize for, because I told the truth, and sooner or later Mother was bound to find out anyway. I seem to be indifferent to Mother's tears and Father's glances, and I am, because both of them are now feeling what I've always felt. I can only feel sorry for Mother, who will have to decide what her attitude should be all by herself. For my part, I will continue to remain silent and aloof, and I don't intend to shrink from the truth, because the longer it's postponed, the harder it will be for them to accept it when they do hear it!

Yours, Anne

Dearest Kitty,

The house is still trembling from the after-effects of the quarrels. Everyone is angry with everyone else: Mother and I, Mr van Daan and Father, Mother and Mrs van D. Terrific atmosphere, don't you think? Once again Anne's usual list of shortcomings has been extensively aired.

Our German visitors were back last Saturday. They stayed until six. We all sat upstairs, not daring to move an inch. If there's no one else working in the building or in the neighbourhood, you can hear every single step in the private office. I've got ants in my pants again from having to sit still so long.

Mr Voskuijl has been hospitalized, but Mr Kleiman's back at the office. His stomach stopped bleeding sooner than it normally does. He told us that the Register Office took an extra beating because the firemen flooded the entire building instead of just putting out the fire. That does my heart good!

The Carlton Hotel has been destroyed. Two British planes loaded with firebombs landed right on top of the German Officers' Club. The entire corner of Vijzelstraat and Singel has gone up in flames. The number of air strikes on German cities is increasing daily. We haven't had a good night's rest in ages, and I have bags under my eyes from lack of sleep.

Our food is terrible. Breakfast consists of plain, unbuttered bread and ersatz coffee. For the last two weeks lunch has been either spinach or cooked lettuce with huge potatoes that have a rotten, sweetish taste. If you're trying to slim, the Annexe is the place to be! Upstairs they complain bitterly, but we don't think it's such a tragedy.

All the Dutch men who either fought or were mobilized in 1940 have been called up to work in prisoner-of-war camps. I bet they're taking this precaution because of the invasion!

Yours, Anne

SATURDAY, 1 MAY 1943

Dearest Kitty,

Yesterday was Dussel's birthday. At first he acted as if he didn't want to celebrate it, but when Miep arrived with a large shopping bag overflowing with gifts, he was as excited as a little child. His darling 'Lotje' had sent him eggs, butter, biscuits, lemonade, bread, cognac, spice cake, flowers, oranges, chocolate, books and writing paper. He piled his presents on a table and displayed them for no fewer than three days, the ridiculous old fool!

You mustn't get the idea that he's starving. We found bread, cheese, jam and eggs in his cupboard. It's absolutely disgraceful that Dussel, whom we've treated with such kindness and whom we took in to save from destruction, should stuff himself behind our backs and not give us anything. After all, we've shared all we had with him! But what's worse, in our opinion, is that he's so stingy with respect to Mr Kleiman, Mr Voskuijl and Bep. He doesn't give them a thing. In Dussel's view the oranges that Kleiman so badly needs for his sick stomach will benefit his own stomach even more.

Tonight the guns have been banging away so much that I've already had to gather up my belongings four times. Today I packed a suitcase with the stuff I'd need in case we had to flee, but as Mother correctly noted, 'Where would you go?'

All of Holland is being punished for the workers' strikes. Martial law has been declared, and everyone is going to get one less butter coupon. What naughty children.

I washed Mother's hair this evening, which is no easy task these days. We have to use a very sticky liquid cleanser because there's no more shampoo. Besides that, Mums had a hard time combing her hair because the family comb has only ten teeth left.

Yours, Anne

*W*hen I think about our lives here, I usually come to the conclusion that we live in a paradise compared with the Jews who aren't in hiding. All the same, later on, when everything has returned to normal, I'll probably wonder how we, who always lived in such comfortable circumstances, could have 'sunk' so low. With respect to manners, I mean. For example, the same oilcloth has covered the dining-table ever since we've been here. After so much use, it's hardly what you'd call spotless. I do my best to clean it, but since the dishcloth was also purchased before we went into hiding and consists of more holes than cloth, it's a thankless task. The van Daans have been sleeping all winter long on the same flannelette sheet, which can't be washed because soap powder is rationed and in short supply. Besides, it's of such poor quality that it's practically useless. Father is walking around in frayed trousers, and his tie is also showing signs of wear and tear. Mummy's corset snapped today and is beyond repair, while Margot is wearing a bra that's two sizes too small. Mother and Margot have shared the same three vests the entire winter, and mine are so small they don't even cover my stomach. These are all things that can be overcome, but I sometimes wonder: how can we, whose every possession, from my knickers to Father's shaving brush, is so old and worn, ever hope to regain the position we had before the war?

The Attitude of the Annexe Residents Towards the War

*M*r *van Daan*. In the opinion of us all, this revered gentleman has great insight into politics. Nevertheless, he predicts we'll have to stay here until the end of '43. That's a very long time, and yet it's possible to hold out until then. But who can assure us that this war, which has caused nothing but pain and sorrow, will then be over? And that nothing will have happened to us and our helpers long before that time? No one! That's why each and every day is filled with tension. Expectation and hope generate tension, as does fear – for example, when we hear a noise inside or outside the house, when the guns go off or when we read new 'proclamations' in the paper, since we're afraid our helpers might be forced to go into hiding themselves sometime. These days everyone is talking about having to hide. We don't know how many people are actually in hiding; of course, the number is relatively small compared with the general population, but later on we'll no doubt be astonished at how many good people in Holland were willing to take Jews and Christians, with or without money, into their homes. There're also an unbelievable number of people with false identity papers.

Mrs van Daan. When this beautiful damsel (by her own account) heard that it was getting easier these days to obtain false IDs, she immediately proposed that we each have one made. As if there were nothing to it, as if Father and Mr van Daan were made of money.

Mrs van Daan is always saying the most ridiculous things, and her Putti is often exasperated. But that's not surprising, because one day Kerli announces, 'When this is all over, I'm going to have myself baptized'; and the next, 'As long as I can remember, I've wanted to go to Jerusalem. I only feel at home with other Jews!'

Pim is a big optimist, but he always has his reasons.

Mr Dussel makes up everything as he goes along, and anyone wishing to contradict His Majesty had better think twice. In Albert Dussel's home his word is law, but that doesn't suit Anne Frank in the least.

What the other members of the Annexe family think about the war doesn't matter. When it comes to politics, these four are the only ones who count. Actually, only two of them do, but Madame van Daan and Dussel include themselves as well.

TUESDAY, 18 MAY 1943

Dearest Kit,

I recently witnessed a fierce dogfight between German and English pilots. Unfortunately, a couple of Allied airmen had to jump out of their burning plane. Our milkman, who lives in Halfweg, saw four Canadians sitting along the side of the road, and one of them spoke fluent Dutch. He asked the milkman if he had a light for his cigarette, and then told him the crew had consisted of six men. The pilot had been burned to death, and the fifth crew member had hidden himself somewhere. The German Security Police came to pick up the four remaining men, none of whom was injured. After parachuting out of a flaming plane, how can anyone have such presence of mind?

Although it's undeniably hot, we have to light a fire every other day to burn our vegetable peelings and rubbish. We can't throw anything into the dustbins, because the warehouse employees might see it. One small act of carelessness and we're done for!

All university students are being asked to sign an official statement to the effect that they 'sympathize with the Germans and approve of the New Order'. Eighty per cent have decided to obey the dictates of their conscience, but the penalty will be severe. Any student refusing to sign will be sent to a German labour camp. What's to become of the youth of our country if they've all got to do hard labour in Germany?

Last night the guns were making so much noise that Mother shut the window; I was in Pim's bed. Suddenly, right above our heads, we heard Mrs van D. leap up, as if she'd been bitten by Mouschi. This was followed by a loud boom, which sounded as if a firebomb had landed beside my bed. 'Lights! Lights!' I screamed.

Pim switched on the lamp. I expected the room to burst into flames any minute. Nothing happened. We all rushed upstairs to see what was going on. Mr and Mrs van D. had seen a red glow through the open window, and he thought there was a fire near by, while she was certain· our house was ablaze. Mrs van D. was already standing beside her bed with her knees knocking when the boom came. Dussel stayed upstairs to smoke a cigarette, and we crawled back into bed. Less than fifteen minutes later the shooting started again. Mrs van D. sprang out of bed and went downstairs to Dussel's room to seek the comfort she was unable to find with her spouse. Dussel welcomed her with the words 'Come into my bed, my child!'

We burst into peals of laughter, and the roar of the guns bothered us no more; our fears had all been swept away.

Yours, Anne

SUNDAY, 13 JUNE 1943

Dearest Kitty,

*T*he poem Father composed for my birthday is too nice to keep to myself.

Since Pim writes his verses only in German, Margot volunteered to translate it into Dutch. See for yourself whether Margot hasn't done herself proud. It begins with the usual summary of the year's events and then continues:

As youngest among us, but small no more,
Your life can be trying, for we have the chore
Of becoming your teachers, a terrible bore.
'We've got experience! Take it from me!'
'We've done this all before, you see.
We know the ropes, we know the game.
Since time immemorial, always the same.
One's own shortcomings are nothing but fluff,
But everyone else's are heavier stuff.
Fault-finding comes easy when this is our plight,
But it's hard for your parents, try as they might,
To treat you with fairness, and kindness as well;
Nit-picking's a habit that's hard to dispel.
When you're living with old folk, all you can do
Is put up with their nagging – it's hard but it's true.
The pill may be bitter, but down it must go,
For it's meant to keep the peace, you know.
The many months here have not been in vain,
Since wasting time goes against your grain.
You read and study nearly all the day,
Determined to chase the boredom away.
The more difficult question, much harder to bear,
Is 'What on earth do I have to wear?
I've got no more knickers, my clothes are too tight,
My vest is a loincloth, I'm really a sight!
To put on my shoes I must cut off my toes,
Oh dear, I'm plagued with so many woes!'

Margot had trouble getting the part about food to
rhyme, so I'm leaving it out. But aside from that, don't
you think it's a good poem?

For the rest, I've been thoroughly spoiled and have received a number of lovely presents, including a big book on my favourite subject, Greek and Roman mythology. Nor can I complain about the lack of sweets; everyone had dipped into their last reserves. As the Benjamin of the Annexe, I got more than I deserve.

Yours, Anne

TUESDAY, 15 JUNE 1943

Dearest Kitty,

*H*eaps of things have happened, but I often think I'm boring you with my dreary chitchat and that you'd just as soon have fewer letters. So I'll keep the news brief.

Mr Voskuijl wasn't operated on for his ulcer after all. Once the doctors had him on the operating table and opened him up, they saw that he had cancer. It was in such an advanced stage that an operation was pointless. So they stitched him up again, kept him in hospital for three weeks, fed him well and sent him back home. But they made an unforgivable error: they told the poor man exactly what was in store for him. He can't work any more, and he's just sitting at home, surrounded by his eight children, brooding about his approaching death. I feel very sorry for him and hate not being able to go out;

otherwise, I'd visit him as often as I could and help take his mind off matters. Now the good man can no longer let us know what's being said and done in the warehouse, which is a disaster for us. Mr Voskuijl was our greatest source of help and support when it came to safety measures. We miss him very much.

Next month it's our turn to hand over our radio to the authorities. Mr Kleiman has a small set hidden in his home that he's giving us to replace our beautiful Philips. It's a pity we have to turn in our big one, but when you're in hiding, you can't afford to bring the authorities down on your heads. Of course, we'll put the 'baby' radio upstairs. What's a clandestine radio when there are already clandestine Jews and clandestine money?

All over the country people are trying to get hold of an old radio that they can hand over instead of their 'morale booster'. It's true: as the reports from outside grow worse and worse, the radio, with its wondrous voice, helps us not to lose heart and to keep telling ourselves, 'Cheer up, keep your spirits high, things are bound to get better!'

Yours, Anne

Dear Kitty,

*T*o get back to the subject of child-rearing (for the umpteenth time), let me tell you that I'm doing my best to be helpful, friendly and kind and to do all I can to keep the rain of rebukes down to a light drizzle. It's not easy trying to behave like a model child with people you can't stand, especially when you don't mean a word of it. But I can see that a little hypocrisy gets me a lot further than my old method of saying exactly what I think (even though no one ever asks my opinion or cares one way or another). Of course, I often forget my role and find it impossible to curb my anger when they're unfair, so that they spend the next month saying I'm the cheekiest girl in the world. Don't you think I'm to be pitied sometimes? It's a good thing I'm not a moaner, because then I might become sour and bad-tempered. I can usually see the humorous side of their scoldings, but it's easier when somebody else is being hauled over the coals.

Further, I've decided (after a great deal of thought) to drop the shorthand. First, so that I have more time for my other subjects, and second, because of my eyes. That's a sad story. I've become very short-sighted and should have had glasses ages ago. (Ugh, won't I look like a muggins!) But as you know, people in hiding can't . . .

Yesterday all anyone here could talk about was Anne's eyes, because Mother had suggested I go to the specialist

with Mrs Kleiman. Just hearing this made my knees weak,
since it's no small matter. Going outside! Just think of it,
walking down the *street*! I can't imagine it. I was petrified
at first, and then glad. But it's not as simple as all that;
the various authorities who had to approve such a step
were unable to reach a quick decision. They first had to
carefully weigh all the difficulties and risks, though Miep
was ready to set off immediately with me in tow. In the
mean time, I'd taken my grey coat from the wardrobe,
but it was so small it looked as if it might have belonged
to my little sister. We lowered the hem, but I still couldn't
button it. I'm really curious to see what they decide, only
I don't think they'll ever work out a plan, because the
British have landed in Sicily and Father's all set for a
'quick finish'.

Bep's been giving Margot and me a lot of office work
to do. It makes us both feel important, and it's a big help
to her. Anyone can file letters and make entries in a sales
book, but we do it with remarkable accuracy.

Miep has so much to carry she looks like a pack mule.

She goes out nearly every day in search of vegetables, and then cycles back with her purchases in large shopping bags. She's also the one who brings five library books with her every Saturday. We long for Saturdays because that means books. We're like a lot of little children with a present. Ordinary people don't know how much books can mean to someone who's cooped up. Our only diversions are reading, studying and listening to the wireless.

Yours, Anne

TUESDAY, 13 JULY 1943

The Best Little Table

Yesterday afternoon Father gave me permission to ask Mr Dussel whether he would please be so good as to allow me (see how polite I am?) to use the table in our room two afternoons a week, from four to five-thirty. I already sit there every day from two-thirty to four while Dussel has a nap, but the rest of the time the room and the table are out of bounds to me. It's impossible to study next door in the afternoon, because there's too much going on. Besides, Father sometimes likes to sit at the desk during the afternoon.

So it seemed like a reasonable request, and I asked Dussel very politely. What do you think the learned gentleman's reply was? 'No.' Just plain 'No'!

I was incensed and wasn't about to let myself be put off like that. I asked him the reason for his 'No', but this didn't get me anywhere. The gist of his reply was: 'I have to study too, you know, and if I can't do that in the afternoons, I won't be able to fit it in at all. I have to finish the task I've set for myself; otherwise, there's no point in starting. Besides, you aren't serious about your studies. Mythology – what kind of work is that? Reading and knitting don't count either. I use that table and I'm not going to give it up!'

I replied, 'Mr Dussel, I do take my work seriously. I can't study next door in the afternoons, and I would appreciate it if you would reconsider my request!'

Having said these words, the insulted Anne turned round and pretended the learned doctor wasn't there. I was seething with rage and felt that Dussel had been incredibly rude (which he certainly had been) and that I'd been very polite.

That evening, when I managed to get hold of Pim, I told him what had happened and we discussed what my next step should be, because I had no intention of giving up and preferred to deal with the matter myself. Pim gave me a rough idea of how to approach Dussel, but cautioned me to wait until the next day, since I was in such a flap. I ignored this last piece of advice and waited for Dussel after I'd done the washing-up. Pim was sitting next door and that had a calming effect.

I began, 'Mr Dussel, you seem to believe further discussion of the matter is pointless, but I beg you to reconsider.'

Dussel gave me his most charming smile and said, 'I'm always prepared to discuss the matter, even though it's already been settled.'

I went on talking, despite Dussel's repeated interruptions. 'When you first came here,' I said, 'we agreed that the room was to be shared by the two of us. If we were to divide it fairly, you'd have the entire morning and I'd have the entire afternoon! I'm not asking for that much, but two afternoons a week does seem reasonable to me.'

Dussel leapt out of his chair as if he'd sat on a pin. 'You have no business talking about your rights to the room. Where am I supposed to go? Maybe I should ask Mr van Daan to build me a cubbyhole in the attic. You're not the only one who can't find a quiet place to work. You're always looking for a fight. If your sister Margot, who has more right to work space than you do, had come to me with the same request, I'd never even have thought of refusing, but you . . .'

And once again he brought up the business about the mythology and the knitting, and once again Anne was insulted. However, I showed no sign of it and let Dussel finish: 'But no, it's impossible to talk to you. You're shamefully self-centred. No one else matters, as long as you get your way. I've never seen such a child. But after all is said and done, I'll be obliged to let you have your way, since I don't want people saying later on that Anne Frank failed her exams because Mr Dussel refused to relinquish his table!'

He went on and on until there was such a deluge of words I could hardly keep up. For one fleeting moment.

I thought, 'Him and his lies. I'll smack his ugly mug so hard he'll go bouncing off the wall!' But the next moment I thought, 'Calm down, he's not worth getting so upset about!'

At long last Mr Dussel's fury was spent, and he left the room with an expression of triumph mixed with wrath, his coat pockets bulging with food.

I went running over to Father and recounted the entire story, or at least those parts he hadn't been able to follow himself. Pim decided to talk to Dussel that very same evening, and they spoke for more than half an hour. They first discussed whether Anne should be allowed to use the table, yes or no. Father said that he and Dussel had dealt with the subject once before, at which time he'd professed to agree with Dussel because he didn't want to contradict the elder in front of the younger, but that, even then, he hadn't thought it was fair. Dussel felt I had no right to talk as if he were an intruder laying claim to everything in sight. But Father protested strongly, since he himself had heard me say nothing of the kind. And so the conversation went back and forth, with Father defending my 'selfishness' and my 'pointless activities' and Dussel grumbling the whole time.

Dussel finally had to give in, and I was granted the opportunity to work without interruption two afternoons a week. Dussel looked very sullen, didn't speak to me for two days and made sure he occupied the table from five to five-thirty – all very childish, of course.

Anyone who's so petty and pedantic at the age of fifty-four was born that way and is never going to change.

Dearest Kitty,

There's been another break-in, but this time a real one! Peter went down to the warehouse this morning at seven, as usual, and noticed at once that both the warehouse door and the street door were open. He immediately reported this to Pim, who went to the private office, tuned the radio to a German station and locked the door. Then they both went back upstairs. In such cases our orders are 'not to wash ourselves or run any water, to be quiet, to be dressed by eight and not to go to the lavatory', and as usual we followed these to the letter. We were all glad we'd slept so well and hadn't heard anything. For a while we were indignant because no one from the office came upstairs the entire morning; Mr Kleiman left us on tenterhooks until eleven-thirty. He told us that the burglars had forced the outside door and the warehouse door with a crowbar, but when they didn't find anything worth stealing, they tried their luck on the next floor. They stole two cash-boxes containing 40 guilders, blank chequebooks and, worst of all, coupons for 330 pounds of sugar, our entire allotment. It won't be easy to wangle new ones.

Mr Kugler thinks this burglar belongs to the same gang as the one who made an unsuccessful attempt six weeks ago to open all three doors (the warehouse door and the two outside doors).

The burglary caused another stir, but the Annexe seems

to thrive on excitement. Naturally, we were glad the cash register and the typewriters had been safely tucked away in our wardrobe.

Yours, Anne

PS. Landing in Sicily. Another step closer to the . . . !

MONDAY, 19 JULY 1943

Dearest Kitty,

North Amsterdam was very heavily bombed on Sunday. There was apparently a great deal of destruction. Entire streets are in ruins, and it will take a while for them to dig out all the bodies. So far there have been two hundred dead and countless wounded; the hospitals are bursting at the seams. We've been told of children searching forlornly in the smouldering ruins for their dead parents. It still makes me shiver to think of the dull, distant drone that signified the approaching destruction.

*B*ep is currently able to get hold of exercise-books, especially journals and ledgers, useful for my book-keeping sister! Other kinds are for sale as well, but don't ask what they're like or how long they'll last. At the moment they're all labelled 'No Coupons Needed'! Like everything else you can purchase without ration stamps, they're totally worthless. They consist of twelve sheets of grey paper with narrow lines that slant across the page. Margot is thinking about taking a course in calligraphy; I've advised her to go ahead and do it. Mother won't let me because of my eyes, but I think that's silly. Whether I do that or something else, it all comes down to the same thing.

Since you've never been through a war, Kitty, and since you know very little about life in hiding, in spite of my letters, let me tell you, just for fun, what we each want to do first when we're able to go outside again.

Margot and Mr van Daan wish, above all else, to have a hot bath, filled to the brim, which they can lie in for more than half an hour. Mrs van Daan would like a cake, Dussel can think of nothing but seeing his Charlotte, and Mother is dying for a cup of real coffee. Father would like to visit Mr Voskuijl, Peter would go into town, and as for me, I'd be so overjoyed I wouldn't know where to begin.

Most of all I long to have a home of our own, to be

able to move around freely and have someone help me with my homework again, at last. In other words, to go back to school!

Bep has offered to get us some fruit, at so-called bargain prices: grapes 2.50 guilders a pound, gooseberries 70 cents a pound, one peach 50 cents, melons 75 cents a pound. No wonder the papers write every evening in big, fat letters: 'Play Fair and Keep Prices Down'!

MONDAY, 26 JULY 1943

Dear Kitty,

Yesterday was a very tumultuous day, and we're still all wound up. Actually, you may wonder if there's ever a day that passes without some kind of excitement.

The first warning siren went off in the morning while we were at breakfast, but we paid no attention, because it only meant that the planes were crossing the coast. I had a terrible headache, so I lay down for an hour after breakfast and then went to the office at about two. At two-thirty Margot had finished her office work and was just gathering her things together when the sirens began wailing again. So she and I trooped back upstairs. None too soon, it seems, for less than five minutes later the guns were booming so loudly that we went and stood in the passage. The house shook and the bombs kept falling. I was clutching my 'escape bag', more because I wanted to have something to hold on to than because I wanted to run away. I know we can't leave here, but if we had to, being seen on the streets would be just as dangerous as getting caught in an air raid. After half an hour the drone of engines faded and the house began to hum with activity again. Peter emerged from his lookout post in the front attic, Dussel remained in the front office, Mrs van D. felt safest in the private office, Mr van Daan had been watching from the loft, and those of us on the landing spread out to watch the columns of smoke rising from the harbour. Before long the smell of fire was everywhere, and outside it looked as if the city were enveloped in a thick fog.

A big fire like that is not a pleasant sight, but fortunately for us it was all over, and we went back to our various jobs. Just as we were starting dinner: another air-raid alarm. The food was good, but I lost my appetite the moment I heard the siren. Nothing happened, however, and forty-five minutes later the all-clear was sounded. After the washing-up: another air-raid warning, gunfire and swarms of planes. 'Oh, gosh, twice in one day,' we thought, 'that's twice too many.' Little good that did us, because once again the bombs rained down, this time on the other side of the city. According to British reports, Schiphol Airport was bombed. The planes dived and climbed, the air was abuzz with the drone of engines. It was very scary, and the whole time I kept thinking, 'Here it comes, this is it.'

I can assure you that when I went to bed at nine, my

legs were still shaking. At the stroke of midnight I woke up again: more planes! Dussel was undressing, but I took no notice and leapt up, wide awake, at the sound of the first shot. I stayed in Father's bed until one, in my own bed until one-thirty, and was back in Father's bed at two. But the planes kept on coming. At last they stopped firing and I was able to go back 'home' again. I finally fell asleep at half past two.

Seven o'clock. I awoke with a start and sat up in bed. Mr van Daan was with Father. My first thought was: burglars. 'Everything,' I heard Mr van Daan say, and I thought everything had been stolen. But no, this time it was wonderful news, the best we've had in months, maybe even since the war began. Mussolini has resigned and the King of Italy has taken over the government.

We jumped for joy. After the awful events of yesterday, finally something good happens and brings us . . . hope! Hope for an end to the war, hope for peace.

Mr Kugler popped in and told us that the Fokker aircraft factory had been hit hard. Meanwhile, there was another air-raid alarm this morning, with planes flying over, and another warning siren. I've had it up to here with alarms. I've hardly slept, and the last thing I want to do is work. But now the suspense about Italy and the hope that the war will be over by the end of the year are keeping us awake . . .

Yours, Anne

Dearest Kitty,

Mrs van Daan, Dussel and I were doing the washing-up, and I was extremely quiet. This is very unusual for me and they were sure to notice, so in order to avoid any questions, I quickly racked my brains for a neutral topic. I thought the book *Henry from Across the Street* might fit the bill, but I couldn't have been more wrong; if Mrs van Daan doesn't jump down my throat, Mr Dussel does. It all boiled down to this: Mr Dussel had recommended the book to Margot and me as an example of excellent writing. We thought it was anything but that. The little boy had been portrayed well, but as for the rest . . . the less said the better. I mentioned something to that effect while we were washing up, and Dussel launched into a veritable tirade.

'How can you possibly understand the psychology of a man? That of a child isn't so difficult [!]. But you're far too young to read a book like that. Even a twenty-year-old man would be unable to comprehend it.' (So why did he go out of his way to recommend it to Margot and me?)

Mrs van D. and Dussel continued their harangue: 'You know far too much about things you're not supposed to. You've been brought up all wrong. Later on, when you're older, you won't be able to enjoy anything any more. You'll say, "Oh, I read that twenty years ago in some book." You'd better hurry if you want to catch a husband or fall in love, since everything is bound to be a disappointment to you. You already know all there is to know in theory. But in practice? That's another story!'

Can you imagine how I felt? I astonished myself by calmly replying, 'You may think I haven't been raised properly, but many people would disagree!'

They apparently believe that good child-rearing includes trying to pit me against my parents, since that's all they ever do. And not telling a girl my age about grown-up subjects is fine. We can all see what happens when people are raised that way.

At that moment I could have slapped them both for poking fun at me. I was beside myself with rage, and if I only knew how much longer we had to put up with each other's company, I'd start counting the days.

Mrs van Daan's a fine one to talk! She sets an example all right – a bad one! She's known to be exceedingly pushy, egotistical, cunning, calculating and perpetually dissatisfied. Add to that, vanity and coquettishness and there's no question about it: she's a thoroughly despicable person. I could write an entire book about Madame van Daan, and who knows, maybe someday I will. Anyone can put on a charming exterior when they want to. Mrs van D. is friendly to strangers, especially men, so it's easy to make a mistake when you first get to know her.

Mother thinks that Mrs van D. is too stupid for words, Margot that she's too unimportant, Pim that she's too ugly (literally and figuratively!), and after long observation (I'm never prejudiced at the beginning), I've come to the conclusion that she's all three of the above, and lots more besides. She has so many bad traits, why should I single out just one of them?

Yours, Anne

PS. Will the reader please take into consideration that this story was written before the writer's fury had cooled?

TUESDAY, 3 AUGUST 1943

Dearest Kitty,

Things are going well on the political front. Italy has banned the Fascist Party. The people are fighting the Fascists in many places – even the army has joined the fight. How can a country like that continue to wage war against England?

Our beautiful radio was taken away last week. Dussel was very angry at Mr Kugler for turning it in on the appointed day. Dussel is slipping lower and lower in my estimation, and he's already below zero. Whatever he says about politics, history, geography or anything else is so ridiculous that I hardly dare repeat it: Hitler will fade from history; the harbour in Rotterdam is bigger than the one in Hamburg; the English are idiots for not taking the opportunity to bomb Italy to smithereens; etc., etc.

We just had a third air raid. I decided to grit my teeth and practise being courageous.

Mrs van Daan, the one who always said 'Let them fall'

155

and 'Better to end with a bang than not to end at all', is the most cowardly one among us. She was shaking like a leaf this morning and even burst into tears. She was comforted by her husband, with whom she recently declared a truce after a week of squabbling; I nearly got sentimental at the sight.

Mouschi has now proved, beyond a shadow of a doubt, that having a cat has disadvantages as well as advantages. The whole house is crawling with fleas, and it's getting worse each day. Mr Kleiman sprinkled yellow powder in every nook and cranny, but the fleas haven't taken the slightest notice. It's making us all very jittery; we're forever imagining a bite on our arms and legs or other parts of our bodies, so we leap up and do a few exercises, since it gives us an excuse to take a better look at our arms or necks. But now we're paying the price for having had so little physical exercise; we're so stiff we can hardly turn our heads. The real calisthenics fell by the wayside long ago.

Yours, Anne

Dearest Kitty,

Now that we've been in hiding for a little over a year, you know a great deal about our lives. Still, I can't possibly tell you everything, since it's all so different compared with ordinary times and ordinary people. Nevertheless, to give you a closer look into our lives, from time to time I'll describe part of an ordinary day. I'll start with the evening and night.

Nine in the evening. Bedtime always begins in the Annexe with an enormous hustle and bustle. Chairs are shifted, beds pulled out, blankets unfolded – nothing stays where it is during the daytime. I sleep on a small divan, which is only five feet long, so we have to add a few chairs to make it longer. Eiderdown, sheets, pillows, blankets: everything has to be removed from Dussel's bed, where it's kept during the day.

In the next room there's a terrible creaking: that's Margot's folding bed being set up. More blankets and pillows, anything to make the wooden slats a bit more comfortable. Upstairs it sounds like thunder, but it's only Mrs van D.'s bed being shoved against the window so that Her Majesty, arrayed in her pink bed jacket, can sniff the night air through her delicate little nostrils.

Nine o'clock. After Peter's finished, it's my turn for the bathroom. I wash myself from head to toe, and more often than not I find a tiny flea floating in the sink (only during the hot months, weeks or days). I brush my teeth,

157

curl my hair, manicure my nails and dab peroxide on my upper lip to bleach the black hairs – all this in less than half an hour.

Nine-thirty. I throw on my dressing-gown. With soap in one hand, and potty, hairpins, knickers, curlers and cotton wool in the other, I hurry out of the bathroom. The next person in invariably calls me back to remove the gracefully curved but unsightly hairs that I've left in the sink.

Ten o'clock. Time to put up the black-out screen and say good night. For the next fifteen minutes, at least, the house is filled with the creaking of beds and the sigh of broken springs, and then, provided our upstairs neighbours aren't having a marital tiff in bed, all is quiet.

Eleven-thirty. The bathroom door creaks. A narrow strip of light falls into the room. Squeaking shoes, a large coat, even larger than the man inside it . . . Dussel is returning from his nightly work in Mr Kugler's office. I hear him shuffling back and forth for ten whole minutes, the rustle of paper (from the food he's tucking away in his cupboard) and the bed being made up. Then the figure disappears again, and the only sound is the occasional suspicious noise from the lavatory.

Approximately three o'clock. I have to get up to use the tin under my bed, which, to be on the safe side, has a rubber mat underneath in case of leaks. I always hold my breath while I go, since it clatters into the tin like a brook down a mountainside. The potty is returned to its place, and the figure in the white nightdress (the one that causes Margot to exclaim every evening, 'Oh, that indecent nightie!') climbs back into bed. A certain somebody lies awake for about fifteen minutes, listening to the sounds of the night. In the first place, to hear whether there are any burglars downstairs, and then to the various beds – upstairs, next door and in my room – to tell whether the others are asleep or half awake. This is no fun, especially when it concerns a member of the family named Dr Dussel. First, there's the sound of a fish gasping for air, and this is repeated nine or ten times. Then, the lips are moistened profusely. This is alternated with little smacking sounds, followed by a long period of tossing and turning and rearranging the pillows. After five minutes of perfect quiet, the same sequence repeats itself three more times, after which he's presumably lulled himself back to sleep for a while.

Sometimes the guns go off during the night, between one and four. I'm never aware of it before it happens, but all of a sudden I find myself standing beside my bed, out of sheer habit. Occasionally I'm dreaming so deeply (of irregular French verbs or a quarrel upstairs) that I realize only when my dream is over that the shooting has stopped and that I've remained quietly in my room. But usually I wake up. Then I grab a pillow and a handkerchief, throw on my dressing-gown and slippers and dash next door to Father, just the way Margot described in this birthday poem:

> *When shots ring out in the dark of night,*
> *The door creaks open and into sight*
> *Come a hanky, a pillow, a figure in white . . .*

Once I've reached the big bed, the worst is over, except when the shooting is extra loud.

Six forty-five. Brrring . . . the alarm clock, which raises its shrill voice at any hour of the day or night, whether you want it to or not. Creak . . . wham . . . Mrs van D. turns it off. Screak . . . Mr van D. gets up, puts on the water and races to the bathroom.

Seven-fifteen. The door creaks again. Dussel can go to the bathroom. Alone at last, I remove the black-out screen . . . and a new day begins in the Annexe.

Yours, Anne

THURSDAY, 5 AUGUST 1943

Dearest Kitty,

Today let's talk about the lunch break.
    It's twelve-thirty. The whole gang breathes a sigh of relief: Mr van Maaren, the man with the shady past, and Mr de Kok have gone home for lunch.

Upstairs you can hear the thud of the vacuum cleaner on Mrs van D.'s beautiful and only rug. Margot tucks a few books under her arm and heads for the class for 'slow learners', which is what Dussel seems to be. Pim goes and sits in a corner with his constant companion, Dickens, in hopes of finding a bit of peace and quiet. Mother hastens upstairs to help the busy little housewife, and I tidy up both the bathroom and myself at the same time.

Twelve forty-five. One by one they trickle in: first Mr Gies and then either Mr Kleiman or Mr Kugler, followed by Bep and sometimes even Miep.

One. Clustered round the radio, they all listen raptly to the BBC. This is the only time the members of the Annexe family don't interrupt each other, since even Mr van Daan can't argue with the speaker.

One-fifteen. Food distribution. Everyone from downstairs gets a cup of soup, plus pudding, if there happens to be any. A contented Mr Gies sits on the divan or leans against the desk with his newspaper, cup and usually the cat at his side. If one of the three is missing, he doesn't hesitate to let his protest be heard. Mr Kleiman relates the latest news from town, and he's an excellent source. Mr Kugler hurries up the stairs, gives a short but solid knock on the door and comes in either wringing his hands or rubbing them in glee, depending on whether he's quiet and in a bad mood or talkative and in a good mood.

One forty-five. Everyone rises from the table and goes about their business. Margot and Mother do the washing-up, Mr and Mrs van D. head for the divan, Peter for the attic, Father for his divan, Dussel too, and Anne does her homework.

What comes next is the quietest hour of the day; when they're all asleep, there are no disturbances. To judge by his face, Dussel is dreaming of food. But I don't look at him long, because the time whizzes by and before you know it, it'll be 4.00 p.m. and the pedantic Dr Dussel will be standing with the clock in his hand because I'm one minute late clearing off the table.

Yours, Anne

Dearest Kitty,

A few weeks ago I started writing a story, something I made up from beginning to end, and I've enjoyed it so much that the products of my pen are piling up.

Yours, Anne

Dearest Kitty,

*W*e now continue with a typical day in the Annexe. Since we've already had lunch, it's time to describe dinner.

Mr van Daan. Is served first, and takes a generous portion of whatever he likes. Usually joins in the conversation, never fails to give his opinion. Once he's spoken, his word is final. If anyone dares to suggest otherwise, Mr van D. can put up a good fight. Oh, he can hiss like a cat . . . but I'd rather he didn't. Once you've seen it, you never want to see it again. His opinion is the best, he knows the most about everything. Granted, the man has a good head on his shoulders, but it's swelled to no small degree.

Madame. Actually, the best thing would be to say nothing. Some days, especially when a foul mood is on the way, her face is hard to read. If you analyse the discussions, you realize she's not the subject, but the guilty party! A fact everyone prefers to ignore. Even so, you could call her the instigator. Stirring up trouble, now *that's* what Mrs van Daan calls fun. Stirring up trouble between Mrs Frank and Anne. Margot and Mr Frank aren't quite as easy.

But let's return to the table. Mrs van D. may think she doesn't always get enough, but that's not the case. The choicest potatoes, the tastiest morsel, the tenderest bit of whatever there is, that's Madame's motto. The others can all have their turn, as long as I get the best. (Exactly what she accuses Anne Frank of doing.) Her second watchword is: keep talking. As long as somebody's listening, it doesn't seem to occur to her to wonder whether they're interested. She must think that whatever Mrs van Daan says will interest everyone.

Smile coquettishly, pretend you know everything, offer everyone a piece of advice and mother them – that's sure to make a good impression. But if you take a better look, the good impression fades. One, she's hardworking; two, cheerful; three, coquettish – and sometimes a pretty face. That's Petronella van Daan.

The third diner. Says very little. Young Mr van Daan is usually quiet and hardly makes his presence known. As far as his appetite is concerned, he's a Danaïdean vessel that never gets full. Even after the most substantial meal, he can look you calmly in the eye and claim he could have eaten twice as much.

Number four – Margot. Eats like a bird and doesn't talk at all. She eats only vegetables and fruit. 'Spoiled', in the opinion of the van Daans. 'Too little exercise and fresh air', in ours.

Beside her – Mummy. Has a hearty appetite, does her share of the talking. No one has the impression, as they do with Mrs van Daan, that this is a housewife. What's the difference between the two? Well, Mrs van D. does the cooking and Mother washes up and polishes the furniture.

Numbers six and seven. I won't say much about Father and me. The former is the most modest person at the table. He always looks to see whether the others have been served first. He needs nothing for himself; the best things are for the children. He's goodness personified. Seated next to him is the Annexe's little bundle of nerves.

Dussel. Help yourself, keep your eyes on the food, eat and don't talk. And if you have to say something, then for goodness' sake talk about food. That doesn't lead to quarrels, just to bragging. He consumes enormous portions, and 'no' is not part of his vocabulary, whether the food is good or bad.

Trousers that come up to his chest, a red jacket, black patent-leather slippers and horn-rimmed glasses – that's how he looks when he's at work at the little table, always studying and never progressing. This is interrupted only by his afternoon nap, food and – his favourite spot – the lavatory. Three, four or five times a day there's bound to be someone waiting outside the door, hopping impatiently from one foot to another, trying to hold it in and barely managing. Does Dussel care? Not a whit. From seven-fifteen to seven-thirty, from twelve-thirty to one, from two to two-fifteen, from four to four-fifteen, from six to six-fifteen, from eleven-thirty to twelve. You can set your watch by them; these are the times for his 'regular sessions'. He never deviates or lets himself be swayed by the voices outside the door, begging him to open up before a disaster occurs.

Number nine is not part of our Annexe family, although she does share our house and table. Bep has a healthy appetite. She cleans her plate and isn't choosy. Bep's easy to please and that pleases us. She can be characterized as follows: cheerful, good-humoured, kind and willing.

TUESDAY, 10 AUGUST 1943

Dearest Kitty,

A new idea: during meals I talk more to myself than to the others, which has two advantages. First, they're glad they don't have to listen to my continuous chatter, and second, I don't have to get annoyed by their opinions. I don't think my opinions are stupid but other people do, so it's better to keep them to myself. I apply the same tactic when I have to eat something I loathe. I put the dish in front of me, pretend it's delicious, avoid looking at it as much as possible, and it's gone before I've had time to realize what it is. When I get up in the morning, another very disagreeable moment, I leap out of bed, think to myself, 'You'll be slipping back under the covers soon,' walk to the window, take down the black-out screen, sniff at the crack until I feel a bit of fresh air, and I'm awake. I strip the bed as fast as I can so I won't be tempted to get back in. Do you know what Mother calls this sort of thing? The art of living. Isn't that a funny expression?

We've all been a little confused this past week because our dearly beloved Westertoren bells have been carted off to be melted down for the war, so we have no idea of the exact time, either night or day. I still have hopes that they'll come up with a substitute, made of tin or copper or some such thing, to remind the neighbourhood of the clock.

Everywhere I go, upstairs or down, they all cast admiring glances at my feet, which are adorned by a pair of exceptionally beautiful (for times like these!) shoes. Miep managed to snap them up for 27.50 guilders. Burgundy-coloured suede and leather with medium-sized high heels. I feel as if I'm on stilts, and look even taller than I already am.

Yesterday was my unlucky day. I pricked my right

thumb with the blunt end of a big needle. As a result, Margot had to peel potatoes for me (take the good with the bad), and writing was awkward. Then I bumped into the cupboard door so hard it nearly knocked me over, and was scolded for making such a racket. They wouldn't let me run water to bathe my forehead, so now I'm walking around with a giant lump over my right eye. To make matters worse, the little toe on my right foot got stuck in the vacuum cleaner. It bled and hurt, but my other ailments were already causing me so much trouble that I let this one slide, which was stupid of me, because now I'm walking around with an infected toe. What with the ointment, the gauze and the tape, I can't get my heavenly new shoe on my foot.

Dussel has put us in danger for the umpteenth time. He actually had Miep bring him a book, an anti-Mussolini tirade, which has been banned. On the way here she was knocked down by an SS motorcycle. She lost her head and shouted 'You brutes!' and went on her way. I don't dare think what would have happened if she'd been taken down to headquarters.

Yours, Anne

A Daily Chore in Our Little Community:
Peeling Potatoes!

One person goes to get some newspapers; another, the knives (keeping the best for himself, of course); the third, the potatoes; and the fourth, the water.

Mr Dussel begins. He may not always peel them very well, but he does peel non-stop, glancing left and right to see if everyone is doing it the way he does. No, they're not!

'Look, Anne, I am taking peeler in my hand like so and going from the top to bottom! *Nein*, not so . . . but so!'

'I think my way is easier, Mr Dussel,' I say tentatively.

'But this is best way, Anne. This you can take from me. Of course, it is no matter, you do the way you want.'

We go on peeling. I glance at Dussel out of the corner of my eye. Lost in thought, he shakes his head (over me, no doubt), but says no more.

I keep on peeling. Then I look at Father, on the other side of me. To Father, peeling potatoes is not a chore, but precision work. When he reads, he has a deep wrinkle in the back of his head. But when he's preparing potatoes, beans or vegetables, he seems to be totally absorbed in his task. He puts on his potato-peeling face, and when it's set in that particular way, it would be impossible for him to turn out anything less than a perfectly peeled potato.

I keep on working. I glance up for a second, but that's all the time I need. Mrs van D. is trying to attract Dussel's attention. She starts by looking in his direction, but Dussel pretends not to notice. She winks, but Dussel goes on peeling. She laughs, but Dussel still doesn't look up. Then Mother laughs too, but Dussel pays them no notice. Having failed to achieve her goal, Mrs van D. is obliged to change tactics. There's a brief silence. Then she says, 'Putti, why don't you put on an apron? Otherwise, I'll have to spend all day tomorrow trying to get the spots out of your suit!'

'I'm not getting it dirty.'

Another brief silence. 'Putti, why don't you sit down?'

'I'm fine this way. I like standing up!'

Silence.

'Putti, look out, *du spritzt schon!*'★

'I know, Mummy, but I'm being careful.'

Mrs van D. casts about for another topic. 'Um, Putti, why aren't the British carrying out any bombing raids today?'

'Because the weather's bad, Kerli!'

★ Now you're splashing!

'But yesterday it was such nice weather and they weren't flying then either.'

'Let's drop the subject.'

'Why? Can't a person talk about that or offer an opinion?'

'No!'

'Well, why in the world not?'

'Oh, be quiet, *Mammichen*!'★

'Mr Frank always answers *his* wife.'

Mr van D. is trying to control himself. This remark always rubs him up the wrong way, but Mrs van D.'s not one to quit: 'Oh, there's never going to be an invasion!'

Mr van D. goes white, and when she notices it, Mrs van D. turns red, but she's not about to be deterred: 'The British aren't doing a thing!'

The bomb bursts. 'And now shut up, *Donnerwetter noch mal*!'†

Mother can barely stifle a laugh, and I stare straight ahead.

Scenes like these are repeated almost daily, unless they've just had a terrible row. In that case, neither Mr nor Mrs van D. says a word.

It's time for me to get some more potatoes. I go up to the attic, where Peter is busy picking fleas from the cat. He looks up, the cat notices it, and whoosh . . . he's gone. Out of the window and into the rain gutter.

Peter swears; I laugh and slip out of the room.

★ Mummy.
† For crying out loud!

Freedom in the Annexe

Five-thirty. Bep's arrival signals the beginning of our nightly freedom. Things get going right away. I go upstairs with Bep, who usually has her pudding before the rest of us. The moment she sits down, Mrs van D. begins stating her wishes. Her list usually starts with 'Oh, by the way, Bep, something else I'd like . . .' Bep winks at me. Mrs van D. doesn't miss a chance to make her wishes known to whoever comes upstairs. It must be one of the reasons none of them likes to go up there.

Five forty-five. Bep leaves. I go down two floors to have a look around: first to the kitchen, then to the private office and then to the coal store to open the cat door for Mouschi.

After a long tour of inspection, I land up in Mr Kugler's office. Mr van Daan is combing all the drawers and files for today's mail. Peter picks up Boche and the warehouse key; Pim lugs the typewriters upstairs; Margot looks around for a quiet place to do her office work; Mrs van D. puts a kettle of water on the gas ring; Mother comes down the stairs with a pan of potatoes; we all know our jobs.

Soon Peter comes back from the warehouse. The first question they ask him is whether he's remembered the bread. No, he hasn't. He crouches before the door to the front office to make himself as small as possible and crawls on his hands and knees to the steel cabinet, takes out the bread and starts to leave. At any rate, that's what he intends to do, but before he knows what's happened,

Mouschi has jumped over him and gone to sit under the desk.

Peter looks all around him. Aha, there's the cat! He crawls back into the office and grabs the cat by the tail. Mouschi hisses, Peter sighs. What has he accomplished? Mouschi's now sitting by the window licking herself, very pleased at having escaped Peter's clutches. Peter has no choice but to lure her with a piece of bread. Mouschi takes the bait, follows him out, and the door closes.

I watch the entire scene through a crack in the door.

Mr van Daan is angry and slams the door. Margot and I exchange looks and think the same thing: he must have worked himself into a rage again because of some blunder on Mr Kugler's part, and he's forgotten all about the Keg Company next door.

Another step is heard in the passage. Dussel comes in, goes towards the window with an air of propriety, sniffs . . . coughs, sneezes and clears his throat. He's out of luck – it was pepper. He continues to the front office. The curtains are open, which means he can't get at his writing paper. He disappears with a scowl.

Margot and I exchange another glance. 'One less page for his sweetheart tomorrow,' I hear her say. I nod in agreement.

An elephant's tread is heard on the stairway. It's Dussel, seeking comfort in his favourite spot.

We continue working. Knock, knock, knock . . . Three taps means dinnertime!

Wenn Die Uhr Halb Neune Schlägt . . . ⋆

 argot and Mother are nervous. 'Shh . . . Father.
Be quiet, Otto. Shh . . . Pim! It's eight-thirty.
Come here, you can't run the water any more. Walk
softly!' A sample of what's said to Father in the bathroom.
At the stroke of half past eight, he has to be in the
living-room. No running water, no flushing toilet, no
walking around, no noise whatsoever. As long as the
office staff hasn't arrived, sounds travel more easily to the
warehouse.

The door opens upstairs at eight-twenty, and this is
followed by three gentle taps on the floor . . . Anne's
porridge. I clamber up the stairs to get my dog-bowl.

Back downstairs, everything has to be done quickly,
quickly: I comb my hair, put away the potty, shove the
bed back in place. Quiet! The clock is striking eight-
thirty! Mrs van D. changes her shoes and shuffles through
the room in her slippers; Mr van D. too – a veritable
Charlie Chaplin. All is quiet.

The ideal family scene has now reached its high point.
I want to read or study and Margot does too. Father and
Mother ditto. Father is sitting (with Dickens and the
dictionary, of course) on the edge of the sagging, squeaky
bed, which doesn't even have a decent mattress. Two

⋆ When the clock strikes half past eight.

bolsters can be piled on top of each other. 'I don't need these,' he thinks. 'I can manage without them!'

Once he starts reading, he doesn't look up. He laughs now and then and tries to get Mother to read a passage.

'I don't have the time right now!'

He looks disappointed, but then continues to read. A little while later, when he comes across another interesting bit, he tries again: 'You *have* to read this, Mother!'

Mother sits on the folding bed, either reading, sewing, knitting or studying, whichever is next on her list. An idea suddenly occurs to her, and she quickly says, so as not to forget, 'Anne, remember to . . . Margot, jot this down . . .'

After a while it's quiet again. Margot slams her book shut; Father knits his forehead, his eyebrows forming a funny curve and his wrinkle of concentration reappearing at the back of his head, and he buries himself in his book again; Mother starts chatting with Margot; and I get curious and listen too. Pim is drawn into the conversation . . . Nine o'clock. Breakfast!

FRIDAY, 10 SEPTEMBER 1943

Dearest Kitty,

*E*very time I write to you, something special has happened, usually unpleasant rather than pleasant.

This time, however, something wonderful is going on.

On Wednesday, 8 September we were listening to the seven o'clock news when we heard an announcement: 'Here is some of the best news of the war so far: Italy has capitulated.' Italy has unconditionally surrendered! The Dutch broadcast from England began at eight-fifteen with the news: 'Listeners, an hour and fifteen minutes ago, just as I finished writing my daily report, we received the wonderful news of Italy's capitulation. I tell you, I never tossed my notes into the wastepaper basket with more delight than I did today!'

'God Save the King', the American national anthem and the Russian 'Internationale' were played. As always, the Dutch programme was uplifting without being too optimistic.

The British have landed in Naples. Northern Italy is occupied by the Germans. The truce was signed on Friday, 3 September, the day the British landed in Italy. The Germans are ranting and raving in all the newspapers at the treachery of Badoglio and the Italian king.

Still, there's bad news as well. It's about Mr Kleiman. As you know, we all like him very much. He's unfailingly cheerful and amazingly brave, despite the fact that he's always ill and in pain and can't eat much or do a lot of walking. 'When Mr Kleiman enters a room, the sun begins to shine,' Mother said recently, and she's absolutely right.

Now it seems he has to go into hospital for a very difficult operation on his stomach, and will have to stay there for at least four weeks. You should have seen him when he said good-bye to us. He acted so normally, as though he were just off to run an errand.

Yours, Anne

THURSDAY, 16 SEPTEMBER 1943

Dearest Kitty,

Relationships here in the Annexe are getting worse all the time. We don't dare open our mouths at mealtime (except to slip in a bite of food), because no matter what we say, someone is bound to resent it or take it the wrong way. Mr Voskuijl occasionally comes to visit us. Unfortunately, he's not doing very well. He isn't making it any easier for his family, because his attitude seems to be: what do I care, I'm going to die anyway! When I think how touchy everyone is here, I can just imagine what it must be like at the Voskuijls'.

I've been taking valerian every day to fight the anxiety and depression, but it doesn't stop me from being even more miserable the next day. A good hearty laugh would help more than ten valerian drops, but we've almost forgotten how to laugh. Sometimes I'm afraid my face is going to sag with all this sorrow and that my mouth is going to permanently droop at the corners. The others aren't doing any better. Everyone here is dreading the great terror known as winter.

Another fact that doesn't exactly brighten up our days is that Mr van Maaren, the man who works in the warehouse, is getting suspicious about the Annexe. A person with any brains must have noticed by now that Miep sometimes says she's going to the lab, Bep to the files and Mr Kleiman to the Opekta stores, while Mr Kugler claims the Annexe doesn't belong to this building at all, but to the one next door.

We wouldn't care what Mr van Maaren thought of the situation except that he's known to be unreliable and to possess a high degree of curiosity. He's not one who can be put off with a flimsy excuse.

One day Mr Kugler wanted to be extra cautious, so at twenty past twelve he put on his coat and went to the chemist round the corner. Less than five minutes later he was back, and he sneaked up the stairs like a thief to visit us. At one-fifteen he started to leave, but Bep met him on the landing and warned him that van Maaren was in the office. Mr Kugler did an about-turn and stayed with us until one-thirty. Then he took off his shoes and went in his stockinged feet (despite his cold) to the front attic and down the other stairway, taking one step at a time to avoid the creaks. It took him fifteen minutes to negotiate the stairs, but he ended up safely in the office after having entered from the outside.

In the mean time, Bep had got rid of van Maaren and come to get Mr Kugler from the Annexe. But he'd already left and at that moment was still tiptoeing down the stairs. What must the passers-by have thought when they saw the manager putting on his shoes outside? Hey, you there, in the socks!

Yours, Anne

Dearest Kitty,

It's Mrs van Daan's birthday. Other than one ration coupon each for cheese, meat and bread, all she received from us was a pot of jam. Her husband, Dussel and the office staff gave her nothing but flowers and also food. Such are the times we live in!

Bep had a nervous fit last week because she had so many errands to do. Ten times a day people were sending her out for something, each time insisting she go right away or go again or that she'd done it all wrong. And when you think that she has her regular office work to do, that Mr Kleiman is ill, that Miep is home with a cold and that Bep herself has a sprained ankle, boyfriend troubles and a grumpy father, it's no wonder she's at the end of her tether. We comforted her and told her that if she'd put her foot down once or twice and say she didn't have the time, the shopping lists would shrink of their own accord.

Saturday there was a big drama, the likes of which have never been seen here before. It started with a discussion of van Maaren and ended in a general argument and tears. Dussel complained to Mother that he was being treated like a leper, that no one was friendly to him and that, after all, he hadn't done anything to deserve it. This was followed by a lot of sweet talk, which luckily Mother didn't fall for this time. She told him we were disappointed in him and that, on more than one occasion, he'd been a source of great annoyance. Dussel promised her the moon, but, as usual, we haven't seen so much as a beam.

There's trouble brewing with the van Daans, I can tell! Father's furious because they're cheating us: they've been holding back meat and other things. Oh, what kind of bombshell is about to burst now? If only I weren't so involved in all these skirmishes! If only I could leave here! They're driving us crazy!

Yours, Anne

SUNDAY, 17 OCTOBER 1943

Dearest Kitty,

*M*r Kleiman is back, thank goodness! He looks a bit pale, and yet he cheerfully set off to sell some clothes for Mr van Daan.

The disagreeable fact is that Mr van Daan has run out of money. He lost his last hundred guilders in the warehouse, which is still creating trouble for us: the men are wondering how a hundred guilders could land up in the warehouse on a Monday morning. Suspicion abounds. Meanwhile, the hundred guilders have been stolen. Who's the thief?

But I was talking about the money shortage. Mrs van D. has piles of dresses, coats and shoes, none of which she feels she can do without. Mr van D.'s suit is difficult to shift, and Peter's bike was put up for sale but is back again, since nobody wanted it. But the story doesn't end there. You see, Mrs van. D. is going to have to part with her fur coat. In her opinion, the firm should pay for our upkeep, but that's ridiculous. They just had a flaming row about it and have entered the 'oh, my sweet Putti' and 'darling Kerli' stage of reconciliation.

My mind boggles at the profanity this honourable house has had to endure in the past month. Father walks around with his lips pressed together, and whenever he hears his name, he looks up in alarm, as if he's afraid he'll be called upon to resolve another delicate problem. Mother's so overwrought her cheeks are blotched with red, Margot complains of headaches, Dussel can't sleep, Mrs van D. frets and fumes all day long, and I've gone completely round the bend. To tell you the truth, I sometimes forget who we're at odds with and who we're not.

The only way to take my mind off it is to study, and I've been doing a lot of that lately.

Yours, Anne

My dearest Kitty,

*M*r Kleiman is out again: his stomach won't give him a moment's peace. He doesn't even know whether it's stopped bleeding. He came to tell us he wasn't feeling well and was going home, and for the first time he seemed really down.

Mr and Mrs van D. have had more raging battles. The reason is simple: they're broke. They wanted to sell an overcoat and a suit of Mr van D.'s, but were unable to find any buyers. His prices were much too high.

Some time ago Mr Kleiman was talking about a furrier he knows. This gave Mr van D. the idea of selling his wife's fur coat. It's made of rabbit skin, and she's had it for seventeen years. Mrs van D. got 325 guilders for it, an enormous amount. She wanted to keep the money herself to buy new clothes after the war, and it took some doing before Mr van D. could make her understand that it was desperately needed to cover household expenses.

You can't imagine the screaming, shouting, stamping of feet and swearing that went on. It was terrifying. My family stood holding its breath at the bottom of the stairs, in case it might be necessary to drag them apart. All the bickering, tears and nervous tension have become such a stress and strain that I fall into my bed at night crying and thanking my lucky stars that I have half an hour to myself.

I'm doing fine, except I've got no appetite. I keep

hearing: 'Goodness, you look awful!' I must admit they're doing their best to keep me fit: they're plying me with dextrose, cod-liver oil, brewer's yeast and calcium. My nerves often get the better of me, especially on Sundays; that's when I really feel miserable. The atmosphere is stifling, sluggish, leaden. Outside, you don't hear a single bird, and a deathly, oppressive silence hangs over the house and clings to me as if it were going to drag me into the deepest regions of the underworld. At times like these, Father, Mother and Margot don't matter to me in the least. I wander from room to room, climb up and down the stairs and feel like a songbird whose wings have been ripped off and who keeps hurling itself against the bars of its dark cage. 'Let me out, where there's fresh air and laughter!' a voice within me cries. I don't even bother to reply any more, but lie down on the divan. Sleep makes the silence and the terrible fear go by more quickly, helps pass the time, since it's impossible to kill it.

Yours, Anne

WEDNESDAY, 3 NOVEMBER 1943

Dearest Kitty,

To take our minds off matters as well as to develop them, Father ordered a catalogue from a correspondence school. Margot pored through the thick brochure three times without finding anything to her liking and within her budget. Father was easier to satisfy and decided to write and ask for a trial lesson in 'Elementary Latin'. No sooner said than done. The lesson arrived, Margot set to work enthusiastically and decided to take the course, despite the expense. It's much too hard for me, though I'd really like to learn Latin.

To give me a new project as well, Father asked Mr Kleiman for a children's Bible so I could finally learn something about the New Testament.

'Are you planning to give Anne a Bible for Hanukkah?' Margot asked, somewhat perturbed.

'Yes . . . Well, maybe St Nicholas' Day would be a better occasion,' Father replied.

Jesus and Hanukkah don't exactly go together.

Since the vacuum cleaner's broken, I have to take an old brush to the rug every night. The window's closed, the light's on, the stove's burning, and there I am brushing away at the rug. 'That's sure to be a problem,' I thought to myself the first time. 'There're bound to be complaints.' I was right: Mother got a headache from the thick clouds of dust whirling around the room, Margot's new Latin dictionary was caked with dirt, and Pim grumbled that the floor didn't look any different anyway. Small thanks for my pains.

We've decided that from now on the stove is going to be lit at seven-thirty on Sunday mornings instead of five-thirty. I think it's risky. What will the neighbours think of our smoking chimney?

It's the same with the curtains. Ever since we first went

into hiding, they've been tacked firmly to the windows. Sometimes one of the ladies or gentlemen can't resist the urge to peek outside. The result: a storm of reproaches. The response: 'Oh, nobody will notice.' That's how every act of carelessness begins and ends. No one will notice, no one will hear, no one will pay the least bit of attention. Easy to say, but is it true?

At the moment, the tempestuous quarrels have subsided; only Dussel and the van Daans are still at loggerheads. When Dussel is talking about Mrs van D., he invariably calls her 'that old bat' or 'that stupid hag', and conversely, Mrs van D. refers to our ever so learned gentleman as an 'old maid' or a 'touchy neurotic spinster', etc.

The pot calling the kettle black!

Yours, Anne

MONDAY EVENING, 8 NOVEMBER 1943

Dearest Kitty,

*I*f you were to read all my letters in one sitting, you'd be struck by the fact that they were written in a variety of moods. It annoys me to be so dependent on the moods here in the Annexe, but I'm not the only one: we're all subject to them. If I'm engrossed in a book, I have to rearrange my thoughts before I can mingle with other people, because otherwise they might think I was strange. As you can see, I'm currently in the middle of a depression. I couldn't really tell you what set it off, but I think it stems from my cowardice, which confronts me at every turn. This evening, when Bep was still here, the doorbell rang long and loud. I instantly turned white, my stomach churned, and my heart beat wildly – and all because I was afraid.

At night in bed I see myself alone in a dungeon, without Father and Mother. Or I'm roaming the streets, or the Annexe is on fire, or they come in the middle of the night to take us away and I crawl under my bed in desperation. I see everything as if it were actually taking place. And to think it might all happen soon!

Miep often says she envies us because we have such peace and quiet here. That may be true, but she's obviously not thinking about our fear.

I simply can't imagine the world will ever be normal again for us. I do talk about 'after the war', but it's as if I were talking about a castle in the air, something that can never come true.

I see the eight of us in the Annexe as if we were a patch of blue sky surrounded by menacing black clouds. The perfectly round spot on which we're standing is still safe, but the clouds are moving in on us, and the ring between us and the approaching danger is being pulled tighter and tighter. We're surrounded by darkness and danger, and in our desperate search for a way out we keep bumping into each other. We look at the fighting down below and the peace and beauty up above. In the mean time, we've been cut off by the dark mass of clouds, so that we can go neither up nor down. It looms before us like an impenetrable wall, trying to crush us, but not yet able to. I can only cry out and implore, 'Oh, ring, ring, open wide and let us out!'

Yours, Anne

THURSDAY, 11 NOVEMBER 1943

Dearest Kitty,

I have a good title for this chapter:

Ode to My Fountain Pen
In Memoriam

My fountain pen was always one of my most prized possessions; I valued it highly, especially because it had a thick nib, and I can only write neatly with thick nibs. It has led a long and interesting fountain-pen life, which I will summarize below.

When I was nine, my fountain pen (packed in cotton wool) arrived as a 'sample of no commercial value' all the way from Aachen, where my grandmother (the kindly donor) used to live. I lay in bed with flu, while the February winds howled around our flat. This splendid fountain pen came in a red leather case, and I showed it to my girlfriends the first chance I got. Me, Anne Frank, the proud owner of a fountain pen.

When I was ten, I was allowed to take the pen to school, and to my surprise, the teacher even let me write with it. When I was eleven, however, my treasure had to be tucked away again, because my sixth-form teacher allowed us to use only school pens and ink-pots. When I was twelve, I started at the Jewish Lyceum and my fountain pen was given a new case in honour of the occasion. Not only did it have room for a pencil, it also had a zip, which was much more impressive. When I was thirteen, the fountain pen went with me to the Annexe, and together we've raced through countless diaries and compositions. I'd turned fourteen and my fountain pen was enjoying the last year of its life with me when . . .

It was just after five on Friday afternoon. I came out of my room and was about to sit down at the table to write when I was roughly pushed to one side to make room for Margot and Father, who wanted to practise their Latin. The fountain pen remained unused on the table, while its owner, sighing, was forced to make do with a very tiny corner of the table, where she began rubbing beans. That's how we remove mould from the beans and restore them to their original state. At a quarter to six I swept the floor, dumped the dirt into a newspaper, along with the rotten beans, and tossed it into the stove. A giant flame shot up, and I thought it was wonderful that the stove, which had been gasping its last breath, had made such a miraculous recovery.

All was quiet again. The Latin students had left, and I sat down at the table to pick up where I'd left off. But no matter where I looked, my fountain pen was nowhere in sight. I took another look. Margot looked, Mother looked, Father looked, Dussel looked. But it had vanished.

'Maybe it fell in the stove, along with the beans!' Margot suggested.

'No, it couldn't have!' I replied.

But that evening, when my fountain pen still hadn't turned up, we all assumed it had been burned, especially because celluloid is highly inflammable. Our darkest fears were confirmed the next day when Father went to empty the stove and discovered the clip, used to fasten it to a pocket, among the ashes. Not a trace of the gold nib was left. 'It must have melted into stone,' Father conjectured.

I'm left with one consolation, small though it may be: my fountain pen was cremated, just as I would like to be some day.

Yours, Anne

Dearest Kitty,

*R*ecent events have the house rocking on its founda-
tions. Owing to an outbreak of diphtheria at Bep's,
she won't be allowed to come in contact with us for six
weeks. Without her, the cooking and shopping will be
very difficult, not to mention how much we'll miss her
company. Mr Kleiman is still in bed and has eaten nothing
but gruel for three weeks. Mr Kugler is up to his neck
in work.

Margot sends her Latin lessons to a teacher, who cor-
rects and then returns them. She's registered under Bep's
name. The teacher's very nice, and witty too. I bet he's
glad to have such a clever pupil.

Dussel is in a turmoil and we don't know why. It all
began with Dussel's saying nothing when he was upstairs;
he didn't exchange so much as a word with either Mr
or Mrs van Daan. We all noticed it. This went on for a
few days, and then Mother took the opportunity to warn
him about Mrs van D., who could make life miserable
for him. Dussel said Mr van Daan had started the silent
treatment and he had no intention of breaking it. I should
explain that yesterday was 16 November, the first anniversary of his living in the Annexe. Mother received a
plant in honour of the occasion, but Mrs van Daan, who
had alluded to the date for weeks and made no bones
about the fact that she thought Dussel should treat us to
dinner, received nothing. Instead of making use of the

opportunity to thank us – for the first time – for unselfishly taking him in, he didn't utter a word. And on the morning of the sixteenth, when I asked him whether I should offer him my congratulations or my condolences, he replied that either one would do. Mother, having cast herself in the role of peacemaker, made no headway whatsoever, and the situation finally ended in a draw.

I can say without exaggeration that Dussel has definitely got a screw loose. We often laugh to ourselves because he has no memory, no fixed opinions and no common sense. He's amused us more than once by trying to pass on the news he's just heard, since the message invariably gets garbled in transmission. Furthermore, he answers every reproach or accusation with a load of fine promises, which he never manages to keep.

> *'Der Mann hat einen grossen Geist*
> *Und ist so klein von Taten!'* ★

Yours, Anne

★ A well-known expression: 'The spirit of the man is great, / How puny are his deeds.'

Dearest Kitty,

*L*ast night, just as I was falling asleep, Hanneli suddenly appeared before me.

I saw her there, dressed in rags, her face thin and worn. She looked at me with such sadness and reproach in her enormous eyes that I could read the message in them: 'Oh, Anne, why have you deserted me? Help me, help me, rescue me from this hell!'

And I can't help her. I can only stand by and watch while other people suffer and die. All I can do is pray to God to bring her back to us. I saw Hanneli, and no one else, and I understood why. I misjudged her, wasn't mature enough to understand how difficult it was for her. She was devoted to her friend, and it must have seemed as though I were trying to take her away. The poor thing, she must have felt awful! I know, because I recognize the feeling in myself! I had an occasional flash of understanding, but then got selfishly wrapped up again in my own problems and pleasures.

It was horrible of me to treat her that way, and now she was looking at me, oh so helplessly, with her pale face and beseeching eyes. If only I could help her! Dear God, I have everything I could wish for, while fate has her in its deadly clutches. She was as devout as I am, maybe even more so, and she too wanted to do what was right. But then why have I been chosen to live, while she's probably going to die? What's the difference between us? Why are we now so far apart?

To be honest, I hadn't thought of her for months – no, for at least a year. I hadn't forgotten her entirely, and yet it wasn't until I saw her before me that I thought of all her suffering. ·

Oh, Hanneli, I hope that if you live to the end of the war and return to us, I'll be able to take you in and make up for the wrong I've done you.

But even if I were ever in a position to help, she wouldn't need it more than she does now. I wonder if she ever thinks of me, and what she's feeling?

Merciful God, comfort her, so that at least she won't be alone. Oh, if only You could tell her I'm thinking of her with compassion and love, it might help her go on.

I've got to stop dwelling on this. It won't get me anywhere. I keep seeing her enormous eyes, and they haunt me. Does Hanneli really and truly believe in God, or has religion merely been foisted upon her? I don't even know that. I never took the trouble to ask.

Hanneli, Hanneli, if only I could take you away, if only I could share everything I have with you. It's too late. I can't help, or undo the wrong I've done. But I'll never forget her again and I'll always pray for her!

Yours, Anne

Dearest Kitty,

The closer it got to St Nicholas' Day, the more we all thought back to last year's festively decorated basket. More than anyone, I thought it would be terrible to skip a celebration this year. After long deliberation, I finally came up with an idea, something funny. I consulted Pim, and a week ago we set to work writing a verse for each person.

Sunday evening at a quarter to eight we trooped upstairs carrying the big laundry basket, which had been decorated with cutouts and bows made of pink and blue carbon paper. On top was a large piece of brown wrapping paper with a note attached. Everyone was rather amazed at the sheer size of the gift. I removed the note and read it aloud:

> *'Once again St Nicholas' Day*
> *Has even come to our hideaway;*
> *It won't be quite as fun, I fear,*
> *As the happy day we had last year.*
> *Then we were hopeful, no reason to doubt*
> *That optimism would win the bout,*
> *And by the time this year came round,*
> *We'd all be free, and safe and sound.*
> *Still, let's not forget it's St Nicholas' Day,*
> *Though we've nothing left to give away.*

We'll have to find something else to do:
So everyone please look in their shoe!'

As each person took their own shoe out of the basket, there was a roar of laughter. Inside each shoe was a little paper parcel addressed to its owner.

Yours, Anne

WEDNESDAY, 22 DECEMBER 1943

Dearest Kitty,

A bad case of flu has prevented me from writing to you until today. Being ill here is dreadful. With every cough, I had to duck under the blanket – once, twice, three times – and try to keep from coughing any more. Most of the time the tickle refused to go away, so

I had to drink milk with honey, sugar or cough drops. I get dizzy just thinking about all the cures I've been subjected to: sweating out the fever, steam treatment, wet compresses, dry compresses, hot drinks, swabbing my throat, lying still, heating pad, hot-water bottles, lemonade and, every two hours, the thermometer. Will these remedies really make you better? The worst part was when Mr Dussel decided to play doctor and lay his pomaded head on my bare chest to listen to the sounds. Not only did his hair tickle, but I was embarrassed, even though he went to school thirty years ago and does have some kind of medical degree. Why should he lay his head on my heart? After all, he's not my boyfriend! For that matter, he wouldn't be able to tell a healthy sound from an unhealthy one. He'd have to have his ears cleaned first, since he's becoming alarmingly hard of hearing. But enough about my illness. I'm fit as a fiddle again. I've grown almost half an inch and gained two pounds. I'm pale, but itching to get back to my books.

*Ausnahmsweise** (the only word that will do here), we're all getting on well together. No squabbles, though that probably won't last long. There hasn't been such peace and quiet in this house for at least six months.

Bep is still in isolation, but any day now her sister will no longer be contagious.

For Christmas, we're getting extra cooking oil, sweets and treacle. For Hanukkah, Mr Dussel gave Mrs van Daan and Mother a beautiful cake, which he'd asked

---

* By way of exception.

Miep to bake. On top of all the work she has to do! Margot and I received a brooch made out of a penny, all bright and shiny. I can't really describe it, but it's lovely.

I also have a Christmas present for Miep and Bep. For a whole month I've saved up the sugar I put on my porridge, and Mr Kleiman has used it to have fondant made.

The weather is drizzly and overcast, the stove stinks, and the food lies heavily on our stomachs, producing a variety of rumbles.

The war is at an impasse, spirits are low.

Yours, Anne

FRIDAY, 24 DECEMBER 1943

Dear Kitty,

*A*s I've written many times before, moods have a tendency to affect us quite a bit here, and in my case it's been getting worse lately. '*Himmelhoch jauchzend, zu Tode betrübt*'* certainly applies to me. I'm 'on top of the world' when I think of how fortunate we are and compare myself to other Jewish children, and 'in the

---

* A famous line from Goethe: 'On top of the world, or in the depths of despair.'

depths of despair' when, for example, Mrs Kleiman comes by and talks about Jopie's hockey club, canoe trips, school plays and afternoon teas with friends.

I don't think I'm jealous of Jopie, but I long to have a really good time for once and to laugh so hard it hurts. We're stuck in this house like lepers, especially during winter and the Christmas and New Year holidays. Actually, I shouldn't even be writing this, since it makes me seem so ungrateful, but I can't keep everything to myself, so I'll repeat what I said at the beginning: 'Paper is more patient than people.'

Whenever someone comes in from outside, with the wind in their clothes and the cold on their cheeks, I feel like burying my head under the blankets to keep from thinking, 'When will we be allowed to breathe fresh air again?' I can't do that – on the contrary, I have to hold my head up high and put a bold face on things, but the thoughts keep coming anyway. Not just once, but over and over.

Believe me, if you've been shut up for a year and a half, it can get to be too much for you sometimes. But feelings can't be ignored, no matter how unjust or ungrateful they seem. I long to ride a bike, dance, whistle, look at the world, feel young and know that I'm free, and yet I can't let it show. Just imagine what would happen if all eight of us were to feel sorry for ourselves or walk around with the discontent clearly visible on our faces. Where would that get us? I sometimes wonder if anyone will ever understand what I mean, if anyone will ever overlook my ingratitude and not worry about whether or not I'm Jewish and merely see me as a teen-ager badly in need of some good plain fun. I don't know, and I wouldn't be able to talk about it with anyone, since I'm sure I'd start to cry. Crying can bring relief, as long as you don't cry alone. Despite all my theories and efforts, I miss – every day and every hour of the day – having a mother who understands me. That's why with every-thing I do and write, I imagine the kind of mum I'd like to be to my children later on. The kind of mum who doesn't take everything people say too seriously, but who does take *me* seriously. I find it difficult to describe what I mean, but the word 'mum' says it all. Do you know what I've come up with? In order to give me the feeling of calling my mother something that sounds like 'Mum', I often call her 'Mumsie'. Sometimes I shorten it to 'Mums': an imperfect 'Mum'. I wish I could honour her by removing the 's'. It's a good thing she doesn't realize this, since it would only make her unhappy.

Well, that's enough of that. My writing has raised me somewhat from 'the depths of despair'.

Yours, Anne

*I*t's the day after Christmas, and I can't help thinking about Pim and the story he told me this time last year. I didn't understand the meaning of his words then as well as I do now. If only he'd bring it up again, I might be able to show him I understood what he meant!

I think Pim told me because he, who knows the 'intimate secrets' of so many others, needed to express his own feelings for once; Pim never talks about himself, and I don't think Margot has any inkling of what he's been through. Poor Pim, he can't fool me into thinking he's forgotten that girl. He never will. It's made him very accommodating, since he's not blind to Mother's faults. I hope I'm going to be a little like him, without having to go through what he has!

Anne

MONDAY, 27 DECEMBER 1943

*F*riday evening, for the first time in my life, I received a Christmas present. Mr Kleiman, Mr Kugler and the girls had prepared a wonderful surprise for us. Miep made a delicious Christmas cake with 'Peace 1944' written on top, and Bep provided biscuits that were up to pre-war standards.

There was a pot of yoghurt for Peter, Margot and me, and a bottle of beer for each of the adults. And once again everything was wrapped so nicely, with pretty pictures glued to the parcels. For the rest, the holidays passed by quickly for us.

Anne

I was very sad again last night. Grandma and Hanneli came to me once more. Grandma, oh, my sweet Grandma. How little we understood what she suffered, how kind she always was and what an interest she took in everything that concerned us. And to think that all that time she was carefully guarding her terrible secret.*

Grandma was always so loyal and good. She would never have let any of us down. Whatever happened, no matter how much I misbehaved, Grandma always stuck up for me. Grandma, did you love me, or did you not understand me either? I don't know. How lonely Grandma must have been, in spite of us. You can be lonely even when you're loved by many people, since you're still not anybody's 'one and only'.

And Hanneli? Is she still alive? What's she doing? Dear God, watch over her and bring her back to us. Hanneli, you're a reminder of what my fate might have been. I keep seeing myself in your place. So why am I often miserable about what goes on here? Shouldn't I be happy, contented and glad, except when I'm thinking of Hanneli and those suffering along with her? I'm selfish and cowardly. Why do I always think and dream the most awful things and want to scream in terror? Because, in spite of everything, I still don't have enough faith in God. He's

---

* Anne's grandmother was terminally ill.

given me so much, which I don't deserve, and yet each day I make so many mistakes!

Thinking about the suffering of those you hold dear can reduce you to tears; in fact, you could spend the whole day crying. The most you can do is pray for God to perform a miracle and save at least some of them. And I hope I'm doing enough of that!

Anne

THURSDAY, 30 DECEMBER 1943

Dearest Kitty,

Since the last raging quarrels, things have settled down here, not only between ourselves, Dussel and 'upstairs', but also between Mr and Mrs van D. Nevertheless, a few dark thunderclouds are heading this way, and all because of . . . food. Mrs van D. came up with the ridiculous idea of frying fewer potatoes in the morning and saving them for later in the day. Mother and Dussel and the rest of us didn't agree with her, so now we're dividing up the potatoes as well. It seems the fats and oils aren't being doled out fairly, and Mother's going to have to put a stop to it. I'll let you know if there are any interesting developments. For the last few months now we've been splitting up the meat (theirs with fat, ours without), the soup (they eat it, we don't), the potatoes (theirs peeled, ours not), the extras and now the fried potatoes too.

If only we could split up completely!

Yours, Anne

PS. Bep had a picture postcard of the entire Royal Family copied for me. Juliana looks very young, and so does the Queen. The three little girls are adorable. It was incredibly nice of Bep, don't you think?

SUNDAY, 2 JANUARY 1944

Dearest Kitty,

This morning, when I had nothing to do, I leafed through the pages of my diary and came across so many letters dealing with the subject of 'Mother' in such strong terms that I was shocked. I said to myself, 'Anne, is that really you talking about hate? Oh, Anne, how could you?'

I continued to sit with the open book in my hand and wonder why I was filled with so much anger and hate that I had to confide it all to you. I tried to understand the Anne of last year and make apologies for her, because as long as I leave you with these accusations and don't attempt to explain what prompted them, my conscience won't be clear. I was suffering then (and still do) from moods that kept my head under water (figuratively speaking) and allowed me to see things only from my own perspective, without calmly considering what the others – those whom I, with my mercurial temperament, had hurt or offended – had said, and then behaving as they would have done.

I hid inside myself, thought of no one but myself and calmly wrote down all my joy, sarcasm and sorrow in my diary. Because this diary has become a kind of scrap-book, it means a great deal to me, but I could easily write 'over and done with' on many of its pages.

I was furious at Mother (and still am a lot of the time). It's true, she didn't understand me, but I didn't understand her either. Because she loved me, she was tender and affectionate, but because of the difficult situations I put her in, and the sad circumstances in which she found herself, she was nervous and irritable, so I can understand why she was often short with me.

I was offended, took it far too much to heart and was insolent and beastly to her, which, in turn, made her unhappy. We were caught in a vicious circle of unpleasantness and sorrow. Not a very happy period for either of us, but at least it's coming to an end. I didn't want to see what was going on, and I felt very sorry for myself, but that's understandable too.

Those violent outbursts on paper are simply expressions of anger that, in normal life, I could have worked off by locking myself in my room and stamping my foot a few times or calling Mother names behind her back.

The period of tearfully passing judgement on Mother

is over. I've grown wiser and Mother's nerves are a bit steadier. Most of the time I manage to hold my tongue when I'm annoyed, and she does too; so on the surface, we seem to be getting along better. But there's one thing I can't do, and that's to love Mother with the devotion of a child.

I soothe my conscience with the thought that it's better for unkind words to be down on paper than for Mother to have to carry them around in her heart.

Yours, Anne

THURSDAY, 6 JANUARY 1944

Dearest Kitty,

Today I have two things to confess. It's going to take a long time, but I have to tell them to someone, and you're the most likely candidate, since I know you'll keep a secret, no matter what happens.

The first is about Mother. As you know, I've frequently complained about her and then tried my best to be nice. I've suddenly realized what's wrong with her. Mother has said that she sees us more as friends than as daughters. That's all very nice, of course, except that a friend can't take the place of a mother. I need my mother to set a good example and be a person I can respect, but in most matters she's an example of what *not* to do. I have the feeling that Margot thinks so differently about these things that she'd never be able to understand what I've just told you. And Father avoids all conversations having to do with Mother.

I imagine a mother as a woman who, first and foremost, possesses a great deal of tact, especially towards her adolescent children, and not one who, like Mumsie, pokes fun at me when I cry. Not because I'm in pain, but because of other things.

This may seem trivial, but there's one incident I've never forgiven her for. It happened one day when I had to go to the dentist. Mother and Margot planned to go with me and agreed I should take my bicycle. When the dentist was finished and we were back outside, Margot and Mother very sweetly informed me that they were going into town to buy or look at something, I don't remember what, and of course I wanted to go along. But they said I couldn't come because I had my bike with me. Tears of rage rushed to my eyes, and Margot and Mother began laughing at me. I was so furious that I stuck my tongue out at them, right there on the street. A little old lady happened to be passing by, and she looked terribly shocked. I cycled home and must have cried for hours. Strangely enough, even though Mother has wounded me thousands of times, this particular wound still stings whenever I think of how angry I was.

I find it difficult to confess the second one because it's about myself. I'm not prudish, Kitty, and yet every time they give a blow-by-blow account of their trips to the lavatory, which they often do, my whole body rises in revolt.

Yesterday I read an article on blushing by Sis Heyster. It was as if she'd addressed it directly to me. Not that I blush easily, but the rest of the article did apply. What she basically says is that during puberty girls withdraw into themselves and begin thinking about the wondrous changes taking place in their bodies. I feel that too, which probably accounts for my recent embarrassment over Margot, Mother and Father. On the other hand, Margot is a lot shyer than I am, and yet she's not in the least embarrassed.

I think that what's happening to me is so wonderful, and I don't just mean the changes taking place on the outside of my body, but also those on the inside. I never discuss myself or any of these things with others, which is why I have to talk about them to myself. Whenever I have my period (and that's only been three times), I have the feeling that in spite of all the pain, discomfort and mess, I'm carrying around a sweet secret. So even though it's a nuisance, in a certain way I'm always looking forward to the time when I'll feel that secret inside me once again.

Sis Heyster also writes that girls my age feel very insecure about themselves and are just beginning to discover that they're individuals with their own ideas, thoughts and habits. I'd just turned thirteen when I came here, so I started thinking about myself and realized that I've become an 'independent person' sooner than most girls. Sometimes when I lie in bed at night I feel a terrible urge to touch my breasts and listen to the quiet, steady beating of my heart.

Unconsciously, I had these feelings even before I came here. Once when I was spending the night at Jacque's, I could no longer restrain my curiosity about her body, which she'd always hidden from me and which I'd never seen. I asked her whether, as proof of our friendship, we could touch each other's breasts. Jacque refused. I also had a terrible desire to kiss her, which I did. Every time I see a female nude, such as the Venus in my art history book, I go into ecstasy. Sometimes I find them so exquisite I have to struggle to hold back my tears. If only I had a girlfriend!

THURSDAY, 6 JANUARY 1944

Dearest Kitty,

*M*y longing for someone to talk to has become so unbearable that I somehow took it into my head to select Peter for this role. On the few occasions when I have gone to Peter's room during the day, I've always thought it was nice and cosy. But Peter's too polite to show someone the door when they're bothering him, so I've never dared to stay long. I've always been afraid he'd think I was a pest. I've been looking for an excuse to linger in his room and get him talking without his noticing, and yesterday I got my chance. Peter, you see, is currently going through a crossword-puzzle craze, and he doesn't do anything else all day. I was helping him, and we soon ended up sitting across from each other at his table, Peter on the chair and me on the divan.

It gave me a wonderful feeling when I looked into his dark blue eyes and saw how bashful my unexpected visit had made him. I could read his innermost thoughts, and in his face I saw a look of helplessness and uncertainty as to how to behave, and at the same time a flicker of awareness of his masculinity. I saw his shyness, and I melted. I wanted to say, 'Tell me about yourself. Look beneath my chatty exterior.' But I found that it was easier to think up questions than to ask them.

The evening came to a close, and nothing happened, except that I told him about the article on blushing. Not what I wrote you, of course, just that he would grow more secure as he got older.

That night I lay in bed and cried my eyes out, all the while making sure no one could hear me. The idea that I had to beg Peter for favours was simply revolting. But people will do almost anything to satisfy their longings; take me, for example, I've made up my mind to visit Peter more often and, somehow, get him to talk to me.

You mustn't think I'm in love with Peter, because I'm not. If the van Daans had had a daughter instead of a son, I'd have tried to make friends with her.

This morning I woke up just before seven and immediately remembered what I'd been dreaming about. I was sitting on a chair and across from me was Peter . . . Peter Schiff. We were looking at Mary Bos's sketchbook. The dream was so vivid I can even remember some of the drawings. But that wasn't all – the dream went on. Peter's eyes suddenly met mine, and I stared for a long time into those velvety brown eyes. Then he said very softly, 'If I'd only known, I'd have come to you long ago!' I turned abruptly away, overcome by emotion. And then I felt a soft, oh-so-cool and gentle cheek against mine, and it felt so good, so good . . .

At that point I woke up, still feeling his cheek against mine and his brown eyes staring deep into my heart, so deep that he could read how much I'd loved him and how much I still do. Again my eyes filled with tears, and I was sad because I'd lost him once more, and yet at the same time glad because I knew with certainty that Peter is still the only one for me.

It's funny, but I often have such vivid images in my dreams. One night I saw Grammy* so clearly that I could even make out her skin of soft, crinkly velvet. Another time Grandma appeared to me as a guardian angel. After that it was Hanneli, who still symbolizes to me the suffering of my friends as well as that of Jews in general, so that when I'm praying for her, I'm also praying for all the Jews and all those in need.

And now Peter, my dearest Peter. I've never had such a clear mental image of him. I don't need a photograph, I can see him oh so well.

Yours, Anne

* Grammy is Anne's grandmother on her father's side, and Grandma her grandmother on her mother's side.

Dearest Kitty,

I'm such an idiot. I forgot that I haven't yet told you the story of my one true love.

When I was a little girl, way back in nursery school, I took a liking to Sally Kimmel. His father was gone, and he and his mother lived with an aunt. One of Sally's cousins was a good-looking, slender, dark-haired boy named Appy, who later turned out to look like a matinée idol and aroused more admiration than the short, comical, chubby Sally. For a long time we went everywhere together, but aside from that, my love was unrequited until Peter crossed my path. I had an absolute crush on him. He liked me too, and we were inseparable for one whole summer. I can still see us walking hand in hand through our neighbourhood, Peter in a white cotton suit and me in a short summer dress. At the end of the summer holidays he moved up a form to the next school, while I stayed in the sixth form. He'd collect me on the way home, or I'd pick him up. Peter was the ideal boy: tall, slim and good-looking, with a serious, quiet and intelligent face. He had dark hair, beautiful brown eyes, ruddy cheeks and a nicely pointed nose. I was crazy about his smile, which made him look so boyish and mischievous.

I'd gone to the country during the summer holidays, and when I came back, Peter was no longer at his old address; he'd moved and was living with a much older boy, who apparently told him I was just a child, because

Peter stopped seeing me. I loved him so much that I didn't want to face the truth. I kept clinging to him until the day I finally realized that if I continued to chase after him, people would say I was mad about boys.

The years went by. Peter went around with girls his own age and no longer bothered to say hello to me. I started school at the Jewish Lyceum, and several boys in my class were in love with me. I enjoyed it and felt honoured by their attentions, but that was all. Later on, Hello had a terrible crush on me, but as I've already told you, I never fell in love again.

There's a saying: 'Time heals all wounds.' That's how it was with me. I told myself I'd forgotten Peter and no longer liked him in the least. But my memories of him were so strong that I had to admit to myself that the only reason I no longer liked him was that I was jealous of the other girls. This morning I realized that nothing has changed; on the contrary, as I've grown older and more mature, my love has grown along with me. I can understand now that Peter thought I was childish, and yet it still hurts to think he'd forgotten me completely. I saw his face so clearly; I knew for certain that no one but Peter could have stuck in my mind that way.

I've been in an utter state of confusion today. When Father kissed me this morning, I wanted to shout, 'Oh, if only you were Peter!' I've been thinking of him constantly, and all day long I've been repeating to myself, 'Oh, Petel, my darling, darling Petel . . .'

Where can I find help? I simply have to go on living and praying to God that, if we ever get out of here,

Peter's path will cross mine and he'll gaze into my eyes, read the love in them and say, 'Oh, Anne, if I'd only known, I'd have come to you long ago.'

Once when Father and I were talking about sex, he said I was too young to understand that kind of desire. But I thought I did understand it, and now I'm sure I do. Nothing is as dear to me now as my darling Petel!

I saw my face in the mirror, and it looked so different. My eyes were clear and deep, my cheeks were rosy, which they hadn't been in weeks, my mouth was much softer. I looked happy, and yet there was something so sad in my expression that the smile immediately faded from my lips. I'm not happy, since I know Petel's not thinking of me, and yet I can still feel his beautiful eyes gazing at me and his cool, soft cheek against mine . . . Oh, Petel, Petel, how am I ever going to free myself from your image? Wouldn't anyone who took your place be a poor substitute? I love you, with a love so great that it simply couldn't keep growing inside my heart, but had to leap out and reveal itself in all its magnitude.

A week ago, even a day ago, if you'd asked me, 'Which of your friends do you think you'd be most likely to marry?' I'd have answered, 'Sally, since he makes me feel good, peaceful and safe!' But now I'd cry, 'Petel, because I love him with all my heart and all my soul. I surrender myself completely!' Except for that one thing: he may touch my face, but that's as far as it goes.

This morning I imagined I was in the front attic with Petel, sitting on the floor by the windows, and after talking for a while, we both began to cry. Moments later I felt his mouth and his wonderful cheek! Oh, Petel, come to me. Think of me, my dearest Petel!

WEDNESDAY, 12 JANUARY 1944

Dearest Kitty,

*B*ep's been back for the last two weeks, though her sister won't be allowed back at school until next week. Bep herself spent two days in bed with a bad cold. Miep and Jan were also out for two days, with upset stomachs.

I'm currently going through a dance and ballet craze and am diligently practising my dance steps every evening. I've made an ultra-modern dance costume out of a lacy lavender petticoat belonging to Mumsie. Tape is threaded through the top and tied just above the bust. A pink corded ribbon completes the ensemble. I tried to turn my gym shoes into ballet slippers, but with no success. My stiff limbs are well on the way to becoming as supple as they used to be. A terrific exercise is to sit on the floor, place a heel in each hand and raise both legs in the air. I have to sit on a cushion, because otherwise my poor backside really takes a beating.

Everyone here is reading a book called *A Cloudless Morning*. Mother thought it was extremely good because it describes a number of adolescent problems. I thought to myself, a bit ironically, 'Why don't you take more interest in your own adolescents first!'

I think Mother believes that Margot and I have a better relationship with our parents than anyone in the whole wide world, and that no mother is more involved in the lives of her children than she is. She must have my sister in mind, since I don't believe Margot has the same problems and thoughts as I do. Far be it from me to point out to Mother that one of her daughters is not at all what she imagines. She'd be completely bewildered, and anyway, she'd never be able to change; I'd like to spare her that grief, especially since I know that everything would remain the same. Mother does sense that Margot loves her much more than I do, but she thinks I'm just going through a phase.

Margot's much nicer. She seems a lot different from what she used to be. She's not nearly as catty these days and is becoming a real friend. She no longer thinks of me as a little baby who doesn't count.

It's funny, but I can sometimes see myself as others see me. I take a leisurely look at the person called 'Anne Frank' and browse through the pages of her life as though she were a stranger.

Before I came here, when I didn't think about things as much as I do now, I occasionally had the feeling that I didn't belong to Mumsie, Pim and Margot and that I would always be an outsider. I sometimes went around for six months at a time pretending I was an orphan. Then I'd chastise myself for playing the victim, when really, I'd always been so fortunate. After that I'd force myself to be friendly for a while. Every morning when I heard footsteps on the stairs, I hoped it would be Mother coming to say good morning. I'd greet her warmly, because I honestly did look forward to her affectionate glance. But then she'd snap at me for having made some comment or other and I'd go off to school feeling completely discouraged. On the way home I'd make excuses for her, telling myself that she had so many worries. I'd arrive home in high spirits, chatting nineteen to the dozen, until the events of the morning would repeat themselves and I'd leave the room with my satchel in my hand and a pensive look on my face. Sometimes I'd decide to stay angry, but then I always had so much to talk about after school that I'd forget my resolution and want Mother to stop whatever she was doing and lend a willing ear. Then the time would come once more when I no longer listened for the steps on the stairs and felt lonely and cried into my pillow every night.

Everything has become much worse here. But you already knew that. Now God has sent someone to help me: Peter. I fondle my pendant, press it to my lips and think, 'What do I care! Petel is mine and nobody knows it!' With this in mind, I can rise above every nasty remark. Which of the people here would suspect that so much is going on in the mind of a teenage girl?

My dearest Kitty,

There's no reason for me to go on describing all our quarrels and arguments down to the last detail. It's enough to tell you that we've divided many things like meat and fats and oils and are frying our own potatoes. Recently we've been eating a little extra rye bread because by four o'clock we're so hungry for dinner we can barely control our rumbling stomachs.

Mother's birthday is rapidly approaching. She received some extra sugar from Mr Kugler, which sparked off jealousy on the part of the van Daans, because Mrs van D. didn't receive any on her birthday. But what's the point of boring you with harsh words, spiteful conversations and tears when you know they bore us even more?

Mother has expressed a wish, which isn't likely to come true any time soon: not to have to see Mr van Daan's face for two whole weeks. I wonder if everyone who shares a house sooner or later ends up at odds with their fellow residents. Or have we just had a stroke of bad luck? At mealtimes, when Dussel helps himself to a quarter of the half-filled gravy boat and leaves the rest of us to do without, I lose my appetite and feel like jumping to my feet, knocking him off his chair and throwing him out of the door.

Are most people so stingy and selfish? I've gained some insight into human nature since I came here, which is good, but I've had enough for the present. Peter says the same.

The war is going to go on despite our quarrels and our longing for freedom and fresh air, so we should try to make the best of our stay here.

I'm preaching, but I also believe that if I live here much longer, I'll turn into a dried-up old beanstalk. And all I really want is to be an honest-to-goodness teenager!

Yours, Anne

WEDNESDAY EVENING, 19 JANUARY 1944

Dearest Kitty,

I (there I go again!) don't know what's happened, but since my dream I keep noticing how I've changed. By the way, I dreamed about Peter again last night and once again I felt his eyes penetrate mine, but this dream was less vivid and not quite as beautiful as the last.

You know that I always used to be jealous of Margot's relationship with Father. There's not a trace of my jealousy left now; I still feel hurt when Father's nerves cause him to be unreasonable towards me, but then I think, 'I can't blame you for being the way you are. You talk so much about the minds of children and adolescents, but you don't know the first thing about them!' I long for more than Father's affection, more than his hugs and kisses. Isn't it awful of me to be so preoccupied with myself? Shouldn't I, who wants to be good and kind, forgive them first? I forgive Mother too, but every time she makes a sarcastic remark or laughs at me, it's all I can do to control myself.

I know I'm far from being what I should; will I ever be?

Anne Frank

PS. Father asked if I told you about the cake. For Mother's birthday, she received a real mocha cake, prewar quality, from the office. It was a really nice day! But at the moment there's no room in my head for things like that.

SATURDAY, 22 JANUARY 1944

Dearest Kitty,

Can you tell me why people go to such lengths to hide their real selves? Or why I always behave very differently when I'm in the company of others? Why do people have so little trust in one another? I know there must be a reason, but sometimes I think it's horrible that you can't ever confide in anyone, not even those closest to you.

It seems as if I've grown up since the night I had that dream, as if I've become more independent. You'll be amazed when I tell you that even my attitude towards the van Daans has changed. I've stopped looking at all the discussions and arguments from my family's biased point of view. What's brought on such a radical change? Well, you see, I suddenly realized that if Mother had been different, if she'd been a real mum, our relationship would have been very, very different. Mrs van Daan is by no means a wonderful person, yet half the arguments could have been avoided if Mother hadn't been so hard to deal with every time they got on to a tricky subject. Mrs van Daan does have one good point, though: you can talk to her. She may be selfish, stingy and underhanded, but she'll readily back down as long as you don't provoke her and make her unreasonable. This tactic doesn't work every time, but if you're patient, you can keep trying and see how far you get.

All the conflicts about our upbringing, about not pampering children, about the food – about everything, absolutely everything – might have taken a different turn if we'd remained open and on friendly terms instead of always seeing the worst side.

I know exactly what you're going to say, Kitty. 'But, Anne, are these words really coming from your lips? From you, who have had to put up with so many unkind words from upstairs? From you, who are aware of all the injustices?'

And yet they are coming from me. I want to take a fresh look at things and form my own opinion, not just ape my parents, as in the proverb 'The apple never falls far from the tree.' I want to re-examine the van Daans and decide for myself what's true and what's been blown out of proportion. If I end up being disappointed in them,

I can always side with Father and Mother. But if not, I can try to change their attitude. And if that doesn't work, I'll have to stick with my own opinions and judgement. I'll take every opportunity to speak openly to Mrs van D. about our many differences and not be afraid – despite my reputation as a smart aleck – to offer my impartial opinion. I won't say anything negative about my own family, though that doesn't mean I won't defend them if somebody else does, and as of today, my gossiping is a thing of the past.

Up till now I was absolutely convinced that the van Daans were entirely to blame for the quarrels, but now I'm sure the fault was largely ours. We were right as far as the issues were concerned, but intelligent people (such as ourselves!) should have more insight into how to deal with others.

I hope I've got at least a touch of that insight, and that I'll find an occasion to put it to good use.

Yours, Anne

MONDAY, 24 JANUARY 1944

Dearest Kitty,

A very strange thing has happened to me. (Actually, 'happened' isn't quite the right word.)

Before I came here, whenever anyone at home or at

school talked about sex, they were either secretive or disgusting. Any words having to do with sex were spoken in a low whisper, and those who weren't in the know were often laughed at. That struck me as odd, and I often wondered why people were so mysterious or obnoxious when they talked about this subject. But because I couldn't change things, I said as little as possible or asked my girlfriends for information.

After I'd learned quite a lot, Mother once said to me, 'Anne, let me give you some good advice. Never discuss this with boys, and if they bring it up, don't answer them.'

I still remember my exact reply. 'No, of course not,' I exclaimed. 'Imagine!' And nothing more was said.

When we first went into hiding, Father often told me about things I'd rather have heard from Mother, and I learned the rest from books or things I picked up in conversations.

Peter van Daan wasn't ever as obnoxious about this subject as the boys at school. Or maybe just once or twice, in the beginning, though he wasn't trying to get me to talk. Mrs van Daan once told us she'd never discussed these matters with Peter, and as far as she knew, neither had her husband. Apparently she didn't even know how much Peter knew or where he got his information.

Yesterday, when Margot, Peter and I were peeling potatoes, the conversation somehow turned to Boche. 'We're still not sure whether Boche is a boy or a girl, are we?' I asked.

'Yes we are,' he answered. 'Boche is a tomcat.'

I began to laugh. 'Some tomcat if he's pregnant.'

Peter and Margot joined in the laughter. You see, a month or two ago Peter informed us that Boche was sure to have kittens before long, because her stomach was rapidly swelling. However, Boche's fat tummy turned out to be due to a bunch of stolen bones. No kittens were growing inside, much less about to be born.

Peter felt called upon to defend himself against my accusation. 'Come with me. You can see for yourself. I was horsing around with the cat one day, and I could definitely see it was a "he".'

Unable to restrain my curiosity, I went with him to the warehouse. Boche, however, wasn't receiving visitors at that hour, and was nowhere in sight. We waited for a while, but when it got cold, we went back upstairs.

Later that afternoon I heard Peter go downstairs for the second time. I mustered the courage to walk through the silent house by myself and reached the warehouse. Boche was on the packing table, playing with Peter, who was getting ready to put him on the scales and weigh him.

'Hello, do you want to have a look?' Without any preliminaries, he picked up the cat, turned him over on his back, deftly held his head and paws and began the lesson. 'This is the male sexual organ, these are a few stray hairs, and that's his backside.'

The cat flipped himself over and stood up on his little white feet.

If any other boy had pointed out the 'male sexual

organ' to me, I would never have given him a second glance. But Peter went on talking in a normal voice about what is otherwise a very awkward subject. Nor did he have any ulterior motives. By the time he'd finished, I felt so much at ease that I started acting normally too. We played with Boche, had a good time, chatted a bit and finally sauntered through the long warehouse to the door.

'Were you there when Mouschi was fixed?'

'Yes, of course. It doesn't take long. Naturally, they give the cat an anaesthetic.'

'Do they take something out?'

'No, the vet just snips the tube. There's nothing to see on the outside.'

I had to get up my nerve to ask a question, since it wasn't as 'normal' as I thought. 'Peter, the German word *Geschlechtsteil* means "sexual organ", doesn't it? But then the male and female ones have different names.'

'I know that.'

'The female one is a vagina, that I know, but I don't know what it's called in males.'

'Hmm.'

'Oh well,' I said. 'How are we supposed to know these words? Most of the time you just come across them by accident.'

'Why wait? I'll ask my parents. They know more than I do and they've had more experience.

We were already on the stairs, so nothing more was said.

Yes, it really did happen. I'd never have talked to a

girl about this in such a normal tone of voice. I'm also certain that this isn't what Mother meant when she warned me about boys.

All the same, I wasn't exactly my usual self for the rest of the day. When I thought back to our talk, it struck me as odd. But I've learned at least one thing: there are young people, even those of the opposite sex, who can discuss these things naturally, without cracking jokes.

Is Peter really going to ask his parents a lot of questions? Is he really the way he seemed yesterday?

Oh, what do I know?!!!

Yours, Anne

FRIDAY, 28 JANUARY 1944

Dearest Kitty,

*I*n recent weeks I've developed a great liking for family trees and the genealogical tables of royal families. I've come to the conclusion that once you begin your search, you have to keep digging deeper and deeper into the past, which leads you to even more interesting discoveries.

Although I'm extremely diligent when it comes to my schoolwork and can pretty much follow the BBC Home Service on the radio, I still spend many of my Sundays sorting out and looking over my film-star collection, which has grown to a very respectable size. Mr Kugler makes me happy every Monday by bringing me a copy of *Cinema & Theatre* magazine. The less worldly members of our household often refer to this small indulgence as a waste of money, yet they never fail to be surprised at how accurately I can list the actors in any given film, even after a year. Bep, who often goes to the cinema with her boyfriend on her day off, tells me on Saturday the name of the film they're going to see, and I then proceed to rattle off the names of the leading actors and actresses and the reviews. Mums recently remarked that I wouldn't need to go to the cinema later on, because I know all the plots, the names of the stars and the reviews by heart.

Whenever I come sailing in with a new hairstyle, I can read the disapproval on their faces, and I can be sure someone will ask which film star I'm trying to imitate. My reply, that it's my own invention, is greeted with scepticism. As for the hair-do, it doesn't hold its set for more than half an hour. By that time I'm so sick and tired of their remarks that I race to the bathroom and restore my hair to its normal mass of curls.

Yours, Anne

Dearest Kitty,

*T*his morning I was wondering whether you ever felt like a cow, having to chew my stale news over and over again until you're so fed up with the monotonous fare that you yawn and secretly wish Anne would dig up something new.

Sorry, I know you find it dull as ditchwater, but imagine how sick and tired I am of hearing the same old stuff. If the talk at mealtimes isn't about politics or good food, then Mother or Mrs van D. trot out stories about their childhood that we've heard a thousand times before, or Dussel goes on and on about beautiful racehorses, his Charlotte's extensive wardrobe, leaky rowing-boats, boys who can swim at the age of four, aching muscles and frightened patients. It all boils down to this: whenever one of the eight of us opens his mouth, the other seven can finish the story for him. We know the punch line of every joke before it gets told, so that whoever's telling it is left to laugh alone. The various milkmen, grocers and butchers of the two former housewives have been praised to the skies or run into the ground so many times that in our imaginations they've grown as old as Methuselah; there's absolutely no chance of anything new or fresh being brought up for discussion in the Annexe.

Still, all this might be bearable if only the grown-ups weren't in the habit of repeating the stories we hear from Mr Kleiman, Jan or Miep, each time embellishing them with a few details of their own, so that I often have to pinch my arm under the table to keep myself from setting the enthusiastic storyteller on the right track. Little children, such as Anne, must never, ever correct their elders, no matter how many blunders they make or how often they let their imaginations run away with them.

Jan and Mr Kleiman love talking about people who have gone underground or into hiding; they know we're eager to hear about others in our situation and that we truly sympathize with the sorrow of those who've been arrested as well as the joy of prisoners who've been freed.

Going underground or into hiding has become as routine as the proverbial pipe and slippers that used to await the man of the house after a long day at work. There are many resistance groups, such as Free Netherlands, that forge identity cards, provide financial support to those in hiding, organize hiding places and find work for young Christians who go underground. It's amazing how much these generous and unselfish people do, risking their own lives to help and save others.

The best example of this is our own helpers, who have managed to pull us through so far and will hopefully bring us safely to shore, because otherwise they'll find themselves sharing the fate of those they're trying to protect. Never have they uttered a single word about the burden we must be, never have they complained that we're too much trouble. They come upstairs every day and talk to the men about business and politics, to the women about food and wartime difficulties and to the children about books and newspapers. They put on their most cheerful expressions, bring flowers and gifts for birthdays and special occasions and are always ready to do what they can. That's something we should never forget; while others display their heroism in battle or against the Germans, our helpers prove theirs every day by their good spirits and affection.

The most bizarre stories are making the rounds, yet most of them are really true. For instance, Mr Kleiman reported this week that a football match was held in the province of Gelderland; one team consisted entirely of men who had gone underground, and the other of eleven Military Policemen. In Hilversum, new registration cards were issued. In order for the many people in hiding to get their rations (you have to show this card to obtain your ration book or else pay 60 guilders a book), the registrar asked all those hiding in that district to pick up their cards at a specified hour, when the documents could be collected at a separate table.

All the same, you have to be careful that stunts like these don't reach the ears of the Germans.

Yours, Anne

My dearest Kit,

Another Sunday has rolled around; I don't mind them as much as I did in the beginning, but they're boring enough.

I still haven't gone to the warehouse yet, but maybe sometime soon. Last night I went downstairs in the dark, all by myself, after having been there with Father a few nights before. I stood at the top of the stairs while German planes flew back and forth, and I knew I was on my own, that I couldn't count on others for support. My fear vanished. I looked up at the sky and trusted in God.

I have an intense need to be alone. Father has noticed I'm not my usual self, but I can't tell him what's bothering me. All I want to do is scream 'Let me be, leave me alone!'

Who knows, perhaps the day will come when I'm left alone more than I'd like!

Anne Frank

Dearest Kitty,

*I*nvasion fever is mounting daily throughout the country. If you were here, I'm sure you'd be as impressed as I am at the many preparations, though you'd no doubt laugh at all the fuss we're making. Who knows, it may all be for nothing!

The papers are full of invasion news and are driving everyone insane with such statements as: 'In the event of a British landing in Holland, the Germans will do what they can to defend the country, even flooding it, if necessary.' They've published maps of Holland with the potential flood areas marked. Since large portions of Amsterdam were shaded in, our first question was what we should do if the water in the streets rose to above our waists. This tricky question elicited a variety of responses:

'It'll be impossible to walk or ride a bike, so we'll have to wade through the water.'

'Don't be silly. We'll have to try and swim. We'll all put on our bathing suits and caps and swim underwater as much as we can, so nobody can see we're Jews.'

'Rubbish! I can just imagine the ladies swimming with the rats biting their legs!' (That was a man, of course; we'll see who screams loudest!)

'We won't even be able to leave the house. The warehouse is so unstable it'll collapse if there's a flood.'

'Listen, everyone, all joking aside, we really ought to try and get a boat.'

'Why bother? I have a better idea. We can each take a packing case from the attic and row with a wooden spoon.'

'I'm going to walk on stilts. I used to be a wizard at it when I was young.'

'Jan Gies won't need to. He'll let his wife ride piggyback, and then Miep will be on stilts.'

So now you have a rough idea of what's going on, don't you, Kit? This light-hearted banter is all very amusing, but reality will prove otherwise. The second question about the invasion was bound to arise: what should we do if the Germans evacuate Amsterdam?

'Leave the city along with the others. Disguise ourselves as well as we can.'

'Whatever happens, don't go outside! The best thing to do is to stay put! The Germans are capable of herding the entire population of Holland into Germany, where they'll all die.'

'Of course we'll stay here. This is the safest place. We'll try to talk Kleiman and his family into coming here to live with us. We'll somehow get hold of a bag of wood shavings, so we can sleep on the floor. Let's ask Miep and Kleiman to bring some blankets, just in case. And we'll order some extra grain to supplement the sixty-five pounds we already have. Jan can try to find some more beans. At the moment we've got about sixty-five pounds of beans and ten pounds of split peas. And don't forget the fifty tins of vegetables.

'What about the rest, Mother? Give us the latest figures.'

'Ten tins of fish, forty tins of milk, twenty pounds of powdered milk, three bottles of oil, four pots of butter, four jars of meat, two big jars of strawberries, two jars of raspberries, twenty jars of tomatoes, ten pounds of oatmeal, nine pounds of rice. That's it.'

Our supplies are holding out fairly well. All the same, we have to feed the office staff, which means dipping into our reserves every week, so it's not as much as it seems. We have enough coal and firewood, candles too.

'Let's all make little moneybags to hide in our clothes so we can take our money with us if we need to leave here.'

'We can make lists of what to take first in case we have to run for it, and pack our rucksacks in advance.'

'When the time comes, we'll put two people on lookout, one in the loft at the front of the house and one at the back.'

'Hang on, what's the use of so much food if there isn't any water, gas or electricity?'

'We'll have to cook on the stove. Filter the water and boil it. We should clean some big jugs and fill them with water. We can also store water in the three pans we use for preserving, and in the tin bath.'

'Besides, we still have about two hundred and thirty pounds of winter potatoes in the spice storeroom.'

All day long that's all I hear. Invasion, invasion, nothing but invasion. Arguments about going hungry, dying, bombs, fire extinguishers, sleeping bags, identity cards, poison gas, etc., etc. Not exactly cheerful.

A good example of the explicit warnings of the male contingent is the following conversation with Jan:

Annexe: 'We're afraid that when the Germans retreat, they'll take the entire population with them.'

Jan: 'That's impossible. They haven't got enough trains.'

Annexe: 'Trains? Do you really think they'd put civilians on trains? Absolutely not. Everyone would have to hoof it.' (Or, as Dussel always says, *per pedes apostolorum.*)

Jan: 'I can't believe that. You're always looking on the dark side. What reason would they have to round up all the civilians and take them along?'

Annexe: 'Don't you remember Goebbels saying that if the Germans have to go, they'll slam the doors to all the occupied territories behind them?'

Jan: 'They've said a lot of things.'

Annexe: 'Do you think the Germans are too noble or humane to do it? Their reasoning is: if we go under, we'll drag everyone else down with us.'

Jan: 'You can say what you like, I just don't believe it.'

Annexe: 'It's always the same old story. No one wants to see the danger until it's staring them in the face.'

Jan: 'But you don't know anything for sure. You're just making an assumption.'

Annexe: 'Because we've already been through it all ourselves. First in Germany and then here. What do you think's happening in Russia?'

Jan: 'You shouldn't include the Jews. I don't think anyone knows what's going on in Russia. The British and the Russians are probably exaggerating for propaganda purposes, just like the Germans.'

Annexe: 'Absolutely not. The BBC has always told the truth. And even if the news is slightly exaggerated, the facts are bad enough as they are. You can't deny that millions of peace-loving citizens in Poland and Russia have been murdered or gassed.'

I'll spare you the rest of our conversations. I'm very calm and take no notice of all the fuss. I've reached the point where I hardly care whether I live or die. The world will keep on turning without me, and I can't do anything to change events anyway. I'll just let matters take their course and concentrate on studying and hope that everything will be all right in the end.

Yours, Anne

TUESDAY, 8 FEBRUARY 1944

Dear Kitty,

I can't tell you how I feel. One minute I'm longing for peace and quiet, and the next for a little fun. We've forgotten how to laugh ⊤ I mean, laughing so hard you can't stop.

This morning I had the giggles; you know, the kind we used to have at school. Margot and I were giggling like real teenagers.

Last night there was another scene with Mother. Margot was tucking her woollen blanket around her when suddenly she leapt out of bed and carefully examined the blanket. What do you think she found? A pin! Mother had patched the blanket and forgotten to take it out. Father shook his head meaningfully and made a comment about how careless Mother is. Soon afterwards Mother came in from the bathroom, and just to tease her I said, *'Du bist doch eine echte Rabenmutter.'**

Of course, she asked me why I'd said that, and we told her about the pin she'd overlooked. She immediately assumed her haughtiest expression and said, 'You're a fine one to talk. When you're sewing, the entire floor is covered with pins. And look, you've left the manicure set lying around again. You never put that away either!'

I said I hadn't used it, and Margot backed me up, since she was the guilty party.

Mother went on talking about how messy I was until I got fed up and said, rather curtly, 'I wasn't even the one who said you were careless. I'm always getting blamed for other people's mistakes!'

Mother fell silent, and less than a minute later I was obliged to kiss her good night. This incident may not have been very important, but these days everything gets on my nerves.

Anne Mary Frank

* Oh, you *are* cruel.

Dearest Kitty,

*T*he sun is shining, the sky is deep blue, there's a magnificent breeze, and I'm longing – really longing – for everything: conversation, freedom, friends, being alone. I long . . . to cry! I feel as if I were about to explode. I know crying would help, but I can't cry. I'm restless. I walk from one room to another, breathe through the crack in the window frame, feel my heart beating as if to say, 'Fulfil my longing at last . . .'

I think spring is inside me. I feel spring awakening, I feel it in my entire body and soul. I have to force myself to act normally. I'm in a state of utter confusion, don't know what to read, what to write, what to do. I only know that I'm longing for something . . .

Yours, Anne

Dearest Kitty,

A lot has changed for me since Saturday. What's happened is this: I was longing for something (and still am), but . . . a small, a very small, part of the problem has been resolved.

On Sunday morning I noticed, to my great joy (I'll be honest with you), that Peter kept looking at me. Not in the usual way. I don't know, I can't explain it, but I suddenly had the feeling he wasn't as in love with Margot as I used to think. All day long I tried not to look at him too much, because whenever I did, I caught him looking at me and then – well, it made me feel wonderful inside, and that's not a feeling I should have too often.

Sunday evening everyone, except Pim and me, was clustered round the radio, listening to the 'Immortal Music of the German Masters'. Dussel kept twisting and turning the knobs, which annoyed Peter, and the others too. After restraining himself for half an hour, Peter asked somewhat irritably if he would stop fiddling with the radio. Dussel replied in his haughtiest tone, '*Ich mach' das schon!*'★ Peter became angry and made an insolent remark. Mr van Daan sided with him, and Dussel had to back down. That was it.

The reason for the disagreement wasn't particularly interesting in and of itself, but Peter has apparently taken the matter very much to heart, because this morning, when I was rummaging around in the crate of books in the attic, Peter came up and began telling me what had happened. I didn't know anything about it, but Peter soon realized he'd found an attentive listener and started warming to his subject.

'Well, it's like this,' he said. 'I don't usually talk much, since I know beforehand I'll just be tongue-tied. I start

★ I'll decide that.

stuttering and blushing and I twist my words around so much I finally have to stop, because I can't find the right words. That's what happened yesterday. I meant to say something entirely different, but once I started, I got all mixed up. It's awful. I used to have a bad habit, and sometimes I wish I still did: whenever I was angry with someone, I'd beat them up instead of arguing with them. I know this method won't get me anywhere, and that's why I admire you. You're never at a loss for words: you say exactly what you want to say and aren't in the least bit shy.'

'Oh, you're wrong about that,' I replied. 'Most of what I say comes out very differently from the way I'd planned. Plus I talk too much and too long, and that's just as bad.'

'Maybe, but you have the advantage that no one can see you're embarrassed. You don't blush or go to pieces.'

I couldn't help being secretly amused at his words. However, since I wanted him to go on talking quietly about himself, I hid my laughter, sat down on a cushion on the floor, wrapped my arms around my knees and gazed at him intently.

I'm glad there's someone else in this house who flies into the same rages as I do. Peter seemed relieved that he could criticize Dussel without being afraid I'd tell. As for me, I was pleased too, because I sensed a strong feeling of fellowship, which I only remember having had with my girlfriends.

Yours, Anne

*T*he minor run-in with Dussel had several repercussions, for which he had only himself to blame.
Monday evening Dussel came in to see Mother and told
her triumphantly that Peter had asked him that morning
if he'd slept well, and then added how sorry he was about
what had happened Sunday evening – he hadn't really
meant what he'd said. Dussel assured him he hadn't taken
it to heart. So everything was right as rain again. Mother
passed this story on to me, and I was secretly amazed that
Peter, who'd been so angry with Dussel, had humbled
himself, despite all his assurances to the contrary.

I couldn't refrain from sounding Peter out on the subject, and he instantly replied that Dussel had been lying.
You should have seen Peter's face. I wish I'd had a
camera. Indignation, rage, indecision, agitation and much
more crossed his face in rapid succession.

That evening Mr van Daan and Peter really told Dussel
off. But it couldn't have been all that bad, since Peter
had another dental appointment today.

Actually, they never wanted to speak to each other
again.

*P*eter and I hadn't talked to each other all day, except for a few meaningless words. It was too cold to go up to the attic, and anyway, it was Margot's birthday. At twelve-thirty he came to look at the presents and hung around chatting longer than was strictly necessary, something he'd never have done otherwise. But I got my chance in the afternoon. Since I felt like spoiling Margot on her birthday, I went to get the coffee, and after that the potatoes. When I came to Peter's room, he immediately took his papers off the stairs, and I asked if I should close the trapdoor to the attic.

'Yes,' he said, 'go ahead. When you're ready to come back down, just knock and I'll open it for you.'

I thanked him, went upstairs and spent at least ten minutes searching around in the barrel for the smallest potatoes. My back started aching, and the attic was cold. Naturally, I didn't bother to knock but opened the trapdoor myself. But he obligingly got up and took the pan out of my hands.

'I did my best, but I couldn't find any smaller ones.'

'Did you look in the big barrel?'

'Yes, I've been through them all.'

By this time I was at the bottom of the stairs, and he examined the pan of potatoes he was still holding. 'Oh, but these are fine,' he said, and added, as I took the pan from him, 'My compliments!'

As he said this, he gave me such a warm, tender look

that I started glowing inside. I could tell he wanted to please me, but since he couldn't make a long complimentary speech, he said everything with his eyes. I understood him so well and was very grateful. It still makes me happy to think back to those words and that look!

When I went downstairs, Mother said she needed more potatoes, this time for dinner, so I volunteered to go back up. When I entered Peter's room, I apologized for disturbing him again. As I was going up the stairs, he stood up, went over to stand between the stairs and the wall, grabbed my arm and tried to stop me.

'I'll go,' he said. 'I have to go upstairs anyway.'

I replied that it wasn't really necessary, that I didn't have to get only the small ones this time. Convinced, he let go of my arm. On my way back, he opened the trapdoor and once again took the pan from me. Standing by the door, I asked, 'What are you working on?'

'French,' he replied.

I asked if I could take a look at his lessons. Then I went to wash my hands and sat down across from him on the divan.

After I'd explained some French to him, we began to talk. He told me that after the war he wanted to go to the Dutch East Indies and live on a rubber plantation. He talked about his life at home, the black market and what a hopeless case he is. I told him he had a big inferiority complex. He talked about the war, saying that Russia and England were bound to go to war against each other, and about the Jews. He said life would have been much easier if he'd been a Christian or could become one after the war. I asked if he wanted to be baptized, but that wasn't what he meant either. He said he'd never be able to feel like a Christian, but that after the war he'd make sure nobody would know he was Jewish. I felt a momentary pang. It's such a shame he still has a touch of dishonesty in him.

Peter added, 'The Jews have been and always will be the chosen people!'

I answered, 'Just this once, I hope they'll be chosen for something good!'

But we went on chatting very pleasantly, about Father, about judging human character and all sorts of things, so many that I can't even remember them all.

I left at a quarter past five, because Bep had arrived.

That evening he said something else I thought was nice. We were talking about the picture of a film star I'd once given him, which has been hanging in his room for at least a year and a half. He liked it so much that I offered to give him a few more.

'No,' he replied, 'I'd rather keep the one I've got. I look at it every day, and the people in it have become my friends.'

I now have a better understanding of why he always hugs Mouschi so tightly. He obviously needs affection too. I forgot to mention something else he was talking about. He said, 'No, I'm not afraid, except when it comes to things about myself, but I'm working on that.

Peter has a huge inferiority complex. For example, he always thinks he's so stupid and we're so clever. When

I help him with French, he thanks me a thousand times. One of these days I'm going to say, 'Oh, cut it out! You're much better at English and geography!'

Anne Frank

THURSDAY, 17 FEBRUARY 1944

Dear Kitty,

I was upstairs this morning, since I promised Mrs van D. I'd read her some of my stories. I began with 'Eva's Dream', which she liked a lot, and then I read a few passages from 'The Secret Annexe', which had her in stitches. Peter also listened for a while (just the last part) and asked if I'd come to his room sometime to read more. I decided I had to take a chance right then and there, so I got my exercise-book and let him read that bit where Cady and Hans talk about God. I can't really tell what kind of impression it made on him. He said something I don't quite remember, not about whether it was good, but about the idea behind it. I told him I just wanted him to see that I didn't write only amusing things. He nodded, and I left the room. We'll see if I hear anything more!

Yours, Anne Frank

My dearest Kitty,

Whenever I go upstairs, it's always so I can see 'him'. Now that I have something to look forward to, my life here has improved greatly.

At least the object of my friendship is always here, and I don't have to be afraid of rivals (except for Margot). Don't think I'm in love, because I'm not, but I do have the feeling that something beautiful is going to develop between Peter and me, a kind of friendship and a feeling of trust. I go and see him whenever I get the chance, and it's not the way it used to be, when he didn't know what to make of me. On the contrary, he's still talking away as I'm heading out of the door. Mother doesn't like me going upstairs. She always says I'm bothering Peter and that I should leave him alone. Honestly, can't she credit me with some intuition? She always looks at me so oddly when I go to Peter's room. When I come down again, she asks me where I've been. It's terrible, but I'm beginning to hate her!

Yours, Anne M. Frank

Dearest Kitty,

*I*t's Saturday again, and that should tell you enough. This morning all was quiet. I spent nearly an hour upstairs making meatballs, but I only spoke to 'him' in passing.

When everyone went upstairs at two-thirty to either read or take a nap, I went downstairs, with blanket and all, to sit at the desk and read or write. Before long I couldn't take it any more. I put my head in my arms and sobbed my heart out. The tears streamed down my cheeks, and I felt desperately unhappy. Oh, if only 'he' had come to comfort me.

It was past four by the time I went upstairs again. At five o'clock I set off to get some potatoes, hoping once again that we'd meet, but while I was still in the bathroom fixing my hair, he went to see Boche.

I wanted to help Mrs van D. and went upstairs with my book and everything, but suddenly I felt the tears coming back. I raced downstairs to the lavatory, grabbing the mirror on the way. I sat there on the toilet, fully dressed, long after I was through, my tears leaving dark spots on the red of my apron, and I felt utterly dejected.

Here's what was going through my mind: 'Oh, I'll never reach Peter this way. Who knows, maybe he doesn't even like me and he doesn't need anyone to confide in. Maybe he only thinks of me in a casual sort of way. I'll have to go back to being alone, without anyone to confide in and without Peter, without hope, comfort or anything to look forward to. Oh, if only I could rest my head on his shoulder and not feel so hopelessly alone and deserted! Who knows, maybe he doesn't care for me at all and looks at the others in the same tender way. Maybe I only imagined it was especially for me. Oh, Peter, if only you could hear me or see me. If the truth is disappointing, I won't be able to bear it.'

A little later I felt hopeful and full of expectation again, though my tears were still flowing – on the inside.

Yours, Anne M. Frank

SUNDAY, 20 FEBRUARY 1944

*W*hat happens in other people's houses during the rest of the week happens here in the Annexe on Sundays. While other people put on their best clothes and go strolling in the sun, we scrub, sweep and do the washing.

Eight o'clock. Though the rest of us prefer to lie in, Dussel gets up at eight. He goes to the bathroom, then downstairs, then up again and then to the bathroom, where he devotes a whole hour to washing himself.

Nine-thirty. The stoves are lit, the black-out screen is taken down, and Mr van Daan heads for the bathroom.

One of my Sunday morning ordeals is having to lie in bed and look at Dussel's back when he's praying. I know it sounds strange, but a praying Dussel is a terrible sight to behold. It's not that he cries or gets sentimental, not at all, but he does spend a quarter of an hour – an entire fifteen minutes – rocking from his toes to his heels. Back and forth, back and forth. It goes on for ever, and if I don't shut my eyes tight, my head starts to spin.

Ten-fifteen. The van Daans whistle; the bathroom's free. In the Frank family quarters, the first sleepy faces are beginning to emerge from their pillows. Then everything happens fast, fast, fast. Margot and I take turns doing the washing. Since it's quite cold downstairs, we put on trousers and head scarves. Meanwhile, Father is busy in the bathroom. Either Margot or I have a turn in the bathroom at eleven, and then we're all clean.

Eleven-thirty. Breakfast. I won't dwell on this, since there's enough talk about food without my bringing the subject up as well.

Twelve-fifteen. We each go our separate ways. Father, clad in overalls, gets down on his hands and knees and brushes the rug so vigorously that the room is enveloped in a cloud of dust. Mr Dussel makes the beds (all wrong, of course), always whistling the same Beethoven violin concerto as he goes about his work. Mother can be heard shuffling around the attic as she hangs up the washing. Mr van Daan puts on his hat and disappears into the lower regions, usually followed by Peter and Mouschi. Mrs van D. dons a long apron, a black woollen jacket and overshoes, winds a red woollen scarf around her head, scoops up a bundle of dirty laundry and, with a well-rehearsed washerwoman's nod, heads downstairs. Margot and I do the dishes and tidy up the room.

My dearest Kitty,

The weather's been wonderful since yesterday, and I've perked up quite a bit. My writing, the best thing I have, is coming along well. I go to the attic almost every morning to get the stale air out of my lungs. This morning when I went there, Peter was busy cleaning up. He finished quickly and came over to where I was sitting on my favourite spot on the floor. The two of us looked out at the blue sky, the bare chestnut tree glistening with dew, the seagulls and other birds glinting with silver as they swooped through the air, and we were so moved and entranced that we couldn't speak. He stood with his head against a thick beam, while I sat. We breathed in the air, looked outside and both felt that the spell shouldn't be broken with words. We remained like this for a long while, and by the time he had to go to the loft to chop wood, I knew he was a good, decent boy. He climbed the ladder to the loft, and I followed; during the fifteen minutes he was chopping wood, we didn't say a word either. I watched him from where I was standing, and could see he was obviously doing his best to chop the right way and show off his strength. But I also looked out of the open window, letting my eyes roam over a large part of Amsterdam, over the rooftops and on to the horizon, a strip of blue so pale it was almost invisible.

'As long as this exists,' I thought, 'this sunshine and this cloudless sky, and as long as I can enjoy it, how can I be sad?'

The best remedy for those who are frightened, lonely or unhappy is to go outside, somewhere they can be alone, alone with the sky, nature and God. For then and only then can you feel that everything is as it should be and that God wants people to be happy amid nature's beauty and simplicity.

As long as this exists, and that should be for ever, I know that there will be solace for every sorrow, whatever the circumstances. I firmly believe that nature can bring comfort to all who suffer.

Oh, who knows, perhaps it won't be long before I can share this overwhelming feeling of happiness with someone who feels the same as I do.

Yours, Anne

PS. Thoughts: To Peter.

We've been missing out on so much here, so very much, and for such a long time. I miss it just as much as you do. I'm not talking about external things, since we're well provided for in that sense; I mean the internal things. Like you, I long for freedom and fresh air, but I think we've been amply compensated for their loss. On the inside, I mean.

This morning, when I was sitting in front of the window and taking a long, deep look outside at God and nature, I was happy, just plain happy. Peter, as long as people feel that kind of happiness within themselves, the joy of nature, health and much more besides, they'll always be able to recapture that happiness.

Riches, prestige, everything can be lost. But the happiness in your own heart can only be dimmed; it will always be there, as long as you live, to make you happy again.

Whenever you're feeling lonely or sad, try going to the loft on a beautiful day and looking outside. Not at the houses and the rooftops, but at the sky. As long as you can look fearlessly at the sky, you'll know that you're pure within and will find happiness once more.

My dearest Kitty,

*F*rom early in the morning till late at night, all I do is think about Peter. I fall asleep with his image before my eyes, dream about him and wake up with him still looking at me.

I have the strong feeling that Peter and I aren't really as different as we may seem on the surface, and I'll explain why: neither Peter nor I have a mother. His is too superficial, likes to flirt and doesn't concern herself much with what goes on in his head. Mine takes an active interest in my life, but has no tact, sensitivity or motherly understanding.

Both Peter and I are struggling with our innermost feelings. We're still unsure of ourselves and are too vulnerable, emotionally, to be dealt with so roughly. Whenever that happens, I want to run outside or hide my feelings. Instead, I bang the pots and pans, splash the water and am generally noisy, so that everyone wishes I were miles away. Peter's reaction is to shut himself away, say little, sit quietly and daydream, all the while carefully hiding his true self.

But how and when will we finally reach each other?

I don't know how much longer I can continue to keep this yearning under control.

Yours, Anne M. Frank

My dearest Kitty,

*I*t's like a nightmare, one that goes on long after I'm awake. I see him nearly every hour of the day and yet I can't be with him, I can't let the others notice, and I have to pretend to be cheerful, though my heart is aching.

Peter Schiff and Peter van Daan have melted into one Peter, who's good and kind and whom I long for desperately. Mother's horrible, Father's nice, which makes him even more exasperating, and Margot's the worst, since she takes advantage of my smiling face to claim me for herself, when all I want is to be left alone.

Peter didn't join me in the attic, but went up to the loft to do some carpentry work. At every rasp and bang, another chunk of my courage broke off and I was even more unhappy. In the distance a clock was tolling 'Be pure in heart, be pure in mind!'

I'm sentimental, I know. I'm despondent and foolish, I know that too.

Oh, help me!

Yours, Anne M. Frank

WEDNESDAY, 1 MARCH 1944

Dearest Kitty,

My own affairs have been pushed to the background by . . . a break-in. I'm boring you with all my break-ins, but what can I do when burglars take such pleasure in honouring Gies & Co. with their presence? This incident is much more complicated than the last one, in July 1943.

Last night at seven-thirty Mr van Daan was heading, as usual, for Mr Kugler's office when he saw that both the glass door and the office door were open. He was surprised, but he went on through and was even more astonished to see that the alcove doors were open as well and that there was a terrible mess in the front office. 'There's been a burglary' flashed through his mind. But just to make sure, he went downstairs to the front door, checked the lock and found everything closed. 'Bep and Peter must just have been very careless this evening,' Mr van D. concluded. He remained for a while in Mr Kugler's office, switched off the lamp and went upstairs without worrying much about the open doors or the messy office.

Early this morning Peter knocked at our door to tell us that the front door was wide open and that the projector and Mr Kugler's new briefcase had disappeared from the cupboard. Peter was instructed to lock the door. Mr van Daan told us about his discoveries of the night before, and we were extremely worried.

The only explanation is that the burglar must have had a duplicate key, since there were no signs of a forced entry. He must have sneaked in early in the evening, shut the door behind him, hidden himself when he heard Mr van Daan, fled with the loot after Mr van Daan went upstairs and, in his hurry, not bothered to shut the door.

Who could have our key? Why didn't the burglar go to the warehouse? Was it one of our own warehouse employees, and will he turn us in, now that he's heard Mr van Daan and maybe even seen him?

It's really scary, since we don't know whether the burglar will take it into his head to try and get in again. Or was he so startled when he heard someone else in the building that he'll stay away?

Yours, Anne

PS. We'd be delighted if you could search out a good detective for us. Obviously, there's one condition: he must be relied upon not to inform on people in hiding.

THURSDAY, 2 MARCH 1944

Dearest Kitty,

*M*argot and I were in the attic together today. I can't enjoy being there with her the way I imagine it'd be with Peter (or someone else). I know she feels the same about most things as I do!

While washing up, Bep began talking to Mother and Mrs van Daan about how discouraged she gets. What help did those two offer her? Our tactless mother, especially, only made things go from bad to worse. Do you know what her advice was? That she should think about all the other people in the world who are suffering! How can thinking about the misery of others help if you're miserable yourself? I said as much. Their response, of course, was that I should stay out of conversations of this sort.

The grown-ups are such idiots! As if Peter, Margot, Bep and I didn't all have the same feelings. The only thing that helps is a mother's love, or that of a very, very close friend. But these two mothers don't understand the first thing about us! Perhaps Mrs van Daan does, a bit more than Mother. Oh, I wish I could have said something to poor Bep, something that I know from my own experience would have helped. But Father came between us, pushing me roughly aside. They're all so stupid!

I also talked to Margot about Father and Mother, about how nice it could be here if they weren't so aggravating. We'd be able to organize evenings in which everyone could take turns discussing a given subject. But we've already been through all that. It's impossible for me to talk here! Mr van Daan goes on the offensive, Mother gets sarcastic and can't say *anything* in a normal voice, Father doesn't feel like taking part, nor does Mr Dussel, and Mrs van D. is attacked so often that she just sits there with a red face, hardly able to put up a fight any more. And what about us? We aren't allowed to have an opinion! My, my, aren't they progressive! Not have an opinion! People can tell you to shut up, but they can't keep you from having an opinion. You can't forbid someone to have an opinion, no matter how young they are! The only thing that would help Bep, Margot, Peter and me would be great love and devotion, which we don't get here. And no one, especially not the idiotic sages around here, is capable of understanding us, since we're more sensitive and much more advanced in our thinking than any of them ever suspect!

Love, what is love? I don't think you can really put it into words. Love is understanding someone, caring for him, sharing his joys and sorrows. This eventually includes physical love. You've shared something, given something away and received something in return, whether or not you're married, whether or not you have a baby. Losing your virtue doesn't matter, as long as you know that for as long as you live you'll have someone at your side who understands you, and who doesn't have to be shared with anyone else!

Yours, Anne M. Frank

At the moment, Mother's grumbling at me again; she's clearly jealous because I talk to Mrs van Daan more than to her. What do I care!

I managed to get hold of Peter this afternoon, and we talked for at least forty-five minutes. He wanted to tell me something about himself, but didn't find it easy. He finally got it out, though it took a long time. I honestly didn't know whether it was better for me to stay or to go. But I wanted so much to help him! I told him about

Bep and how tactless our mothers are. He told me that his parents argue constantly, about politics and cigarettes and all kinds of things. As I've told you before, Peter's very shy, but not too shy to admit that he'd be perfectly happy not to see his parents for a year or two. 'My father isn't as nice as he looks,' he said. 'But in the matter of the cigarettes, Mother's absolutely right.'

I also told him about my mother. But he came to Father's defence. He thought he was a 'terrific chap'.

Tonight when I was hanging up my apron after washing up, he called me over and asked me not to say anything downstairs about his parents' having had another argument and not being on speaking terms. I promised, though I'd already told Margot. But I'm sure Margot won't pass it on.

'Oh no, Peter,' I said, 'you don't have to worry about me. I've learned not to blab everything I hear. I never repeat what you tell me.'

He was glad to hear that. I also told him what terrible gossips we are, and said, 'Margot's quite right, of course, when she says I'm not being honest, because as much as I want to stop gossiping, there's nothing I like better than discussing Mr Dussel.'

'It's good that you admit it,' he said. He blushed, and his sincere compliment almost embarrassed me too.

Then we talked about 'upstairs' and 'downstairs' some more. Peter was really rather surprised to hear that we don't like his parents. 'Peter,' I said, 'you know I'm always honest, so why shouldn't I tell you this as well? We can see their faults too.'

I added, 'Peter, I'd really like to help you. Will you let me? You're caught in an awkward position, and I know, even though you don't say anything, that it upsets you.'

'Oh, your help is always welcome!'

'Maybe it'd be better for you to talk to Father. You can tell him anything, he won't pass it on.'

'I know, he's a real pal.'

'You like him a lot, don't you?'

Peter nodded, and I continued, 'Well, he likes you too, you know!'

He looked up quickly and blushed. It was really touching to see how happy these few words made him. 'You think so?' he asked.

'Yes,' I said. 'You can tell from the little things he lets slip now and then.'

Then Mr van Daan came in to do some dictating. Peter's a 'terrific chap', just like Father!

Yours, Anne M. Frank

FRIDAY, 3 MARCH 1944

My dearest Kitty,

When I looked into the candle tonight, I felt calm and happy again. It seems Grandma is in that candle, and it's Grandma who watches over and protects me and makes me feel happy again. But . . . there's someone else who governs all my moods and that's . . . Peter. I went to get the potatoes today, and while I was standing on the stairway with my pan full, he asked, 'What did you do during lunch break?'

I sat down on the stairs, and we began to talk. The potatoes didn't make it to the kitchen until five-fifteen (an hour after I'd gone to get them). Peter didn't say anything more about his parents; we just talked about books and about the past. Oh, he gazes at me with such warmth in his eyes; I don't think it will take much for me to fall in love with him.

He brought the subject up this evening. I went to his room after peeling potatoes and remarked on how hot it was. 'You can tell the temperature by looking at Margot and me, because we turn white when it's cold and red when it's hot,' I said.

'In love?' he asked.

'Why should I be in love?' It was a pretty silly answer (or, rather, question).

'Why not?' he said, and then it was time for dinner.

What did he mean? Today I finally managed to ask him whether my chatter bothered him. All he said was, 'Oh, it's fine with me!' I can't tell how much of his reply was due to shyness.

Kitty, I sound like someone who's in love and can talk about nothing but her dearest darling. And Peter is a darling. Will I ever be able to tell him that? Only if he thinks the same of me, but I'm the kind of person you have to treat with kid gloves, I know that all too well.

And he likes to be left alone, so I don't know how much he likes me. In any case, we're getting to know each other a little better. I wish we dared to say more. But who knows, maybe that time will come sooner than I think! Once or twice a day he gives me a knowing glance, I wink back, and we're both happy. It seems insane to talk about his being happy, and yet I have the overwhelming feeling he thinks the same way I do.

Yours, Anne M. Frank

SATURDAY, 4 MARCH 1944

Dear Kitty,

This is the first Saturday in months that hasn't been tiresome, dreary and boring. The reason is Peter. This morning as I was on my way to the attic to hang up my apron, Father asked whether I wanted to stay and practise my French, and I said yes. We spoke French together for a while and I explained something to Peter, and then we worked on our English. Father read aloud from Dickens, and I was in seventh heaven, since I was sitting on Father's chair, close to Peter.

I went downstairs at quarter to eleven. When I went back up at eleven-thirty, Peter was already waiting for me on the stairs. We talked until quarter to one. Whenever I leave the room, for example after a meal, and Peter has a chance and no one else can hear, he says, 'Cheerio, Anne, see you later.'

Oh, I'm so happy! I wonder if he's going to fall in love with me after all? In any case, he's a nice boy, and you have no idea how good it is to talk to him!

Mrs van D. thinks it's all right for me to talk to Peter, but today she asked me teasingly, 'Can I trust you two up there?'

'Of course,' I protested. 'I take that as an insult!' Morning, noon and night, I look forward to seeing Peter.

Yours, Anne M. Frank

PS. Before I forget, last night everything was blanketed in snow. Now it's thawed and there's almost nothing left.

MONDAY, 6 MARCH 1944

Dearest Kitty,

*E*ver since Peter told me about his parents, I've felt a certain sense of responsibility towards him – don't you think that's strange? It's as though their quarrels were just as much my business as his, and yet I don't dare bring it up any more, because I'm afraid it makes him uncomfortable. I wouldn't want to intrude, not for all the money in the world.

I can tell by Peter's face that he ponders things just as deeply as I do. Last night I was annoyed when Mrs van

D. scoffed, 'The thinker!' Peter flushed and looked embarrassed, and I nearly blew my top.

Why don't these people keep their mouths shut? You can't imagine what it's like to have to stand on the sidelines and see how lonely he is, without being able to do anything. I can imagine, as if I were in his place, how despondent he must sometimes feel at the quarrels. And about love. Poor Peter, he needs to be loved so much!

It sounded so cold when he said he didn't need any friends. Oh, he's so wrong! I don't think he means it. He clings to his masculinity, his solitude and his feigned indifference so he can maintain his role, so he'll never, ever have to show his feelings. Poor Peter, how long can he keep it up? Won't he explode from this superhuman effort?

Oh, Peter, if only I could help you, if only you would let me! Together we could banish our loneliness, yours and mine!

I've been doing a great deal of thinking, but not saying much. I'm happy when I see him, and happier still if the sun shines when we're together. I washed my hair yesterday, and because I knew he was next door, I was very rambunctious. I couldn't help it; the more quiet and serious I am on the inside, the noisier I get on the outside! Who will be the first to discover the chink in my armour?

It's just as well that the van Daans don't have a daughter. My conquest could never be so challenging, so beautiful and so nice with someone of the same sex!

Yours, Anne M. Frank

PS. You know I'm always honest with you, so I think I should tell you that I live from one encounter to the next. I keep hoping to discover that he's dying to see me, and I'm in raptures when I notice his bashful attempts. I think he'd like to be able to express himself as easily as I do; little does he know it's his awkwardness that I find so touching.

TUESDAY, 7 MARCH 1944

Dearest Kitty,

When I think back to my life in 1942, it all seems so unreal. The Anne Frank who enjoyed that heavenly existence was completely different from the one who has grown wise within these walls. Yes, it was heavenly. Five admirers on every street corner, twenty or so friends, the favourite of most of my teachers, spoiled rotten by Father and Mother, bags full of sweets and loads of pocket money. What more could anyone ask for?

You're probably wondering how I could have charmed all those people. Peter says it's because I'm 'attractive', but that isn't it entirely. The teachers were amused and entertained by my clever answers, my witty remarks, my smiling face and my critical mind. That's all I was: a terrible flirt, coquettish and amusing. I had a few plus points, which kept me in everybody's good graces:

I was hardworking, honest and generous. I would never have refused anyone who wanted to peek at my answers, I was magnanimous with my sweets, and I wasn't stuck-up.

Would all that admiration eventually have made me overconfident? It's a good thing that, at the height of my glory, I was suddenly plunged into reality. It took me more than a year to get used to doing without admiration.

How did they see me at school? As the class comedian, the eternal ringleader, never in a bad mood, never a cry-baby. Was it any wonder that everyone wanted to cycle to school with me or do me little favours?

I look back at that Anne Frank as a pleasant, amusing, but superficial girl, who has nothing to do with me. What did Peter say about me? 'Whenever I saw you, you were surrounded by a flock of girls and at least two boys, you were always laughing, and you were always the centre of attention!' He was right.

What's remained of that Anne Frank? Oh, I haven't forgotten how to laugh or toss off a remark, I'm just as good, if not better, at hauling people over the coals, and I can still flirt and be amusing, if I want to be . . .

But there's the catch. I'd like to live that seemingly carefree and happy life for an evening, a few days, a week. At the end of that week I'd be exhausted, and would be grateful to the first person to talk to me about something meaningful. I want friends, not admirers. People who respect me for my character and my deeds, not my flattering smile. The circle around me would be much smaller, but what does that matter, as long as they're sincere?

In spite of everything, I wasn't altogether happy in 1942; I often felt I'd been deserted, but because I was on the go all day long, I didn't think about it. I enjoyed myself as much as I could, trying consciously or unconsciously to fill the void with jokes.

Looking back, I realize that this period of my life has irrevocably come to a close; my happy-go-lucky, carefree schooldays are gone for ever. I don't even miss them. I've outgrown them. I can no longer just be frivolous, since my serious side is always there.

I see my life up till New Year 1944 as if I were looking through a powerful magnifying glass. When I was at home, my life was filled with sunshine. Then, in the middle of 1942, everything changed overnight. The quarrels, the accusations – I couldn't take it all in. I was caught off guard, and the only way I knew how to keep my bearings was to talk back.

The first half of 1943 brought crying spells, loneliness and the gradual realization of my faults and shortcomings, which were numerous and seemed even more so. I filled the day with chatter, tried to draw Pim closer to me and failed. This left me on my own to face the difficult task of improving myself so I wouldn't have to hear their reproaches, because they made me so despondent.

The second half of the year was slightly better. I became a teenager, and was treated more like a grown-up. I began to think about things and to write stories, finally coming to the conclusion that the others no longer had anything to do with me. They had no right to swing me back and forth like a pendulum on a clock. I wanted to change myself in my own way. I realized I could manage without my mother, completely and totally, and that hurt. But what affected me even more was the realization that I was never going to be able to confide in Father. I didn't trust anyone but myself.

After New Year the second big change occurred: my dream, through which I discovered my longing for . . . a boy; not for a girlfriend, but for a boyfriend. I also discovered an inner happiness underneath my superficial and cheerful exterior. From time to time I was quiet. Now I live only for Peter, since what happens to me in the future depends largely on him!

I lie in bed at night, after ending my prayers with the words '*Ich danke dir für all das Gute und Liebe und Schöne*',⋆ and I'm filled with joy. I think of going into hiding, my health and my whole being as *das Gute*; Peter's love (which is still so new and fragile and which neither of us dares to say aloud), the future, happiness and love as *das Liebe*; the world, nature and the tremendous beauty of everything, all that splendour, as *das Schöne*.

At such moments I don't think about all the misery, but about the beauty that still remains. This is where Mother and I differ greatly. Her advice in the face of melancholy is: 'Think about all the suffering in the world and be thankful you're not part of it.' My advice is: 'Go outside, to the country, enjoy the sun and all nature has to offer. Go outside and try to recapture the happiness

⋆ Thank you, God, for all that is good and dear and beautiful.

within yourself; think of all the beauty in yourself and in everything around you and be happy.'

I don't think Mother's advice can be right, because what are you supposed to do if you become part of the suffering? You'd be completely lost. On the contrary, beauty remains, even in misfortune. If you just look for it, you discover more and more happiness and regain your balance. A person who's happy will make others happy; a person who has courage and faith will never die in misery!

Yours, Anne M. Frank

WEDNESDAY, 8 MARCH 1944

*M*argot and I have been writing each other notes, just for fun, of course.

Anne: It's strange, but I can only remember the day after what has happened the night before. For example, I suddenly remembered that Mr Dussel was snoring loudly last night. (It's now quarter to three on Wednesday afternoon and Mr Dussel is snoring again, which is why it flashed through my mind, of course.) When I had to use the potty, I deliberately made more noise to get the snoring to stop.

Margot: Which is better, the snoring or the gasping for air?

Anne: The snoring's better, because it stops when I make a noise, without waking the person in question.

What I didn't write to Margot, but what I'll confess to you, dear Kitty, is that I've been dreaming of Peter a great deal. The night before last I dreamed I was skating right here in our living-room with that little boy from the Apollo skating-rink; he was with his sister, the girl with the spindly legs who always wore the same blue dress. I introduced myself, overdoing it a bit, and asked him his name. It was Peter. In my dream I wondered just how many Peters I actually knew!

Then I dreamed we were standing in Peter's room, facing each other beside the stairs. I said something to him; he gave me a kiss, but replied that he didn't love me all that much and that I shouldn't flirt. In a desperate and pleading voice I said, 'I'm not flirting, Peter!'

When I woke up, I was glad Peter hasn't said it after all.

Last night I dreamed we were kissing each other, but Peter's cheeks were very disappointing: they weren't as soft as they looked. They were more like Father's cheeks – the cheeks of a man who already shaves.

My dearest Kitty,

The proverb 'Misfortunes never come singly' definitely applies to today. Peter just said so. Let me tell you all the awful things that have happened and that are still hanging over our heads.

First, Miep is ill, as a result of Henk and Aagje's wedding yesterday. She caught a cold in the Westerkerk, where the service was held. Second, Mr Kleiman hasn't returned to work since the last time his stomach started bleeding, so Bep's been left to hold the fort alone. Third, the police have arrested a man (whose name I won't put in writing). It's terrible not only for him, but for us as well, since he's been supplying us with potatoes, butter and jam. Mr M., as I'll call him, has five children under the age of thirteen, and another on the way.

Last night we had another little scare: we were in the middle of dinner when suddenly someone knocked on the wall next door. For the rest of the evening we were nervous and gloomy.

Lately I haven't been at all in the mood to write down what's been going on here. I've been more wrapped up in myself. Don't get me wrong, I'm terribly upset about what's happened to poor, good-hearted Mr M., but there's not much room for him in my diary.

Tuesday, Wednesday and Thursday I was in Peter's room from four-thirty to five-fifteen. We worked on our French and chatted about one thing and another. I really look forward to that hour or so in the afternoon, but best of all is that I think Peter's just as pleased to see me.

Yours, Anne M. Frank

Dearest Kitty,

I haven't been able to sit still lately. I wander upstairs and down and then back again. I like talking to Peter, but I'm always afraid of being a nuisance. He's told me a bit about the past, about his parents and about himself, but it's not enough, and every five minutes I wonder why I find myself longing for more. He used to think I was a real pain in the neck, and the feeling was mutual. I've changed my mind, but how do I know he's changed his? I think he has, but that doesn't necessarily mean we have to become the best of friends, although as far as I'm concerned, it would make our time here more bearable. But I won't let this drive me crazy. I spend enough time thinking about him and don't have to get you worked up as well, simply because I'm so miserable!

Dearest Kitty,

*T*hings are getting crazier here as the days go by. Peter hasn't looked at me since yesterday. He's been behaving as if he's cross with me. I'm doing my best not to chase after him and to talk to him as little as possible, but it's not easy! What's going on, what makes him keep me at arm's length one minute and rush back to my side the next? Perhaps I'm imagining that it's worse than it really is. Perhaps he's just moody like me, and tomorrow everything will be all right again!

I have the hardest time trying to maintain a normal façade when I'm feeling so wretched and sad. I have to talk, help around the house, sit with the others and, above all, act cheerful! Most of all I miss the outdoors and having a place where I can be alone for as long as I want! I think I'm getting everything all mixed up, Kitty, but then, I'm in a state of utter confusion: on the one hand, I'm half mad with desire for him, can hardly be in the same room without looking at him; and on the other hand, I wonder why he should matter to me so much and why I can't be calm again!

Day and night, during every waking hour, I do nothing but ask myself, 'Have you given him enough chance to be alone? Have you been spending too much time upstairs? Do you talk too much about serious subjects he's not yet ready to talk about? Maybe he doesn't even like you? Has it all been your imagination? But then why has he told you so much about himself? Is he sorry he did?' And a whole lot more.

Yesterday afternoon I was so worn out by the sad news from the outside that I lay down on my divan for a nap. All I wanted was to sleep and not have to think. I slept until four, but then I had to go next door. It wasn't easy, answering all Mother's questions and inventing an excuse to explain my nap to Father. I pleaded a headache, which wasn't a lie, since I did have one . . . on the inside!

Ordinary people, ordinary girls, teenagers like myself, would think all this self-pity is a little crazy. But that's just it. I pour my heart out to you, and the rest of the time I'm as impudent, cheerful and self-confident as possible to avoid questions and keep from getting on my own nerves.

Margot is very kind and would like me to confide in her, but I can't tell her everything. She takes me too seriously, far too seriously, and spends a lot of time thinking about her loony sister, looking at me closely whenever I open my mouth and wondering, 'Is she acting, or does she really mean it?'

It's because we're always together. I don't want the person I confide in to be around me all the time.

When will I untangle my jumbled thoughts? When will I find inner peace again?

Yours, Anne

Dearest Kitty,

*I*t might be amusing for you (though not for me) to hear what we're going to eat today. The cleaning lady is working downstairs, so at the moment I'm seated at the van Daans' oilcloth-covered table with a handkerchief sprinkled with fragrant pre-war perfume pressed to my nose and mouth. You probably don't have the faintest idea what I'm talking about, so let me 'begin at the beginning'. The people who supply us with food coupons have been arrested, so we have just our five black-market ration books – no coupons, no fats and oils. Since Miep and Mr Kleiman are ill again, Bep can't manage the shopping. The food is wretched, and so are we. As of tomorrow, we won't have a scrap of fat, butter or margarine. We can't eat fried potatoes for breakfast (which we've been doing to save on bread), so we're having porridge instead, and because Mrs van D. thinks we're starving, we bought some milk and some cream. Lunch today consists of mashed potatoes and pickled kale. This explains the precautionary measure with the handkerchief. You wouldn't believe how much kale can stink when it's a few years old! The kitchen smells like a mixture of spoiled plums, rotten eggs and brine. Ugh, just the thought of having to eat that muck makes me want to be sick! Besides that, our potatoes have contracted such strange diseases that one out of every two buckets of *pommes de terre* ends up in the dustbin. We entertain ourselves by trying to work out which disease they've got, and we've reached the conclusion that they suffer from cancer, smallpox and measles. Honestly, being in hiding during the fourth year of the war is no picnic. If only the whole stinking mess were over!

To tell you the truth, the food wouldn't matter so much to me if life here were more pleasant in other ways. But that's just it: this tedious existence is starting to make us all disagreeable. Here are the opinions of the five grown-ups on the present situation (children aren't allowed to have opinions, and for once I'm sticking to the rules):

Mrs van Daan: 'I'd stopped wanting to be queen of the kitchen long ago. But sitting around doing nothing was boring, so I went back to cooking. Still, I can't help complaining: it's impossible to cook without oil, and all those disgusting smells make me feel like retching. Besides, what do I get in return for my efforts? Ingratitude and rude remarks. I'm always the black sheep; I get blamed for everything. What's more, it's my opinion that the war is making very little progress. The Germans will win in the end. I'm terrified that we're going to starve, and when I'm in a bad mood, I snap at everyone who comes near.'

Mr van Daan: 'I just smoke and smoke and smoke. Then the food, the political situation and Kerli's moods don't seem so bad. Kerli's a sweetheart. If I don't have anything to smoke, I feel ill, then I need to eat meat, life becomes unbearable, nothing's good enough, and there's bound to be a flaming row. My Kerli's an idiot.'

Mrs Frank: 'Food's not very important, but I'd love a slice of rye bread right now, because I'm so hungry. If I were Mrs van Daan, I'd have put a stop to Mr van Daan's smoking long ago. But I desperately need a cigarette now, because my head's in such a whirl. The van Daans are horrible people; the British may make a lot of mistakes, but the war is progressing. I should keep my mouth shut and be grateful I'm not in Poland.'

Mr Frank: 'Everything's fine, I don't need a thing. Stay calm, we've got plenty of time. Just give me my potatoes, and I'll be quiet. Better set aside some of my rations for Bep. The political situation is improving, I'm extremely optimistic.'

Mr Dussel: 'I must complete the task I've set for myself, everything must be finished on time. The political situation is looking "*gut*", it's "eempossible" for us to get caught. Me, me, me . . . !'

Yours, Anne

Dearest Kitty,

*W*hew! Released from the gloom and doom for a few moments! All I've been hearing today is: 'If this and that happens, we're in trouble, and if so-and-so falls ill, we'll be left to fend for ourselves, and if . . .'

Well, you know the rest, or at any rate I assume you're familiar enough with the residents of the Annexe to guess what they'd be talking about.

The reason for all the 'ifs' is that Mr Kugler has been called up for a six-day work detail, Bep is down with a bad cold and will probably have to stay home tomorrow, Miep hasn't got over her flu, and Mr Kleiman's stomach bled so much he lost consciousness. What a tale of woe!

We think Mr Kugler should go directly to a reliable doctor for a medical certificate of ill health, which he can present to the Town Hall in Hilversum. The warehouse employees have been given a day off tomorrow, so Bep will be alone in the office. If (there's another 'if') Bep has to stay at home, the door will remain locked and we'll have to be as quiet as mice so the Keg Company won't hear us. At one o'clock Jan will come for half an hour to check on us poor forsaken souls, like a zoo-keeper.

This afternoon, for the first time in ages, Jan gave us some news of the outside world. You should have seen us gathered around him; it looked exactly like a print: 'At Grandmother's Knee'.

He regaled his grateful audience with talk of – what else? – food. Mrs P., a friend of Miep's, has been cooking his meals. The day before yesterday Jan ate carrots with green peas, yesterday he had the leftovers, today she's cooking marrowfat peas, and tomorrow she's planning to mash the remaining carrots with potatoes.

We asked about Miep's doctor.

'Doctor?' said Jan. 'What doctor? I called him this morning and got his receptionist on the line. I asked for a flu prescription and was told I could come and pick it up tomorrow morning between eight and nine. If you've got a particularly bad case of flu, the doctor himself comes to the phone and says, "Stick out your tongue and say 'aah'. Oh, I can hear it, your throat's infected. I'll write out a prescription and you can take it to the chemist's. Good day." And that's that. Easy job he's got, diagnosis by phone. But I shouldn't blame the doctors. After all, a person has only two hands, and these days there're too many patients and too few doctors.'

Still, we all had a good laugh at Jan's phone call. I can just imagine what a doctor's waiting-room looks like these days. Doctors no longer turn up their noses at the poorer patients, but at those with minor illnesses. 'Hey, what are you doing here?' they think. 'Go to the end of the queue; real patients have priority!'

Yours, Anne

Dearest Kitty,

*T*he weather is gorgeous, indescribably beautiful; I'll be going up to the attic in a moment.

I now know why I'm so much more restless than Peter. He has his own room, where he can work, dream, think and sleep. I'm constantly being chased from one corner to another. I'm never alone in the room I share with Dussel, though I long to be so much. That's another reason I take refuge in the attic. When I'm there, or with you, I can be myself, at least for a little while. Still, I don't want to whinge. On the contrary, I want to be brave!

Thank goodness the others notice nothing of my innermost feelings, except that every day I'm growing cooler and more contemptuous of Mother, less affectionate to Father and less willing to share a single thought with Margot; I'm closed up tighter than a drum. Above all, I have to maintain my air of confidence. No one must know that my heart and mind are constantly at war with each other. Up till now reason has always won the battle, but will my emotions get the upper hand? Sometimes I fear they will, but more often I actually hope they do!

Oh, it's so terribly hard not to talk to Peter about these things, but I know I have to let him begin; it's so hard to act during the daytime as if everything I've said and done in my dreams had never taken place! Kitty, Anne is crazy, but then these are crazy times and even crazier circumstances.

The nicest part is being able to write down all my thoughts and feelings; otherwise, I'd absolutely suffocate. I wonder what Peter thinks about all these things? I keep thinking I'll be able to talk to him about them one day. He must have guessed something about the inner me, since he couldn't possibly love the outer Anne he's known so far! How could someone like Peter, who loves peace and quiet, possibly stand my bustle and noise? Will he be the first and only person to see what's beneath my granite mask? Will it take him long? Isn't there some old saying about love being akin to pity? Isn't that what's happening here as well? Because I often pity him as much as I do myself!

I honestly don't know how to begin, I really don't, so how can I expect Peter to when talking is so much harder for him? If only I could write to him, then at least he'd know what I was trying to say, since it's so hard to say it out loud!

Yours, Anne M. Frank

My dearest darling,

*E*verything turned out all right after all; Bep just had a sore throat, not flu, and Mr Kugler got a medical certificate to excuse him from the work detail. The entire Annexe breathed a huge sigh of relief. Everything's fine here! Except that Margot and I are rather tired of our parents.

Don't get me wrong. I still love Father as much as ever and Margot loves both Father and Mother, but when you're as old as we are, you want to make a few decisions for yourself, get out from under their thumb. Whenever I go upstairs, they ask what I'm going to do, they won't let me salt my food, Mother asks me every evening at eight-fifteen if it isn't time for me to change into my nightie, and they have to approve every book I read. I must admit, they're not at all strict about that and let me read nearly everything, but Margot and I are sick and tired of having to listen to their comments and questions all day long.

There's something else that displeases them: I no longer feel like giving them little kisses morning, noon and night. All those little nicknames seem so affected, and Father's fondness for talking about farting and going to the lavatory is disgusting. In short, I'd like nothing better than to do without their company for a while, and they don't understand that. Not that Margot and I have ever said any of this to them. What would be the point? They wouldn't understand anyway.

Margot said last night, 'What really bothers me is that if you happen to put your head in your hands and sigh once or twice, they immediately ask whether you have a headache or don't feel well.'

For both of us, it's been quite a blow to suddenly realize that very little remains of the close and harmonious family we used to be at home! This is mostly because everything's out of kilter here. By that I mean that we're treated like children when it comes to external matters, while, inwardly, we're much older than other girls our age. Even though I'm only fourteen, I know what I want, I know who's right and who's wrong, I have my own opinions, ideas and principles, and though it may sound odd coming from a teenager, I feel I'm more of a person than a child – I feel I'm completely independent of others. I know I'm better at debating or carrying on a discussion than Mother, I know I'm more objective, I don't exaggerate as much, I'm much tidier and better with my hands, and because of that I feel (this may make you laugh) that I'm superior to her in many ways. To love someone, I have to admire and respect the person, but I feel neither respect nor admiration for Mother!

Everything would be all right if only I had Peter, since I admire him in many ways. He's so decent and capable!

Yours, Anne M. Frank

Dearest Kitty,

I've told you more about myself and my feelings than I've ever told a living soul, so why shouldn't that include sex?

Parents, and people in general, are very peculiar when it comes to sex. Instead of telling their sons and daughters everything at the age of twelve, they send the children out of the room the moment the subject arises and leave them to find out everything on their own. Later on, when parents notice that their children have, somehow, come by their information, they assume they know more (or less) than they actually do. So why don't they try to make amends by asking them what's what?

A major stumbling block for the adults – though in my opinion it's no more than a pebble – is that they're afraid their children will no longer look upon marriage as sacred and pure once they realize that, in most cases, this purity is a lot of nonsense. As far as I'm concerned, it's not wrong for a man to bring a little experience to a marriage. After all, it has nothing to do with the marriage itself, does it?

Soon after I turned eleven, they told me about menstruation. But even then, I had no idea where the blood came from or what it was for. When I was twelve and a half, I learned some more from Jacque, who wasn't as ignorant as I was. My own intuition told me what a man and a woman do when they're together; it seemed like a crazy idea at first, but when Jacque confirmed it, I was proud of myself for having worked it out!

It was also Jacque who told me that children didn't come out of their mother's tummies. As she put it, 'Where the ingredients go in is where the finished product comes out!' Jacque and I found out about the hymen, and quite a few other details, from a book on sex education. I also knew that you could keep from having children, but how that worked inside your body remained a mystery. When I came here, Father told me about prostitutes, etc., but all in all there are still unanswered questions.

If mothers don't tell their children everything, they hear it in bits and pieces, and that can't be right.

Even though it's Saturday, I'm not bored! That's because I've been up in the attic with Peter. I sat there dreaming with my eyes closed, and it was wonderful.

Yours, Anne M. Frank

SUNDAY, 19 MARCH 1944

Dearest Kitty,

Yesterday was a very important day for me. After lunch everything was as usual. At five I put on the potatoes, and Mother gave me some blood sausage to take to Peter. I didn't want to at first, but I finally went.

He wouldn't accept the sausage, and I had the dreadful feeling it was still because of that argument we'd had about distrust. Suddenly I couldn't bear it a moment longer and my eyes filled with tears. Without another word, I returned the plate to Mother and went to the lavatory to have a good cry. Afterwards I decided to talk things out with Peter. Before dinner the four of us were helping him with a crossword puzzle, so I couldn't say anything. But as we were sitting down to eat, I whispered to him, 'Are you going to practise your shorthand tonight, Peter?'

'No,' was his reply.

'I'd like to talk to you later on.'

He agreed.

After the washing-up, I went to his room and asked if he'd refused the sausage because of our last quarrel. Luckily, that wasn't the reason; he just thought it was bad manners to seem so eager. It had been very hot downstairs and my face was as red as a lobster. So after taking down some water for Margot, I went back up to get a little fresh air. For the sake of appearances, I first went and stood beside the van Daans' window before going to Peter's room. He was standing on the left side of the open window, so I went over to the right side. It's much easier to talk next to an open window in semi-darkness than in broad daylight, and I think Peter felt the same way. We told each other so much, so very much, that I can't repeat it all. But it felt good; it was the most wonderful evening I've ever had in the Annexe. I'll give you a brief description of the various subjects we touched on.

First we talked about the quarrels and how I see them in a very different light these days, and then about how we've become alienated from our parents. I told Peter about Mother and Father and Margot and myself. At one point he asked, 'You always give each other a good-night kiss, don't you?'

'One? Dozens of them. You don't, do you?'

'No, I've never really kissed anyone.'

'Not even on your birthday?'

'Yes, on my birthday I have.'

We talked about how neither of us really trusts our parents, and how his parents love each other a great deal and wish he'd confide in them, but that he doesn't want to. How I cry my heart out in bed and he goes up to the loft and swears. How Margot and I have only recently got to know each other and yet still tell each other very little, since we're always together. We talked about every imaginable thing, about trust, feelings and ourselves. Oh, Kitty, he was just as I thought he would be.

Then we talked about the year 1942, and how different we were back then; we don't even recognize ourselves from that period. How we couldn't stand each other at first. He'd thought I was a noisy pest, and I'd quickly concluded that he was nothing special. I didn't understand why he didn't flirt with me, but now I'm glad. He also mentioned how he often used to retreat to his room. I said that my noise and exuberance and his silence were two sides of the same coin, and that I also liked peace and quiet but don't have anything for myself alone, except my diary, and that everyone would rather see the back of me, starting with Mr Dussel, and that I don't always want to sit with my parents. We discussed how glad he is that my parents have children and how glad I am that he's here. How I now understand his need to withdraw and his relationship with his parents, and how much I'd like to help him when they argue.

'But you're always a help to me!' he said.

'How?' I asked, greatly surprised.

'By being cheerful.'

That was the nicest thing he said all evening. He also told me that he didn't mind my coming to his room the way he used to; in fact, he liked it. I also told him that all of Father's and Mother's pet names were meaningless, that a kiss here and there didn't automatically lead to trust. We also talked about doing things your own way, the diary, loneliness, the difference between everyone's inner and outer selves, my mask, etc.

It was wonderful. He must have come to love me as a friend, and, for the time being, that's enough. I'm so grateful and happy, I can't find the words. I must apologize, Kitty, since my style is not up to my usual standard today. I've just written whatever came into my head!

I have the feeling that Peter and I share a secret. Whenever he looks at me with those eyes, with that smile and that wink, it's as if a light goes on inside me. I hope things will stay like this and that we'll have many, many more happy hours together.

Your grateful and happy Anne

Dearest Kitty,

*T*his morning Peter asked me if I'd come again one evening. He swore I wouldn't be disturbing him, and said that where there was room for one, there was room for two. I said I couldn't see him every evening, since my parents didn't think it was a good idea, but he thought I shouldn't let that bother me. So I told him I'd like to come some Saturday evening and also asked him if he'd let me know when you could see the moon.

'Fine,' he said, 'maybe we can go downstairs and look at the moon from there.' I agreed; I'm not really so scared of burglars.

In the mean time, a shadow has fallen on my happiness. For a long time I've had the feeling that Margot likes Peter. Just how much I don't know, but the whole situation is very unpleasant. Now every time I go and see Peter I'm hurting her, without meaning to. The funny thing is that she hardly lets it show. I know I'd be insanely jealous, but Margot just says I shouldn't feel sorry for her.

'I think it's so awful that you've become the odd one out,' I added.

'I'm used to that,' she replied, somewhat bitterly.

I don't dare tell Peter. Maybe later on, but he and I need to discuss so many other things first.

Mother gave me a warning tap last night, which I deserved. I mustn't carry my indifference and contempt for her too far. In spite of everything, I should try once again to be friendly and keep my remarks to myself!

Even Pim isn't as nice as he used to be. He's been trying not to treat me like a child, but now he's much too cold. We'll just have to see what comes of it! He's warned me that if I don't do my algebra, I won't get any extra tuition after the war. I could simply wait and see what happens, but I'd like to start again, provided I get a new book.

That's enough for now. I do nothing but gaze at Peter, and I'm filled to overflowing!

Yours, Anne M. Frank

Evidence of Margot's goodness. I received this today, 20 March 1944:

Anne, yesterday when I said I wasn't jealous of you, I wasn't being entirely honest. The situation is this: I'm not jealous of either you or Peter. I'm just sorry I haven't found anyone with whom to share my thoughts and feelings, and I'm not likely to in the near future. But that's why I wish, from the bottom of my heart, that you will both be able to place your trust in each other. You're already missing out on so much here, things other people take for granted.

On the other hand, I'm certain I'd never have got as far with Peter, because I think I'd need to feel very close to a person before I could share my thoughts. I'd want to have the feeling that he understood me through and through, even if I didn't say much. For this reason it would have to be someone I felt was intellectually superior to me, and that isn't the case with Peter. But I can imagine your feeling close to him.

So there's no need for you to reproach yourself because you think you're taking something I was entitled to; nothing could be further from the truth. You and Peter have everything to gain by your friendship.

My answer:

Dearest Margot,

Your letter was extremely kind, but I still don't feel completely happy about the situation, and I don't think I ever will.

At the moment, Peter and I don't trust each other as much as you seem to think. It's just that when you're standing beside an open window at twilight, you can say more to each other than in bright sunshine. It's also easier to whisper your feelings than to shout them from the rooftops. I think you've begun to feel a kind of sisterly affection for Peter and would like to help him, just as much as I would. Perhaps you'll be able to do that some day, though that's not the kind of trust we have in mind. I believe that trust has to come from both sides; I also think that's the reason why Father and I have never really grown so close. But let's not talk about it any more. If there's anything you still want to discuss, please write, because it's easier for me to say what I mean on paper than face-to-face. You know how much I admire you, and only hope that some of your goodness and Father's goodness will rub off on me, because, in that sense, you two are a lot alike.

Yours, Anne

WEDNESDAY, 22 MARCH 1944

Dearest Kitty,

I received this letter last night from Margot:

Dear Anne,

After your letter of yesterday I have the unpleasant feeling that your conscience bothers you whenever you go to Peter's to work or talk; there's really no reason for that. In my heart, I know there's someone who deserves my trust (as I do his), and I wouldn't be able to tolerate Peter in his place.

However, as you wrote, I do think of Peter as a kind of brother . . . a younger brother; we've been sending out feelers, and a brotherly and sisterly affection may or may not develop at some later date, but it's certainly not reached that stage yet. So there's no need for you to feel sorry for me. Now that you've found companionship, enjoy it as much as you can.

In the mean time, things are getting more and more wonderful here. I think, Kitty, that true love may be developing in the Annexe. All those jokes about marrying Peter if we stayed here long enough weren't so silly after all. Not that I'm thinking of marrying him, mind you. I don't even know what he'll be like when he grows up. Or if we'll even love each other enough to get married.

I'm sure now that Peter loves me too; I just don't know in what way. I can't decide if he wants only a good friend, or if he's attracted to me as a girl or as a sister. When he said I always helped him when his parents were arguing, I was tremendously happy; it was one step towards making me believe in his friendship. I asked him yesterday what he'd do if there were a dozen Annes who kept popping in to see him. His answer was: 'If they were all like you, it wouldn't be so bad.' He's extremely hospitable, and I think he really likes to see me. Meanwhile, he's been working hard at learning French, even studying in bed until ten-fifteen.

Oh, when I think back to Saturday night, to our words, our voices, I feel satisfied with myself for the very first time; what I mean is, I'd still say the same and wouldn't want to change a thing, the way I usually do. He's so handsome, whether he's smiling or just sitting still. He's so sweet and good and beautiful. I think what surprised him most about me was when he discovered that I'm not at all the superficial, worldly Anne I appear to be, but a dreamer, like he is, with just as many troubles!

Last night after washing up, I waited for him to ask me to stay upstairs. But nothing happened; I went away. He came downstairs to tell Dussel it was time to listen to the radio and hung around the bathroom for a while, but when Dussel took too long, he went back upstairs. He paced up and down his room and went to bed early.

The entire evening I was so restless I kept going to the bathroom to splash cold water on my face. I read a bit, daydreamed some more, looked at the clock and waited, waited, waited, all the while listening to his footsteps. I went to bed early, exhausted.

Tonight I have to take a bath, and tomorrow? Tomorrow's so far away!

Yours, Anne M. Frank

My answer:

Dearest Margot,

I think the best thing is simply to wait and see what happens. It can't be much longer before Peter and I will have to decide whether to go back to the way we were or do something else. I don't know how it'll turn out; I can't see any farther than the end of my nose.

But I'm certain of one thing: if Peter and I do

become friends, I'm going to tell him you're also very fond of him and are prepared to help him if he needs you. You wouldn't want me to, I'm sure, but I don't care; I don't know what Peter thinks of you, but I'll ask him when the time comes. It's certainly nothing bad – on the contrary! You're welcome to join us in the attic, or wherever we are. You won't be disturbing us, because we have an unspoken agreement to talk only in the evenings when it's dark.

Keep your spirits up! I'm doing my best, though it's not always easy. Your time may come sooner than you think.

Yours, Anne

THURSDAY, 23 MARCH 1944

Dearest Kitty,

*T*hings are more or less back to normal here. Our coupon men have been released from prison, thank goodness!

Miep's been back since yesterday, but today it was her husband's turn to take to his bed – shivers and a temperature, the usual flu symptoms. Bep is better, though she still has a cough, and Mr Kleiman will have to stay at home for a long time.

Yesterday a plane crashed near by. The crew was able to parachute out in time. It crashed on top of a school, but luckily there were no children inside. There was a small fire and a couple of people were killed. As the airmen made their descent, the Germans sprayed them with bullets. The Amsterdammers who saw it seethed with rage at such a dastardly deed. We – by which I mean the ladies – were also scared out of our wits. Brrr, I hate the sound of gunfire.

Now about myself.

I was with Peter yesterday and, somehow, I honestly don't know how, we ended up talking about sex. I'd made up my mind a long time ago to ask him a few things. He knows everything; when I said that Margot and I weren't very well informed, he was amazed. I told him a lot about Margot and me and Mother and Father and said that lately I didn't dare ask them anything. He offered to enlighten me, and I gratefully accepted: he described how contraceptives work, and I asked him very boldly how boys could tell they were grown up. He had to think about that one; he said he'd tell me tonight. I told him what had happened to Jacque, and said that girls are defenceless against strong boys. 'Well, you don't have to be afraid of me,' he said.

When I came back that evening, he told me how it is with boys. Slightly embarrassing, but still awfully nice to be able to discuss it with him. Neither he nor I had ever imagined we'd be able to talk so openly to a girl or a boy, respectively, about such intimate matters. I think I know everything now. He told me a lot about what he called *Präsentivmitteln*★ in German.

That night in the bathroom Margot and I were talking about Bram and Trees, two friends of hers.

This morning I was in for a nasty surprise: after breakfast Peter beckoned me upstairs. 'That was a dirty trick you played on me,' he said. 'I heard what you and Margot were saying in the bathroom last night. I think you just wanted to find out how much Peter knew and then have a good laugh!'

I was stunned! I did everything I could to talk him out of that outrageous idea; I could understand how he must have felt, but it just wasn't true!

'Oh no, Peter,' I said. 'I'd never be so rotten. I told you I wouldn't pass on anything you said to me and I won't. To put on an act like that and then deliberately be so mean . . . No, Peter, that's not my idea of a joke. It wouldn't be fair. I didn't say anything, honest. Won't you believe me?' He assured me he did, but I think we'll have to talk about it again sometime. I've done nothing all day but worry about it. Thank goodness he came right out and said what was on his mind. Imagine if he'd gone around thinking I could be that horrible. He's so sweet!

Now I'll have to tell him everything!

Yours, Anne

★ Should be *Präservativmitteln*: prophylactics.

Dear Kitty,

I often go up to Peter's room after dinner nowadays to breathe in the fresh evening air. You can get around to meaningful conversations more quickly in the dark than with the sun tickling your face. It's cosy and snug sitting beside him on a chair and looking outside. The van Daans and Dussel make the silliest remarks when I disappear into his room. '*Annes zweite Heimat*',★ they say, or 'Is it proper for a gentleman to receive young girls in his room at night with the lights out?' Peter has amazing presence of mind in the face of these so-called witticisms. My mother, incidentally, is also bursting with curiosity and simply dying to ask what we talk about, only she's secretly afraid I'd refuse to answer. Peter says the grown-ups are just jealous because we're young and that we shouldn't take their obnoxious comments to heart.

Sometimes he comes downstairs to get me, but that's awkward too, because in spite of all his precautions his face turns bright red and he can hardly get the words out of his mouth. I'm glad I don't blush; it must be extremely unpleasant.

Besides, it bothers me that Margot has to sit downstairs all by herself, while I'm upstairs enjoying Peter's company. But what can I do about it? I wouldn't mind it if she came, but she'd just be the odd one out, sitting there like a lump.

★ Anne's second home.

I've had to listen to countless remarks about our sudden friendship. I can't tell you how often the conversation at meals has been about an Annexe wedding, should the war last another five years. Do we take any notice of this parental chitchat? Hardly, since it's all so silly. Have my parents forgotten that they were young once? Apparently they have. At any rate, they laugh at us when we're serious, and they're serious when we're joking.

I don't know what's going to happen next, or whether we'll run out of things to say. But if it goes on like this, we'll eventually be able to be together without talking. If only his parents would stop acting so strangely. It's probably because they don't like seeing me so often; Peter and I certainly never tell them what we talk about. Imagine if they knew we were discussing such intimate things.

I'd like to ask Peter whether he knows what girls look like down there. I don't think boys are as complicated as girls. You can easily see what boys look like in photographs or pictures of male nudes, but with women it's different. In women, the genitals, or whatever they're called, are hidden between their legs. Peter has probably never seen a girl up close. To tell you the truth, neither have I. Boys are a lot easier. How on earth would I go about describing a girl's parts? I can tell from what he said that he doesn't know exactly how it all fits together. He was talking about the '*Muttermund*',* but that's on the inside, where you can't see it. Everything's pretty well arranged in us women. Until I was eleven or twelve, I

* Cervix.

didn't realize there was a second set of labia on the inside, since you couldn't see them. What's even funnier is that I thought urine came out of the clitoris. I asked Mother once what that little bump was, and she said she didn't know. She can really play dumb when she wants to!

But to get back to the subject. How on earth can you explain what it all looks like without any models? Shall I try anyway? Okay, here goes!

When you're standing up, all you see from the front is hair. Between your legs there are two soft, cushiony things, also covered with hair, which press together when you're standing, so you can't see what's inside. They separate when you sit down, and they're very red and quite fleshy on the inside. In the upper part, between the outer labia, there's a fold of skin that, on second thought, looks like a kind of blister. That's the clitoris. Then come the inner labia, which are also pressed together in a kind of crease. When they open up, you can see a fleshy little mound, no bigger than the top of my thumb. The upper part has a couple of small holes in it, which is where the urine comes out. The lower part looks as if it were just skin, and yet that's where the vagina is. You can barely find it, because the folds of skin hide the opening. The hole's so small I can hardly imagine how a man could get in there, much less how a baby could come out. It's hard enough trying to get your index finger inside. That's all there is, and yet it plays such an important role!

Yours, Anne M. Frank

Dearest Kitty,

You never realize how much you've changed until after it's happened. I've changed quite drastically, everything about me is different: my opinions, ideas, critical outlook. Inwardly, outwardly, nothing's the same. And, I might safely add, since it's true, I've changed for the better. I once told you that, after years of being adored, it was hard for me to adjust to the harsh reality of grown-ups and rebukes. But Father and Mother are largely to blame for my having to put up with so much. At home they wanted me to enjoy life, which was fine, but here they shouldn't have encouraged me to agree with them and only shown me 'their' side of all the quarrels and gossip. It was a long time before I discovered the score was fifty-fifty. I now know that many blunders have been committed here, by young and old alike. Father and Mother's biggest mistake in dealing with the van Daans is that they're never candid and friendly (admittedly, the friendliness might have to be feigned). Above all, I want to keep the peace, and to neither quarrel nor gossip. With Father and Margot that's not difficult, but it is with Mother, which is why I'm glad she gives me an occasional rap on the knuckles. You can win Mr van Daan over to your side by agreeing with him, listening quietly, not saying much and most of all . . . responding to his teasing and his corny jokes with a joke of your own. Mrs van D. can be won over by talking openly to her and admitting when you're wrong. She also frankly admits her faults, of which she has many. I know all too well that she doesn't think as badly of me as she did in the beginning. And that's simply because I'm honest and tell people right to their faces what I think, even when it's not very flattering. I want to be honest; I think it gets you further and also makes you feel better about yourself.

Yesterday Mrs van D. was talking about the rice we gave Mr Kleiman. 'All we do is give, give, give. But at a certain point I think that enough is enough. If he'd only take the trouble, Mr Kleiman could find his own rice. Why should we give away all our supplies? We need them just as badly.'

'No, Mrs van Daan,' I replied. 'I don't agree with you. Mr Kleiman may very well be able to get hold of a little rice, but he doesn't like having to worry about it. It's not our place to criticize the people who are helping us. We should give them whatever they need if we can possibly spare it. One less plate of rice a week won't make that much difference; we can always eat beans.'

Mrs van D. didn't see it my way, but she added that, even though she disagreed, she was willing to back down, and that was an entirely different matter.

Well, I've said enough. Sometimes I know what my place is and sometimes I have my doubts, but I'll eventually get where I want to be! I know I will! Especially now that I have help, since Peter helps me through many a rough patch and rainy day!

I honestly don't know how much he loves me and

whether we'll ever get as far as a kiss; in any case, I don't want to force the issue! I told Father I often go and see Peter and asked if he approved, and of course he did!

It's much easier now to tell Peter things I'd normally keep to myself; for example, I told him I want to write later on, and if I can't be a writer, to write in addition to my work.

I don't have much in the way of money or worldly possessions, I'm not beautiful, intelligent or clever, but I'm happy, and I intend to stay that way! I was born happy, I love people, I have a trusting nature, and I'd like everyone else to be happy too.

Your devoted friend, Anne M. Frank

An empty day, though clear and bright,
Is just as dark as any night.

(I wrote this a few weeks ago and it no longer holds true, but I included it because my poems are so few and far between.)

MONDAY, 27 MARCH 1944

Dearest Kitty,

At least one long chapter on our life in hiding should be about politics, but I've been avoiding the subject, since it interests me so little. Today, however, I'll devote an entire letter to politics.

Of course, there are many different opinions on this topic, and it's not surprising to hear it frequently discussed in times of war, but . . . arguing so much about politics is just plain stupid! Let them laugh, swear, make bets, grumble and do whatever they want as long as they stew in their own juice. But don't let them argue, since that only makes things worse. The people who come from outside bring us a lot of news that later proves to be untrue; however, until now our radio has never lied. Jan, Miep, Mr Kleiman, Bep and Mr Kugler go up and down in their political moods, though Jan least of all.

Here in the Annexe the mood never varies. The endless debates over the invasion, air raids, speeches, etc., etc., are accompanied by countless exclamations such as 'Eempossible!, *Um Gottes Willen*,★ If they're just getting started now, how long is it going to last!, It's going splendidly, *gut*, great!'

Optimists and pessimists – not to mention the realists – air their opinions with unflagging energy, and as with everything else, they're all certain that they have a monopoly on the truth. It annoys a certain lady that her spouse has such supreme faith in the British, and a certain husband attacks his wife because of her teasing and disparaging remarks about his beloved nation!

And so it goes from early in the morning to late at night; the funny part is that they never get tired of it.

★ Oh, for God's sake.

I've discovered a trick, and the effect is overwhelming, just like pricking someone with a pin and watching them jump. Here's how it works: I start talking about politics. All it takes is a single question, a word or a sentence, and before you know it, the entire family is involved!

As if the German 'Wehrmacht News' and the English BBC weren't enough, they've now added special air-raid announcements. In a word, splendid. But the other side of the coin is that the British Air Force is operating round the clock. Not unlike the German propaganda machine, which is cranking out lies twenty-four hours a day!

So the radio is switched on every morning at eight (if not earlier) and is listened to every hour until nine, ten or even eleven at night. This is the best evidence yet that the adults have infinite patience, but also that their brains have turned to mush (some of them, I mean, since I wouldn't want to insult anyone). One broadcast, two at the most, should be enough to last the entire day. But no, those old nincompoops ... never mind, I've already said it all! 'Music While You Work', the Dutch broadcast from England, Frank Phillips or Queen Wilhelmina, they each get a turn and find a willing listener. If the adults aren't eating or sleeping, they're clustered around the radio talking about eating, sleeping and politics. Whew! It's getting to be a bore, and it's all I can do to keep from turning into a dreary old crone myself! Though with all the oldies around me, that might not be such a bad idea!

Here's a shining example, a speech made by our beloved Winston Churchill.

Nine o'clock, Sunday evening. The teapot, under its cosy, is on the table, and the guests enter the room. Dussel sits to the left of the radio, Mr van D. in front of it and Peter to the side. Mother is next to Mr van D., with Mrs van D. behind them. Margot and I are sitting in the last row and Pim at the table. I realize this isn't a very clear description of our seating arrangements, but it doesn't matter. The men smoke, Peter's eyes close from the strain of listening, Mummy is dressed in her long, dark negligée, Mrs van D. is trembling because of the planes, which take no notice of the speech but fly blithely on towards Essen, Father is slurping his tea, and Margot and I are united in a sisterly way by the sleeping Mouschi, who has taken possession of both our knees. Margot's hair is in curlers and my nightdress is too small, too tight and too short. It all looks so intimate, cosy and peaceful, and for once it really is. Yet I await the end of the speech with dread. They're impatient, straining at the leash to start another argument! Pst, pst, like a cat luring a mouse from its hole, they goad each other into quarrels and dissent.

Yours, Anne

My dearest Kitty,

As much as I'd like to write more on politics, I have lots of other news to report today. First, Mother has virtually forbidden me to go up to Peter's, since, according to her, Mrs van Daan is jealous. Second, Peter's invited Margot to join us upstairs. Whether he really means it or is just saying it out of politeness, I don't know. Third, I asked Father if he thought I should take any notice of Mrs van Daan's jealousy and he said I didn't have to.

What should I do now? Mother's angry, doesn't want me going upstairs, wants me to go back to doing my homework in the room I share with Dussel. She may be jealous herself. Father doesn't begrudge us those few hours and thinks it's nice we get along so well. Margot likes Peter too, but feels that three people can't talk about the same things as two.

Furthermore, Mother thinks Peter's in love with me. To tell you the truth, I wish he were. Then we'd be even, and it'd be a lot easier to get to know each other. She also claims he's always looking at me. Well, I suppose we do give each other the occasional wink. But I can't help it if he keeps admiring my dimples, can I?

I'm in a very difficult position. Mother's against me and I'm against her. Father turns a blind eye to the silent struggle between Mother and me. Mother is sad, because she still loves me, but I'm not at all unhappy, because she no longer means anything to me.

As for Peter . . . I don't want to give him up. He's so sweet and I admire him so much. He and I could have a really beautiful relationship, so why are the old people poking their noses into our business again? Fortunately, I'm used to hiding my feelings, so I manage not to show how insane I am about him. Is he ever going to say anything? Am I ever going to feel his cheek against mine, the way I felt Petel's cheek in my dream? Oh, Peter and Petel, you're one and the same! They don't understand us; they'd never understand that we're content just to sit beside each other and not say a word. They have no idea of what draws us together! Oh, when will we overcome all these difficulties? And yet it's good that we have to surmount them, since it makes the end that much more beautiful. When he lays his head on his arms and closes his eyes, he's still a child; when he plays with Mouschi or talks about her, he's loving; when he carries the potatoes or other heavy loads, he's strong; when he goes to watch the gunfire or walks through the dark house to look for burglars, he's brave; and when he's so awkward and clumsy, he's hopelessly endearing. It's much nicer when he explains something to me than when I have to teach him. I wish he were superior to me in nearly every way!

What do we care about our two mothers? Oh, if only he'd say something.

Father always says I'm conceited, but I'm not, I'm merely vain! I haven't had many people tell me I was pretty, except for a boy at school who said I looked so nice when I smiled. Yesterday Peter paid me a true compliment, and just for fun I'll give you a rough idea of our conversation.

Peter often says, 'Smile!' I thought it was strange, so yesterday I asked him, 'Why do you always want me to smile?'

'Because you get dimples in your cheeks. How do you do that?'

'I was born with them. There's also one in my chin. It's the only mark of beauty I possess.'

'No, no, that's not true!'

'Yes, it is. I know I'm not beautiful. I never have been and I never will be!'

'I don't agree. I think you're pretty.'

'I am not.'

'I say you are, and you'll have to take my word for it!'

So of course I then said the same about him.

Yours, Anne M. Frank

WEDNESDAY, 29 MARCH 1944

Dearest Kitty,

Mr Bolkestein, the Cabinet Minister, speaking on the Dutch broadcast from London, said that after the war a collection would be made of diaries and letters dealing with the war. Of course, everyone pounced on my diary. Just imagine how interesting it would be if I were to publish a novel about the Secret Annexe. The title alone would make people think it was a detective story.

Seriously, though, ten years after the war people would find it very amusing to read how we lived, what we ate and what we talked about as Jews in hiding. Although I tell you a great deal about our lives, you still know very little about us. How frightened the women are during air raids; last Sunday, for instance, when 350 British planes dropped 550 tons of bombs on IJmuiden, so that the houses trembled like blades of grass in the wind. Or how many epidemics are raging here.

You know nothing of these matters, and it would take me all day to describe everything down to the last detail. People have to queue for vegetables and all kinds of goods; doctors can't visit their patients, since their cars and bikes are stolen the moment they turn their backs; burglaries and thefts are so common that you ask yourself what's suddenly got into the Dutch to make them so light-fingered. Little children, eight- and eleven-year-olds, smash the windows of people's homes and steal whatever they can lay their hands on. People don't dare leave the house for even five minutes, since they're liable to come back and find all their belongings gone. Every day the newspapers are filled with reward notices for the return of stolen typewriters, Persian rugs, electric clocks, fabrics, etc. The electric clocks on street corners are dismantled, public phones are stripped down to the last wire.

Morale among the Dutch can't be good. Everyone's hungry; except for the ersatz coffee, a week's food ration doesn't last two days. The invasion's long in coming, the men are being shipped off to Germany, the children are ill or undernourished, everyone's wearing worn-out clothes and run-down shoes. A new sole costs 7.50 guilders on the black market. Besides, few shoemakers will do repairs, or if they do, you have to wait four months for your shoes, which might very well have disappeared in the mean time.

One good thing has come out of this: as the food gets worse and the decrees more severe, the acts of sabotage against the authorities are increasing. The food office, the police, the officials – they're all either helping their fellow citizens or denouncing them and sending them off to prison. Fortunately, only a small percentage of Dutch people are on the wrong side.

Yours, Anne

FRIDAY, 31 MARCH 1944

Dearest Kitty,

Just imagine, it's still fairly cold, and yet most people have been without coal for nearly a month. Sounds awful, doesn't it? There's a general mood of optimism about the Russian front, because that's going great guns!

I don't often write about the political situation, but I must tell you where the Russians are at the moment. They've reached the Polish border and the Prut River in Romania. They're close to Odessa, and they've surrounded Ternopol. Every night we're expecting an extra communiqué from Stalin.

They're firing off so many salutes in Moscow, the city must be rumbling and shaking all day long. Whether they like to pretend the fighting's near by or they simply don't have any other way to express their joy, I don't know!

Hungary has been occupied by German troops. There are still a million Jews living there; they too are doomed.

Nothing special is happening here. Today is Mr van Daan's birthday. He received two packets of tobacco, one serving of coffee, which his wife had managed to save, lemon punch from Mr Kugler, sardines from Miep, eau-de-Cologne from us, lilacs, tulips and, last but not least, a cake with raspberry filling, slightly gluey because of the poor quality of the flour and the lack of butter, but delicious anyway.

All that talk about Peter and me has died down a bit. He's coming to fetch me tonight. Pretty nice of him, don't you think, since he hates doing it! We're very good friends. We spend a lot of time together and talk about every imaginable subject. It's so nice not having to hold back when we come to a delicate topic, the way I would with other boys. For example, we were talking about blood and somehow the conversation turned to menstruation, etc. He thinks we women are quite tough to be able to withstand the loss of blood, and that I am too. I wonder why?

My life here is better now, much better. God has not forsaken me, and He never will.

Yours, Anne M. Frank

My dearest Kitty,

*A*nd yet everything is still so difficult. You do know what I mean, don't you? I long so much for him to kiss me, but that kiss is taking its own sweet time. Does he still think of me as a friend? Don't I mean anything more?

You and I both know that I'm strong, that I can carry most burdens alone. I've never been used to sharing my worries with anyone, and I've never clung to a mother, but I'd love to lay my head on his shoulder and just sit there quietly.

I can't, I simply can't forget that dream of Peter's cheek, when everything was so good! Does he have the same longing? Is he just too shy to say he loves me? Why does he want me near him so much? Oh, why doesn't he say something?

I've got to stop, I've got to be calm. I'll try to be strong again, and if I'm patient, the rest will follow. But

– and this is the worst part – I seem to be chasing him. I'm always the one who has to go upstairs; *he* never comes to *me*. But that's because of the rooms, and he understands why I object. Oh, I'm sure he understands more than I think.

Yours, Anne M. Frank

MONDAY, 3 APRIL 1944

My dearest Kitty,

Contrary to my usual practice, I'm going to write you a detailed description of the food situation, since it's become a matter of some difficulty and importance, not only here in the Annexe, but in all of Holland, all of Europe and even beyond.

In the twenty-one months we've lived here, we've been through a good many 'food cycles' – you'll understand what that means in a moment. A 'food cycle' is a period in which we have only one particular dish or type of vegetable to eat. For a long time we ate nothing but endive. Endive with sand, endive without sand, endive with mashed potatoes, endive and mashed potato casserole. Then it was spinach, followed by kohlrabi, salsify, cucumbers, tomatoes, sauerkraut, etc., etc.

It's not much fun when you have to eat, say, sauerkraut every day for lunch and dinner, but when you're hungry enough, you do a lot of things. Now, however, we're going through the most delightful period so far, because there are no vegetables at all.

Our weekly lunch menu consists of brown beans, split-pea soup, potatoes with dumplings, potato kugel and, by the grace of God, turnip tops or rotten carrots, and then it's back to brown beans. Because of the bread shortage, we eat potatoes at every meal, starting with breakfast, but then we fry them a little. To make soup we use brown beans, haricot beans, potatoes, packets of vegetable soup, packets of chicken soup and packets of bean soup. There are brown beans in everything, including the bread. For dinner we always have potatoes with imitation gravy and – thank goodness we've still got it – beetroot salad. I must tell you about the dumplings. We make them with government-issue flour, water and yeast. They're so gluey and tough that it feels as if you have rocks in your stomach, but oh well!

The high point is our weekly slice of liver sausage,

and the jam on our unbuttered bread. But we're still alive, and much of the time it still tastes good too!

Yours, Anne M. Frank

My dearest Kitty,

*F*or a long time now I didn't know why I was bothering to do any schoolwork. The end of the war still seemed so far away, so unreal, like a fairy tale. If the war isn't over by September, I won't go back to school, since I don't want to be two years behind.

Peter filled my days, nothing but Peter, dreams and thoughts until Saturday night, when I felt so utterly miserable; oh, it was awful. I held back my tears when I was with Peter, laughed uproariously with the van Daans as we drank lemon punch and was cheerful and excited, but the minute I was alone I knew I was going to cry my eyes out. I slid to the floor in my nightie and began by saying my prayers, very fervently. Then I drew my knees to my chest, laid my head on my arms and cried, all huddled up on the bare floor. A loud sob brought me back down to earth, and I choked back my tears, since I didn't want anyone next door to hear me. Then I tried to pull myself together, saying over and over, 'I must, I must, I must . . .' Stiff from sitting in such an unusual position, I fell back against the side of the bed and kept up my struggle until just before ten-thirty, when I climbed back into bed. It was over!

And now it's really over. I finally realized that I must do my schoolwork to keep from being ignorant, to get on in life, to become a journalist, because that's what I want! I *know* I can write. A few of my stories are good, my descriptions of the Secret Annexe are humorous, much of my diary is vivid and alive, but . . . it remains to be seen whether I really have talent.

'Eva's Dream' is my best fairy tale, and the odd thing is that I don't have the faintest idea where it came from. Parts of 'Cady's Life' are also good, but as a whole it's nothing special. I'm my best and harshest critic. I know what's good and what isn't. Unless you write yourself, you can't know how wonderful it is; I always used to bemoan the fact that I couldn't draw, but now I'm over-joyed that at least I can write. And if I don't have the talent to write books or newspaper articles, I can always write for myself. But I want to achieve more than that. I can't imagine having to live like Mother, Mrs van Daan and all the women who go about their work and are then forgotten. I need to have something besides a hus-band and children to devote myself to! I don't want to have lived in vain like most people. I want to be useful or bring enjoyment to all people, even those I've never met. I want to go on living even after my death! And that's why I'm so grateful to God for having given me this gift, which I can use to develop myself and to express all that's inside me!

When I write I can shake off all my cares. My sorrow disappears, my spirits are revived! But, and that's a big question, will I ever be able to write something great, will I ever become a journalist or a writer?

I hope so, oh, I hope so very much, because writing allows me to record everything, all my thoughts, ideals and fantasies.

I haven't worked on 'Cady's Life' for ages. In my mind I've worked out exactly what happens next, but the story doesn't seem to be coming along very well. I might never finish it, and it'll end up in the wastepaper basket or the fire. That's a horrible thought, but then I say to myself, 'At the age of fourteen and with so little experience, you can't write about philosophy.'

So onwards and upwards, with renewed spirits. It'll all work out, because I'm determined to write!

Yours, Anne M. Frank

THURSDAY, 6 APRIL 1944

Dearest Kitty,

You asked me what my hobbies and interests are and I'd like to answer, but I'd better warn you, I have lots of them, so don't be surprised.

First of all: writing, but I don't really think of that as a hobby.

Number two: genealogical charts. I'm looking in every newspaper, book and document I can find for the family trees of the French, German, Spanish, English, Austrian, Russian, Norwegian and Dutch royal families. I've made great progress with many of them, because for a long time I've been taking notes while reading biographies or history books. I even copy out many of the passages on history.

So my third hobby is history, and Father's already bought me numerous books. I can hardly wait for the day when I'll be able to go to the public library and ferret out the information I need.

Number four is Greek and Roman mythology. I have various books on this subject too. I can name the nine Muses and the seven loves of Zeus. I have the wives of Hercules, etc., etc., off pat.

My other hobbies are film stars and family photographs. I'm crazy about reading and books. I adore the history of the arts, especially when it concerns writers, poets and painters; musicians may come later. I loathe algebra, geometry and arithmetic. I enjoy all my other school subjects, but history's my favourite!

Yours, Anne M. Frank

My dearest Kitty,

My head's in a whirl, I really don't know where to begin. Thursday (the last time I wrote to you) everything was as usual. Friday afternoon (Good Friday) we played Monopoly; Saturday afternoon too. The days passed very quickly. At about two o'clock on Saturday, heavy firing began – machine-guns, according to the men. For the rest, everything was quiet.

Sunday afternoon Peter came to see me at four-thirty, at my invitation. At five-fifteen we went to the front attic, where we stayed until six. There was a beautiful Mozart concert on the radio from six to seven-fifteen; I especially enjoyed the *Kleine Nachtmusik*. I can hardly bear to listen in the kitchen, since beautiful music stirs me to the very depths of my soul. Sunday evening Peter couldn't take his bath, because the tub was down in the office kitchen, filled with dirty clothes. The two of us went to the front attic together, and in order to be able to sit comfortably, I took along the only cushion I could find in my room. We seated ourselves on a packing case. Since both the case and the cushion were very narrow, we were sitting quite close, leaning against two other cases; Mouschi kept us company, so we weren't without a chaperon. Suddenly, at quarter to nine, Mr van Daan whistled and asked if we had Mr Dussel's cushion. We jumped up and went downstairs with the cushion, the cat and Mr van Daan. This cushion was the source of much misery. Dussel was angry because I'd taken the one he uses as a pillow, and he was afraid it might be covered with fleas; he had the entire house in an uproar because of this one cushion. In revenge, Peter and I stuck two hard brushes in his bed, but had to take them out again when Dussel unexpectedly decided to go and sit in his room. We had a really good laugh at this little intermezzo.

But our fun was short-lived. At nine-thirty Peter knocked gently on the door and asked Father to come upstairs and help him with a difficult English sentence.

'That sounds fishy,' I said to Margot. 'It's obviously a pretext. You can tell by the way the men are talking that there's been a break-in!' I was right. The warehouse was being broken into at that very moment. Father, Mr van Daan and Peter were downstairs in a flash. Margot, Mother, Mrs van D. and I waited. Four frightened women need to talk, so that's what we did until we heard a bang downstairs. After that all was quiet. The clock struck quarter to ten. The colour had drained from our faces, but we remained calm, even though we were afraid. Where were the men? What was that bang? Were they fighting with the burglars? We were too scared to think; all we could do was wait.

Ten o'clock, footsteps on the stairs. Father, pale and nervous, came inside, followed by Mr van Daan. 'Lights out, tiptoe upstairs, we're expecting the police!'

There wasn't time to be scared. The lights were switched off, I grabbed a jacket, and we sat down up-stairs.

'What happened? Tell us quickly!'

There was no one to tell us; the men had gone back downstairs. The four of them didn't come back up until ten past ten. Two of them kept watch at Peter's open window. The door to the landing was locked, the bookcase shut. We draped a sweater over our night-light, and then they told us what had happened:

Peter was on the landing when he heard two loud bangs. He went downstairs and saw that a large panel was missing from the left half of the warehouse door. He dashed upstairs, alerted the 'Home Guard', and the four of them went downstairs. When they entered the warehouse, the burglars were going about their business. Without thinking, Mr van Daan yelled 'Police!' Hurried footsteps outside; the burglars had fled. The board was put back in the door so the police wouldn't notice the gap, but then a swift kick from outside sent it flying to the floor. The men were amazed at the burglars' audacity. Both Peter and Mr van Daan felt a murderous rage come over them. Mr van Daan slammed an axe against the floor, and all was quiet again. Once more the panel was replaced, and once more the attempt was foiled. Outside, a man and a woman shone a glaring torch through the opening, lighting up the entire warehouse. 'What the . . .' mumbled one of the men, but now their roles had been reversed. Instead of policemen, they were now burglars. All four of them raced upstairs. Dussel and Mr van Daan snatched up Dussel's books, Peter opened the doors and windows in the kitchen and private office, hurled the phone to the ground, and the four of them finally ended up behind the bookcase.

END OF PART ONE

In all probability the man and woman with the torch had alerted the police. It was Sunday night, Easter Sunday. The next day, Easter Monday, the office was going to be closed, which meant we wouldn't be able to move around until Tuesday morning. Think of it, having to sit in such terror for a day and two nights! We thought of nothing, but simply sat there in pitch darkness – in her fear, Mrs van D. had switched off the lamp. We whispered, and every time we heard a creak, someone said, 'Shh, shh.'

It was ten-thirty, then eleven. Not a sound. Father and Mr van Daan took turns coming upstairs to us. Then, at eleven-fifteen, a noise below. Up above you could hear the whole family breathing. For the rest, no one moved a muscle. Footsteps in the house, the private office, the kitchen, then . . . on the staircase. All sounds of breathing stopped, eight hearts pounded. Footsteps on the stairs, then a rattling at the bookcase. This moment is indescribable.

'Now we're done for,' I said, and I had visions of all fifteen of us being dragged away by the Gestapo that very night.

More rattling at the bookcase, twice. Then we heard a tin fall, and the footsteps receded. We were out of danger, so far! A shiver went through everyone's body, I heard several sets of teeth chattering, no one said a word. We stayed like this until eleven-thirty.

There were no more sounds in the house, but a light was shining on our landing, right in front of the bookcase. Was that because the police thought it looked so suspicious or because they simply forgot? Was anyone going to come back and turn it off? We found our tongues again. There were no longer any people inside the building, but perhaps someone was standing guard outside. We then did three things: tried to guess what was going on, trembled with fear and went to the lavatory. Since the buckets were in the attic, all we had was Peter's metal wastepaper basket. Mr van Daan went first, then Father, but Mother was too embarrassed. Father brought the wastebasket to the next room, where Margot, Mrs van Daan and I gratefully made use of it. Mother finally gave in. There was a great demand for paper, and luckily I had some in my pocket.

The wastebasket stank, everything went on in a whisper, and we were exhausted. It was midnight.

'Lie down on the floor and go to sleep!' Margot and I were each given a pillow and a blanket. Margot lay down near the food cupboard, and I made my bed between the table legs. The smell wasn't quite so bad when you were lying on the floor, but Mrs van Daan quietly went and got some powdered bleach and draped a tea-towel over the potty as a further precaution.

Talk, whispers, fear, stench, farting and people continually going to the lavatory; try sleeping through that! By two-thirty, however, I was so tired I dozed off and didn't hear a thing until three-thirty. I woke up when Mrs van D. laid her head on my feet.

'For heaven's sake, give me something to put on!' I said. I was handed some clothes, but don't ask what: a pair of woollen slacks over my pyjamas, a red jumper and a black skirt, white stockings and tattered kneesocks.

Mrs van D. sat back down on the chair, and Mr van D. lay down with his head on my feet. From three-thirty onwards I was engrossed in thought, and still shivering so much that Mr van Daan couldn't sleep. I was preparing myself for the return of the police. We'd tell them we were in hiding; if they were good people, we'd be safe, and if they were Nazi sympathizers, we could try to bribe them!

'We should hide the wireless set!' moaned Mrs van D.

'Right, in the stove,' answered Mr van D. 'If they find us, they might as well find the wireless!'

'Then they'll also find Anne's diary,' added Father.

'So burn it,' suggested the most terrified of the group.

This and the police rattling on the bookcase were the moments when I was most afraid. Oh, not my diary; if my diary goes, I go too! Thank goodness Father didn't say anything more.

There's no point in recounting all the conversations; so much was said. I comforted Mrs van Daan, who was very frightened. We talked about escaping, being interrogated by the Gestapo, phoning Mr Kleiman and being courageous.

'We must behave like soldiers, Mrs van Daan. If our time has come, well then, it'll be for Queen and Country, for freedom, truth and justice, as they're always telling us on the wireless. The only bad thing is that we'll drag the others down with us!'

After an hour Mr van Daan switched places with his wife again, and Father came and sat beside me. The men smoked one cigarette after another, an occasional sigh was heard, somebody made another trip to the potty, and then everything began all over again.

Four o'clock, five, five-thirty. I went and sat with Peter by his window and listened, so close we could feel each other's bodies trembling; we spoke a word or two from time to time and listened intently. Next door they took down the black-out screen. They made a list of everything they were planning to tell Mr Kleiman over the phone, because they intended to ring him at seven and ask him to send someone over. They were taking a big chance, since the police guard at the door or in the warehouse might hear them, but there was an even greater risk that the police would return.

I'm enclosing their list, but for the sake of clarity, I'll copy it here.

Burglary: Police in building, up to *bookcase*, but no farther. Burglars apparently interrupted, forced warehouse door, fled through garden. Main entrance bolted; Kugler *must* have left through second door.

Typewriter and adding machine safe in black chest in private office.

Miep's or Bep's washing in kitchen.

Only Bep or Kugler have key to second door; lock may be broken.

Try to warn Jan and get key, look around office;
   also feed cat.

For the rest, everything went according to plan. Mr Kleiman was phoned, the poles were removed from the doors, the typewriter was put back in the chest. Then we all sat round the table again and waited for either Jan or the police.

Peter had dropped off to sleep and Mr van Daan and I were lying on the floor when we heard loud footsteps below. I got up quietly. 'It's Jan!'

'No, no, it's the police!' they all said.

There was a knocking at our bookcase. Miep whistled. This was too much for Mrs van Daan, who sank limply in her chair, white as a sheet. If the tension had lasted another minute, she would have fainted.

Jan and Miep came in and were met with a delightful scene. The table alone would have been worth a photograph: a copy of *Cinema & Theatre*, opened at a page of dancing girls and smeared with jam and pectin, which we'd been taking to combat the diarrhoea, two jam jars, half a bread roll, a quarter of a bread roll, pectin, a mirror, a comb, matches, ashes, cigarettes, tobacco, an ashtray, books, a pair of pants, a torch, Mrs van Daan's comb, toilet paper, etc.

Jan and Miep were of course greeted with shouts and tears. Jan nailed a pinewood board over the gap in the door and went off again with Miep to inform the police of the break-in. Miep had also found a note under the warehouse door from Sleegers, the night watchman, who had noticed the hole and alerted the police. Jan was also planning to see Sleegers.

So we had half an hour in which to put the house and ourselves to rights. I've never seen such a transformation as in those thirty minutes. Margot and I got the beds ready downstairs, went to the lavatory, brushed our teeth, washed our hands and combed our hair. Then I tidied up the room a bit and went back upstairs. The table had already been cleared, so we got some water, made coffee and tea, boiled the milk and laid the table. Father and Peter emptied our improvised potties and rinsed them with warm water and powdered bleach. The largest one was filled to the brim and was so heavy they had a hard time lifting it. To make things worse, it was leaking, so they had to put it in a bucket.

At eleven o'clock Jan was back and joined us at the table, and gradually everyone began to relax. Jan had the following story to tell:

Mr Sleegers was asleep, but his wife told Jan that her husband had discovered the hole in the door while making his rounds. He called in a policeman, and the two of them searched the building. Mr Sleegers, in his capacity as night watchman, patrols the area every night on his bike, accompanied by his two dogs. His wife said he would come on Tuesday and tell Mr Kugler the rest. No one at the police station seemed to know anything about the break-in, but they made a note to come first thing Tuesday morning to have a look.

On the way back Jan happened to run into Mr van Hoeven, the man who supplies us with potatoes, and told him of the break-in. 'I know,' Mr van Hoeven calmly replied. 'Last night when my wife and I were walking past your building, I saw a gap in the door. My wife wanted to walk on, but I peeked inside with a torch, and that's when the burglars must have run off. To be on the safe side, I didn't ring the police. I thought it wouldn't be wise in your case. I don't know anything, but I have my suspicions.' Jan thanked him and went on. Mr van Hoeven obviously suspects we're here, because he always delivers the potatoes at lunchtime. A decent chap!

It was one o'clock by the time Jan left and we'd washed up. All eight of us went to bed. I woke up at quarter to three and saw that Mr Dussel was already up. My face rumpled with sleep, I happened to run into Peter in the bathroom, just after he'd come downstairs. We agreed to meet in the office. I freshened up a bit and went down.

'After all this, do you still dare go to the front attic?' he asked. I nodded, grabbed my pillow, with a cloth wrapped around it, and we went up together. The weather was gorgeous, and even though the air-raid sirens soon began to wail, we stayed where we were. Peter put his arm around my shoulder, I put mine around his, and we sat quietly like this until four o'clock, when Margot came to fetch us for coffee.

We ate our bread, drank our lemonade and joked (we were finally able to again), and for the rest everything was back to normal. That evening I thanked Peter because he'd been the bravest of us all.

★

None of us has ever been in such danger as we were that night. God was truly watching over us. Just think – the police were right at the bookcase, the light was on, and still no one had discovered our hiding place! 'Now we're done for!' I'd whispered at that moment, but once again we were spared. When the invasion comes and the bombs start falling, it'll be every man for himself, but this time we feared for those good, innocent Christians who are helping us.

'We've been saved, keep on saving us!' That's all we can say.

This incident has brought about a whole lot of changes. As of now, Dussel will be doing his work in the bathroom, and Peter will be patrolling the house between eight-thirty and nine-thirty. Peter isn't allowed to open his window any more, since one of the Keg people noticed it was open. We can no longer flush the toilet after nine-thirty at night. Mr Sleegers has been hired as night watchman, and tonight a carpenter from the underground is coming to make a barricade out of our white Frankfurt bedsteads. Debates are going on left and right in the Annexe. Mr Kugler has reproached us for our carelessness. Jan also said we should never go downstairs. What we have to do now is find out whether Sleegers can be trusted, whether the dogs will bark if they hear someone behind the door, how to make the barricade, all sorts of things.

We've been strongly reminded of the fact that we're Jews in chains, chained to one spot, without any rights, but with a thousand obligations. We must put our feelings aside; we must be brave and strong, bear discomfort without complaint, do whatever is in our power and trust in God. One day this terrible war will be over. The time will come when we'll be people again and not just Jews!

Who has inflicted this on us? Who has set us apart from all the rest? Who has put us through such suffering? It's God who has made us the way we are, but it's also God who will lift us up again. In the eyes of the world, we're doomed, but if, after all this suffering, there are still Jews left, the Jewish people will be held up as an example. Who knows, maybe our religion will teach the world and all the people in it about goodness, and that's the reason, the only reason, we have to suffer. We can never be just Dutch, or just English, or whatever, we will always be Jews as well. And we'll have to keep on being Jews, but then, we'll want to be.

Be brave! Let's remember our duty and perform it without complaint. There will be a way out. God has never deserted our people. Through the ages Jews have had to suffer, but through the ages they've gone on living, and the centuries of suffering have only made them stronger. The weak shall fall and the strong shall survive and not be defeated!

That night I really thought I was going to die. I waited for the police and I was ready for death, like a soldier on a battlefield. I'd gladly have given my life for my country. But now, now that I've been spared, my first wish after the war is to become a Dutch citizen. I love the Dutch, I love this country, I love the language, and I want to work here. And even if I have to write to the Queen herself, I won't give up until I've reached my goal!

I'm becoming more and more independent of my parents. Young as I am, I face life with more courage and have a better and truer sense of justice than Mother. I know what I want, I have a goal, I have opinions, a religion and love. If only I can be myself, I'll be satisfied. I know that I'm a woman, a woman with inner strength and a great deal of courage!

If God lets me live, I'll achieve more than Mother ever did, I'll make my voice heard, I'll go out into the world and work for mankind!

I now know that courage and happiness are needed first!

Yours, Anne M. Frank

FRIDAY, 14 APRIL 1944

Dear Kitty,

*E*veryone here is still very tense. Pim has nearly reached boiling point; Mrs van D. is lying in bed with a cold, grumbling; Mr van D. is growing pale without his cigarettes; Dussel, who's having to give up many of his comforts, is carping at everyone; etc., etc. We seem to have run out of luck lately. The toilet's leaking, and the tap's stuck. Thanks to our many connections, we'll soon be able to get these repaired.

I'm occasionally sentimental, as you know, but from time to time I have reason to be: when Peter and I are sitting close together on a hard wooden crate among the junk and dust, our arms around each other's shoulders, Peter toying with a lock of my hair; when the birds outside are trilling their songs, when the trees are in bud, when the sun beckons and the sky is so blue – oh, that's when I wish for so much!

All I see around me are dissatisfied and grumpy faces, all I hear are sighs and stifled complaints. You'd think our lives had taken a sudden turn for the worse. Honestly, things are only as bad as you make them. Here in the Annexe no one even bothers to set a good example. Everyone has to decide for himself how to get the better of his own mood!

Every day you hear, 'If only it were all over!'

> *Work, love, courage and hope,*
> *Make me good and help me cope!*

I really believe, Kit, that I'm slightly bats today, and I don't know why. My writing's all mixed up, I'm jumping from one thing to another, and sometimes I seriously doubt whether anyone will ever be interested in this drivel. They'll probably call it 'The Musings of an Ugly

Duckling'. *My* diaries certainly won't be of much use to Mr Bolkestein or Mr Gerbrandy.★

Yours, Anne M. Frank

SATURDAY, 15 APRIL 1944

Dearest Kitty,

'There's just one bad thing after another. When will it all end?' You can say that again. Guess what's happened now? Peter forgot to unbolt the front door. As a result, Mr Kugler and the warehouse employees couldn't get in. He went to Keg's, smashed in our office kitchen window and got in that way. The windows in the Annexe were open, and the Keg people saw that too. What must they be thinking? And van Maaren? Mr Kugler's furious. We accuse him of not doing anything to reinforce the doors, and then we do a stupid thing like this! Peter's extremely upset. At the table, Mother said she felt more sorry for Peter than for anyone else, and he nearly began to cry. We're equally to blame, since we usually ask him every day if he's unbolted the door, and so does Mr van Daan. Maybe I can go and comfort him later on. I want to help him so much!

★ Gerrit Bolkestein was the Minister of Education and Pieter Gerbrandy was the Prime Minister of the Dutch government in exile in London. See Anne's letter of 29 March 1944.

Here are the latest news bulletins about life in the Secret Annexe over the last few weeks:

A week ago, on Saturday, Boche suddenly fell ill. He sat quite still and started drooling. Miep immediately picked him up, rolled him in a towel, tucked him in her shopping bag and took him to the dog-and-cat clinic. Boche had some kind of intestinal problem, so the vet gave him medicine. Peter gave it to him a few times, but Boche soon made himself scarce. I bet he was out courting his sweetheart. But now his nose is swollen and he meows whenever you pick him up – he was probably trying to steal food and somebody smacked him. Mouschi lost her voice for a few days. Just when we decided she had to be taken to the vet too, she started getting better.

We now leave the attic window open a crack every night. Peter and I often sit up there in the evening.

Thanks to rubber cement and oil paint, our toilet could quickly be repaired. The broken tap has been replaced.

Luckily, Mr Kleiman is feeling better. He's going to see a specialist soon. We can only hope he won't need an operation.

This month we received eight ration books. Unfortunately, for the next two weeks beans have been substituted for oatmeal or groats. Our latest delicacy is piccalilli. If you're out of luck, all you get is a jar full of cucumber and mustard sauce.

Vegetables are hard to come by. There's only lettuce, lettuce and more lettuce. Our meals consist entirely of potatoes and imitation gravy.

The Russians are in possession of more than half the

Crimea. The British aren't advancing beyond Cassino. We'll have to count on the Western Wall. There have been a lot of unbelievably heavy air raids. The Central Register Office in The Hague was bombed. All Dutch people will be issued new ration registration cards.

Enough for today.

Yours, Anne M. Frank

SUNDAY, 16 APRIL 1944

My dearest Kitty,

Remember yesterday's date, since it was a red-letter day for me. Isn't it an important day for every girl when she gets her first kiss? Well then, it's no less important to me. The time Bram kissed me on my right cheek or Mr Woudstra on my right hand doesn't count. How did I suddenly come by this kiss? I'll tell you.

Last night at eight I was sitting with Peter on his divan and it wasn't long before he put an arm around me. (Since it was Saturday, he wasn't wearing his overalls.) 'Why don't we move over a little,' I said, 'so I won't keep bumping my head against the cupboard.'

He moved so far over he was practically in the corner. I slipped my arm under his and across his back, and he put his arm around my shoulder, so that I was nearly engulfed by him. We've sat like this on other occasions, but never so close as we were last night. He held me firmly against him, my left side against his chest; *my* heart had already begun to beat faster, but there was more to come. He wasn't satisfied until my head lay on his shoulder, with his on top of mine. I sat up again after about five minutes, but before long he took my head in his hands and put it back next to his. Oh, it was so wonderful. I could hardly talk, my pleasure was too intense; he caressed my cheek and arm, a bit clumsily, and played with my hair. Most of the time our heads were touching.

I can't tell you, Kitty, the feeling that ran through me. I was too happy for words, and I think he was too.

At nine-thirty we stood up. Peter put on his gym shoes so he wouldn't make much noise on his nightly round of the building, and I was standing next to him. How I suddenly made the right movement, I don't know, but before we went downstairs, he gave me a kiss, through my hair, half on my left cheek and half on my ear. I tore downstairs without looking back, and I long so much for today.

Sunday morning, just before eleven.

Yours, Anne M. Frank

Dearest Kitty,

*D*o you think Father and Mother would approve of a girl my age sitting on a divan and kissing a seventeen-and-a-half-year-old boy? I doubt they would, but I have to trust my own judgement in this matter. It's so peaceful and safe, lying in his arms and dreaming, it's so thrilling to feel his cheek against mine, it's so wonderful to know there's someone waiting for me. But, and there is a but, will Peter want to leave it at that? I haven't forgotten his promise, but . . . he is a boy!

I know I'm starting at a very young age. Not even fifteen and already so independent – that's a little hard for other people to understand. I'm pretty positive Margot would never kiss a boy unless there was some talk of an engagement or marriage. Neither Peter nor I has any such plans. I'm also sure that Mother never touched a man before she met Father. What would my girlfriends or Jacque say if they knew I'd lain in Peter's arms with my heart against his chest, my head on his shoulder and his head and face against mine!

Oh, Anne, how terribly shocking! But seriously, I don't think it's at all shocking; we're cooped up here, cut off from the world, anxious and fearful, especially lately. Why should we stay apart when we love each other? Why shouldn't we kiss each other in times like these? Why should we wait until we've reached a suitable age? Why should we ask anybody's permission?

I've decided to look out for my own interests. He'd never want to hurt me or make me unhappy. Why shouldn't I do what my heart tells me and makes both of us happy?

Yet I have a feeling, Kitty, that you can sense my doubt. It must be my honesty rising in revolt against all this sneaking around. Do you think it's my duty to tell Father what I'm up to? Do you think our secret should be shared with a third person? Much of the beauty would be lost, but would it make me feel better inside? I'll bring it up with *him*.

Oh, yes, I still have so much I want to discuss with him, since I don't see the point of just cuddling. Sharing our thoughts with each other requires a great deal of trust, but we'll both be stronger because of it!

Yours, Anne M. Frank

PS. We were up at six yesterday morning, because the whole family heard the sounds of a break-in again. It must have been one of our neighbours who was the victim this time. When we checked at seven o'clock, our doors were still shut tight, thank goodness!

Dearest Kitty,

*E*verything's fine here. Last night the carpenter came again to put some sheets of iron over the door panels. Father just finished saying he definitely expects large-scale operations in Russia and Italy, as well as in the West, before 20 May; the longer the war lasts, the harder it is to imagine being liberated from this place.

Yesterday Peter and I finally got round to having the talk we've been postponing for the last ten days. I told him all about girls, without hesitating to discuss the most intimate matters. I found it rather amusing that he thought the opening in a woman's body was simply left out of illustrations. He couldn't imagine that it was actually located between a woman's legs. The evening ended with a mutual kiss, near the mouth. It's really a lovely feeling!

I might take my 'favourite quotes notebook' up with me some time so Peter and I can go into things more deeply. I don't think lying in each other's arms day in and day out is very satisfying, and I hope he feels the same.

After our mild winter we've been having a beautiful spring. April is glorious, not too hot and not too cold, with occasional light showers. Our chestnut tree is in leaf, and here and there you can already see a few small blossoms.

Bep presented us on Saturday with four bouquets of

flowers: three bouquets of daffodils, and one bouquet of grape hyacinths for me. Mr Kugler is supplying us with more and more newspapers.

It's time to do my algebra, Kitty. Cheerio.

Yours, Anne M. Frank

WEDNESDAY, 19 APRIL 1944

Dearest Darling,

(*T*hat's the title of a film with Dorit Kreysler, Ida Wüst and Harald Paulsen!)

What could be nicer than sitting before an open window, enjoying nature, listening to the birds sing, feeling the sun on your cheeks and holding a darling boy in your arms? I feel so peaceful and safe with his arm around me, knowing he's near and yet not having to speak; how can this be bad when it does me so much good? Oh, if only we were never disturbed again, not even by Mouschi.

Yours, Anne M. Frank

FRIDAY, 21 APRIL 1944

My dearest Kitty,

I stayed in bed yesterday with a sore throat, but since I was already bored the very first afternoon and didn't have a temperature, I got up today. My sore throat has nearly '*verschwunden*'.★

Yesterday, as you've probably already discovered, was our Führer's fifty-fifth birthday. Today is the eighteenth birthday of Her Royal Highness Princess Elizabeth of York. The BBC reported that she hasn't yet been declared of age, though royal children usually are. We've been wondering which prince they'll marry this beauty off to, but can't think of a suitable candidate; perhaps her sister, Princess Margaret Rose, can have Crown Prince Baudouin of Belgium!

★ Disappeared.

Here we've been going from one disaster to the next. No sooner have the outside doors been reinforced than van Maaren rears his head again. In all likelihood he's the one who stole the potato flour, and now he's trying to pin the blame on Bep. Not surprisingly, the Annexe is once again in an uproar. Bep is beside herself with rage. Perhaps Mr Kugler will finally have this shady character followed.

The appraiser from Beethovenstraat was here this morning. He offered us 400 guilders for our chest; in our opinion, the other estimates are also too low.

I want to ask the magazine *The Prince* if they'll take one of my fairy tales, under a pseudonym, of course. But so far all my fairy tales have been too long, so I don't think I have much of a chance.

Till the next time, darling.

Yours, Anne M. Frank

TUESDAY, 25 APRIL 1944

Dearest Kitty,

F or the last ten days Dussel hasn't been on speaking terms with Mr van Daan, and all because of the new security measures since the break-in. One of these was that he's no longer allowed to go downstairs in the evenings. Peter and Mr van Daan make the last round every night at nine-thirty, and after that no one may go downstairs. We can't flush the toilet any more after eight at night or after eight in the morning. The windows may be opened only in the morning when the lights go on in Mr Kugler's office, and they can no longer be propped open with a stick at night. This last measure is the reason for Dussel's sulking. He claims that Mr van Daan ticked him off, but he has only himself to blame. He says he'd rather live without food than without air, and that they simply must work out a way to keep the windows open.

'I'll have to speak to Mr Kugler about this,' he said to me.

I replied that we never discussed matters of this sort with Mr Kugler, only within the group.

'Everything's always happening behind my back. I'll have to talk to your father about that.'

He's also not allowed to sit in Mr Kugler's office any more on Saturday afternoons or Sundays, because the manager of Keg's might hear him if he happens to be next door. Dussel promptly went and sat there anyway. Mr van Daan was furious, and Father went downstairs to talk to Dussel, who came up with some flimsy excuse, but even Father didn't fall for it this time. Now Father's keeping his dealings with Dussel to a minimum because Dussel insulted him. Not one of us knows what he said, but it must have been pretty awful.

And to think that that miserable man has his birthday next week. How can you celebrate your birthday when you've got the sulks, how can you accept gifts from people you won't even talk to?

★

Mr Voskuijl is going downhill rapidly. For more than ten days he's had a temperature of almost a hundred and four. The doctor said his condition is hopeless; they think the cancer has spread to his lungs. The poor man, we'd so like to help him, but only God can help him now!

I've written an amusing story called 'Blurry the Explorer', which was a big hit with my three listeners.

I still have a bad cold and have passed it on to Margot, as well as Mother and Father. If only Peter doesn't get it. He insisted on a kiss, and called me his El Dorado. You can't call a person that, silly boy! But he's sweet anyway!

Yours, Anne M. Frank

THURSDAY, 27 APRIL 1944

Dearest Kitty,

*M*rs van D. was in a bad mood this morning. All she did was complain, first about her cold, not being able to get cough drops and the agony of having to blow her nose all the time. Next she grumbled that the sun wasn't shining, the invasion hadn't started, we weren't allowed to look out of the windows, etc., etc. We couldn't help but laugh at her, and it couldn't have been that bad, since she soon joined in.

Our recipe for potato kugel, modified due to lack of onions:

Grate peeled potatoes fine and add a little dry government-issue flour and salt. Grease a mould or ovenproof dish with paraffin wax or stearin and bake for $2\frac{1}{2}$ hours. Serve with rotten strawberry compote. (Onions not available. Nor oil for mould or dough!)

At the moment I'm reading *Emperor Charles V*, written by a professor at the University of Göttingen; he's spent forty years working on this book. It took me five days to read fifty pages. I can't do any more than that. Since the book has 598 pages, you can work out just how long it's going to take me. And that's not even counting the second volume. But . . . very interesting!

The things a schoolgirl has to do in the course of a single day! Take me, for example. First, I translated a passage on Nelson's last battle from Dutch into English. Then, I read more about the Northern War (1700–21) involving Peter the Great, Charles XII, Augustus the Strong, Stanislaus Leczinsky, Mazeppa, von Görz, Brandenburg, Western Pomerania, Eastern Pomerania and Denmark, plus the usual dates. Next, I landed up in Brazil, where I read about Bahia tobacco, the abundance of coffee, the one and a half million inhabitants of Rio de Janeiro, Pernambuco and São Paulo and, last but not least, the Amazon River. Then about Negroes, mulattos, mestizos, whites, the illiteracy rate – over 50 per cent –

and malaria. Since I had some time left, I glanced through a genealogical chart: John the Old, William Louis, Ernest Casimir I, Henry Casimir I, right up to little Margriet Franciska (born in 1943 in Ottawa).

Twelve o'clock: I resumed my studies in the attic, reading about deans, priests, ministers, popes and . . . whew, it was one o'clock!

At two the poor child (ahem) was back at work. Old World and New World monkeys were next. Kitty, tell me quickly, how many toes does a hippopotamus have?

Then came the Bible, Noah's Ark, Shem, Ham and Japheth. After that, Charles V. Then, with Peter, Thackeray's book about the colonel, in English. A French test, and then a comparison between the Mississippi and the Missouri!

Enough for today. Adieu!

Yours, Anne M. Frank

FRIDAY, 28 APRIL 1944

Dearest Kitty,

I've never forgotten my dream of Peter Schiff (see the beginning of January). Even now I can still feel his cheek against mine, and that wonderful glow that made up for all the rest. Once in a while I'd had the same feeling with this Peter, but never so intensely . . . until last night. We were sitting on the divan, as usual, in each other's arms. Suddenly the everyday Anne slipped away and the second Anne took her place. The second Anne, who's never over-confident or amusing, but wants only to love and be gentle.

I sat pressed against him and felt a wave of emotion come over me. Tears rushed to my eyes; those from the left fell on his overalls, while those from the right trickled down my nose and into the air and landed beside the first. Did he notice? He made no movement to show that he had. Did he feel the same way I did? He hardly said a word. Did he realize he had two Annes at his side? My questions went unanswered.

At eight-thirty I stood up and went to the window, where we always say good-bye. I was still trembling, I was still Anne number two. He came over to me, and I threw my arms around his neck and kissed him on his left cheek. I was about to kiss the other cheek when my mouth met his, and we pressed our lips together. In a daze, we embraced, over and over again, never to stop, oh!

Peter needs tenderness. For the first time in his life he's discovered a girl; for the first time he's seen that even the biggest pests also have an inner self and a heart, and are transformed as soon as they're alone with you. For the first time in his life he's given himself and his friendship to another person. He's never had a friend before, boy or girl. Now we've found each other. I, for that matter, didn't know him either, had never had someone I could confide in, and it's led to this . . .

The same question keeps nagging at me: 'Is it right?' Is it right for me to yield so soon, for me to be so passionate, to be filled with as much passion and desire as Peter? Can I, a girl, allow myself to go that far?

There's only one possible answer: 'I'm longing so much . . . and have for such a long time. I'm so lonely and now I've found comfort!'

In the mornings we act normally, in the afternoons too, except now and then. But in the evenings the suppressed longing of the entire day, the happiness and the bliss of all the times before come rushing to the surface, and all we can think about is each other. Every night, after our last kiss, I feel like running away and never looking him in the eyes again. Away, far away into the darkness and alone!

And what awaits me at the bottom of those fourteen stairs? Bright lights, questions and laughter. I have to act normally and hope they don't notice anything.

My heart is still too tender to be able to recover so quickly from a shock like the one I had last night. The gentle Anne makes infrequent appearances, and she's not about to let herself be shoved out of the door so soon after she's arrived. Peter's reached a part of me that no one has ever reached before, except in my dream! He's taken hold of me and turned me inside out. Doesn't everyone need a little quiet time to put themselves to rights again? Oh, Peter, what have you done to me? What do you want from me?

Where will this lead? Oh, now I understand Bep.

Now, now that I'm going through it myself, I understand her doubts; if I were older and he wanted to marry me, what would my answer be? Anne, be honest! You wouldn't be able to marry him. But it's so hard to let go. Peter still has too little character, too little will-power, too little courage and strength. He's still a child, emotionally no older than I am; all he wants is happiness and peace of mind. Am I really only fourteen? Am I really just a silly schoolgirl? Am I really so inexperienced in everything? I have more experience than most; I've experienced something almost no one my age ever has.

I'm afraid of myself, afraid my longing is making me yield too soon. How can it ever go right with other boys later on? Oh, it's so hard, the eternal struggle between heart and mind. There's a time and a place for both, but how can I be sure that I've chosen the right time?

Yours, Anne M. Frank

TUESDAY, 2 MAY 1944

Dearest Kitty,

On Saturday night I asked Peter whether he thinks I should tell Father about us. After we'd discussed it, he said he thought I should. I was glad; it shows he's sensible, and sensitive. As soon as I came downstairs, I went with Father to get some water. While we were on the stairs, I said, 'Father, I expect you've gathered that when Peter and I are together, we don't exactly sit at opposite ends of the room. Do you think that's wrong?'

Father paused before answering: 'No, I don't think it's wrong. But Anne, when you're living so close together, as we do, you have to be careful.' He said some other words to that effect, and then we went upstairs.

On Sunday morning he called me to him and said, 'Anne, I've been thinking about what you said.' (Oh, oh, I knew what was coming!) 'Here in the Annexe it's not such a good idea. I thought you were just friends. Is Peter in love with you?'

'Of course not,' I answered.

'Well, you know I understand both of you. But you must be the one to show restraint; don't go upstairs so often, don't encourage him more than you can help. In matters like these, it's always the man who takes the active role, and it's up to the woman to set the limits. Outside, where you're free, things are quite different. You see other boys and girls, you can go outdoors, take part in sports and all kinds of activities. But here, if you're together too much and want to get away, you can't. You see each other every hour of the day – all the time, in fact. Be careful, Anne, and don't take it too seriously!'

'I don't, Father, but Peter's a decent boy, a nice boy!'

'Yes, but he doesn't have much strength of character. He can easily be influenced to do good, but also to do bad. I hope for his sake that he stays good, because he's basically a good person.'

We talked some more and agreed that Father would speak to him too.

On Sunday afternoon when we were in the front attic, Peter asked, 'Have you talked to your Father yet, Anne?'

'Yes,' I replied, 'I'll tell you all about it. He doesn't think it's wrong, but he says that here, where we're in such close quarters, it could lead to conflicts.'

'We've already agreed not to quarrel, and I plan to keep my promise.'

'Me too, Peter. But Father didn't think we were serious, he thought we were just friends. Do you think we still can be?'

'Yes, I do. How about you?'

'Me too. I also told Father that I trust you. I do trust you, Peter, just as much as I do Father. And I think you're worthy of my trust. You are, aren't you?'

'I hope so.' (He was very shy, and blushing.)

'I believe in you, Peter,' I continued. 'I believe you have a good character and that you'll get on in this world.'

After that we talked about other things. Later I said, 'If we ever get out of here, I know you won't give me another thought.'

He got all fired up. 'That's not true, Anne. Oh no, I won't let you even think that about me!'

Just then somebody called us.

Father did talk to him, he told me on Monday. 'Your Father thought our friendship might turn into love,' he said. 'But I told him we'd keep ourselves under control.'

★

Father wants me to stop going upstairs so often, but I don't want to. Not just because I like being with Peter, but because I've said I trust him. I do trust him, and I want to prove it to him, but I'll never be able to if I stay downstairs out of distrust.

No, I'm going!

In the mean time, the Dussel drama has been resolved. On Saturday evening at dinner he apologized in beautiful Dutch. Mr van Daan was immediately reconciled. Dussel must have spent all day practising his speech.

Sunday, his birthday, passed without incident. We gave him a bottle of good wine from 1919, the van Daans (who can now give their gift after all) presented him with a jar of piccalilli and a packet of razor blades, and Mr Kugler gave him a bottle of lemon syrup (to make lemonade), Miep a book, *Little Martin*, and Bep a plant. He treated everyone to an egg.

Yours, Anne M. Frank

WEDNESDAY, 3 MAY 1944

Dearest Kitty,

*F*irst the weekly news! We're having a break from politics. There's nothing, and I mean absolutely nothing, to report. I'm also gradually starting to believe that the invasion will come. After all, they can't let the Russians do all the dirty work; actually, the Russians aren't doing anything at the moment either.

Mr Kleiman comes to the office every morning now. He got a new set of springs for Peter's divan, so Peter will have to get to work re-upholstering it. Not surprisingly, he isn't at all in the mood. Mr Kleiman also brought some flea powder for the cats.

Have I told you that our Boche has disappeared? We haven't seen hide nor hair of her since last Thursday. She's probably already in cat heaven, while some animal lover has turned her into a tasty dish. Perhaps some girl who can afford it will be wearing a cap made of Boche's fur. Peter is heartbroken.

For the last two weeks we've been eating lunch at eleven-thirty on Saturdays; in the mornings we have to make do with a cup of porridge. Starting tomorrow it'll be like this every day; that saves us a meal. Vegetables are still very hard to come by. This afternoon we had rotten boiled lettuce. Ordinary lettuce, spinach and boiled lettuce, that's all there is. Add to that rotten potatoes, and you have a meal fit for a king!

I hadn't had my period for more than two months, but it finally started last Sunday. Despite the mess and bother, I'm glad it hasn't deserted me.

As you can no doubt imagine, we often say in despair, 'What's the point of the war? Why, oh, why can't people live together peacefully? Why all this destruction?'

The question is understandable, but so far no one has

come up with a satisfactory answer. Why is England manufacturing bigger and better aeroplanes and bombs and at the same time churning out new houses for reconstruction? Why are millions spent on the war each day, while not a penny is available for medical science, artists or the poor? Why do people have to starve when mountains of food are rotting away in other parts of the world? Oh, why are people so crazy?

I don't believe the war is simply the work of politicians and capitalists. Oh no, the common man is every bit as guilty; otherwise, people and nations would have rebelled long ago! There's a destructive urge in people, the urge to rage, murder and kill. And until all of humanity, without exception, undergoes a metamorphosis, wars will continue to be waged, and everything that has been carefully built up, cultivated and grown will be cut down and destroyed, only to start all over again!

I've often been down in the dumps, but never desperate. I look upon our life in hiding as an interesting adventure, full of danger and romance, and every privation as an amusing addition to my diary. I've made up my mind to lead a different life from other girls, and not to become an ordinary housewife later on. What I'm experiencing here is a good beginning to an interesting life, and that's the reason – the only reason – why I have to laugh at the humorous side of the most dangerous moments.

I'm young and have many hidden qualities; I'm young and strong and living through a big adventure; I'm right in the middle of it and can't spend all day complaining because it's impossible to have any fun! I'm blessed with many things: happiness, a cheerful disposition and strength. Every day I feel myself maturing, I feel liberation drawing near, I feel the beauty of nature and the goodness of the people around me. Every day I think what a fascinating and amusing adventure this is! With all that, why should I despair?

Yours, Anne M. Frank

FRIDAY, 5 MAY 1944

Dear Kitty,

*F*ather's unhappy with me. After our talk on Sunday he thought I'd stop going upstairs every evening. He won't have any of that *'Knutscherei'*★ going on. I can't stand that word. Talking about it was bad enough – why does he have to make me feel bad too! I'll have a word with him today. Margot gave me some good advice. Here's more or less what I'd like to say:

> I think you expect an explanation from me, Father, so I'll give you one. You're disappointed in me, you expected more restraint from me, you no doubt

★ Necking.

want me to act the way a fourteen-year-old is supposed to. But that's where you're wrong!

Since we've been here, from July 1942 until a few weeks ago, I haven't had an easy time. If only you knew how much I used to cry at night, how unhappy and despondent I was, how lonely I felt, you'd understand my wanting to go upstairs! I've now reached the point where I don't need the support of Mother or anyone else. It didn't happen overnight. I've struggled long and hard and shed many tears to become as independent as I am now. You can laugh and refuse to believe me, but I don't care. I know I'm an independent person, and I don't feel I need to account to you for my actions. I'm only telling you this because I don't want you to think I'm doing things behind your back. But there's only one person I'm accountable to, and that's me.

When I was having problems, everyone – and that includes you – closed their eyes and ears and didn't help me. On the contrary, all I ever got were admonitions not to be so noisy. I was noisy only to keep myself from being miserable all the time. I was over-confident to keep from having to listen to the voice inside me. I've been putting on an act for the last year and a half, day in, day out. I've never complained or dropped my mask, nothing of the kind, and now . . . now the battle is over. I've won! I'm independent, in both body and mind. I don't need a mother any more, and I've emerged from the struggle a stronger person.

Now that it's over, now that I know the battle has been won, I want to go my own way, to follow the path that seems right to me. Don't think of me as a fourteen-year-old, since all these troubles have made me older; I won't regret my actions, I'll behave the way I think I should!

Gentle persuasion won't keep me from going upstairs. You'll either have to forbid it, or trust me through thick and thin. Whatever you do, just leave me alone!

Yours, Anne M. Frank

SATURDAY, 6 MAY 1944

Dearest Kitty,

*L*ast night before dinner I tucked the letter I'd written into Father's pocket. According to Margot, he read it and was upset for the rest of the evening. (I was upstairs washing up!) Poor Pim, I might have known what the effect of such an epistle would be. He's so sensitive! I immediately told Peter not to ask any questions or say anything more. Pim's said nothing else to me about the matter. Is he going to?

Everything here is more or less back to normal. We can hardly believe what Jan, Mr Kugler and Mr Kleiman tell us about the prices and the people on the outside; half a pound of tea costs 350.00 guilders, half a pound of coffee 80.00 guilders, a pound of butter 35.00 guilders, one egg 1.45 guilders. People are paying 14.00 guilders an ounce for Bulgarian tobacco! Everyone's trading on the black market; every errand boy has something to offer. The baker's delivery boy has supplied us with darning wool – 90 cents for one measly skein – the milkman can get hold of ration books, an undertaker delivers cheese. Break-ins, murders and thefts are daily occurrences. Even the police and night watchmen are getting in on the act. Everyone wants to put food in their stomachs, and since wages have been frozen, people have had to resort to swindling. The police have their hands full trying to track down the many girls of fifteen, sixteen, seventeen and older who are reported missing every day.

I want to try to finish my story about Ellen, the fairy. Just for fun, I can give it to Father on his birthday, together with all the copyrights.

See you later! (Actually, that's not the right phrase. In the German programme broadcast from England they always close with '*Auf wiederhören*'.★ So I suppose I should say, 'Until we write again.')

Yours, Anne M. Frank

SUNDAY MORNING, 7 MAY 1944

Dearest Kitty,

*F*ather and I had a long talk yesterday afternoon. I cried my eyes out, and he cried too. Do you know what he said to me, Kitty?

'I've received many letters in my lifetime, but none as hurtful as this. You, who have had so much love from your parents. You, whose parents have always been ready to help you, who have always defended you, no matter what. You talk of not having to account to us for your actions! You feel you've been wronged and left to your own devices. No, Anne, you've done us a great injustice!

'Perhaps you didn't mean it that way, but that's what you wrote. No, Anne, *we* have done nothing to deserve such a reproach!'

Oh, I've failed miserably. This is the worst thing I've

★ Until we speak again.

ever done in my entire life. I used my tears to show off, to make myself seem important so he'd respect me. I've certainly had my share of unhappiness, and everything I said about Mother is true. But to accuse Pim, who's so good and who's done everything for me – no, that was too cruel for words.

It's good that somebody has finally cut me down to size, has broken my pride, because I've been far too smug. Not everything Mistress Anne does is good! Anyone who deliberately causes such pain to someone they say they love is despicable, the lowest of the low!

What I'm most ashamed of is the way Father has forgiven me; he said he's going to throw the letter in the stove, and he's being so nice to me now, as if *he* were the one who'd done something wrong. Well, Anne, you still have a lot to learn. It's time you made a beginning, instead of looking down on other people and always blaming them!

I've known a lot of sorrow, but who hasn't at my age? I've been putting on an act, but was hardly even aware of it. I've felt lonely, but never desperate! Not like Father, who once ran out into the street with a knife so he could put an end to it all. I've never gone that far.

I should be deeply ashamed of myself, and I am. What's done can't be undone, but at least you can keep it from happening again. I'd like to start all over again, and that shouldn't be difficult, now that I have Peter. With him supporting me, I *know* I can do it! I'm not alone any more. He loves me, I love him, I have my books, my writing and my diary. I'm not all that ugly, or that stupid,

I have a sunny disposition, and I want to develop a good character!

Yes, Anne, you knew full well that your letter was unkind and untrue, but you were actually proud of it! I'll take Father as my example once again, and I *will* improve myself.

Yours, Anne M. Frank

MONDAY, 8 MAY 1944

Dearest Kitty,

*H*ave I ever told you anything about our family? I don't think I have, so let me begin. Father was born in Frankfurt am Main to very wealthy parents: Michael Frank owned a bank and became a millionaire, and Alice Stern's parents were prominent and well-to-do. Michael Frank didn't start out rich; he was a self-made man. In his youth Father led the life of a rich man's son. Parties every week, balls, banquets, beautiful girls, waltzing, dinners, a huge house, etc. After Grandpa died, most of the money was lost, and after the Great War and inflation there was nothing left at all. Until the war there were still quite a few rich relatives. So Father was extremely well-bred, and he had to laugh yesterday because for the first time in his fifty-five years, he scraped out the frying pan at the table.

Mother's family wasn't as wealthy, but still fairly well-off, and we've listened open-mouthed to stories of private balls, dinners and engagement parties with 250 guests.

We're far from rich now, but I've pinned all my hopes on after the war. I can assure you, I'm not so set on a bourgeois life as Mother and Margot. I'd like to spend a year in Paris and London learning the languages and studying art history. Compare that with Margot, who wants to nurse newborn babies in Palestine. I still have visions of gorgeous dresses and fascinating people. As I've told you many times before, I want to see the world and do all kinds of exciting things, and a little money won't hurt!

This morning Miep told us about her cousin's engagement party, which she went to on Saturday. The cousin's parents are rich, and the groom's are even richer. Miep made our mouths water telling us about the food that was served: vegetable soup with meatballs, cheese, meat rolls, hors d'oeuvres made with eggs and roast beef, cheese rolls, gateau, wine and cigarettes, and you could eat as much as you wanted.

Miep drank ten schnapps and smoked three cigarettes – could this be our temperance advocate? If Miep drank all those, I wonder how many her spouse managed to knock back? Everyone at the party was a little tipsy, of course. There were also two officers from the murder squad, who took photographs of the wedding couple. You can see we're never far from Miep's thoughts, since she promptly noted their names and addresses in case anything should happen and we needed contacts with good Dutch people.

Our mouths were watering so much. We, who'd had nothing but two spoonfuls of porridge for breakfast and were absolutely famished; we, who get nothing but half-cooked spinach (for the vitamins!) and rotten potatoes day after day; we, who fill our empty stomachs with nothing but boiled lettuce, raw lettuce, spinach, spinach and more spinach. Maybe we'll end up being as strong as Popeye, though so far I've seen no sign of it!

If Miep had taken us along to the party, there wouldn't have been any rolls left over for the other guests. If we'd been there, we'd have snatched up everything in sight, including the furniture. I tell you, we were practically pulling the words right out of her mouth. We were gathered around her as if we'd never in all our lives heard of delicious food or elegant people! And these are the granddaughters of the distinguished millionaire. The world is a crazy place!

Yours, Anne M. Frank

TUESDAY, 9 MAY 1944

Dearest Kitty,

I've finished my story about Ellen, the fairy. I've copied it out on nice notepaper, decorated it with red ink and sewn the pages together. The whole thing looks quite pretty, but I don't know if it's enough of a birthday present. Margot and Mother have both written poems.

Mr Kugler came upstairs this afternoon with the news that starting Monday, Mrs Broks would like to spend two hours in the office every afternoon. Just imagine! The office staff won't be able to come upstairs, the potatoes can't be delivered, Bep won't get her dinner, we can't use the lavatory, we won't be able to move and all sorts of other inconveniences! We proposed a variety of ways to get rid of her. Mr van Daan thought a good laxative in her coffee might do the trick. 'No,' Mr Kleiman answered, 'please don't, or we'll never get her off the bog!'

A roar of laughter. 'The bog?' Mrs van D. asked. 'What does that mean?' An explanation was given. 'Is it all right to use that word?' she asked in perfect innocence.

'Just imagine,' Bep giggled, 'there you are shopping at The Bijenkorf and you ask the way to the bog. They wouldn't even know what you were talking about!'

Dussel now sits on the 'bog', to borrow the expression, every day at twelve-thirty on the dot. This afternoon I boldly took a piece of pink paper and wrote:

> Mr Dussel's Toilet Timetable
> Mornings from 7.15 to 7.30 a.m.
> Afternoons after 1.00 p.m.
> Otherwise, only as needed!

I tacked this to the green lavatory door while he was still inside. I might well have added 'Transgressors will be subject to confinement!' Because our lavatory can be locked from both the inside and the outside.

Mr van Daan's latest joke:

After a Bible lesson about Adam and Eve, a thirteen-year-old boy asked his father, 'Tell me, Father, how did I get born?'

'Well,' the father replied, 'the stork plucked you out of the ocean, set you down in Mother's bed and bit her in the leg, hard. It bled so much she had to stay in bed for a week.'

Not fully satisfied, the boy went to his mother. 'Tell me, Mother,' he asked, 'how did you get born and how did I get born?'

His mother told him the very same story. Finally, hoping to hear the finer points, he went to his grandfather. 'Tell me, Grandfather,' he said, 'how did you get born and how did your daughter get born?' And for the third time he was told exactly the same story.

That night he wrote in his diary: 'After careful inquiry, I must conclude that there has been no sexual intercourse in our family for the last three generations!'

I still have work to do; it's already three o'clock.

Yours, Anne M. Frank

PS. Since I think I've mentioned the new cleaning lady,

I just want to note that she's married, sixty years old and hard of hearing! Very convenient, in view of all the noise that eight people in hiding are capable of making.

Oh, Kit, it's such lovely weather. If only I could go outside!

WEDNESDAY, 10 MAY 1944

Dearest Kitty,

We were sitting in the attic yesterday afternoon working on our French when suddenly I heard the splatter of water behind me. I asked Peter what it might be. Without pausing to reply, he dashed up to the loft – the scene of the disaster – and shoved Mouschi, who was squatting beside her soggy litter box, back to the right place. This was followed by shouts and squeals, and then Mouschi, who by that time had finished peeing, took off downstairs. In search of something similar to her box, Mouschi had found herself a pile of wood shavings, right over a crack in the floor. The puddle immediately trickled down to the attic and, as luck would have it, landed in and next to the potato barrel. The ceiling was dripping, and since the attic floor has also got its share of cracks, little yellow drops were leaking through the ceiling and on to the dining-table, between a pile of stockings and books.

I was doubled up with laughter, it was such a funny sight. There was Mouschi crouched under a chair, Peter armed with water, powdered bleach and a cloth, and Mr van Daan trying to calm everyone down. The room was soon set to rights, but it's a well-known fact that cat puddles stink to high heaven. The potatoes proved that all too well, as did the wood shavings, which Father collected in a bucket and brought downstairs to burn.

Poor Mouschi! How were you to know it's impossible to get peat for your box?

Anne

THURSDAY, 11 MAY 1944

Dearest Kitty,

A new sketch to make you laugh: Peter's hair had to be cut, and as usual his mother was to be the hairdresser. At seven twenty-five Peter vanished into his room, and reappeared on the stroke of seven-thirty, stripped down to his blue swimming trunks and a pair of gym shoes.

'Are you coming?' he asked his mother.

'Yes, I'll be up in a minute, but I can't find the scissors!'

Peter helped her look, rummaging around in her cosmetics drawer. 'Don't make such a mess, Peter,' she grumbled.

I didn't catch Peter's reply, but it must have been insolent, because she cuffed him on the arm. He cuffed her back, she punched him with all her might, and Peter pulled his arm away with a look of mock horror on his face. 'Come on, old girl!'

Mrs van D. stayed put. Peter grabbed her by the wrists and pulled her all around the room. She laughed, cried, scolded and kicked, but nothing helped. Peter led his prisoner as far as the attic stairs, where he was obliged to let go of her. Mrs van D. came back to the room and collapsed into a chair with a loud sigh.

'*Die Entführung der Mutter*,'★ I joked.

'Yes, but he hurt me.'

I went to have a look and cooled her hot, red wrists with water. Peter, still by the stairs and growing impatient again, strode into the room with his belt in his hand, like a lion-tamer. Mrs van D. didn't move, but stayed by her writing desk, looking for a handkerchief. 'You've got to apologize first.'

'All right, I hereby offer my apologies, but only because if I don't, we'll be here till midnight.'

Mrs van D. had to laugh in spite of herself. She got up and went towards the door, where she felt obliged to give us an explanation. (By us I mean Father, Mother and me; we were busy washing up.) 'He wasn't like this at home,' she said. 'I'd have belted him so hard he'd have gone flying down the stairs [!]. He's never been so

★ *The Abduction of Mother*, a possible reference to Mozart's opera *The Abduction from the Seraglio*.

367

insolent. This isn't the first time he's deserved a good hiding. That's what you get with a modern upbringing, modern children. I'd never have grabbed my mother like that. Did you treat your mother that way, Mr Frank?' She was very upset, pacing back and forth, saying whatever came into her head, and she still hadn't gone upstairs. Finally, at long last, she made her exit.

Less than five minutes later she stormed back down the stairs, with her cheeks all puffed out, and flung her apron on a chair. When I asked if she was through, she replied that she was going downstairs. She tore down the stairs like a tornado, probably straight into the arms of her Putti.

She didn't come up again until eight, this time with her husband. Peter was dragged from the attic, given a merciless scolding and showered with abuse: ill-mannered good-for-nothing brat, bad example, Anne this, Margot that, I couldn't hear the rest.

Everything seems to have calmed down again today!

Yours, Anne M. Frank

PS. Tuesday and Wednesday evening our beloved Queen addressed the country. She's taking a holiday so she'll be in good health for her return to the Netherlands. She used words like 'soon, when I'm back in Holland', 'a swift liberation', 'heroism' and 'heavy burdens'.

This was followed by a speech by Prime Minister Gerbrandy. He had such a squeaky little child's voice that Mother instinctively said, 'Oooh.' A clergyman, who must have borrowed his voice from Mr Edel, concluded by asking God to take care of the Jews, all those in concentration camps and prisons and everyone working in Germany.

THURSDAY, 11 MAY 1944

Dearest Kitty,

Since I've left my entire 'junk box' – including my fountain pen – upstairs and I'm not allowed to disturb the grown-ups during their nap time (until two-thirty), you'll have to make do with a letter in pencil.

I'm terribly busy at the moment, and strange as it may sound, I don't have enough time to get through my pile of work. Shall I tell you briefly what I've got to do? Well then, before tomorrow I have to finish reading the first volume of a biography of Galileo Galilei, since it has to be returned to the library. I started reading it yesterday and have got up to page 220 out of 320 pages, so I'll manage it. Next week I have to read *Palestine at the Crossroads* and the second volume of Galilei. Besides that, I finished the first volume of a biography of Emperor Charles V yesterday, and I still have to work out the many genealogical charts I've collected and the notes I've taken. Next I have three pages of foreign words from my various books, all of which have to be written down, memorized and read aloud. Number four: my film stars are in terrible disarray and are dying to be sorted out, but since it'll take several days to do that and Professor Anne is, as she's already said, up to her ears in work, they'll have to put up with the chaos a while longer. Then there're Theseus, Oedipus, Peleus, Orpheus, Jason and Hercules all waiting to be untangled, since their various deeds are running crisscross through my mind like multicoloured threads in a dress. Myron and Phidias are also urgently in need of attention, or else I'll forget entirely how they fit into the picture. The same applies, for example, to the Seven Years War and the Nine Years War. Now I'm getting everything all mixed up. Well, what can you do with a memory like mine! Just imagine how forgetful I'll be when I'm eighty!

Oh, one more thing. The Bible. How long is it going to take before I come to the story of the bathing Susanna? And what do they mean by Sodom and Gomorrah? Oh, there's still so much to find out and learn. And in the mean time, I've left Charlotte of the Palatine in the lurch.

You can see, can't you, Kitty, that I'm full to bursting?

And now something else. You've known for a long time that my greatest wish is to be a journalist, and later on, a famous writer. We'll have to wait and see if these grand illusions (or delusions!) will ever come true, but till now I've had no lack of topics. In any case, after the war I'd like to publish a book called *The Secret Annexe*. It remains to be seen whether I'll succeed, but my diary can serve as the basis.

I also need to finish 'Cady's Life'. I've thought up the rest of the plot. After being cured in the sanatorium,

Cady goes back home and continues writing to Hans. It's 1941, and it doesn't take her long to discover Hans's Nazi sympathies, and since Cady is deeply concerned with the plight of the Jews and of her friend Marianne, they begin drifting apart. They meet and get back together, but break up when Hans takes up with another girl. Cady is shattered, and because she wants to have a good job, she studies nursing. When she's qualified she accepts a position, at the urging of her father's friends, as a nurse in a TB sanatorium in Switzerland. During her first holiday she goes to Lake Como, where she runs into Hans. He tells her that two years earlier he'd married Cady's successor, but that his wife took her life in a fit of depression. Now that he's seen his little Cady again, he realizes how much he loves her, and once more asks for her hand in marriage. Cady refuses, even though, in spite of herself, she loves him as much as ever. But her pride holds her back. Hans goes away, and years later Cady learns that he's in England, where he's struggling with ill health.

When she's twenty-seven, Cady marries a well-to-do man named Simon. She grows to love him, but not as much as Hans. She has two daughters and a son, Lilian, Judith and Nico. She and Simon are happy together, but Hans is always in the back of her mind until one night she dreams of him and says farewell.

It's not sentimental nonsense: it's based on the story of Father's life.

Yours, Anne M. Frank

SATURDAY, 13 MAY 1944

My dearest Kitty,

Yesterday was Father's birthday, Father and Mother's nineteenth wedding anniversary, a day without the cleaning lady . . . and the sun was shining as it's never shone before in 1944. Our chestnut tree is in full bloom. It's covered with leaves and is even more beautiful than last year.

Father received a biography of Linnaeus from Mr Kleiman, a book on nature from Mr Kugler, *The Canals of Amsterdam* from Dussel, a huge box from the van Daans (wrapped so beautifully it might have been done by a professional), containing three eggs, a bottle of beer, a pot of yoghurt and a green tie. It made our jar of treacle seem rather paltry. My roses smelled wonderful compared with Miep and Bep's red carnations. He was thoroughly spoiled. Fifty petits fours arrived from Siemons' Bakery, delicious! Father also treated us to spice cake, the men to beer and the ladies to yoghurt. Everything was scrumptious!

Yours, Anne M. Frank

TUESDAY, 16 MAY 1944

My dearest Kitty,

Just for a change (since we haven't had one of these in so long) I'll recount a little discussion between Mr and Mrs van D. last night:

Mrs van D.: 'The Germans have had plenty of time to fortify the Atlantic Wall, and they'll certainly do everything within their power to hold back the British. It's amazing how strong the Germans are!'

Mr van D.: 'Oh, yes, amazing!'

Mrs van D.: 'It is!'

Mr van D.: 'So strong they're bound to win the war in the end, is that what you mean?'

Mrs van D.: 'They might. I'm not convinced that they won't.'

Mr van D.: 'I won't even answer that.'

Mrs van D.: 'You always end up answering. You let yourself get carried away, every single time.

Mr van D.: 'No, I don't. I always keep my answers to the bare minimum.'

Mrs van D.: 'But you always do have an answer and you always have to be right! Your predictions hardly ever come true, you know!'

Mr van D.: 'So far they have.

Mrs van D.: 'No they haven't. You said the invasion was going to start last year, the Finns were supposed to have been out of the war by now, the Italian campaign ought to have been over by last winter, and the Russians should already have captured Lemberg. Oh no, I don't set much store by your predictions.'

Mr van D. (leaping to his feet): 'Why don't you shut your trap for a change? I'll show you who's right; some-day you'll get tired of needling me. I can't stand your bellyaching a minute longer. Just wait, one day I'll make you eat your words!' (End of Act One.)

Actually, I couldn't help giggling. Mother couldn't either, and even Peter was biting his lips to keep from laughing. Oh, those stupid grown-ups. They need to learn a few things first before they start making so many remarks about the younger generation!

Since Friday we've been keeping the windows open again at night.

Yours, Anne M. Frank

What Our Annexe Family Is Interested In
(A Systematic Survey of Courses and Reading Matter)

Mr van Daan: No courses; looks up many things in Knaur's Encyclopedia and Lexicon; likes to read detective stories, medical books and love stories, exciting or trivial.

Mrs van Daan: A correspondence course in English; likes to read biographical novels and occasionally other kinds of novels.

Mr Frank: Is learning English (Dickens!) and a bit of Latin; never reads novels, but likes serious, rather dry descriptions of people and places.

Mrs Frank: A correspondence course in English; reads everything except detective stories.

Mr Dussel: Is learning English, Spanish and Dutch with no noticeable results; reads everything; goes along with the opinion of the majority.

Peter van Daan: Is learning English, French (correspondence course), shorthand in Dutch, English and German, commercial correspondence in English, woodworking, economics and sometimes maths; seldom reads, sometimes geography.

Margot Frank: Correspondence courses in English, French and Latin, shorthand in English, German and Dutch, trigonometry, solid geometry, mechanics, physics, chemistry, algebra, geometry, English literature, French literature, German literature, Dutch literature, bookkeeping, geography, modern history, biology, economics; reads everything, preferably on religion and medicine.

Anne Frank: Shorthand in French, English, German

and Dutch, geometry, algebra, history, geography, art history, mythology, biology, Bible history, Dutch literature; likes to read biographies, dull or exciting, and history books (sometimes novels and light reading).

Dearest Kitty,

I felt rotten yesterday. Throwing up (me of all people!), headache, stomach-ache and anything else you can imagine. I'm feeling better today. I'm famished, but I think I'll skip the beans we're having for dinner.

Everything's going fine between Peter and me. The poor boy has an even greater need for tenderness than I do. He still blushes every evening when he gets his good-night kiss, and then begs for another one. Am I merely a better substitute for Boche? I don't mind. He's so happy just knowing somebody loves him.

After my laborious conquest, I've distanced myself a little from the situation, but you mustn't think my love has cooled. Peter's a sweetheart, but I've slammed the door to my inner self; if he ever wants to force the lock again, he'll have to use a harder crowbar!

Yours, Anne M. Frank

Dearest Kitty,

*L*ast night when I came down from the attic, I noticed, the moment I entered the room, that the lovely vase of carnations had fallen over. Mother was down on her hands and knees mopping up the water and Margot was fishing my papers from off the floor. 'What happened?' I asked with anxious foreboding, and before they could reply, I assessed the damage from across the room. My entire genealogy folder, my exercise-books, my textbooks, everything was afloat. I nearly cried, and I was so upset I started speaking German. I can't remember a word, but according to Margot I babbled something about '*unübersehbarer Schaden, schrecklich, entsetzlich, nie zu ersetzen*'* and much more. Father burst out laughing and Mother and Margot joined in, but I felt like crying because all my work and elaborate notes were lost.

I took a closer look and, luckily, the 'incalculable loss' wasn't as bad as I'd expected. Up in the attic I carefully peeled apart the sheets of paper that were stuck together and then hung them on the clothes-line to dry. It was such a funny sight, even I had to laugh. Maria de' Medici alongside Charles V, William of Orange and Marie Antoinette.

'It's *Rassenschande*',† Mr van Daan joked.

* Incalculable loss, terrible, awful, irreplaceable.
† An affront to racial purity.

After entrusting my papers to Peter's care, I went back downstairs.

'Which books are ruined?' I asked Margot, who was going through them.

'Algebra,' Margot said.

But as luck would have it, my algebra book wasn't entirely ruined. I wish it had fallen right in the vase. I've never loathed any book as much as that one. Inside the front cover are the names of at least twenty girls who had it before I did. It's old, yellowed, full of scribbles, crossed-out words and revisions. The next time I'm in a wicked mood, I'm going to tear the flaming thing to pieces!

Yours, Anne M. Frank

MONDAY, 22 MAY 1944

Dearest Kitty,

On 20 May, Father lost his bet and had to give five pots of yoghurt to Mrs van Daan: the invasion still hasn't begun. I can safely say that all of Amsterdam, all of Holland, in fact the entire western coast of Europe, all the way down to Spain, are talking about the invasion day and night, debating, making bets and . . . hoping.

The suspense is rising to fever pitch; by no means has everyone we think of as 'good' Dutch people kept their faith in the British, not everyone thinks the British bluff is a masterful strategical move. Oh no, people want deeds – great, heroic deeds.

No one can see farther than the end of their nose, no one gives a thought to the fact that the British are fighting for their own country and their own people; everyone thinks it's Britain's duty to save Holland, as quickly as possible. What obligations do the British have towards us? What have the Dutch done to deserve the generous help they so clearly expect? Oh no, the Dutch are very much mistaken. The British, despite their bluff, are certainly no more to blame for the war than all the other countries, large and small, that are now occupied by the Germans. The British are not about to offer their excuses; true, they were sleeping during the years Germany was rearming itself, but all the other countries, especially those bordering on Germany, were asleep too. Britain and the rest of the world have discovered that burying your head in the sand doesn't work, and now each of them, especially Britain, is having to pay a heavy price for its ostrich policy.

No country sacrifices its men without reason, and certainly not in the interests of another, and Britain is no exception. The invasion, liberation and freedom will come someday; yet Britain, not the occupied territories, will choose the moment.

To our great sorrow and dismay, we've heard that many people have changed their attitude towards us Jews. We've been told that anti-Semitism has cropped up in circles where once it would have been unthinkable. This fact has affected us all very, very deeply. The reason for the hatred is understandable, maybe even human, but that doesn't make it right. According to the Christians, the Jews are blabbing their secrets to the Germans, denouncing their helpers and causing them to suffer the dreadful fate and punishments that have already been meted out to so many. All of this is true. But as with everything, they should look at the matter from both sides: would Christians act any differently if they were in our place? Could anyone, regardless of whether they're Jews or Christians, remain silent in the face of German pressure? Everyone knows it's practically impossible, so why do they ask the impossible of the Jews?

It's being said in underground circles that the German Jews who emigrated to Holland before the war and have now been sent to Poland shouldn't be allowed to return here. They were granted the right to asylum in Holland, but once Hitler is gone, they should go back to Germany.

When you hear that, you begin to wonder why we're fighting this long and difficult war. We're always being told that we're fighting for freedom, truth and justice! The war isn't even over, and already there's dissension and Jews are regarded as lesser beings. Oh, it's sad, very sad that the old adage has been confirmed for the umpteenth time: 'What one Christian does is his own responsibility, what one Jew does reflects on all Jews.'

To be honest, I can't understand how the Dutch, a nation of good, honest, upright people, can sit in judgement on us the way they do. On *us* – the most oppressed, unfortunate and pitiable people in all the world.

I have only one hope: that this anti-Semitism is just a passing thing, that the Dutch will show their true colours, that they'll never waver from what they know in their hearts to be just, for this is unjust!

And if they ever carry out this terrible threat, the meagre handful of Jews still left in Holland will have to go. We too will have to shoulder our bundles and move on, away from this beautiful country, which once so kindly took us in and now turns its back on us.

I love Holland. Once I hoped it would become a fatherland to me, since I had lost my own. And I hope so still!

Yours, Anne M. Frank

THURSDAY, 25 MAY 1944

Dearest Kitty,

*B*ep's engaged! The news isn't much of a surprise, though none of us is particularly pleased. Bertus may be a nice, steady, athletic young man, but Bep doesn't love him, and to me that's enough reason to advise her against marrying him.

Bep's trying to get on in the world, and Bertus is pulling her back; he's a labourer, without any interests or any desire to make something of himself, and I don't think that'll make Bep happy. I can understand Bep's wanting to put an end to her indecision; four weeks ago she decided to write him off, but then she felt even worse. So she wrote him a letter, and now she's engaged.

There are several factors involved in this engagement. First, Bep's sick father, who likes Bertus very much. Second, she's the oldest of the Voskuijl girls and her mother teases her about being an old maid. Third, she's just turned twenty-four, and that matters a great deal to Bep.

Mother said it would have been better if Bep had simply had an affair with Bertus. I don't know, I feel sorry for Bep and can understand her loneliness. In any case, they can get married only after the war, since Bertus is in hiding, or at any rate has gone underground. Besides, they don't have a penny to their name and nothing in the way of a trousseau. What a sorry prospect for Bep, for whom we all wish the best. I only hope Bertus improves under her influence, or that Bep finds another man, one who knows how to appreciate her!

Yours, Anne M. Frank

THE SAME DAY

There's something happening every day. This morning Mr van Hoeven was arrested. He was hiding two Jews in his house. It's a heavy blow for us, not only because those poor Jews are once again balancing on the edge of an abyss, but also because it's terrible for Mr van Hoeven.

The world's been turned upside down. The most decent people are being sent to concentration camps, prisons and lonely cells, while the lowest of the low rule over young and old, rich and poor. One gets caught for black marketeering, another for hiding Jews or other unfortunate souls. Unless you're a Nazi, you don't know what's going to happen to you from one day to the next.

Mr van Hoeven is a great loss to us too. Bep can't possibly lug such huge amounts of potatoes all the way here, nor should she have to, so our only choice is to eat fewer of them. I'll tell you what we have in mind, but it's certainly not going to make life here any more agreeable. Mother says we'll skip breakfast, eat porridge and bread for lunch and fried potatoes for dinner and, if possible, vegetables or lettuce once or twice a week. That's all there is. We're going to be hungry, but nothing's worse than being caught.

Yours, Anne M. Frank

My dearest Kitty,

At long, long last, I can sit quietly at my table before the crack in the window frame and write you everything, everything I want to say.

I feel more miserable than I have in months. Even after the break-in I didn't feel so utterly broken, inside and out. On the one hand, there's the news about Mr van Hoeven, the Jewish question (which is discussed in detail by everyone in the house), the invasion (which is so long in coming), the awful food, the tension, the miserable atmosphere, my disappointment in Peter. On the other hand, there's Bep's engagement, the Whitsun reception, the flowers, Mr Kugler's birthday, cakes and stories about cabarets, films and concerts. That gap, that enormous gap, is always there. One day we're laughing at the comical side of life in hiding, and the next day (and there are many such days), we're frightened, and the fear, tension and despair can be read on our faces.

Miep and Mr Kugler bear the greatest burden for us, and for all those in hiding – Miep in everything she does and Mr Kugler through his enormous responsibility for the eight of us, which is sometimes so overwhelming that he can hardly speak from the pent-up tension and strain. Mr Kleiman and Bep also take very good care of us, but they're able to put the Annexe out of their minds, even if it's only for a few hours or a few days. They have their own worries, Mr Kleiman with his health and Bep with her engagement, which isn't looking very promising at the moment. But they also have their outings, their visits to friends, their everyday lives as ordinary people, so that the tension is sometimes relieved, if only for a short while, while ours never is, never has been, not once in the two years we've been here. How much longer will this increasingly oppressive, unbearable weight press down on us?

The drains are clogged again. We can't run the water, or if we do, only a trickle; we can't flush the toilet, so we have to use a toilet brush; and we've been putting our dirty water into a big earthenware jar. We can manage for today, but what will happen if the plumber can't mend it on his own? They can't come to do the drains until Tuesday.

Miep sent us a currant loaf with 'Happy Whitsun' written on top. It's almost as if she were mocking us, since our moods and cares are far from 'happy'.

We've all become more frightened since the van Hoeven business. Once again you hear 'shh' from all sides, and we're doing everything more quietly. The police forced the door there; they could just as easily do that here too! What will we do if we're ever . . . no, I mustn't write that down. But the question won't let itself be pushed to the back of my mind today; on the contrary, all the fear I've ever felt is looming before me in all its horror.

I had to go downstairs alone at eight this evening to use the lavatory. There was no one down there, since they were all listening to the radio. I wanted to be brave, but it was hard. I always feel safer upstairs than in that huge, silent house; when I'm alone with those mysterious muffled sounds from upstairs and the honking of horns in the street, I have to hurry and remind myself where I am to keep from getting the shivers.

Miep has been acting much nicer towards us since her talk with Father. But I haven't told you about that yet. Miep came up one afternoon all flushed and asked Father straight out if we thought they too were infected with the current anti-Semitism. Father was stunned and quickly talked her out of the idea, but some of Miep's suspicion has lingered on. They're doing more errands for us now and showing more of an interest in our troubles, though we certainly shouldn't bother them with our woes. Oh, they're such good, noble people!

I've asked myself again and again whether it wouldn't have been better if we hadn't gone into hiding, if we were dead now and didn't have to go through this misery, especially so that the others could be spared the burden. But we all shrink from this thought. We still love life, we haven't yet forgotten the voice of nature, and we keep hoping, hoping for . . . everything.

Let something happen soon, even an air raid. Nothing can be more crushing than this anxiety. Let the end come, however cruel; at least then we'll know whether we are to be the victors or the vanquished.

Yours, Anne M. Frank

Dearest Kitty,

Saturday, Sunday, Monday and Tuesday it was too hot to hold my fountain pen, which is why I couldn't write to you. Friday the drains were clogged, Saturday they were cleared. Mrs Kleiman came for a visit in the afternoon and told us a lot about Jopie; she and Jacque van Maarsen are in the same hockey club. Sunday, Bep dropped in to make sure no one had broken in and stayed for breakfast. On Whit Monday Mr Gies served as the Annexe watchman, and Tuesday we were finally allowed to open the windows. We've seldom had a Whit weekend that was so beautiful and warm. Or maybe 'hot' is a better word. Hot weather is horrible in the Annexe. To give you an idea of the numerous complaints, I'll briefly describe these sweltering days.

Saturday: 'Wonderful, what fantastic weather,' we all said in the morning. 'If only it weren't quite so hot,' we said in the afternoon, when the windows had to be shut.

Sunday: 'The heat's unbearable, the butter's melting, there's not a cool spot anywhere in the house, the bread's drying out, the milk's going off, the windows can't be opened. We poor outcasts are suffocating while everyone else is enjoying their Whitsun holiday.' (According to Mrs van D.)

Monday: 'My feet hurt, I have nothing cool to wear, I can't wash up in this heat!' Grumbling from early in the morning to late at night. It was awful.

I can't stand the heat. I'm glad the wind's come up today, but that the sun's still shining.

Yours, Anne M. Frank

Dear Kitty,

'If you're going to the attic, take an umbrella with you, preferably a large one!' This is to protect you from 'household showers'. There's a Dutch proverb: 'High and dry, safe and sound', but it obviously doesn't apply to wartime (guns!) and to people in hiding (litter box!). Mouschi's got into the habit of relieving herself on some newspapers or between the cracks in the floorboards, so we have good reason to fear the splatters and, even worse, the stench. The new Moortje in the warehouse has the same problem. Anyone who's ever had a cat that's not housebroken can imagine the smells, other than pepper and thyme, that permeate this house.

I also have a brand-new prescription for gunfire jitters: when the shooting gets loud, proceed to the nearest wooden staircase. Run up and down a few times, making sure to stumble at least once. What with the scratches and the noise of running and falling, you won't even be able to hear the shooting, much less worry about it.

Yours truly has put this magic formula to use, with great success!

Yours, Anne M. Frank

MONDAY, 5 JUNE 1944

Dearest Kitty,

New problems in the Annexe. A quarrel between Dussel and the Franks over the division of butter. Capitulation on the part of Dussel. Close friendship between the latter and Mrs van Daan, flirtations, kisses and friendly little smiles. Dussel is beginning to long for female companionship.

The van Daans don't see why we should bake a spice cake for Mr Kugler's birthday when we can't have one ourselves. All very petty. Mood upstairs: bad. Mrs van D. has a cold. Dussel caught with brewer's yeast tablets, while we've got none.

The Fifth Army has taken Rome. The city neither destroyed nor bombed. Great propaganda for Hitler.

Very few potatoes and vegetables. One loaf of bread was mouldy.

Scharminkeltje (name of new warehouse cat) can't stand pepper. She sleeps in the litter box and does her business in the wood shavings. Impossible to keep her.

Bad weather. Continuous bombing of Pas de Calais and the west coast of France.

No one buying dollars. Gold even less interesting. The bottom of our black money-box is in sight. What are we going to live on next month?

Yours, Anne M. Frank

TUESDAY, 6 JUNE 1944

My dearest Kitty,

'This is D-Day,' the BBC announced at twelve. 'This is *the* day.' The invasion has begun!

This morning at eight the British reported heavy bombing of Calais, Boulogne, Le Havre and Cherbourg, as well as Pas de Calais (as usual). Further, as a precautionary measure for those in the occupied territories, everyone living within a zone of twenty miles from the coast was warned to prepare for bombardments. Where possible, the British will drop pamphlets an hour ahead of time.

According to the German news, British paratroopers have landed on the coast of France. 'British landing craft are engaged in combat with German naval units,' according to the BBC.

Conclusion reached by the Annexe while breakfasting at nine: this is a trial landing, like the one two years ago in Dieppe.

BBC broadcast in German, Dutch, French and other languages at ten: the invasion has begun! So this is the 'real' invasion. BBC broadcast in German at eleven: speech by Supreme Commander General Dwight Eisenhower.

BBC broadcast in English: 'This is D-Day.' General Eisenhower said to the French people: 'Stiff fighting will come now, but after this the victory. The year 1944 is the year of complete victory. Good luck!'

BBC broadcast in English at one: 11,000 planes are shuttling back and forth or standing by to land troops and bomb behind enemy lines; 4,000 landing craft and small boats are continually arriving in the area between Cherbourg and Le Havre. British and American troops are already engaged in heavy combat. Speeches by Gerbrandy, the Prime Minister of Belgium, King Haakon of Norway, de Gaulle of France, the King of England and, last but not least, Churchill.

A huge commotion in the Annexe! Is this really the beginning of the long-awaited liberation? The liberation we've all talked so much about, which still seems too good, too much of a fairy tale ever to come true? Will this year, 1944, bring us victory? We don't know yet. But where there's hope, there's life. It fills us with fresh courage and makes us strong again. We'll need to be brave to endure the many fears and hardships and the suffering yet to come. It's now a matter of remaining calm and steadfast, of gritting our teeth and keeping a stiff upper lip! France, Russia, Italy, and even Germany, can cry out in agony, but we don't yet have that right!

Oh, Kitty, the best part about the invasion is that I have the feeling that friends are on the way. Those awful Germans have oppressed and threatened us for so long that the thought of friends and salvation means everything to us! Now it's not just the Jews, but Holland and all of occupied Europe. Maybe, Margot says, I can even go back to school in September or October.

Yours, Anne M. Frank

PS. I'll keep you informed of the latest news!

This morning and last night, dummies made of straw and rubber were dropped from the air behind German lines, and they exploded the minute they hit the ground. Many paratroopers, their faces blackened so they couldn't be seen in the dark, landed as well. The French coast was bombarded with 5,500 tons of bombs during the night, and then, at six in the morning, the first landing craft came ashore. Today there were 20,000 aeroplanes in action. The German coastal batteries were destroyed even before the landing; a small bridgehead has already been formed. Everything's going well, despite the bad weather. The army and the people are 'one will and one hope'

Dearest Kitty,

Great news of the invasion! The Allies have taken Bayeux, a village on the coast of France, and are now fighting for Caen. They're clearly intending to cut off the peninsula where Cherbourg is located. Every evening the war correspondents report on the difficulties, the courage and the fighting spirit of the army. To get their stories, they pull off the most amazing feats. A few of the wounded who are already back in England also spoke on the radio. Despite the miserable weather, the planes are flying diligently back and forth. We heard over the BBC that Churchill wanted to land along with the troops on D-Day, but Eisenhower and the other generals managed to talk him out of it. Just imagine, so much courage for such an old man – he must be at least seventy!

The excitement here has died down somewhat; still, we're all hoping that the war will finally be over by the end of the year. It's about time! Mrs van Daan's constant grizzling is unbearable; now that she can no longer drive us crazy with the invasion, she moans and groans all day about the bad weather. If only we could plonk her down in the loft in a bucket of cold water!

Everyone in the Annexe except Mr van Daan and Peter has read the *Hungarian Rhapsody* trilogy, a biography of the composer, piano virtuoso and child prodigy Franz Liszt. It's very interesting, though in my opinion there's a bit too much emphasis on women; Liszt was not only the greatest and most famous pianist of his time, he was also the biggest womanizer, even at the age of seventy. He had affairs with Countess Marie d'Agoult, Princess Carolyne Sayn-Wittgenstein, the dancer Lola Montez, the pianist Agnes Kingworth, the pianist Sophie Menter, the Circassian princess Olga Janina, Baroness Olga Meyendorff, actress Lilla what's-her-name, etc., etc., and there's no end to it. Those parts of the book dealing with music and the other arts are much more interesting. Some of the people mentioned are Schumann, Clara Wieck, Hector Berlioz, Johannes Brahms, Beethoven, Joachim, Richard Wagner, Hans von Bülow, Anton Rubinstein, Frédéric Chopin, Victor Hugo, Honoré de Balzac, Hiller, Hummel, Czerny, Rossini, Cherubini, Paganini, Mendelssohn, etc., etc.

Liszt appears to have been a decent man, very generous and modest, though exceptionally vain. He helped others, put art above all else, was extremely fond of cognac and women, couldn't bear the sight of tears, was a gentleman, couldn't refuse anyone a favour, wasn't interested in money and cared about religious freedom and the world.

Yours, Anne M. Frank

Dearest Kit,

Another birthday has gone by, so I'm now fifteen. I received quite a few gifts: Springer's five-volume art history book, a set of underwear, two belts, a handkerchief, two pots of yoghurt, a pot of jam, two honey biscuits (small), a botany book from Father and Mother, a gold bracelet from Margot, a sticker album from the van Daans, Biomalt and sweet peas from Dussel, sweets from Miep, sweets and exercise-books from Bep, and the high point: the book *Maria Theresa* and three slices of full-cream cheese from Mr Kugler. Peter gave me a lovely bouquet of peonies; the poor boy had put a lot of effort into finding a present, but nothing quite worked out.

The invasion is still going splendidly, in spite of the miserable weather – pouring rains, strong winds and high seas.

Yesterday Churchill, Smuts, Eisenhower and Arnold visited the French villages that the British have captured and liberated. Churchill was on a torpedo boat that shelled the coast. Like many men, he doesn't seem to know what fear is – an enviable trait!

From our position here in Fort Annexe, it's difficult to gauge the mood of the Dutch. No doubt many people are glad the idle (!) British have finally rolled up their sleeves and got down to work. Those who keep claiming they don't want to be occupied by the British don't realize how unfair they're being. Their line of reasoning boils down to this: Britain must fight, struggle and sacrifice its sons to liberate Holland and the other occupied countries. After that the British shouldn't remain in Holland: they should offer their most abject apologies to all the occupied countries, restore the Dutch East Indies to its rightful owner and then return, weakened and impoverished, to Britain. What a bunch of idiots. And yet, as I've already said, many Dutch people can be counted among their ranks. What would have become of Holland and its neighbours if Britain had signed a peace treaty with Germany, as it's had ample opportunity to do? Holland would have become German, and that would have been the end of that!

All those Dutch people who still look down on the British, scoff at Britain and its government of ageing lords, call them cowards, yet hate the Germans, should be given a good shaking, the way you'd plump up a pillow. Maybe that would straighten out their jumbled brains!

Wishes, thoughts, accusations and reproaches are swirling around in my head. I'm not really as conceited as many people think; I know my various faults and shortcomings better than anyone else, but there's one difference: I also know that I want to change, will change and already have changed greatly!

Why is it, I often ask myself, that everyone still thinks I'm so pushy and such a know-it-all? Am I really so arrogant? Am *I* the one who's so arrogant, or are they? It sounds silly, I know, but I'm not going to cross out that last sentence, because it's not as silly as it seems. Mrs van Daan and Dussel, my two chief accusers, are known to be totally unintelligent and, not to put too fine a point on it, just plain 'stupid'! Stupid people usually can't bear it when others do something better than they do; the best examples of this are those two dunces, Mrs van Daan and Dussel. Mrs van D. thinks I'm stupid because I don't suffer so much from this ailment as she does, she thinks I'm pushy because she's even pushier, she thinks my dresses are too short because hers are even shorter, and she thinks I'm such a know-it-all because she talks twice as much as I do about topics she knows nothing about. The same goes for Dussel. But one of my favourite sayings is 'Where there's smoke there's fire', and I readily admit I'm a know-it-all.

What's so difficult about my personality is that I scold and curse myself much more than anyone else does; if Mother adds her advice, the pile of sermons becomes so thick that I despair of ever getting through them. Then I talk back and start contradicting everyone until the old familiar Anne refrain inevitably crops up again: 'No one understands me!'

This phrase is part of me, and as unlikely as it may seem, there's a kernel of truth in it. Sometimes I'm so deeply buried under self-reproaches that I long for a word of comfort to help me dig myself out again. If only I had someone who took my feelings seriously. Alas, I haven't yet found that person, so the search must go on.

I know you're wondering about Peter, aren't you, Kit? It's true, Peter loves me, not as a girlfriend, but as a friend. His affection grows day by day, but some mysterious force is holding us back, and I don't know what it is.

Sometimes I think my terrible longing for him was over-exaggerated. But that's not true, because if I'm unable to go to his room for a day or two, I long for him as desperately as I ever did. Peter is kind and good, and yet I can't deny that he's disappointed me in many ways. I especially don't care for his dislike of religion, his talk of food and various things of that nature. Still, I'm firmly convinced that we'll stick to our agreement never to quarrel. Peter is peace-loving, tolerant and extremely easygoing. He lets me say a lot of things to him that he'd never accept from his mother. He's making a determined effort to remove the blots from his copy-book and keep his affairs in order. Yet why does he hide his innermost self and never allow me access? Of course, he's much more closed than I am, but I know from experience (even though I'm constantly being accused of knowing all there is to know in theory, but not in practice) that in time, even the most uncommunicative types will long as much, or even more, for someone to confide in.

Peter and I have both spent our contemplative years in the Annexe. We often discuss the future, the past and the present, but as I've already told you, I miss the real thing, and yet I know it exists!

Is it because I haven't been outdoors for so long that I've become so mad about nature? I remember a time when a magnificent blue sky, chirping birds, moonlight and budding blossoms wouldn't have captivated me. Things have changed since I came here. One night during Whitsun, for instance, when it was so hot, I struggled to keep my eyes open until eleven-thirty so I could get a good look at the moon, all on my own for once. Alas, my sacrifice was in vain, since there was too much glare and I couldn't risk opening a window. Another time, several months ago, I happened to be upstairs one night when the window was open. I didn't go back down until it had to be closed again. The dark, rainy evening, the wind, the racing clouds, had me spellbound; it was the first time in a year and a half that I'd seen the night face-to-face. After that evening my longing to see it again was even greater than my fear of burglars, a dark rat-infested house or police raids. I went downstairs all by myself and looked out of the windows in the kitchen and private office. Many people think nature is beautiful, many people sleep from time to time under the starry sky, and many people in hospitals and prisons long for the day when they'll be free to enjoy what nature has to offer. But few are as isolated and cut off as we are from the joys of nature, which can be shared by rich and poor alike.

It's not just my imagination – looking at the sky, the clouds, the moon and the stars really does make me feel calm and hopeful. It's much better medicine than valerian or bromide. Nature makes me feel humble and ready to face every blow with courage!

As luck would have it, I'm only able – except for a few rare occasions – to view nature through dusty curtains tacked over dirt-caked windows; it takes the pleasure out of looking. Nature is the one thing for which there is no substitute!

One of the many questions that have often bothered me is why women have been, and still are, thought to be so inferior to men. It's easy to say it's unfair, but that's not enough for me; I'd really like to know the reason for this great injustice!

Men presumably dominated women from the very beginning because of their greater physical strength; it's men who earn a living, beget children and do as they please . . . Until recently, women silently went along with this, which was stupid, since the longer it's kept up, the more deeply entrenched it becomes. Fortunately, education, work and progress have opened women's eyes. In many countries they've been granted equal rights; many people, mainly women, but also men, now realize how wrong it was to tolerate this state of affairs for so long. Modern women want the right to be completely independent!

But that's not all. Women should be respected as well! Generally speaking, men are held in great esteem in all parts of the world, so why shouldn't women have their share? Soldiers and war heroes are honoured and commemorated, explorers are granted immortal fame, martyrs are revered, but how many people look upon women too as soldiers?

In the book *Men against Death* I was greatly struck by the fact that in childbirth alone, women commonly suffer more pain, illness and misery than any war hero ever does. And what's her reward for enduring all that pain? She gets pushed aside when she's disfigured by birth, her children soon leave, her beauty is gone. Women, who struggle and suffer pain to ensure the continuation of the human race, make much tougher and more courageous soldiers than all those big-mouthed freedom-fighting heroes put together!

I don't mean to imply that women should stop having children; on the contrary, nature intended them to, and that's the way it should be. What I condemn are our system of values and the men who don't acknowledge how great, difficult, but ultimately beautiful women's share in society is.

I agree completely with Paul de Kruif, the author of this book, when he says that men must learn that birth is no longer thought of as inevitable and unavoidable in those parts of the world we consider civilized. It's easy for men to talk – they don't and never will have to bear the woes that women do!

I believe that in the course of the next century the notion that it's a woman's duty to have children will change and make way for the respect and admiration of all women, who bear their burdens without complaint or a lot of pompous words!

Yours, Anne M. Frank

Dearest Kitty,

New problems: Mrs van D. is at her wits' end. She's talking about getting shot, being thrown in prison, being hanged and suicide. She's jealous that Peter confides in me and not in her, offended that Dussel doesn't respond sufficiently to her flirtations and afraid her husband's going to squander all the fur-coat money on tobacco. She quarrels, curses, cries, feels sorry for herself, laughs and starts all over again.

What on earth can you do with such a silly, snivelling specimen of humanity? Nobody takes her seriously, she has no strength of character, she complains to one and all, and you should see what she looks like: *von hinten Lyzeum, von vorne Museum.*★ Even worse, Peter's becoming insolent, Mr van Daan irritable and Mother cynical. Yes, everyone's in quite a state! There's only one rule you need to remember: laugh at everything and forget everybody else! It sounds egotistical, but it's actually the only cure for those suffering from self-pity.

Mr Kugler's supposed to spend four weeks in Alkmaar on a work detail. He's trying to get out of it with a doctor's certificate and a letter from Opekta. Mr Kleiman's hoping his stomach will be operated on soon. Starting at eleven last night, all private phones were cut off.

Yours, Anne M. Frank

★ Mutton dressed as lamb.

Dearest Kitty,

Nothing special going on here. The British have begun their all-out attack on Cherbourg. According to Pim and Mr van Daan, we're sure to be liberated before 10 October. The Russians are taking part in the campaign; yesterday they started their offensive near Vitebsk, exactly three years to the day that the Germans invaded Russia.

Bep's spirits have sunk lower than ever. We're nearly out of potatoes; from now on, we're going to count them out for each person, then everyone can do what they want with them. Starting Monday, Miep's taking a week's holiday. Mr Kleiman's doctors haven't found anything on the X-rays. He's torn between having an operation and letting matters take their course.

Yours, Anne M. Frank

My dearest Kitty,

The mood has changed, everything's going enormously well. Cherbourg, Vitebsk and Zhlobin fell today. They're sure to have captured lots of men and equipment. Five German generals were killed near Cherbourg and two taken captive. Now that they've got a harbour, the British can bring whatever they want on shore. The whole Cotentin Peninsula has been captured just three weeks after the invasion! What a feat!

In the three weeks since D-Day there hasn't been a day without rain and storms, neither here nor in France, but this bad luck hasn't kept the British and the Americans from displaying their might. And how! Of course, the Germans have launched their wonder weapon, but a little firecracker like that will hardly make a dent, except maybe minor damage in England and screaming headlines in the Jerry newspapers. Anyway, when they realize in 'Jerryland' that the Bolsheviks really are getting closer, they'll be shaking in their boots.

All German women who aren't working for the military are being evacuated, together with their children, from the coastal regions to the provinces of Groningen, Friesland and Gelderland. Mussert* has announced that if the invasion reaches Holland, he'll enlist. Is that fat pig planning to fight? He could have done that in Russia long before now. Finland turned down a peace offer some time ago, and now the negotiations have been broken off again. Those numbskulls, they'll be sorry!

How far do you think we'll be on 27 July?

Yours, Anne M. Frank

* The leader of the Dutch National Socialist (Nazi) Party.

Dearest Kitty,

*B*ad weather from one at a stretch to the thirty June.*
Don't I say that well? Oh yes, I already know a little
English; just to prove it I'm reading *An Ideal Husband*
with the help of a dictionary! War's going wonderfully:
Bobruysk, Mogilev and Orsha have fallen, lots of
prisoners.

Everything's all right here. Spirits are improving, our
super-optimists are triumphant, the van Daans are doing
disappearing acts with the sugar, Bep's changed her hair,
and Miep has a week off. That's the latest news!

I've been having really ghastly root-canal work done
on one of my front teeth. It's been terribly painful. It
was so bad Dussel thought I was going to faint, and I
nearly did. Mrs van D. promptly got a toothache as well!

Yours, Anne M. Frank

PS. We've heard from Basle that Berndt† played the part
of the innkeeper in *Minna von Barnhelm*. He has 'artistic
leanings', says Mother.

* Anne's English.
† Cousin Bernhard (Buddy) Elias.

Dearest Kitty,

*M*y blood runs cold when Peter talks about becoming a criminal or a speculator; of course, he's joking, but I still have the feeling he's afraid of his own weakness. Margot and Peter are always saying to me, 'If I had your pluck and your strength, if I had your drive and unflagging energy, I could . . . !'

Is it really such an admirable trait not to let myself be influenced by others? Am I right in following my own conscience?

To be honest, I can't imagine how anyone could say 'I'm weak' and then stay that way. If you know that about yourself, why not fight it, why not develop your character? Their answer has always been: 'Because it's much easier not to!' This reply leaves me feeling rather discouraged. Easy? Does that mean a life of deceit and laziness is easy too? Oh no, that can't be true. It can't be true that people are so readily tempted by ease . . . and money. I've given a lot of thought to what my answer should be, to how I should get Peter to believe in himself and, most of all, to change himself for the better. I don't know whether I'm on the right track.

I've often imagined how nice it would be if someone were to confide everything to me. But now that it's reached that point, I realize how difficult it is to put yourself in someone else's shoes and find the *right* answer.

Especially since 'easy' and 'money' are new and completely alien concepts to me.

Peter's beginning to lean on me and I don't want that, not under any circumstances. It's hard enough standing on your own two feet, but when you also have to remain true to your character and soul, it's harder still.

I've been drifting around at sea, have spent days searching for an effective antidote to that terrible word 'easy'. How can I make it clear to him that, while it may seem easy and wonderful, it will drag him down to the depths, to a place where he'll no longer find friends, support or beauty, so far down that he may never rise to the surface again?

We're all alive, but we don't know why or what for; we're all searching for happiness; we're all leading lives that are different and yet the same. We three have been raised in good families, we have the opportunity to get an education and make something of ourselves. We have many reasons to hope for great happiness, but . . . we have to earn it. And that's something you can't achieve by taking the easy way out. Earning happiness means doing good and working, not speculating and being lazy. Laziness may *look* inviting, but only work gives you *true* satisfaction.

I can't understand people who don't like to work, but that isn't Peter's problem either. He just doesn't have a goal, plus he thinks he's too stupid and inferior to ever achieve anything. Poor boy, he's never known how it feels to make someone else happy, and I'm afraid I can't teach him. He isn't religious, scoffs at Jesus Christ and

takes the Lord's name in vain, and though I'm not Orthodox either, it hurts me every time to see him so lonely,
so scornful, so wretched.

People who are religious should be glad, since not
everyone is blessed with the ability to believe in a higher
order. You don't even have to live in fear of eternal
punishment; the concepts of purgatory, heaven and hell
are difficult for many people to accept, yet religion itself,
any religion, keeps a person on the right path. Not the
fear of God, but upholding your own sense of honour
and obeying your own conscience. How noble and good
everyone could be if, at the end of each day, they were
to review their own behaviour and weigh up the rights
and wrongs. They would automatically try to do better
at the start of each new day and, after a while, would
certainly accomplish a great deal. Everyone is welcome to
this prescription; it costs nothing and is definitely useful.
Those who don't know will have to find out by experience that 'a quiet conscience gives you strength'!

Yours, Anne M. Frank

SATURDAY, 8 JULY 1944

Dearest Kitty,

M r Broks was in Beverwijk and managed to get
hold of strawberries at the produce auction. They

arrived here dusty and full of sand, but in large quantities. No fewer than twenty-four crates for the office and us. That very same evening we bottled the first six jars and made eight jars of jam. The next morning Miep started making jam for the office.

At twelve-thirty the outside door was locked, crates were lugged into the kitchen, with Peter, Father and Mr van Daan stumbling up the stairs. Anne got hot water from the water-heater, Margot went for a bucket, all hands on deck! With a funny feeling in my stomach, I entered the overcrowded office kitchen. Miep, Bep, Mr Kleiman, Jan, Father, Peter: the Annexe contingent and the Supply Corps all mixed up together, and that in the middle of the day! Curtains and windows open, loud voices, banging doors – I was trembling with excitement. I kept thinking, 'Are we really in hiding?' This must be how it feels when you can finally go out into the world again. The pan was full, so I dashed upstairs, where the rest of the family was hulling strawberries around the kitchen table. At least that's what they were supposed to be doing, but more was going into their mouths than into the buckets. They were bound to need another bucket soon. Peter went back downstairs, but then the doorbell rang twice. Leaving the bucket where it was, Peter raced upstairs and shut the bookcase behind him. We sat kicking our heels impatiently; the strawberries were waiting to be rinsed, but we stuck to the house rule: 'No running water when strangers are downstairs – they might hear the drains.'

Jan came up at one to tell us it had been the postman.

Peter hurried downstairs again. Ding-dong . . . the door-bell, about-turn. I listened to hear if anyone was coming, standing first at the bookcase, then at the top of the stairs. Finally Peter and I leaned over the banister, straining our ears like a couple of burglars to hear the sounds from downstairs. No unfamiliar voices. Peter tiptoed halfway down the stairs and called out, 'Bep!' Once more: 'Bep!' His voice was drowned out by the racket in the kitchen. So he ran down to the kitchen while I nervously kept watch from above.

'Go upstairs at once, Peter, the accountant's here, you've got to leave!' It was Mr Kugler's voice. Sighing, Peter came upstairs and closed the bookcase.

Mr Kugler finally came up at one-thirty. 'Gosh, the whole world's turned to strawberries. I had strawberries for breakfast, Jan's having them for lunch, Kleiman's eating them as a snack, Miep's boiling them, Bep's hulling them, and I can smell them everywhere I go. I come upstairs to get away from all that red and what do I see? People washing strawberries!'

The rest of the strawberries were bottled. That evening: two jars came unsealed. Father quickly turned them into jam. The next morning: two more lids popped up; and that afternoon: four lids. Mr van Daan hadn't got the jars hot enough when he was sterilizing them, so Father ended up making jam every evening. We ate porridge with strawberries, buttermilk with strawberries, bread with strawberries, strawberries for dessert, strawberries with sugar, strawberries with sand. For two days there was nothing but strawberries, strawberries, strawberries, and then our supply was either exhausted or in jars, safely under lock and key.

'Hey, Anne,' Margot called out one day, 'Mrs van Hoeven has let us have some peas, twenty pounds!'

'That's nice of her,' I replied. And it certainly was, but it's so much work . . . ugh!

'On Saturday, you've all got to shell peas,' Mother announced at the table.

And sure enough, this morning after breakfast our biggest enamel pan appeared on the table, filled to the brim with peas. If you think shelling peas is boring work, you ought to try removing the inner linings. I don't think many people realize that once you've pulled out the linings, the pods are soft, delicious and rich in vitamins. But an even greater advantage is that you get nearly three times as much as when you eat just the peas.

Stripping pods is a precise and meticulous job that might be suited to pedantic dentists or finicky spice experts, but it's a horror for an impatient teenager like me. We started work at nine-thirty; I sat down at ten-thirty, got up again at eleven, sat down again at eleven-thirty. My ears were humming with the following refrain: snap the end, strip the pod, pull the string, pod in the pan, snap the end, strip the pod, pull the string, pod in the pan, etc., etc. My eyes were swimming: green, green, worm, string, rotten pod, green, green. To fight the boredom and have something to do, I chattered all morning, saying whatever came into my head and making everyone laugh. The monotony was killing me. Every string I pulled made me more certain that I never, ever, want to be just a housewife!

At twelve we finally ate breakfast, but from twelve-thirty to one-fifteen we had to strip pods again. When I stopped, I felt a bit seasick, and so did the others. I had a nap until four, still in a daze because of those wretched peas.

Yours, Anne M. Frank

SATURDAY, 15 JULY 1944

Dearest Kitty,

We've received a book from the library with the challenging title *What Do You Think of the Modern Young Girl?* I'd like to discuss this subject today.

The writer criticizes 'today's youth' from head to toe, though without dismissing them all as 'hopeless cases'. On the contrary, she believes they have it within their power to build a bigger, better and more beautiful world, but that they occupy themselves with superficial things, without giving a thought to true beauty.

In some passages I had the strong feeling that the writer was directing her disapproval at me, which is why I finally want to bare my soul to you and defend myself against this attack.

I have one outstanding character trait that must be obvious to anyone who's known me for any length of time: I have a great deal of self-knowledge. In everything I do, I can watch myself as if I were a stranger. I can stand across from the everyday Anne and, without being biased or making excuses, watch what she's doing, both the good and the bad. This self-awareness never leaves me, and every time I open my mouth, I think, 'You should have said that differently' or 'That's fine the way it is.' I condemn myself in so many ways that I'm beginning to realize the truth of Father's adage: 'Every child has to raise itself.' Parents can only advise their children or point them in the right direction. Ultimately, people shape their own characters. In addition, I face life with an extraordinary amount of courage. I feel so strong and capable of bearing burdens, so young and free! When I first realized this, I was glad, because it means I can more easily withstand the blows life has in store.

But I've talked about these things so often. Now I'd like to turn to the chapter 'Father and Mother Don't

Understand Me'. My parents have always spoiled me rotten, treated me kindly, defended me against the van Daans and done all that parents can. And yet for a long time I've felt extremely lonely, left out, neglected and misunderstood. Father did everything he could to curb my rebellious spirit, but it was no use. I've cured myself by holding my behaviour up to the light and looking at what I was doing wrong.

Why didn't Father support me in my struggle? Why did he fall short when he tried to offer me a helping hand? The answer is: he used the wrong methods. He always talked to me as if I were a child going through a difficult phase. It sounds crazy, since Father's the only one who's given me a sense of confidence and made me feel as if I'm a sensible person. But he overlooked one thing: he failed to see that this struggle to triumph over my difficulties was more important to me than anything else. I didn't want to hear about 'typical adolescent problems', or 'other girls', or 'you'll grow out of it'. I didn't want to be treated the same as all-the-other-girls, but as Anne-in-her-own-right, and Pim didn't understand that. Besides, I can't confide in anyone unless they tell me a lot about themselves, and because I know very little about him, I can't get on a more intimate footing. Pim always acts like the elderly father who once had the same fleeting impulses, but who can no longer relate to me as a friend, no matter how hard he tries. As a result, I've never shared my outlook on life or my long-pondered theories with anyone but my diary and, once in a while, Margot. I've hidden anything having to do with me from Father, never shared my ideals with him, deliberately alienated myself from him.

I couldn't have done it any other way. I've let myself be guided entirely by my feelings. It was egotistical, but I've done what was best for my own peace of mind. I would lose that, plus the self-confidence I've worked so hard to achieve, if I were to be subjected to criticism halfway through the job. It may sound hard-hearted, but I can't take criticism from Pim either, because not only do I never share my innermost thoughts with him, but I've pushed him even further away by being irritable.

This is a point I think about quite often: why is it that Pim annoys me so much sometimes? I can hardly bear to have him teach me, and his affection seems forced. I want to be left alone, and I'd rather he ignored me for a while until I'm more sure of myself when I'm talking to him! I'm still torn with guilt about the vile letter I wrote him when I was so upset. Oh, it's hard to be strong and brave in every way!

Still, this hasn't been my greatest disappointment. No, I think about Peter much more than I do Father. I know very well that he was my conquest, and not the other way round. I created an image of him in my mind, pictured him as a quiet, sweet, sensitive boy badly in need of friendship and love! I needed to pour out my heart to a living person. I wanted a friend who would help me find my way again. I accomplished what I set out to do and drew him, slowly but surely, towards me. When I finally got him to be my friend, it automatically developed into an intimacy that, when I think about it now, seems outrageous. We talked about the most private things, but we haven't yet touched upon the things closest to my heart. I still can't make head or tail of Peter. Is he superficial, or is it shyness that holds him back, even with me? But putting all that aside, I made one mistake: I used intimacy to get closer to him, and in doing so, I ruled out other forms of friendship. He longs to be loved, and I can see he's beginning to like me more with each passing day. Our time together leaves him feeling satisfied, but just makes me want to start all over again. I never broach the subjects I long to bring out into the open. I forced Peter, more than he realizes, to get close to me, and now he's holding on for dear life. I honestly don't see any effective way of shaking him off and getting him back on his own two feet. I soon realized he could never be a kindred spirit, but still tried to help him break out of his narrow world and expand his youthful horizons.

'Deep down, the young are lonelier than the old.' I read this in a book somewhere and it's stuck in my mind. As far as I can tell, it's true.

So if you're wondering whether it's harder for the adults here than for the children, the answer is no, it's certainly not. Older people have an opinion about everything and are sure of themselves and their actions. It's twice as hard for us young people to hold on to our opinions at a time when ideals are being shattered and destroyed, when the worst side of human nature predominates, when everyone has come to doubt truth, just-ice and God.

Anyone who claims that the old people have a more difficult time in the Annexe doesn't realize that the problems have a far greater impact on *us*. We're much too young to deal with these problems, but they keep thrusting themselves on us until, finally, we're forced to think up a solution, though most of the time our solutions crumble when faced with the facts. It's difficult in times like these: ideals, dreams and cherished hopes rise within us, only to be crushed by grim reality. It's a wonder I haven't abandoned all my ideals, they seem so absurd and impractical. Yet I cling to them because I still believe, in spite of everything, that people are truly good at heart.

It's utterly impossible for me to build my life on a foundation of chaos, suffering and death. I see the world being slowly transformed into a wilderness, I hear the approaching thunder that, one day, will destroy us too, I feel the suffering of millions. And yet, when I look up at the sky, I somehow feel that everything will change for the better, that this cruelty too will end, that peace and tranquillity will return once more. In the mean time, I must hold on to my ideals. Perhaps the day will come when I'll be able to realize them!

Yours, Anne M. Frank

Dearest Kitty,

I'm finally getting optimistic. Now, at last, things are going well! They really are! Great news! An assassination attempt has been made on Hitler's life, and for once not by Jewish Communists or British capitalists, but by a German general who's not only a count, but young as well. The Führer owes his life to 'Divine Providence': he escaped, unfortunately, with only a few minor burns and scratches. A number of the officers and generals who were near by were killed or wounded. The head of the conspiracy has been shot.

This is the best proof we've had so far that many officers and generals are fed up with the war and would like to see Hitler sink into a bottomless pit, so they can establish a military dictatorship, make peace with the Allies, rearm themselves and, after a few decades, start a new war. Perhaps Providence is deliberately biding its time getting rid of Hitler, since it's much easier, and cheaper, for the Allies to let the impeccable Germans kill each other off. It's less work for the Russians and the British, and it allows them to start rebuilding their own cities that much sooner. But we haven't reached that point yet, and I'd hate to anticipate the glorious event. Still, you've probably noticed that I'm telling the truth, the whole truth and nothing but the truth. For once, I'm not rattling on about high ideals.

Furthermore, Hitler has been so kind as to announce

to his loyal, devoted people that as of today all military personnel are under orders of the Gestapo, and that any soldier who knows that one of his superiors was involved in this cowardly attempt on the Führer's life may shoot him on sight!

A fine kettle of fish that will be. Little Johnny's feet are sore after a long march and his commanding officer yells at him. Johnny grabs his rifle, shouts, 'You, you tried to kill the Führer. Take that!' One shot, and the snooty officer who dared to reprimand him passes into eternal life (or is it eternal death?). Eventually, every time an officer sees a soldier or gives an order, he'll be practically wetting his pants, because the soldiers have more say-so than he does.

Were you able to follow that, or have I been skipping from one subject to another again? I can't help it, the prospect of going back to school in October is making me too happy to be logical! Oh dear, didn't I just tell you I didn't want to anticipate events? Forgive me, Kitty, they don't call me a bundle of contradictions for nothing!

Yours, Anne M. Frank

Dearest Kitty,

'*A* bundle of contradictions' was the end of my previous letter and is the beginning of this one. Can you please tell me exactly what 'a bundle of contradictions' is? What does 'contradiction' mean? Like so many words, it can be interpreted in two ways: a contradiction imposed from without and one imposed from within. The former means not accepting other people's opinions, always knowing best, having the last word; in short, all those unpleasant traits for which I'm known. The latter, for which I'm not known, is my own secret.

As I've told you many times, I'm split in two. One side contains my exuberant cheerfulness, my flippancy, my joy in life and, above all, my ability to appreciate the lighter side of things. By that I mean not finding anything wrong with flirtations, a kiss, an embrace, a saucy joke. This side of me is usually lying in wait to ambush the other one, which is much purer, deeper and finer. No one knows Anne's better side, and that's why most people can't stand me. Oh, I can be an amusing clown for an afternoon, but after that everyone's had enough of me to last a month. Actually, I'm what a romantic film is to a profound thinker – a mere diversion, a comic interlude, something that is soon forgotten: not bad, but not particularly good either. I hate having to tell you this, but why shouldn't I admit it when I know it's true? My lighter, more superficial side will always steal a march on the deeper side and therefore always win. You can't imagine how often I've tried to push away this Anne, which is only half of what is known as Anne – to beat her down, hide her. But it doesn't work, and I know why.

I'm afraid that people who know me as I usually am will discover I have another side, a better and finer side. I'm afraid they'll mock me, think I'm ridiculous and sentimental and not take me seriously. I'm used to not being taken seriously, but only the 'lighthearted' Anne is used to it and can put up with it; the 'deeper' Anne is too weak. If I force the good Anne into the spotlight for even fifteen minutes, she shuts up like a clam the moment she's called upon to speak, and lets Anne number one do the talking. Before I realize it, she's disappeared.

So the nice Anne is never seen in company. She's never made a single appearance, though she almost always takes the stage when I'm alone. I know exactly how I'd like to be, how I am . . . on the inside. But unfortunately I'm only like that with myself. And perhaps that's why – no, I'm sure that's the reason why – I think of myself as happy on the inside and other people think I'm happy on the outside. I'm guided by the pure Anne within, but on the outside I'm nothing but a frolicsome little goat tugging at its tether.

As I've told you, what I say is not what I feel, which is why I have a reputation for being a boy-chaser, a flirt, a smart aleck and a reader of romances. The happy-go-lucky Anne laughs, gives a flippant reply, shrugs her shoulders and pretends she couldn't care less. The quiet

Anne reacts in just the opposite way. If I'm being completely honest, I'll have to admit that it does matter to me, that I'm trying very hard to change myself, but that I'm always up against a more powerful enemy.

A voice within me is sobbing, 'You see, that's what's become of you. You're surrounded by negative opinions, dismayed looks and mocking faces, people who dislike you, and all because you don't listen to the advice of your own better half.' Believe me, I'd like to listen, but it doesn't work, because if I'm quiet and serious, everyone thinks I'm putting on a new act and I have to save myself with a joke, and then I'm not even talking about my own family, who assume I must be ill, stuff me with aspirins and sedatives, feel my neck and forehead to see if I have a temperature, ask about my bowel movements and berate me for being in a bad mood, until I just can't keep it up any more, because when everybody starts hovering over me, I get cross, then sad, and finally end up turning my heart inside out, the bad part on the outside and the good part on the inside, and keep trying to find a way to become what I'd like to be and what I could be if . . . if only there were no other people in the world.

Yours, Anne M. Frank

ANNE'S DIARY ENDS HERE

were first taken to a prison in Amsterdam and then transferred to Westerbork, the transit camp for Jews in the north of Holland. They were deported on 3 September 1944, in the last transport to leave Westerbork, and arrived three days later in Auschwitz (Poland).

Hermann van Pels (van Daan) was, according to the testimony of Otto Frank, gassed to death in Auschwitz in October or November 1944, shortly before the gas chambers were dismantled.

Auguste van Pels (Petronella van Daan) was transported from Auschwitz to Bergen-Belsen, from there to Buchenwald, then to Theresienstadt on 9 April 1945, and apparently to another concentration camp after that. It is certain that she did not survive, though the date of her death is unknown.

Peter van Pels (van Daan) was forced to take part in the 16 January 1945 'death march' from Auschwitz to Mauthausen (Austria), where he died on 5 May 1945, three days before the camp was liberated.

Fritz Pfeffer (Albert Dussel) died on 20 December 1944, in the Neuengamme concentration camp, where he had been transferred from either Buchenwald or Sachsenhausen.

Edith Frank died in Auschwitz-Birkenau on 6 January 1945, from hunger and exhaustion.

Margot and Anne Frank were transported from Auschwitz at the end of October and taken to Bergen-Belsen, a concentration camp near Hanover (Germany). The typhus epidemic that broke out in the winter of 1944–5, as a result of the horrendous hygiene conditions, killed thousands of prisoners, including Margot and, a few days later, Anne. She must have died in late February or early March. The bodies of both girls were probably dumped in Bergen-Belsen's mass graves. The camp was liberated by British troops on 12 April 1945.

Otto Frank was the only one of the eight to survive the concentration camps. After Auschwitz was liberated by Russian troops, he was repatriated to Amsterdam by way of Odessa and Marseilles. He arrived in Amsterdam on 3 June 1945, and stayed there until 1953, when he moved to Basle (Switzerland), where his sister and her family, and later his brother, lived. He married Elfriede Markovits Geiringer, originally from Vienna, who had survived Auschwitz and lost a husband and son in Mauthausen. Until his death on 19 August 1980, Otto Frank continued to live in Birsfelden, outside Basle, where he devoted himself to sharing the message of his daughter's diary with people all over the world.